The All-Red Route

The All-Red Route

From Halifax to Victoria in a 1912 Reo

John Nicol

McArthur & Company

Toronto

Canadian Cataloguing in Publication Data

Nicol, John D. –
    The all-red route: Halifax to Victoria in a 1912 Reo

ISBN 1-55278-097-X

1. Canada – Description and travel. 2. Automobile travel – Canada. 3. Reo automobile.
4. Automobiles — Social aspects. I. Title.

FC75.N52 1999   917.1'04   C99-931748-2
F1017.N52 1999

Composition & Design by *Michael P. Callaghan*
Cover Illustration by *Rocco Baviera/4 eyes art + design*
Endpaper design by *Jo-Anne Taraba*
Typeset at *Moons of Jupiter, Inc.* (Toronto)
Printed in Canada by *Transcontinental Printing Inc.*

McArthur & Company
322 King Street West, Suite 402
Toronto, ON, M5V 1J2

10 9 8 7 6 5 4 3 2 1

To Ann,
Emma, Alexander and Annika

Contents

1 • PROLOGUE   *A Bridge to the Past*
A rowboat; *Titanic* lifeboat; A self-tipping hat; The Internal Bath; Whither Herbert and Dunlop?; Empty automaker boasts; "Waaaah;" Four Strong Winds; A boat of a Pontiac; Bond—not James Bond; A beguiling boat of freedom.

10 • CHAPTER 1   *Converging on Halifax*
Truck wheels flying; Road rage; The *Ocean Limited*; A transcontinental shaving kit; The lost Reo; A train on the windowsill; The pig and the steel girder; Shogun's Tokaido Road; Spittoons amidst the rain.

28 • CHAPTER 2   *Farewell to Nova Scotia*
A fake fisherman's village; Brothers and friends reunited; A ring of cheers and a crackle of stones; Paying for the CPR's axle grease; Glooscap of the Mi'qmaqs; Kaiser king of the road; *Recirgo* Moncton.

46 • CHAPTER 3   *New Brunswick on the Weld*
A cracked hinge and broken taxi drivers; The Wedding; The box camera; Journey's end?; Preachers who weld and walk; The shock in St-Jacques; Transcontinental runner meets transcontinental driver; The Continental kiss; *Bonne Anniversaire*.

66 • CHAPTER 4   *A Song in La Belle Province*
Road rage; Embarrassed in old Quebec; Fortress Quebec; The Reo in Paradise; The separatist line; The oldest road in North America; Johnnie Courteau; Montreal 1912; Montreal the urban jungle.

86 • CHAPTER 5   *Ontario—Halfway Across to Halfway House*
Goodbye to Courteau—Hello Chateau; A near disaster; Roadkills; The sewer water pilaster; A Deusy; A picnic by the Fort; Tears at the old Quinte; An auto town in an auto world; The home of Toronters.

104 • CHAPTER 6   *In Search of Scotia Junction*

Pullmanized by strip malls; A lost shoe in the middle of the road; Mighty Muskoka Sands; A 1912 and 1997 Dutchie; The Scotia mystery; A man and his goats; The Quintessential Canadian; Shedding a Murphy; Wilby on the verge of quitting.

124 • CHAPTER 7   *Finally Heading West*

Across New Ontario in a train, a tug, a freighter and a train; Sudbury moonscape; The birth of broomball; Betrayal in the boondocks; Troutless Trout Creek; The adage from Antigonish; A purgatory of pavement in the Soo.

144 • CHAPTER 8   *Sailing Across Superior*

Ambling on the *Ames*; Wilby's circular tour of the U.S.; The Danish invasion; "Clark Gable is hardly able"; See Port Arthur and Live; Niagara of the North; Sun ignites in Ignace; Rat Portage; Kiplings for Canada!

162 • CHAPTER 9   *Waylaid in Winnipeg*

Husky the Muskie; Winnipeg—Queen of the Prairies, King of the wide roads; Bomberville; Gobsmacked by gumbo; Sunbeam, the car; Fix-Or-Repair-Daily versus Gutless Motors; Prince of Wales, world's most eligible bachelor.

180 • CHAPTER 10   *The Manitoba Mystery*

The Countess of Dufferin; Tin Lizzie; Biblical brotherliness in Portage; The gauge of two horses' asses; Bill the landlord, dance teacher, chef, masseur...; Ike and the marriage that wasn't; The marriage that was— 49 years ago.

200 • CHAPTER 11   *A Rough Ride in Saskatchewan*

School inspectors for pilots and landlords; Indian images for a quarter; Indian Head steak for $5.95; Museum for a boxer and a Mighty Duck; The Regina Cyclone; Moosegaw; Haney in-laws in Swift Current; Buffalo trails swiftly disappearing.

220 • CHAPTER 12   *Cowboy Country*
Prairie chicken season; Cowboy country; Piapot and Payepot's tobacco pouch; Ike, and now Irv, the collector; Reo owners and recycled teenagers; The Big Rodeo; Passion-filled Packards; The schoolhouse; Goggles for the foothills of the Rockeries.

244 • CHAPTER 13   *Beautiful British Columbia*
Frank devastation; The Crowsnest; Wand'ring Stars and reporters; Cranbrook Hotel & Strip Joint; Go West, young Al Hunter; On the tracks at Yahk; Astride Goat River Gorge; Kootenay Landing; Nirvana in Nelson; Rattenbury's realm; A lost son?

270 • CHAPTER 14   *The Valleys of the Okanagan and the Similkameen*
Grass-widowerhood; Lincoln leads to land of Lincoln; The Pot-Smoking Mayor; Doukhobors; Anarchist Mountain and Munson's Mount; Penticton boy makes good; Penny Farthing at the Keremeos carousel; "Naaaaneee!"; Meriting a Merritt parade.

290 • CHAPTER 15   *The Fraser Path to the Pacific*
Bonaparte Indian Cemetery; Snow on Cache Creek; The fulminating Fraser; The Hanging Judge; An oil lamp to the rescue; Cataline the Cariboo Freighter; Findlay family surprise; The Hope horseback ride; Eastman at Vedder Crossing; The Pacific!

312 • CHAPTER 16   *Vancouver to Victoria*
Sox-Giants in eighth game of World Series; Kostyniuk on Kitsilano; Airplane to archives; Ferry to Nanaimo; Dunlop Traction Tread tires; Haney airbrushed from photo; Cathedral Grove; Alberni argument; Malahat Drive; Victorious in Victoria.

332 • EPILOGUE   *Victoria to Kyoto on the Tokaido Road*
Back to St. Catharines, New York, Boston, Bath, San Luis Obispo and oblivion?

354 • ENDNOTES; PHOTOGRAPHIC CREDITS; BIBLIOGRAPHY; ACKNOWLEDGMENTS

Reo Motor Car Company of Canada in St. Catharines, Ontario. Every employee had a hand in building the transcontinental car.

Prologue

A Bridge to the Past

August 24, 1997—St. Catharines, Ontario

The journey began to feel like an adventure with the first blast of the train's horn announcing our approach through the Niagara countryside. We slid past empty Sunday morning roads, apple trees laden with a summer's work and grape vines queuing up for harvest. Then came the stillness of Jordan marsh. A lone rowboat drifted next to the reeds, but there was no sign of the rower who had either slipped into the water, never to be seen again, or was lying down, enjoying the sweet solitude of late summer. The sun was low, like newly lit coals, not offering as much heat as promised. It was 8:10 a.m. on the first day of a two-month journey.

As I turned to watch the rowboat from the train, the window framed the old stone piers of the Grand Trunk Railway bridge rising from the marsh. I felt I wanted to reconnect the span so that trains could trundle over it again. I've always liked the idea of rebuilding bridges. In fact, that is what this whole trip is about.

For starters, I was in Jack Haney's seat, or at least a seat he would have taken in 1912, 85 years before, heading by train from St. Catharines, Ontario, in the Niagara Peninsula south of Toronto, to Halifax, Nova Scotia. In Halifax, Haney would unload a 1912 Reo Special touring car and attempt to drive it across a sparse country to the Pacific, and then take the train home again.

I was going to do the same thing, but on this trip I'd be taking the seat of his passenger, a British writer named Thomas Wilby. Along with driver Lorne Findlay, the 70-year-old owner of a 1912 Reo, we would follow Haney and Wilby's trip over the same 53 days, driving the same roads, sleeping in the same hotels, standing in the same spots and snapping the same photos. I wanted to straddle that long bridge back to 1912, look back and forth on then and now, and see how Canada had changed.

1

News of the Day

Nineteen-twelve was late Edwardian, early Borden, and the end of Taft. It was the year of the *R.M.S. Titanic*, when on the clear night of April 14–15, the "unsinkable ship" sank and 1,513 lives were lost. All through the summer, stories continued to trickle out about the tragedy. There was a requiem mass sung on the hour that Rev. Thomas R. Byles was supposed to officiate at his brother's marriage—he was last seen leading a group in prayer on the second cabin deck of the *Titanic* as it sank. At a reunion in New York, Thomas McCormick, one of only four male Irish survivors, showed the scars on his face from blows struck by sailors who tried to prevent him from entering a lifeboat. And newspapers seemed joyful that the *Titanic's* barber, August F. Welkman of Palmyra, New Jersey, was rescued in the water but was not content to remain ashore—he got a job as chief barber on the *Lusitania*, which three years later would be struck by a torpedo from a German U-boat, killing all 1,198 aboard.

In August 1912, the Great War was two years away. Even though Canada was 45 years old, Mother Britain was trying to goad it into building up its navy. Robert Borden, Canada's eighth prime minister (who distinguished himself by wearing patent leather high-cut shoes to support his weak ankles), had just returned from Britain. On August 24, U.S. President William Howard Taft signed the Panama Canal bill; the canal was still two years from opening. Taft's decision to run for re-election split the Republican Party—Theodore Roosevelt started the Progressive Party earlier that month (it allowed Democrat Woodrow Wilson to win the November election). Also that month, Norwegian explorers Christian Leaden and Harold Thalow returned from Northern Canada where they collected a phonographic record of the folksongs of various Indian tribes to compare them with songs of the Eskimos or Inuit.

Robert Falcon Scott had died earlier in the year after reaching the South Pole, as did pioneering aviator Wilbur Wright—one of Haney's heroes—who succumbed to typhoid. Still, it was the age for daredevils and adventurers and those willing to take a chance. Inventors, trying to come up with a discovery to make their fortune, were putting in patents for a tornado-proof house, mechanical goats (for those secret societies who couldn't find one to initiate new members), eyeglasses for chickens (to stop them from pecking out each other's eyes), and my favourite—the self-tipping hat.

Everyone wore hats—the men wore fedoras and Stetsons and bowlers. It was a year that marked the centenary of trousers, which had been re-introduced for popular use by Napoleon's army. Women wore large hats, carried handbags, donned the aptly named hobble skirt, which went to the ankles and made walking difficult. The large-bosomed, small-waisted woman was still admired, that is, when she was not expected to be in the kitchen. Newspapers spread concern about the growing suffragette movement in Britain. Women swarmed Borden during his trip, vowing to use militant methods in Canada to gain the vote.

Men, of course, were "only 50 per cent efficient," according to a popular newspaper ad. "The reason is that the human system does not, and will not, rid itself of all the waste which it accumulates under our present mode of living. No matter how regular we are, the food we eat and the sedentary lives we live make it impossible. Waste does to us exactly what clinkers do to a stove: make the fire burn low and inefficiently until enough clinkers have accumulated and prevent its burning at all. Just write Dr. Charles Tyrell for his interesting treatise called 'The What, The Why, The Way' of The Internal Bath." While writing down Tyrell's address, I noticed that 13-year-old George Kneeble would be defending his "Swat-That-Fly" contest title. In August 1911, young George killed 266,640 flies, edging out Theodore Bedore who killed 264,660 in Minneapolis, where 3,028,575 met their death during the competition. One of the unsolved mysteries of my research was never knowing if young Kneeble picked up another $50 prize, or whether a few gajillion flies decided to swarm him to death.

The country had 8 million citizens, even though 3.25 million Canadians had emigrated to the U.S. since Confederation. Immigrants were streaming into the United States and Canada, but with a greater impact on Canada's relatively uninhabited west, which former prime minister Sir Wilfrid Laurier had dubbed "the last, best west." His boast that this would be "Canada's century" did not seem far-fetched.

Canada's top athlete was Tom Longboat, the long-distance runner who won the 1907 Boston Marathon and in 1912 set a professional record of 1:18:10 for a 15-mile run. The Canadian Olympic team had just returned from the Stockholm games where two Georges—Goulding in the 10,000-metre walk and Hodgson in 400- and 15-metre swims—beat the best of 27 other countries (Hodgson set world records that stood until Johnny Weissmuller, better known as Tarzan, beat them in 1924). McGill University economics and political science professor Stephen Leacock, noted as a humourist on the lecture circuit, had just come out with his *Sunshine Sketches of a Little Town*, which competed in the bookstores with poet Robert Service's third book, *Rhymes of a Rolling Stone*.

Prince Edward Island author Lucy Maud Montgomery, newly married to a minister and now living in Ontario, was busy writing sequels to her successful 1908 first novel, *Anne of Green Gables*. The British Canadian Theatrical Organization Society, made up of British actors, had just formed to counter the dominance of American theatrical touring companies in Canada. And in Winnipeg, suffragette Nellie McClung, 49, had just formed the Political Equality League.

The issues of the day included the fooforaw in British Columbia about the Doukhobors defying authorities. James Flemming, the premier of New Brunswick, delivered a speech to the Canadian Club in Vancouver on national unity, but he was referring to east-west conflicts rather than Quebec. A respected New York engineer had come up with a plan to open the ice-bound harbours of Eastern Canada, do away with the fogs of the Atlantic coast and end the wandering icebergs that sank the *Titanic*. Carroll Livingstone Riker dreamed of directing the warm Gulf Stream waters into the heart of the Arctic, "melting the pole" and forcing the earth to swing around on its polar axis to direct sunrays on heretofore uninhabitable places (now we fear the poles melting because greenhouse gases, many of which are created by cars, are eroding the protective ozone layer above the poles).

Engineers were in high demand to build the infrastructure of a burgeoning nation, which in those days meant they went into the bush with surveyors to find routes for railway lines. Trains were looked upon as the dominant form of transportation, a means of getting to unexploited parts of the country ever since the "last spike" had been driven in the Canadian Pacific Railway's transcontinental line on November 7, 1885. Mind you, many people seemed to resent the power of the railways, which virtually had a monopoly and could charge what they wanted, despite the massive public investment in rails.

That's why, at the turn of the century, the automobile was welcomed with such enthusiasm. It meant freedom—not restricted to rails. For many, like Prairie farmers, it ended their isolation, allowing them to get their crops to markets and to railway stations. Businessmen quickly jumped on the bandwagon, vowing their customers would increase if only the roads were better. An oft-heard comment at the time was: "Everybody is getting cars these days. They won't go where they can't drive. Now if we just had a road here..." A one-cylinder Winton was the first gasoline-powered car to enter Canada in 1898, purchased by a John Moodie of Hamilton, Ontario. By 1904 there were 600 cars in the country, more than 2,000 by 1907 and nearly 47,000 when Pathfinders Haney and Wilby began their trip. In 1912 alone, Ford opened 7,000 dealerships across North America. Autos were spawning other businesses, too, such as garages and car insurance. The safest car, deemed by that year's Detroit conference for insurance companies, was the Studebaker.

Autos advertised—they dared the horse-and-buggy crowd not to be left behind in the new age. Cars were shown at fall fairs as time-saving appliances that could not be overworked—drivers didn't have to feed them each morning or be concerned about their health. For four years they had been used in Montreal to sell real estate, showing the upper classes that they weren't restricted to living in urban areas, that they could enjoy an estate in the countryside and the culture of the city. The only paved highway in the country was a 16-kilometre concrete stretch from Montreal to Ste-Rose, built in 1910.

Cars were usually driven from May until November, but could be run longer if weather permitted and the roads were passable. Automobile clubs were forming across the country to lobby for better roads, better signage and to organize rallies.

The naysayers pointed out that automobiles were being used for abductions and as getaway cars in robberies, and that they'd consign Old Jack—the faithful ambulance horse who'd saved many lives—to the glue factory. And cars were dangerous. Newspapers were full of gruesome accidents—more than 20,000 insurance claims were made daily in the United States in 1912. They were a nuisance to pedestrians even if they didn't get hit. Roadways had expanded so much to accommodate them that New York sidewalks were too narrow for pedestrians. Some lawmakers tried to put drivers in their place. Auto speeders began to be fined heavily in Montreal, with one man being charged $25 for what the magistrate called "scorching" on Westmount streets. In British Columbia, horse-drawn or engine-propelled vehicles had to pull over to the side of the road if overtaken by another vehicle or horses, or risk a $50 fine. In New Brunswick, drivers had to pin a badge conspicuously to their clothing to show they had permission to operate a motor vehicle.

By August 1912, crossing the United States by motor car was old hat—the only record set that summer was by an Alco truck which made the first coast to coast delivery of merchandise from Philadelphia to San Francisco. Motoring in Canada, for the most part, was something done within provinces. Herbert Gilley of British Columbia vowed to change that, setting out that summer to cross Canada by auto and to capture the gold medal being offered by the Victoria Automobile Club for the first adventurer to do so. He never made it. Dr. H.G. Percival, editor of *Health Magazine* and a long-distance motorist, wrote about his desire to be the pioneer Western pathfinder, but Percival, one newspaper said, "declined to attempt a tour which seemed fraught with countless difficulties, and almost foredoomed to failure." D.A. Dunlop of Toronto, a prominent member of the Ontario Motor League, boasted to the Toronto papers that he would drive through Detroit, Chicago, Minneapolis, Winnipeg, Regina, Calgary and Vancouver. He too would not make it.

Automobile makers, like John Willys of the Willys-Overland company, had the audacity to claim: "Never will the automobile be better made than it is today. Motor cars are as near perfect as mechanical genius." Even Ransom E. Olds boasted that the Reo the Fifth, or a Reo Special as it was known in Canada, was "The Car that marks my limit. I have no quarrel with men who ask more for their cars—none with men who ask less. I have only to say that, after 25 years—after creating 24 models and building tens of thousands of cars—here's the best I know. I call it my Farewell Car." Olds had no intention of retiring, but that was one of the advertising ploys of the time, just as it was common to show women in ads in order to convey the idea that cars were so simple to drive even a woman could do it. Cars became such an allure, such a must in the early part of the century, that men were known to mortgage everything they possessed, to let their families go short and neglect their children's education, in order to own one.

The Trip

Eighty-five years on, in 1997, I wasn't sure I could drive the Reo. I got my first ride in one when Lorne Findlay came to my home in Niagara-on-the-Lake, Ontario. The Reo was on a trailer behind his camper. Lorne and his wife Irene were on their way from Vancouver to meet me in Halifax. Joining us by plane in Halifax would be their son, Peter, a Vancouver music and computer teacher who would drive the camper behind the Reo, spell Lorne in driving the Reo, and update the Internet web page he set up for the trip.

In 1989 I had called Lorne to find out how a 1912 Reo worked for another book I had written about Jack Haney. He proved to be an invaluable contact. He was an encyclopedia about cars, had researched the 1912 trip, and had even sought out and bought

the same-model, same-year car as Haney drove. He said that one day he would duplicate the trip, and I told him to save me a seat. In November of 1996 he wrote to say he
was going to dip his Reo's wheels in the Atlantic on August 27, 1997.

Lorne had a good sense of humour. He told the story of a man he met on his way
to the home of Reos in Lansing, Michigan. At a North Dakota rest stop, a man with a
southern accent grilled Lorne about his adventure. "Just before he left he said:
'Waaaah?'" recalled Lorne. Lorne didn't understand so he asked the man, who turned
out to be from Louisiana, to repeat himself. "Waaaah?" the man blustered. When Lorne
didn't understand him again, he said, "Waaaah you doin' it?"

I had wanted to do this trip for a decade, ever since I became familiar with the
story of the first attempt to find a motor route across Canada. It was a captivating tale
of two men who grew to despise each other, who struggled to get the car across the second largest country in the world, across the batter made out of roads by maritime mon-
soons, across the rocks and swamp of the Canadian Shield, the sucking black clay called
gumbo in the Prairies, and not one but three mountain ranges in British Columbia. I
had become attached to Haney, a man so much of his time but also ahead of his time. I
wanted to tell his story properly, to try to experience what he did and to uncover what
evidence there might be of his trip in the libraries, museums and archives across
Canada.

Lorne's answer coincided with my own—a love of history, of adventure and a
chance to pay tribute to Jack Haney, who persevered to get that car across the country.
More so than I, Lorne also wanted to draw attention to the accomplishment of the
Trans-Canada Highway and our road network. He's the kind of guy who drives his
family nuts pointing out remnants of older highways lying in disuse beside the modern highway, and admits his "mind wanders and conjures up pictures of a road that
caused one to travel at a much slower pace." A mechanic, Lorne once ran his own
garage, and was a tour bus driver who still took the odd tour out. He has worked as an
auto historian, is slight and spry as a teenager, and his mechanic's fingers know more
about cars than my brain ever did.

The night before Lorne drove on to Halifax, we went to a patriotic dinner show in
Niagara Falls called *Oh Canada Eh!* There it became clear we both had a love for
Canada, and for old songs. The humming of "Four Strong Winds" or "Farewell to Nova
Scotia" competed with the hum of the Reo throughout the trip.

At least that's what I knew of the Findlays at the start. Would we recreate the animosity between driver and passenger that threatened the original trip? Would my attitudes change much in two months? What would I think of cars and roads at trip's end? And what would I feel about the country?

Those were some of my thoughts as I sat on the train, feeling awkward about trying to fill the seat that Haney had sat in eighty-five years before. I couldn't ignore the irony of someone like me—whose grandest display of ease with cars is a preference for a standard-gearshift rather than automatic—being in the place of a man who could build a car from scratch and couldn't wait to try out new models and find out how they worked. Then again, Haney was as typical of his era as I was of mine.

For the next 53 days I'd be immersed in a car culture, with men and women for whom a handshake wasn't complete unless they looked under the hood of your car. I might have taken more of an interest in cars, since my father worked as a machinist in a car factory. But he was like a journalist who doesn't like to write when he gets home from work; he never really tinkered with cars other than to clean his spark plugs and change his own oil. Then again, he was 45 when I was born, and perhaps past his car-tinkering prime when I would have noticed. One of my brothers is an executive with a car parts firm, but he agrees with what Louis B. Mayer quipped when he met Albert Einstein: "I have a theory of relativity too," said the film mogul to the physicist. "Never mix relatives and work." I stayed away. The General Motors car factory in St. Catharines (the Reo stopped making cars there in 1914) for years sustained the community that sustained *The Standard* newspaper that sustained me. And my neighbour toiled in a car factory—in fact, one in six Ontarians and one in seven Canadians labour in a field connected to the car.

Horseless carriages, of course, have had an impact on my life. I chose to live on a narrow, quiet street in Niagara-on-the-Lake where I didn't readily fear my kids being struck by speeding cars. Cars dampened my enthusiasm for winter—cleaning the runoff of boots on the car's carpet, chiselling the ice off windshields, ever watchful for black ice, wondering how I should apply my brakes and when, and hoping the operator of that oncoming car is sober enough, and salient enough, about winter driving. In 23 years of driving (in Ontario most teens get their licence at the minimum legal age of 16), I have met the odd snowbank.

My first car, a hand-me-down from my dad, was an off-green 1966 Pontiac Laurentian, which seemed big enough to save half the passengers of the Titanic. The first time it needed oil I filled the engine casing right up to the top, which led to one smoky trip across my native Niagara Falls to my high school basketball game. My next car was another hand-me-down, a 1970 Chevy 2. I took possession of both cars eight years after their birth. Both were gas guzzlers, a way to get around. After university, I spent two years in Europe, where I neither needed or wanted a car, and when I returned I had a brief experience with a 1975 Toyota Corolla. The car probably would have survived had I not picked up a stone in the radiator while pulling over to let in a hitch-hiker a few months later. When I couldn't keep enough water in the radiator as I went from assignment to assignment at *The St. Catharines Standard*, the engine seized on me. Two Nissan Pulsars, both purchased new, followed. Although they were hardly the Aston Martin I dreamed of in my youth—a dream influenced by my first dinky toy, the car of secret agent 007, James Bond—they were efficient slices of cheese, easy to park and good on gas.

So for the trip with Lorne, essentially a 53-day march in celebration of the car, I was like a bass drum player in the high school band—I couldn't contribute to the harmony, but I could keep the beat for the parade.

Haney sat on that Grand Trunk train from St. Catharines with three small suitcases carefully put away in the baggage rack. In them were a few changes of clothes to work on the car, and one set of formal duds—a white shirt with round collars, black knitted tie, sensible black pants and high-cut leather shoes. Next to him on his seat were an overcoat and cap, necessary appointments in motoring costumes, and his diary, in which he would record his expenses and some thoughts. I had one bag for clothes, and another bag for a computer, camera equipment and several notepads, but never enough paper for the experiences that would bombard our senses.

I don't know about Haney, but as a child I was enthralled with history and travel and the tales of explorers like Vasco de Gama and James Cook. All I ever wanted were some history books, a chance to see the world and strawberries to put on my Corn Flakes, just like the picture on the cereal box. Here was an adventure of a lifetime: two months to roam the country, two months to cross bridges to the past. I felt like the richest man in the world.

BRITAIN AND THE AMERICAN AUTOS, August, 1912, Saint John, N.B.—

A United States firm is selling automobiles in England at £50 a piece. That is $250. In England they are not called automobiles but motor cars. The United States adopted the French, and we from the United States. We needed another word to distinguish them from street cars, which the English call trams. In England, to sell automobile cars at £50 a piece is spoken of as almost equivalent to robbery. Not because they are too dear, but because they are too cheap. The motor car owes much of its attraction to its costliness. Can the auto itself survive the cut? A price of £50 puts them within the reach of clerks, and when it comes to second-hand bargains, almost within the reach of errand boys. But it is not economical to carry from one to two tons along with one wherever he may want to go. And it is hard on the roads, congesting to city traffic, and a performance that fills the air with dust.

ROAD RAGE NOT "RIGHT" IN CLASS-BASED ENGLAND, August, 1997, London, England—

Frances Cernuschi has gone to prison for five months in a court case that focused attention on a worldwide phenomenon—road rage. In a country where tourists marvel at the polite queues in stores and on the street, it was, indeed, sensational. The accused wasn't a yob from some slum; wasn't some drunken lout, but a white, 47-year-old married woman from the suburbs. Cernuschi ran down a cyclist on Kensington Road when the 21-year-old man clipped her side mirror and scratched her car. Cernuschi swerved her car into the bike, tossing him to the road and then drove over the bike and accelerated away, leaving the injured man lying in the street.

Chapter 1

Converging on Halifax

August 24—Halifax/Via Rail

Of the seven characters converging on Halifax for this journey, I felt I was the most comfortable. After riding the noon train from Toronto to Montreal, I climbed aboard a sleeper on the 6:59 p.m. *Ocean Limited* from Montreal. Two of the others were travelling in a camper, towing a trailer behind; one was flying economy from Vancouver to Halifax; and two had the difficult task of stepping out of the past to join us. The main character, the one that transcended both 1912 and 1997, was tied to the trailer, its feet blocked and its legs strapped to the floor. Like Gulliver, it was a traveller, a giant in its field. It went by the name Reo Special Touring Car.

As in 1912, the success of the trip rested on the broad shoulders of the dark green Reo, a tall five-seater with a crank start and wooden-spoked wheels. Its most beguiling feature was a bulb horn: it had no electronic dash, no four-wheel drive, no compact-disc player or surround-sound stereo. Its convertible mohair top was the only thing stopping the outside from being inside—with no side windows, it had natural air conditioning years before the 1939 Packard introduced the artificial kind. The openness allowed gawkers to climb inside and stretch their legs in both the front and back seats, examine its speedometer/odometer in miles per hour, step on the gas pedal or the brake which was really a parking brake, and then depress the clutch halfway to move the stick shift into high, low, medium and reverse. The jiggery-pokery is the clutch—when fully depressed, it becomes the brake. It was tricky enough to stop me from asking for the key to go cruise the streets.

Yet, at the time, the Reo ads were directed at all-thumbs motorists like myself: "Anybody could drive it: no engineering education to understand every part, no fear of breakdowns." And at $1,500 "the price is the price a good car should cost—no more, no less." Magazine ads called it the "Car of Instinct: If you had lived in Stephenson's day—you would have gone to see the Rocket. If you had lived near the Wrights—you would have seen the first aeroplane. Now—here's a Reo car built in your very city—which possesses features that have lifted the motor car into the realm of permanent investment." During the 1912 trip, Reo ads boasted that it was "best fitted to undertake the rough work of mapping out the all-Canadian Motor Highway from Halifax to Vancouver. That the Reo was built as a pathfinding car proves that it is built to stand up to all tests."

The Reo was the star of this 1997 venture, yet it was being shepherded by Lorne and Irene on a rickety trailer across the byways of the Eastern United States and Canada. Then again, the last time a 1912 Reo was sent to Halifax, it got lost for a few days in the switchyards of the Canadian Pacific Railway. That wouldn't happen this time.

Joining the Findlays and me from the past were driver/mechanic Jack Haney and British writer Thomas William Wilby: the first men to attempt to find a motor route across Canada. Later on, in Regina, we'd be joined by the ghost of Earl Wise, a mechanic who had helped them with those rather large obstacles in B.C., and more importantly, who kept Haney and Wilby from choking each other to death.

Haney was the trip's second star. Born in Huntingdon, Indiana, the 23-year-old was bred for this adventure. Jack's mother died of typhoid fever when he was two. His father Joseph then gave up teaching to work as a cooper, leading a nomadic life travelling to sawmills up and down the Mississippi. Jack followed, becoming inured to loading up the horse and wagon, moving from boarding house to boarding house, from one school to another. His one constant was the summers spent with his Uncle Jack in a cabin at Clarksville, Missouri. His uncle was a river rat who gathered stray logs on the Mississippi and collected snakes to sell to zoos. Young Jack got to nurture his own sense of adventure and self-dependence when, at age 11, he was given a motorboat by a wealthy family whose son had died in a mishap. To explore the river, Jack became intimately familiar with its motor, a skill he adapted to car motors when he landed his first job at 14, helping out at a garage in North Baltimore, Ohio. Before he was 16, Jack picked up cars from plants in Flint, Michigan, and Toledo, Ohio, to deliver to garage clients. In 1905, with barely a Grade 10 education from a high school in Detroit, he set off for Lansing, Michigan, to work for the new Reo Motor Car Company, opened by Ransom E. Olds, founder of the Oldsmobile.

Olds began tinkering with creating a motor vehicle in the 1880s, and by 1886, a year after Wilhelm Daimler and Karl Benz produced their car, Olds had built a steam-driven carriage. He was 22. Nine years later, in 1895, Olds built a gasoline-powered vehicle, long before Ford built his first. He instituted the assembly line before Ford, invented the carburetor, and built a push-button electric starter as early as 1899. Starting the Olds Motor Vehicle Company in Lansing in 1897, he drew many of the early automobile pioneers, such as Jonathan Maxwell, Hugh Chalmers and Bobby Hupp, who went on to build their own cars. Olds moved his factory to Detroit in 1901. That fall, he used the long-distance drive—an unheard-of venture from Detroit to New York (via Windsor and Niagara Falls, Canada)—to popularize his Curved Dash Olds at an auto show. The 1903 version of that car was the first to be mass-produced, selling for only $650. In 1904, Olds had a disagreement with his group of investors and left to return to Lansing. The investors flopped on their own and sold out in 1908 to William Durant, who later formed General Motors. (Six days before our trip began, thousands of Oldsmobile owners converged on Lansing, Michigan, to celebrate the centenary of "Ranny's" first car.) Olds began the Reo company in Lansing in August 1904 and produced the prototype of a Reo two months later. Since Olds gave his name to his first company, he said he had nothing but his initials to give to his second—the first man to have two cars named after him. He continued to grab newspaper headlines for his cars, whether it was Percy Megargel's first double transcontinental trip in a Reo in 1905, the first public ride of a U.S. president in an automobile (Olds took Teddy Roosevelt for a jaunt in 1907), or the Reo's 1910 destruction of the New York-to-San Francisco speed record by 5 days, crossing in 10 days, 15 hours and 13 minutes.

That same year, Haney left Lansing to work for Reo's year-old Canadian subsidiary, the Reo Motor Car Company of Canada, in St. Catharines. Haney became the company's star troubleshooter, crossing the country by train to fix broken-down Reos. Wearing a tight motoring cap, he would also go whizzing around the Niagara Peninsula road testing new cars for 160 kilometres before the body was added. Each summer they sent him up to the Canadian National Exhibition in Toronto to talk about motors at the Reo display. Haney was the obvious choice as driver and mechanic when Wilby proposed the idea of a transcontinental trip to the Reo Company in the spring of 1912. The 23-year-old got to know a bit of the Canadian West while troubleshooting. He was the company's most capable mechanic, and he was caught up so much with the age of invention, he believed he could solve any problem along the way, as long as he had a helping hand when faced with predicaments that demanded two men.

Haney would have enjoyed my trip out East by train, where I learned much about roads by being on the rails. At Toronto's grand Union Station—it was only on a drawing board in 1912, but its elegance reflects the early century when the railway ruled—I grabbed a seat beside a trucking executive on the Montreal train. He told me why trucks were losing tires on highways, a hot topic in 1997. It had something to do with impact guns securing tires at 800-foot torque pounds rather than at 250-foot torque pounds. In other words, the nuts were on so tight that when the truck hit a pothole, "Bang," said the guy, "there goes your wheels." His company only had one set of wheels come off, which struck an oncoming truck. Luckily, no one was hurt. Besides the bolt problem, he told me some companies neglected to maintain their trucks. "Everyone is cutting rates to keep market share. The bottom line is they don't have the money to do maintenance or purchase new equipment."

Then he explained that trucks were the biggest culprits for creating potholes. He referred to a Transport Canada video which showed how trucks pummel the roads, especially trucks with multiple axles—they don't give the road a chance to bounce back. Whereas some states prevent entire trucks from weighing more than 80,000 pounds and having more than two axles, Ontario allows multiple axles and for trucks to carry payloads of 88,000 pounds—a sure-fire way to spend a fortune on road construction. I argued that I preferred to see the government subsidize trains the way they subsidize roads, and get the big traffic off the highways, but the amiable guy said trains take too long to deliver goods, especially over short distances. They were better handling goods for the West. It was a conversation I'd remember when Prairie trains serenaded me to sleep, and wakened me hours later.

Haney would have had a choice of six trains leaving St. Catharines that day; I had one. As it had in 1912, the *Ocean Limited* still rolled overnight from Montreal to Halifax, although my trip would be eight hours shorter. Haney had already taken the train to Halifax by August 22 and checked into the Halifax Hotel. Both he and Wilby expected to depart two days later. But the Reo, which every employee at the Reo company had a hand in building, was nowhere to be found, even though it had been consigned to railway authorities 12 days before.

The Reo's disappearance on the CPR's freight train network gave the pair no end of embarrassment. August 24, 1912, was a day of radiant sky and brisk wind. The mayor was all set to perform a formal send-off, and all the papers had been alerted to the departure—but there was no Reo. Haney regularly reported its failure to arrive to Wilby, who would go to the station to try to talk the Reo into existence. No amount of cajoling or threatening could produce the car, so Wilby retreated to the Carlton Hotel, with its spacious, manly, smoky lobby, its tiled floor, wooden armchairs, gigantic brass spittoons and a small counter that sold newspapers and tobacco.

Montreal had been Canada's largest city in 1912 and remained so for the next sixty years. When I arrived in 1997, remnants of Expo 67 dotted the island, a shoreline of trees buffered the blue of the St. Lawrence, and Montreal's towers, compared to Toronto's, seemed on a more human scale. It reminded me of my first time in Montreal 30 years earlier, the promise of Expo, the thrill of the centennial, the experimental architecture. My last visit had been for the rally before the 1995 referendum. Fears of what would happen to Quebec still lingered and coloured my impression as I arrived. I was happy to see the words to the national anthem etched in stone in both languages up high on the station rotunda. The ear became attuned to French on the way in, but the brain still had much dust to sweep away if I planned to carry on any conversations.

Fortunately, the *lingua franca* of train travel is pro-public transit. Many of the passengers were on the train because they disliked or were disinterested in driving cars on swollen highways. At dinner on the *Ocean Limited* I ended up at a table with Mike Gushue, vice president of customer relations for VIA Rail, Canada's passenger rail network. He told a story he heard on TV about road rage. A Haitian man in the United States had his car break down on a busy highway. As he was pushing it off, he was shot and killed by another man who thought he blocked traffic for too long. "Road rage," says Gushue. That's just one reason he's optimistic about the future of train travel. He said that federal transportation minister David Collenette thinks about trains as part of a network. "We believe in the future," said Gushue. "I wouldn't have said that three years ago. We want to bring back the ambience of train travel, stop impediments to business, allow passengers to work on the Windsor to Montreal corridor, and leave when people want to leave." Ultimately, he said, "The demographics are in our favour." The rising number of seniors will opt for relaxation on rails rather than competing with 17.5 million other vehicles on Canadian roads.

That night the domecar attendant told me to watch for the lights of Old Quebec: "It's a beautiful site as the train nears the water." I did watch at 10:30 p.m., but the view was marred by a foreground of loosely knit buildings and a requisite four-lane road. I wished I could pick the buildings up like lego blocks and place them close together near the heart of the next town, improve their architecture and make them alluring. It was a sentiment I'd have often over the next eight weeks.

August 25—Halifax

The real joy of train travel emerged before daybreak near Matapédia, on the Gaspé peninsula where the Restigouche and Matapédia rivers meet. As dawn broke, the colours of the firmament retreated to the sky. The black river became blue, and the brooding brown knob of a mountain silhouetted across the water turned out to be forest green. The sky was yellow and orange, in an inviting way, not like smog over a city. The only blight on the horizon was a monstrosity of a mill, with its retaining pools to treat the poison it emits. Below the mill, canoes sat at the shore, angled as if anxious to go for a paddle with or without a passenger, just like that rowboat in Jordan. It was exhilarating—where else could you lie in bed and enjoy the world rambling by. I thought I was a bit better off than Haney. Did the Reo Motor Car Company of St. Catharines offer him a sleeper, or was he supposed to be the dutiful employee, act like a member of his class and sit up on his journey to the coast?

Lunch was spent with Bernard, a Montrealer who promotes radio stations and enjoys living in a city where he doesn't have to own a car. "When you are in a car, you are like the prey of an eagle, waiting for the police to swoop down upon you," he said as the train cut through a valley of evergreens cushioning gentle slopes. "I don't use the car in Montreal. If you don't have the car, you have liberty and no stress—you don't need to find a meter, you don't have to worry about your car. Also, you walk." When he was stationed in Vancouver, his wife visited and wondered why so many people knew him. "I told her I had been walking in the neighbourhood for eight months. That's how you get to know people. If you're not in a car, it is the best way to find out what a city is like." In Vancouver, he'd take the sky train and buses, which he thought was wise from a business perspective: "You can smell the city, see which sector is more rich. You can touch it."

Outside the window, lakes and forests appeared, one after another, alongside the rails, as if situated by a cinematographer. It was an indication of the vastness we would experience over the next two months. The clouds were high, like islands, or sky-communities on the *Jetsons*, the futuristic 1960s cartoon. It made me wonder what forced the Jetsons to live in the sky—overpopulation, or too much pollution?

The train made a slow entrance to Halifax, along Bedford Basin, underneath the Dartmouth bridge and along a shoreline that was too often given over to industry. Suddenly the smell of the sea told me we were near the ocean. The railway station had changed locations since Haney's day, and he would have arrived at 10:45 at night, not at 2:30 in the afternoon. But Haney must have been just as excited. For him, what lay ahead would have been his greatest challenge, a chance to show just how ingenious he could be to keep a car going. When he was asked to do the trip, he called his father for advice. Joseph Haney, whose own life had been one adventure after another, thought the task too difficult and told Jack not to do it, even though he often said his son "had wheels in his head." Jack, who was taught to be independent, wrote back and said, "Thanks, but I'm going anyway."

The writer Wilby wished he had taken his father's advice. For some reason he did not want to travel with an American-born driver, and he asked the Reo company to find him someone else besides Haney. Perhaps his driver the year before, when he had completed a circular New York-to-San Francisco-to-Tijuana-to-Washington tour, was a Canadian or Brit. More than likely Wilby wanted respect from a colonial Canadian toward a son of England. As Wilby would later write in his book, *A Motor Tour Through Canada*,

> Canada owes loyalty to herself. But she owes love and devotion and
> gratitude to the great Mother that fought and bled and spent of her
> treasures that she might found for her children this new Empire for
> them beyond the seas.

Wilby made a pitch to several car companies that they supply him with a car and driver in his attempt to find an "All-Red Route." In those days, countries loyal to the British crown were painted red on maps, so an all-red route was a road across

Canada, totally within its borders. The Reo Motor Car Company accepted, insisting he take Haney.

Born in Norwich, England, just days before Canada was born—on June 6, 1867— Wilby told reporters that he was 42 when he was really 45. He began his journalism career with his hometown *Norwich Daily News*, and later became a "special corre- spondent" of the London Morning Post in Vienna, and of the *Daily Express* in Cairo, and had spent some time in other European capitals such as Paris, Warsaw and Berlin, perhaps as a correspondent for the *London Leader* or *New York World*, two other papers for which he claimed to write. He first came to North America in 1900, arriv- ing in the Port of Quebec and then making his way down to New York by train. It was on a ship to Cairo in late 1903 that he met a New Zealand artist named Frances Hodgkins. The smitten Wilby immediately sent her a scarab for good luck, "as it may have done some forgotten owner of ancient Egypt 4,000 years ago." His Cairo address was the Letter Call Office, but within a year he was based in New York, working for the travel agency Gillespie-Kinports. They wrote back and forth, and by the end of 1904 they were engaged to be married. In January of 1905, Wilby wrote Frances's mother, saying Frances had promised to make him "the happiest of men in his wife and mother-in-law." He told her he wanted to be married in New Zealand, but it would be difficult for him to get away. He ends the letter, referring to his betrothed: "I know her whole life and nature through my heart." The plan was to meet Frances in London or Paris, which is where he wanted to make his home. Instead, while Frances was busily preparing for their reunion, Wilby called off the April wedding before Hodgkins' departure from Wellington.

Wilby did make it to the altar on July 2, 1908, to marry Agnes Andrews, 8 years his junior, in her Massachusetts hometown. The moustachioed Brit might have reminded Agnes of her father Sidney Andrews, a journalist and an adventurer who died when she was only five years old. The Wilbys' first home was in New York. He is listed in the 1907 New York city directory as head of Thomas W. Wilby Tours on Broadway, while maintaining that France was his home. But after the wedding Wilby is listed as running Boughton (his mother's maiden name) Wilby Tours and Wilby Foreign Automobile Tours from a New York residence. Among his auto trips in Europe was a drive around Lincolnshire in 1909. He wrote a story for *Travel* magazine to mark the 100th anniversary of the birth of Alfred Tennyson, one of his idols. In

1910–11 he is listed as a superintendent—not of roads, but of an apartment building, like Norton on the *Honeymooners* TV show. The next year he is listed simply as a writer, which may be a reflection of his failure as a superintendent and as a tour guide, or his success as a writer.

In 1911 Wilby had convinced the Ohio Motor Car Company to chauffeur him and his wife, Agnes Andrews of Brookline, Massachusetts, from New York to San Diego and back in a 90-day circular tour of the United States. On that adventure he was an officer of the Touring Club of America, which he helped found in 1909, and an agent for the federal Office of Public Roads, which commissioned him to log and take photos of his route. On the way the *Omaha World-Leader* hailed Wilby as "a road expert of unquestioned ability. He has travelled in every country of the world by automobile and is a motor enthusiast of the first water"—if not a first-class, self-promoter. After that trip Wilby wrote a romantic novel called *On the Trail to Sunset*, in which the protagonist, a journalist in love with a socially conscious Chicago girl, chases her to New Mexico. If it was at all significant, it portrayed love from male and female perspectives, not unexpected since his wife Agnes was his acknowledged co-writer. The novel's opening line is "Winthrop Hammond walked." The hero chided the tide of traffic, "a ceaseless surge of carriaged and motoring humanity, which left the pedestrian stranded like a glacial moraine upon the stony ledge of the sidewalk." The widened avenue was altered forever, and palatial mansions were "mutilated and shorn of architectural adornments, banks and stores stealing a march upon his favorite haunts." To cater to this faster world, myriad signs, daring and upstart, attracted passersby. It was, for Winthrop, "a vandalism which sacrificed time-honored, cherished associations." Yet, Wilby was a vociferous advocate of cars and roads.

In the Halifax of 1912, where future Second World War munitions minister Clarence Decatur Howe was teaching engineering, there were fewer than 200 cars. Production of the McKay motor car had just begun in Nova Scotia, and $4 could hire a car for an hour. A week before, the city gave Prince Arthur—the Duke of Connaught and Canada's Governor General—a rousing reception at Halifax city hall. It would not be the last time Wilby would be upstaged by the Duke, who was conducting a cross-Canada trip at the same time, although by train. Early in the year pundits speculated that the Duke would conduct his tour by motor, but *Maclean's* magazine suggested he would be "smothered in dust, covered with mud and jolted into semi-insensibility over some of the worst roads and through some of the loveliest scenery in the Empire.... It is an axiom that you cannot see a country from a railway carriage; yet outside a railway carriage there is no hope for comfortable travel in present-day Canada."

Wilby had arrived in Halifax sometime around August 22, either from New York or from Quebec, where he and his wife spent the winter writing *On the Trail to Sunset*. He told newspapers in the East he was from Quebec, either because of his frequent landings from overseas there or to ingratiate himself as a Canadian. By the time he reached the west coast he was referred to as the writer from New York City. At the time he had been contributing articles to *Travel* magazine, a slick publication out of New York. What is more of a mystery is not where he came from but why he came so ill-prepared. For his American trip he prided himself on packing lightly, so there was little evidence of the Wilbys doing anything other than a Sunday drive. But this wasn't a trip on pre-existing roads heading toward the Mexican border. Although it was the same time of year, Wilby arrived for a much cooler Canadian trip toting writing materials, a shaving kit and a change of socks. He was already wearing a fedora, a three-piece tweed suit and the duster on his back—he must have expected to put them to good use. A charmer, Wilby may have felt he was like Oscar Wilde, who entertained author Graham Greene's parents one Christmas with the only currency he had—his wit.

Ever the responsible one, Haney contacted his bosses in St. Catharines to see what he should do about Wilby's lack of preparation. By phone they told him to outfit Wilby for the trip. Haney bought him a change of clothes and gave him two of his own cases, which Wilby accepted as if he had planned it all along. It was clear from the start that Wilby expected to be treated as the star, and made it known to Haney that he wanted to be called "Sir."

For many weeks it seemed as if the trip would have to be abandoned, for there was no hope of getting beyond the Great Lakes. But Wilby told the newspapers that a scouting party sent out to investigate conditions north of Lake Superior reported that they had found a route that appeared passable. Such tips showed how little was known of possible routes across the country. Even in British Columbia, they expected to cross the Hope Mountains, which was supposed to be the most difficult of the whole undertaking. In that case at Princeton, B.C. "an experienced packer will be waiting with horses, which it is expected will be necessary in crossing the two divides on the Hope mountains."

At the time, enthusiasts boasted that the wagon roads built a century ago in eastern Ontario by British military engineers were still the best roads in the western hemisphere. But as the scattered parts of British North America were united politically, the distances proved so vast that no attempt to link wagon roads was even imagined. Iron horse and steel road were the sole means of cross-country travel. The advance of motor cars revived an almost dead interest in highways—all parts of Canada were taking stock of their road assets and wondering how they could be connected. British Columbia had the most stunning challenges, looking for a way to integrate the historic Yale-Cariboo Road with humble trails built by miners with provincial assistance. The Canadian Highway Association was formed in 1910 with the intent of furthering the cause, and, in the 1911 election, the Tories campaigned and won on the promise to aid municipalities in road-building. The Borden government introduced such a bill, but it was defeated in the Senate. Only Nova Scotia and Prince Edward Island had provincial control over roads. Otherwise, the quality of highways was left up to boards, councils and committees across the country. Road enthusiasts even made a military argument for a road—if Canada was invaded, a few sticks of dynamite on the rails could separate east from west.

In a long *Halifax Herald* piece, Wilby primed the public for his adventure. The Maritimes had been explored by three Saint John motorists driving a Reo in 1910, and by Americans in a Reo the following year, but his goals were much grander. He was going to do what fur trade explorer Alexander Mackenzie had first done in 1793—reach the Pacific by land. Wilby intended to make a log of the trip and was aiming for an arrow on a signpost planted May 4 at Alberni on Vancouver Island.

> It is the concrete expression of a great Canadian ideal. It is the first of a series of posts which will stretch for 4,000 miles across mountain and plain, prairie and forest, until at your fine old Acadian city, they have spanned a continent and linked an empire. By a strange twist of historical circumstance, the west is coming to the east and I think the east ought not to sit passively looking on...The great white way—the king's highway and All-Red route of the empire—will not come of itself. The difficulties which the first motorist across will encounter will be as nothing compared with the good he can do in calling attention, by his attempt to lead the way, to the urgent need of forging this link...

Wilby felt it was a serious indictment of Canada that 1,440 kilometres north of Lake Superior remained "a no-man's land."

> That grim solid fact that western Ontario is trail-less and unopened —nothing but forest and muskeg, much broken by rivers and lakes —almost takes one's breath away. One realizes with painful vividness that there is in truth two Canadas—the golden west and the silver east, connected only by the precarious thread of a railroad.... Railroad people and highway engineers of Toronto tell me that only a flying machine can get thru this region.

He said it would take five years to build the highway, in time for Canada's semicentennial, but if citizens sought the backing of the Dominion government, they could have it ready for the Pan-Pacific Exposition in San Francisco in 1915. Wilby knew American roads were not that good. If Canada got on the ball, they could beat the Americans and lure all the tourist traffic through its provinces. Such quick work would go some way to help pay for itself, he reasoned. He was waiting for the day the highway would be not only a great military road and a valuable auxiliary route in the transport of grain from the West to the markets, but the finest and longest highway in the world. With a cross-Canada road built, a national tourist organization on the Swiss model could exploit it, for Canada could boast scenery like the Swiss mountain valleys. He felt the wardens and headquarters of the highway ought to be in Halifax—beginning early his penchant for kissing one where one sat on Saturday nights.

Back in Halifax, the lost Reo posed a problem for the heavily planned trip. For months, Canadian Highway Association officers had prepared maps, plans and charts and organized a chain of pilots to direct the Reo in and out of cities. "Those in eastern Canada, as far as the great lakes, have been selected by different automobile clubs in these districts, while west of this point the men have been appointed by the CHA," he announced. "In most cases the pilot is a member, frequently an officer of the association, and it is his intention to accompany the Pathfinders for at least 100 miles on this journey, resigning his services as guide when the district served by another officer is reached." Not only would pilots be waiting, but several of the towns, especially the bigger cities, were planning receptions and dinners for Wilby. The delay in the car arriving jeopardized their October 1 due date in Vancouver.

Wilby took out his irritation by maligning his digs at the Carlton Hotel (in 1997, it had become apartments for naval veterans). He railed against the uniformed boy who seized his suitcase "as though it was his long-lost property," and didn't have much time for the clerk "gravely sucking a toothpick" who asked him to sign in on a register "bristling with advertisements, toothpicks, and matches."

> The boy hurried me into the lift, shot me up a couple of floors, rushed me down a corridor and into a bedroom, containing little more than a shiny brass bed, a black telephone, a white sink, and a rigid, brown looking-glass at a distressing distance from the light, real or artificial, and then exclaimed with a hard, mechanical abruptness: "Ice water?" The offer of the shivering stuff having been refused with true British indifference, the youth banged down the suit-case and banged himself out into the corridor.

In 1997, when Lorne Findlay arrived in Halifax, he had no trouble finding the Reo: it was on the trailer behind his camper. He went to an antique car show, where he met Eric Davidson, a blind Reo fanatic who ran his hands over every part of the car—its black fenders, the metal casing for its acetylene gas headlights, climbing in behind the tall wooden steering wheel and honking its rubber bulb horn. Eric had lost his eyesight in the famous 1917 Halifax explosion, but from age 10, he was around cars as much as he could be, feeling them on his way to school, or in junkyards, learning what they felt like, what they looked like. At 17 he got a 1925 Chev to work on, and then an old Studebaker, before he began work as a mechanic at Citadel Motors in Halifax. He went to Ottawa to work for a Chrysler dealership, but ended up back in Halifax where he had fixed the city's cars and trucks for 25 years. His keen senses kept him safe.

"I can't hear as well now as I used to. I could get around a garage, avoid falling over jacks. You can go by feel. I can lift the hood of an engine and just know what I'm looking at. I have to know where the fan is, for you can get your fingers hit pretty bad if you go barging in like that. Once I learned what an engine was, what it looked like, what it felt like, I could go ahead and work on it. All mechanics don't know just by looking. They can't see everything at one time." What he does see, or feel, is that older cars had more style. "Now I can't tell one make from the other. They're all the same shape, with so many different names I don't remember half of them. I don't take that much interest in them now."

With one day left in Halifax, I was determined to visit Eric, hear his story, and ask him about the significance of a car that had not been built since 1936.

August 26—Halifax

The day before our departure was filled with a sense of wonder at what lay ahead. The Findlays took me to Peggy's Cove, where a red and white lighthouse stands on the ocean's edge. The Atlantic was calm that day, lazily washing over rock-armoured coast as if the boulders were just whales coming up for air. The Atlantic doesn't convey much from an airplane, but up close you can't escape thoughts of all those who crossed clinging to the rails of ships in sickness, and clinging to dreams of new lives and new opportunities. I didn't realize I had an affinity to Halifax until I connected the harbour to my father's story of his days in the merchant marine. He was a Scottish sailor and his ship was on this side of the Atlantic when the Second World War broke out. He ended up being in the first convoy out of Halifax. He returned to that same city with my eldest brother, when they came to immigrate on April 1, 1951. On our return to Halifax from Peggy's Cove I went by Pier 21, the gateway for 1.5 million immigrants between 1928 and 1971.

Outside is a sign that says "Passage to a New Beginning," with photos of immigrants, ships, soldiers going off to war, health inspections, and line-ups at the immigration officer's desk. It is typically Canadian, understated and self-critical. In four paragraphs of English writing, it devotes one paragraph to those denied entry: "Canada's welcome was not always universal. Some immigrants never got past Pier 21. They were rejected for medical reasons or because of their ethnic origins, and deported. Even among those who were accepted, some would encounter discrimination and hatred. Nevertheless they persevered, survived and prospered." Inside there was nothing to indicate that it had welcomed 100,000 refugees, 50,000 war brides and their 22,000 children, 368,000 Canadian troops or the 3,000 child "guests" who were sent to Canada to wait out the Second World War. It was barren: steel girders, steel staircases and cement floors. Some of its rooms had been turned over to artists, but there was no sign of them. A place that was once so full of life was devoid of it, until a man, a woman and two children appeared. Paul Millington, who grew up in Halifax, was showing his new wife from Brooklyn, N.Y., the place where he landed from England at age three in 1949.

"I was on the *Empress of France*," he said. "I remember it was Christmas time. It had a Santa Claus on it, and he gave me a stuffed dog." Back in Halifax to clear out an old family garage, he had just thrown out that dog a few weeks before. The docks and nearby railyard were his playground. His older brother had been a translator at Pier 21. "The big ships landed here. Most of them unloaded on the second floor. My brother came home one day and told us the story of a woman from Italy who tried to get off the boat with a live pig under her arm. It was illegal to bring live animals into the country, so they wouldn't let her off. She asked if she could keep it if it was dead. When the guy said 'Yeah,' she took the pig by the hind legs and smacked his head up against one of these steel columns. It was dead all right, so they let her through."

Paul directed my eyes to what looked like remnants of giant juice cans near the container pier. During the war, submarine nets used to guard this, the world's second-best natural harbour. Chain mail was strung from the mainland across to McNabs Island between these giant cans. It allowed fishing boats to zig-zag out, and when it became such a problem, they figured out a system similar to cow gates—it allowed boats to zig-zag out—but not let any torpedoes in.

When the topic turned to Wilby and Haney, and to cars, Paul pondered what the country would be like without them. "Have you ever read *Shogun*, or seen the movie?" he asked. "It was about Tokugawa, the last of the great warlords to rule Japan. He made a variety of rules, including a total ban on the use of wheels. He didn't want anybody to amass a force against him, so he forced everyone to carry things on their back. It stopped the rapid movement of arms or an army. It worked. There were no insurrections. Everything moved slowly on people's backs. You had to walk to get anywhere along the Tokaido Road, from Kyoto to what is now Tokyo. It took almost two months to get across. They built 53 way stations for travellers to sleep at night."

Coincidentally, Wilby and Haney would take 53 days to get across Canada, I told him, and I wondered about a world without wheels, and what it would be like if the car didn't dominate our lives. Paul said we romanticize the car, but we can just as easily romanticize the alternative. His great uncle had no qualms about walking the 28 miles into town to buy a shirt. The horse was needed in the field so he wouldn't take the cart. He knew people all along the way. But then Millington defended the car: "I love driving fast on the gas, fast on the brake." His wife broke in: "There aren't enough challenges in life. New York driving is a challenge."

By this time fog covered the harbour. The next morning we'd be off on our own challenge, looking for our own way stations across the century and across the country. For the next 53 days I'd be immersed in automobile heaven, with people who had spent their lifesavings on cars, who worshipped cars, whose identities were wrapped up in cars. While daydreaming, I realized I had to track down Eric Davidson. After a few phone calls, a taxi sped me to the old part of town where Eric lived.

"It was nine o'clock in the morning on December 6, 1917," he said, talking about the last time he could see. "I was two years old, and I was home with my mother that day, my sister and I. She was only three years old. My father was on his way to work. We could all hear the ships in the harbour, blowing their whistles."

At 8:45 a.m., in The Narrows which lead from Halifax Harbour to the Bedford Basin, where ships assembled for First World War convoys, a Belgian hospital ship *Imo* collided with the *Mont Blanc*, a French munitions carrier. Sparks ignited the benzol on the *Mont Blanc*'s deck. Its hold contained 2,766 tonnes of explosives. At 9:06 a.m., Eric was running his toy train back and forth on the windowsill while his mother gazed at the fire in the harbour. "She was showing me what collisions meant when the ammunition went. It blew the north end of Halifax all to pieces. And the glass broke in on my eyes. That's how I lost my sight, my vision. My sister was scalded pretty bad from pots falling off the stove. My mother had her jugular vein cut. My father came home and saw everything was wrecked, my sister was crying and hollering. Everything was in turmoil all over the place, not only in our home. They were going around in horses and wagons, taking the people who were hurt, a few mobile trucks doing the same thing. My mother held her jugular until they took her to hospital. She was able to save her life. That night came a big snowstorm. They had to get people off the street. Some people froze to death."

The explosion killed 1,600 and injured 9,000. Eric was one of 200 blinded by flying glass. "A lot lost arms and legs, and lots had one eye blown out. Some people were deafened. My father got one ear drum blown out. He always said he couldn't hear, but I thought he heard pretty good. Me and my brothers weren't angels. He caught us misbehavin'." Eric spent the winter in hospital, and when he emerged he explored the city on foot with his dad. "My father would take me around the place, fields of old lumber, kindling, wood from houses shattered, old wrecks of wagons. I couldn't see at the time, I had to feel. I learned a lot. They showed me the lumber and explained to me as best they could. I remember my father showing me the old church bell lying on the ground on Duffus Street. He showed me the wreckage of homes, the foundations...explained to me what it was like. The city has changed."

He still likes Halifax, but he prefers the days when cows grazed on fields in the west end, and the city wasn't so spread out. "In the spring you used to hear frogs croaking in the night, birds singing all day long. You could pick blueberries in the middle of summer—there were blueberry bushes around here, and partly a swamp. A good place for kids to coast, a good place to skate in the wintertime. Things were nice in those days. Not the same now. More people coming into the city, a lot of building went on. Some crazy developers, they don't care where they build. There were farms where the Halifax shopping centre is now."

For someone who feels his way around and hears people describe the world around him, he knows the city is not as pretty, that shoppers have abandoned the picturesque buildings downtown for shopping centres built without any style. "Concrete blocks, concrete," he said, "all concrete." He also knows the car—his preoccupation most of his life, his occupation and his hobby, has contributed to this world he now finds hostile.

Eric let me use his phone. Lorne's Reo, I learned, had trouble starting—we were to begin our long journey tomorrow morning. When I told Eric, the idea of tackling that problem got him excited "Maybe the magneto needs points cleaned up in it. Something like that, probably."

I had to leave, to turn my attention now to what Hugh MacLennan called in his novel about the Halifax explosion—*Barometer Rising*—"this anomalous land, this sprawling waste of timber and rock and water where the only living sounds were the footfalls of animals or the fantastic laughter of a loon, this empty tract of primordial silences and winds and erosions and shifting colours." Eric escorted me to the edge of his porch and looked up as if he could see the canopy of maple trees that shaded his two-and-a-half-storey house. He gave me directions through his cozy neighbourhood of front porches and back lanes to a bus stop, and then asked, "Will you see it all right?" I trotted off into the darkness, only wishing I could see as well as Eric Davidson.

ESTABLISHING TWO NEW INTERESTING RECORDS, August, 1912, New York, N.Y.

—Walter Johnson, star pitcher of the Washington Americans, and Nap Rucker, champion southpaw of the Brooklyn, recently established two new records. They succeeded in timing the speed of a pitched ball for the first time in the history of the world, and in order to do this made a record-breaking run in an automobile from New York to Bridgeport, Connecticut and return. The trip was taken on Saturday morning and both pitchers had to be in New York for games that afternoon. They left New York at an early hour in a big Franklin touring car. The distance traveled was 55 miles (88 kilometres) and in returning to New York the distance had to be made in less than two hours. This was a record run considering the fact that most of it was over city pavement.

ALCOHOL-RELATED HIGHWAY DEATHS DECLINING, August, 1997, Halifax, N.S.

—Despite a perception that drunk drivers have taken over the roads, bolstered by two recent high-profile fatalities in the Halifax area, statistics tell a different story. Last year 29 people died in 553 alcohol-related accidents, compared to 42 in 1991 and 89 in 1986. RCMP attribute the decrease to greater awareness about drinking and driving, the use of designated drivers and taxis by drinkers, and the use of cellular phones by people reporting erratic driving.

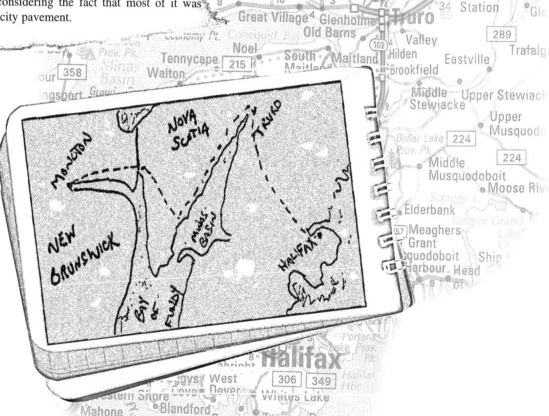

Chapter 2

Farewell to Nova Scotia

August 27—Halifax

On the morning of departure, I hesitated inside the doorway of the Waverley Inn, which had once played host to Oscar Wilde and P.T. Barnum, and noticed a map with the distances to Southampton (2,540 miles) and Liverpool (2,485 miles). I was heading in the other direction, about 4,000 miles, but it was easy to understand why one hundred years ago settlers would have had more affinity to what Wilby called "Mother England" than to British Columbia.

It was imperative to cross the harbour to get to our launch point at Eastern Passage by 7 a.m.—the timing of our start was dictated by a local Breakfast TV program—so I bought passage on the Dartmouth ferry. However, I ended up getting a ride from the Brothers Crowe, Gord and Geoff, who had reunited to surprise Lorne before his departure. Gord, 59, a Northwest Airlines pilot, said he and Geoff "hadn't done anything together since we discovered girls," which was at least 45 years ago. Geoff, 64, a tour bus driver and mechanic like Lorne, assured me they had got the Reo running, all right, and nothing should stop our excursion. He also guaranteed the sun would burn off the fog shrouding our trip over the Dartmouth bridge.

Wilby and Haney's trip began in the shoreline stones across from Oland's garage in Halifax, an area now inaccessible to cars. Haney had backed the Reo into the water and Wilby had put some of the Atlantic into a flask. After photos, including one of Wilby standing in the Reo, he yelled, "All on board for Vancouver!" Next stop was Halifax city hall, where Wilby wrote that the eyes of the crowd "twinkled ever so slightly" as the Reo pulled up for a 3 p.m. ceremony. Flanked by several aldermen, the deputy mayor fell for Wilby's "whim" and gave him a civic letter of greeting for the mayor of Vancouver. "For forty-nine days I was to treasure that documentary evidence of the seriousness of my undertaking as the riders of the Pony Express treasured their mails across the same regions!" wrote Wilby in *The Car*, a British magazine. After speeches and the presentation of pennants from the Canadian Highway Association and from Halifax, they were off. Six of the only 200 licensed cars in Halifax escorted the Reo several kilometres along the main road from Halifax to Truro. "A quarter of an hour and we had passed the city limits, had passed the melancholy spot where lie so many of the unknown victims of the *Titanic* disaster," Wilby told his British readers. The Pathfinders were aiming for Parrsboro, N.B., but because of their 4 p.m. start, they settled for Truro.

In the Ontario Motor League's *Motoring* magazine, Haney, the reluctant writer, describes the launch:

> As this is out of my line it seems more a job than the trip itself, but I will try and give some idea of the fun we had. First we backed the car into the Atlantic to wet her wheels, but I think this was superfluous as they had no chance to get dry until after we left Winnipeg, for it rains sometimes in Canada! We got a send off from the Deputy Mayor and a few "Mobile Bugs" who were not afraid of a little rain. We reached Truro that night over wet, muddy roads with no trouble.

The Halifax newspapers in 1912 said the Reo, up until it got its feet wet, had only been used for demonstration purposes, and that it would tackle about 1,760 kilometres "over which the only travel has been on horse back." The plan was to drive it all the way to the Pacific except for the 1,120-kilometre stretch in the wilderness of Northwestern Ontario, where the car would be shipped by lake steamer to Port Arthur. One headline began the coast-to-coast misspellings of their names: "F.M. Wilby left with Chauffeur Hanly for Vancouver in 35 days."

The 1997 trip embarked from a fake village on the shore of Eastern Passage. The phony fishermen's cottages, set up with government buyout money when Ottawa partially closed down the nearby Canadian Forces Base Shearwater, were an apt setting because we would find so many places across the country trying to mimic the past, trying to hook people longing for what once was. But the façades offer no grittiness; even the greasy breakfasts in the diners seemed too grease-free. Mind you, I didn't try the breakfast-salt-cod-and-pork-scraps specialty at the Tea by the Sea café.

The ceremony drew a crowd of antique car buffs and their cars (technically, any car over 25 years qualifies). There was a '61 Triumph TR4, a '61 Chev Impala, a '64 T-Bird and a baby blue '60 Chevy Bel-Air, which had a sixties wedding theme spilling out an open door. It had a presentation pillow pictured with the same baby blue car at oceanside, a mannequin in a white wedding dress, presents on the ground, and for ambience, an old radio on a chair. In the grogginess of the early morning, I thought the guy just had bad taste—I didn't realize he was advertising his car to anyone who might want to rent it for a wedding. As well there was a red '54 Bel-Air, a red Lincoln Premier with whitewalls, and a black Silver Streak 1948 Pontiac with its gearshift on the steering column and an insignia of Pontiac the Indian chief's head as the hood ornament.

After Breakfast TV, the Findlays and car buffs gathered in a diner adorned by a print of the *Titanic*. Lorne said he was just relieved the car started. Rod Burgland, who owned the black Silver Streak, told us we were more fortunate than owners of Stanley Steamers. "It took an hour-and-a-half to get going in the morning," said the antique car dealer who had lived in Toronto for 25 years before returning to the coast he missed. "They had to drain the water out every night and put it in every morning," not to mention pumping air into the pressure tank, igniting the gasoline under threat of losing one's eyebrows, and then waiting for the water to boil. These contraptions were the brainchild of Francis and Freelan Stanley, the Massachusetts brothers who made the Steamers from 1897 until after the First World War.

Our Reo went for one last tune-up at Burgland's house, to make sure it had enough water in the radiator. This gave time for a closer inspection of the Silver Streak. It had whitewall tires, fog lights and factory signal lights trimmed in chrome, and three lines of chrome down the hood to the Pontiac Indian chief insignia, which also graced the bulging grill, radio, glove box and high-beams. Inside it had two heaters, one for defrost and one for warmth. The back seat had chrome handles to help you in and out, and side windows that slid backwards. "Everyone wanted a car after the war," said Burgland. "All the car companies retooled during the war to make tanks and jeeps. They didn't make cars. There are some '45s around but they're rare." He believes the widespread sentiment for old cars has to do with their crafts-manship. "Today you screw in a bolt or mould a piece of plastic. When they built cars then, they were pretty picky. As well, the technology for the car has stopped. The options are performance or drive line. You can have different motors or more computers. It's like an airplane. It's never going to change its basic shape."

At 11:14 a.m. we departed with Peter and Irene following in the camper, and Norman Brunt in the Reo acting as pilot, just like the original Pathfinders had. No sooner had we begun our journey than we spotted a helicopter overhead, the Esso Imperial Acadia oil tanker at dock and a float plane, as if the other forms of transportation were bidding us adieu. The only thing missing was the replica of John Cabot's ship *The Matthew*, which had left the harbour three days before. We did, however, pass a truck with bold lettering "Haney and Greenwood." (It was as if Jack was nodding to us from the heavens, wishing us to fulfil his goal of getting that Reo across to Greenwood, B.C., and then the Pacific, totally on Canadian soil.)

On the way out of town we passed an image that greeted us across the country: a mall. The signature building was the Wal-Mart big box with the McDonald's logo in its corner, a union of two elements of the car culture—fast food and discount stores. When big boxes land in our communities, they promise umpteen jobs. As a columnist I had discovered these stores in fact provide few jobs, and end up killing mom-and-pop stores and downtown life, where there's public transit and appealing architecture. As well, malls send people scurrying by car to big parking lots to hand money to corporations that care little for the communities where they plop their blacktop. To be kind, I didn't have much affection for them.

Our escape was along a ring road, and then we found 318 north. Our wheels were finally in the tracks of Haney and Wilby. The scenery justified the need for a car. In fact, early motorists boasted that this stretch, as seen from the road, was far superior to the scenery from the train. First was Banook Lake, where the world canoeing championships had just been held, then Lake MicMac, Lake Charles, Lake William, Waverley Lake, Grand Lake. Each conveyed its own colours, each offered its own quiet enchantment. If lakes are the eyes of the earth, as Henry David Thoreau alleged, our every move was being followed. By Waverley, an hour later, the sun had indeed burned off the fog, and a glorious day lay before us. If this two-laned, tree-lined meander of a back road was any indication, we had nothing but 8,000 kilometres of joy ahead of us before we reached the Pacific.

Brunt, our pilot, told us that roads are the only way to get across Nova Scotia. Other than the thrice-weekly *Ocean Limited* from Montreal, no other passenger trains exist.

Of the several things we couldn't duplicate from 1912, one was the weather. Whereas Haney and Wilby arrived in the Maritimes following six weeks of rain that had turned roads into a "batter pudding," we had a smooth highway out of town in good weather. Another thing we didn't do, out of prudence, was drive on the same side of the road as they did. In 1912, cars in the Maritimes and British Columbia drove on the left-hand side of the road. The rest of the country, and the rest of North America and continental Europe for that matter, had chosen to drive on the right. It wouldn't be until 1923 that Nova Scotia switched (1912 for British Columbia).

If not for the rain, Nova Scotia roads of 1912 should have been good. The province had been settled since the early 17th century, with sparse groups of French, or Acadians, and English contesting the land of the Maritimes. The English gained control in the early 18th century, and its governor, Richard Philipps, discouraged road-building because he thought it had a "sinister" goal. He felt there was safety in not having roads, because the Bay of Fundy and shallow tidal rivers helped the British defend against invasion. Despite Philipps, roads developed following the old Indian trails from Port Royal to the Minas Basin, and eventually from Windsor to Halifax. Then the philosophy changed. In the 1750s, roads were deemed necessary to deport Acadians and to secure the British settlements. The demand for roads increased with the flow of Loyalists into the Maritimes after the American Revolution, and with the success of Napoleon in Europe, roads increasingly were seen as a means to stop invasions.

It was only with the establishment of a provincial roads department in 1908 that citizens were no longer expected to spend time or money building and repairing roads. Increased traffic and the cost of grading machines made this a provincial responsibility. The year before, country folk in Nova Scotia had wanted to pass a law forbidding cars on the narrow country roads certain days of the week so that farmers could come to market without having their horses scared. The 1908 Motor Vehicle Act gave every town decision power to prohibit automobile use on its highways, and car owners were responsible for any damage caused by frightened horses. These rules were quite lenient, however, compared to the Farmer's Anti-Automobile Society of Wisconsin, which wanted drivers to pull over for an approaching team of horses and to cover the car with a blanket painted to correspond with the scenery.

The big issue on Nova Scotia roads in 1912 was when and where autos should be permitted. Some people believed the confounded machines shouldn't be used on Sundays. An editorial in a Halifax paper debated:

> Is it reasonable, that the mass of the people, who will never own an auto, will give up the roads they made and practically own to the devil machines? Is it reasonable to believe that the legislature will take the roads of the country people away and transfer them to the rich men who may wish to make motor tracks of them?...In this province, where the country is hilly and the roads narrow, if an automobile comes suddenly over a hill in the face of a horse unacquainted with them, 10 men would not keep him from going over the bank with the wagon to which it may be attached. Automobiles have not come to stay. Just wait until they kill a few people by tumbling the wagon in which those people are traveling peacefully along. They haven't come to stay on country roads, and they won't stay.

Wilby's pilot car, wisely, had left him five kilometres out of town at a dingy wooden inn, like a tugboat would, he said, "convoy and nose mighty ocean liners out into broad deep channels." They went inside for a drink or a "stirrup cup," literally an alcoholic drink for the road that was offered horsemen ready to ride away. Eighty-five years later that wouldn't be such a good idea.

[In 1997, the Halifax papers had just reported a decline in drinking and driving, such that only 29 people had died in Nova Scotia in alcohol-related accidents (89 had died a decade before). What the mortality rates don't consider are that cars are designed for crashes: stretchable seatbelts, airbags, better padding on the dashboard and roof supports, energy-absorbing bumpers, crushable fronts and rears protecting rigid passenger compartments, headrests to stop passengers from snapping their necks, fuel tanks placed where they are least susceptible, and fuel lines fitted with automatic cutoff switches.]

Inside the "smoke-laden, comfortless tap room were men who smelt like lumber-jacks" and stared at the Pathfinders suspiciously until the pilot let their bold adventure be known. These men, who Wilby thought had never been far from the woods or bad drinks, wandered outside to examine the car as a seafarer might sniff "at a fresco by Botticelli or a clergyman examining a boxing-glove once worn by Jem

Mace. Vancouver awoke only vague geographical associations. It had no connection with their lives; it suggested a journey to the moon."

As "leaden clouds raced toward dusk," Wilby and Haney stopped at Shubenacadie to ignite their acetylene gas headlights. The tank for the acetylene gas had been moved underneath the car between the axles from its usual spot on the driver's running board, to free up the running boards for two long trunks. In the trunks were two reserve petrol tanks, which gave them a carrying capacity of 23 gallons, oil cans, six extra inner tubes and a power pump to fill the tires, two mud hooks, anti-skid wheel chains and the pulleys of the block and wire tackle. Wilby was pleased to conceal their tools because he took pride in "the neat, ship-shape appearance of the car—its clean, straight lines."

With the Reo's dull lights casting their first shadows, they ploughed through dark woods, over clay gravel paths, through mud and deep ruts filled with water, spraying anything within metres of the road. They made it into Truro by 8:30 p.m., dropping the car at Chamber's Garage and proceeding to the Stanley House for the night. By the time they had arranged everything for their first evening's stop, the hotel restaurant was closed, so they proceeded to the railway station buffet for good sandwiches and bad tea. While there, Chambers was disappointed to learn that Wilby would be leaving at 7 a.m. "Too bad!" said Chambers in Wilby's book. "We'd thought of giving you a send-off by ringing the town fire-bell. But the citizens would never turn out at that hour."

The modern drive to Truro took less than two hours, which gave me time to go downtown looking for the place where Wilby and Haney had stayed. At the Colchester Historical Museum I discovered that Truro was founded in 1703 by Acadians, and when they were expelled in the 1750s, it was occupied by 53 families from New England. North America's first Bible Society was formed there in 1810, and 10 years later the first oatmeal was manufactured—sturdy folk, those early settlers. Sturdier, it seems, than the Stanley House, which a Colchester archivist Nan Harvey told me is now the parking lot for McQuarrie's Pharmacy. "No," she corrected herself. "That was the Learmont Hotel. The Stanley House is now the parking lot for IGA." It was not the last time I'd find no trace of the hotels where Wilby and Haney stayed. They often slept at old railway hotels, which were usually downtown, but the fall in passenger rail travel led to the demise of such hotels, and to the increase in motor hotels—mo-tels—just off the highway. As well, many hotels were made of wood. Once boarded up, they often became the targets of arsonists. The Stanley burned down in the 1950s; because older downtowns had not been designed for cars, entrepreneurs turned empty spaces into parking lots.

Since they had a camper following the Reo, the Findlays planned to stay in campgrounds across Canada. The local antique auto club booked me a room at a motel near the junction of the highway and the town's four-lane artery. The street was littered with Sobey's, Canadian Tire, McDonald's, Burger King, Zellers, Swiss Chalet, Tim Horton's, Wendy's, Kent Building Supplies and an Irving Gas Station. If not for the Irving filling station telling me I was in the Maritimes, I could have been anywhere in North America. It was a strip, or as Humphrey Carver called it in his book *Compassionate Landscape*, "the promiscuous use of land...the hunt-and-peck form of real estate development." I opted instead for a bed and breakfast called Ann's Farmhouse nearer the Findlays.

At the campground the local car club held a barbecue to greet us and show off their cars, arriving almost in unison, pulling in and then parking with their front ends out for a display. Among the group was a black man named Herbert Upshaw, who was driving a purple '48 Ford. While Halifax was struggling with racial problems at a local school, in the antique car club everyone was colourless.

Herbert, 74, has been in love with cars ever since he piled into his father's as a six-year-old and turned the wheel as if he were driving. His father had a '27 Model T he used to take into town, but one day he couldn't get it back into low gear while going up a hill. It ran backwards and slid into a telephone pole. "After that he put it in the barn and left it there," said Herbert. "The roof caved in and it was full of hay seeds, but I'd sit in it and pretend I was driving it. I figured when I was big enough I was going to fix it up. One day I came home and he had sold it for junk. He had paid $200 for it and now he had sold it for $4." Herbert was heartbroken, but now he has his own antique car.

Frank Hoyt, president of the Golden Age Auto Club, said he became attached to old cars because they reminded him of the cars he drove as a young man. He enjoys the "power, the rumbling noise, the interest it creates when you drive them." He likes the people he meets at events and appreciates the construction of the cars—"the old styles looked good."

August 28 — Truro

The Stanley House was wide awake when the Reo left at 7:30 a.m. Wilby witnessed the hotel's evacuation for the eastbound train, and spied a clean-cut Englishman shining the hotel brasswork. In his book Wilby waxed on about how well-mannered the gentleman was compared to North American-born employees. He wondered how long it would be before this Englishman, who so neatly repacked Wilby's suitcase and placed his bags in the car for him, a man who deftly said "Sir" in the deferential English manner, would lose his obliging manner, before his vocabulary worsened, before he lost the English softness to his voice, before he became an independent, self-reliant North American. "May some good Providence prevent me from meeting him then!"

It's easy to understand why animosity grew between Haney and Wilby. Haney was North American. Worse yet in Wilby's eyes, he was an American. He wrote disparagingly that Haney was like those "sturdy self-contained" drivers he had seen in the States—"fellows with the sense of relationship to their fellow-men hopelessly confused by their own free interpretation of democracy and equality." Haney was loyal to his job and to Reo's goal of getting the car across the country, but he may not have been loyal to someone who considered himself from an upper class. Haney preached equality of blacks long before it was popular, and later, when he owned a garage, he employed a black man whom he treated like a brother. Wilby, on the other hand, considered most people less than his equal, and was accustomed to making racist remarks. In *The Car*, a British magazine, he said his car trip "broke away from the hackneyed method of taking a first-class sleeper on the railroad, dining under the espionage of the Negro waiter, and lolling and dozing in the luxurious chair of the observation car along a thousand or two miles of unfamiliar territory, until at Montreal or Winnipeg the entire social and political and economic life of the country was coolly passed in critical review."

Among the pilots that morning in 1912 were Chambers and Duncan McNutt, who, along with two doctors in town, owned the same model Reo. They escorted Wilby and Haney to Dickson's blacksmith shop in Onslow where they wished them *bon voyage* amid the cheers of a small crowd. Chambers, who loved the latest inventions—he was the first in town to have electric lights in his home—told the *Truro News* that while the project of finding a road to cross the country seemed absurd, it must be put in perspective. His own father, an MP, made speeches in the House of Commons saying the CPR would never "pay for the axle grease" required to carry its trains over the Rocky Mountains in winter. As well, Truro had already seen autos from Los Angeles, Georgia and Tennessee, and cars arrived from New England almost every other day. The first long-distance car to visit came in 1904 from Chicago, which included Marshall Field Jr. of the department store family. One auto had stopped in Truro on its fifth trip from Toronto to Florida. Routes through the more populous United States were more common and less hazardous.

Robert Stanfield, scion of a Canadian business family, future premier of Nova Scotia and national Progressive Conservative leader, would not be born in Truro for two more years. But already his family had established a successful factory for the production of men's briefs. Wilby and Haney passed it on their way to Parrsboro. They headed west to Parrsboro, instead of north to Amherst, because the route had been established 150 years before by the British to defend against Acadians.

Our 8:30 a.m. start nearly ended at 8:35. We were cut off by a Nova Scotia Power truck pulling a trailer, but Lorne deftly eluded it. Had it been a fatal collision, at least I would have felt at home—as a first-generation Scottish-Canadian—in the nearby cemetery amidst the MacDonalds, McKenzies and McCullochs. Then we were held up by a common occurrence: road construction. "I've never seen so much road construction in my life," said Lorne. "Everywhere we drove as we came across the States there was construction."

Just then, a woman at the side of the road gave Lorne and his Reo a big smile, to which Lorne added, "At my age, you take what you can get."

We checked out the Salmon River tidal bore—a function of Bay of Fundy tides coming up through a narrower channel in a rush of water. Bores are a bore unless you catch them at the right time of day, which we didn't. We went past corn fields and blueberry and strawberry patches heading to the Glooscap Trail. On the way Lorne spotted an old Standard Vanguard, a British car, on a farm, and a green '47 Ford truck in a driveway. I always wondered why he was nodding instead of laughing at my attempts at humour, but for the next 52 days he would be listening to make sure the car fired on all cylinders, and trying to spy every antique car in fields from coast to coast.

Our Truro escort led us to what seemed like an automobile menagerie owned by Burchell Fulmore, a semi-retired Halifax man who had spent 30 years in the refrigeration industry. He welcomed us warmly into his home. He sold cars as a hobby; that is, when he wasn't buying them and fixing them up. His house, a three-storey wooden frame home built for a sea captain 180 years before, is decorated with quilts, old dolls and antiques. During the local clam festival weekend, it has room for 15 family members and two dogs. Burt's ancestors were shipbuilders, so he bought the place to form a link with his family's past. But it was his yard that was the biggest link to yesteryear. He had a maroon '37 GM truck, a blue '34 Chev Standard two-door sedan, an orange-red '57 Chevy Bel-Air convertible with hooded headlights and a continental kit with spare in the back, a red '49 Chevy truck, and a car to end all cars, a yellow '34 Chevy Master cabriolet with a rumble seat.

"There were only 148 made in Canada; 3,276 were made in total," said Burt. "You could distinguish a cabriolet from a roadster because they had a roll-up window." It had dual, side-mounted tires, fender skirts over the back tires, a metal luggage rack behind the rumble seat, and chrome trumpet horns which, when new, only cost $8 a pair. The three-speed had come from Montreal with a built-in GM radio and cigarette lighter, and although it was derelict, Burt restored it with its original upholstery pattern—beige leatherette. "My uncle had a '34 Chev which he let me drive when I was a kid. I always thought it was special."

After being plied with tea, coffee, homemade cakes and cookies, we headed toward what Maritimers thought would be a big hurdle—Economy Mountain. The Reo rose up and up and over as if it were a bump in the road.

> Wilby had been struck by the unexpected beauty of the Bay of Fundy coast:
> the sunlit vales, lovely woods and beautiful, peaceful villages set
> amid orchards, white-steepled churches and towering barns tra-
> versed by red gravel and clay roads. A simple everyday girl was
> drawing water from a modern well; an ordinary boy was eating live
> snails; a bearded farmer sat in a buggy; an itinerant butcher hawked
> his wares from a queer, closed wagon, while a long-headed and long-
> legged farm-hand squatted on a split-log fence.

If not for pavement and the ubiquitous hydro wires, we were in 1912. The trees rippled down to meet us. Catching sight of the bay inspired awe. Wilby said his fingers "twitched to daub a canvas with lapis lazuli waters, indigo hills, purple sands, green weirs, seaweed-tinted rocks and the tawny red mud, shiny pink in the middle distance, and dull heliotrope in the offing." When I first read his words I thought he must have been testing out his liver too early in the morning, or perhaps he had decided to wear rose-coloured goggles. But anyone who travels past the Bay of Fundy at various times of the day knows what the light can do, to shade mountains bluish purple one minute, and chestnut brown the next.

In Parrsboro, Wilby had unearthed a sandwich, a glass of orange beer drawn from a keg, and a few cakes. We found the Dinatour (create-your-own-tourist-attraction) Geology Museum, the Fundy Shore Ecology centre and the Parrsboro war memorial—a little town like Parrsboro had several men fall at Ypres, Rossi, Somme and Vimy. The town boasted the world's highest tide, and a great place to survey the tide's vigour, Ottawa House. The wooden frame building, built in 1775, was once a summer home for Sir Charles Tupper, Canada's sixth prime minister. The house looked neglected, but it wasn't—its perch meant it took the full force of the salt-bearing seawinds, necessitating a paint job every 18 months. One of the hostesses pointed to what used to be an island, but a gale in 1869 had lifted the sand and filled in the gap between the island and land. This lofty site would have been a great place to watch nature, as well as the occasional historic arrival, such as the 1607 landing of explorer Samuel de Champlain. He took amethysts from the beach which were later included in the crown jewels of France, and his crew found an iron cross here that indicated Europeans had preceded them.

Before we left town, we saw a statue of Glooscap for whom the trail had been named. He was the chief God of the Mi'kmaq tribe that inhabited Nova Scotia and the woodlands of Eastern North America. Wilby had been told that Glooscap was famous for his kettle, his wailing loons, his stone moose that swam across the bay, and his little vest-pocket dogs that increased to gigantic proportions whenever he needed their services. As I panned over the wide mud flats left by the Bay of Fundy, I couldn't help but think as the natives did, that we are but Lilliputians in a giant's playground.

We regretted, as did Wilby, turning away from the beauty of Cobequid Bay and Minas Basin and heading inland, though it is silly to think of leaving all beauty behind. More always seemed to be just around a curve in the road, or above the brow of a hill. The tourist consciously takes it for granted; unconsciously it is soothing their soul, easing their stress, bringing a smile to their face. Not even two days out of Halifax, I began to feel giddy with the sumptuous feast before us.

A cemetery sign in Southampton said the town had been there since 1784. We were met here by Wellsley Crossman and his 1951 Kaiser Special Deluxe, which cruised in front of us like a hovercraft skimming the land. The Kaiser had the largest windshield of any car in its day. It could comfortably sit three adults in front and boasted no blindspots because of its slim, slant-back cornerposts. When it came out, it had been hailed as a triumph of design—every feature of the body and chassis had been engineered to serve the needs of the human anatomy. It looked roomy, comfortable, and it had a neat atomic-age hood ornament. The Kaiser, Lorne said, was built by an American industrialist who made cars for a short time after the Second World War. Kaiser began making his fortune when he took over a contract in 1913 from a Canadian road-building company that went bust. The Kaiser was discontinued in 1953 due to a car sales slump and the cost of competing with GM, Ford and Chrysler. It hung on, however, to its production of the Willys-Overland Jeep, which just happened to be the other car escorting us into Amherst. At least it was until it ran into trouble and we left it at the roadside. Ironically, the Pathfinders had also left their pilot car behind when it ran out of gas, but that was after Amherst.

The last stretch of red clay roads for Wilby and Haney, past long, flat marsh lands, protected by dikes, and the fields of hay and potatoes, ended around Amherst. It was here that Haney noted in *Motoring Magazine*, "our spare tires had taken a notion to part company with us, but they were soon secured and we hiked on with a pilot ahead of us." (The pilot was Sheriff Davidson who would have led them to Sackville had he filled up his tank.) Amherst at the time had a railway-car factory that employed 2,000, and factories that made woollen goods and pianos—it was the same size then, about 10,000 residents, as it was when we arrived. We drew a cast of characters downtown. A local newspaper reporter and others were embarrassed that the first people to greet us were vagrants; but we also met Victor Matheson, a car fanatic from Pugwash, the little town made famous by favourite son Cyrus Eaton who, after becoming a successful industrialist in the United States, established a Thinkers' Conference in his hometown with philosophers, statesmen and businessmen. Matheson was driving a four-door '31 Chevy, but back in his stable he had a '30 Model A, a '41 Lincoln Zephyr two-door convertible, a '25 Star touring car, a '26 Model T touring car, and a four-door '31 Olds with dual side-mounted tires.

Lunch counters still would have been relatively new for Wilby. In 1912 visitors to Amherst—where we had lunch—would have been greeted at their table with glasses of ice water, would have selected sausage rolls from beneath covers protecting them from flies, and would have lunched listening to the whir of fans sucking air in through the window screens. We found an old Amherst diner that fit the bill, complete with the ice water when we sat down. It even had conversations that dated from 1912—talk in the diner was about a mother of two who had been the victim of a hit-and-run.

"Wouldn't that be terrible, a tragedy," said Irene to the waitress. "A single mother leaving boys six and five. That's a tragedy."

The waitress replied with a cheery note, "That's been happening a lot lately."

Back in the Reo, Lorne told the story behind the visit to the Fulmores. Burt said "You came at a great time for us. My wife's cancer just reappeared and we needed something to take our minds off the moping." Mrs. Fulmore got to show off her cars and her house, her quilts and her dolls, and Burt got a chance to commiserate with Geoff Crowe, whose own wife was battling cancer.

The 1953 Korean War–era Jeep caught up to us, and led us out of town past a train car used for tourist information. The Jeep was owned by Bob Esterbrook, who had driven the same Jeep when he was in the militia in the early fifties. He took us out to a dirt road, and then a gravel road where we saw nothing but cows, bales of straw and electrical wires, as if we were following telegraph poles the way Wilby and Haney did. The route led to the High Marsh Road Covered Bridge, just inside New Brunswick. The bridge, with the surrounding undeveloped tidal lands, gave us the sensation of driving the original Reo. The covered bridges had roofs to protect the wooden floor planks and make them last longer.

A sign, "Blueberries, Rakers Wanted," prompted Lorne to talk about his childhood days when he worked in the fruit orchards of the Okanagan Valley. He remembered loving cars even at age 11, when he lived in the village of Kaleden near Penticton. "For excitement," he said, "I'd ride my bike out to the highway to try to identify cars that came by. I was just the average kid loving cars."

Next came Sackville, the home of Mount Allison University, which always ranks as Canada's best small university in the annual *Maclean's* magazine study. The town had green pennants hanging from poles, "Downtown Sackville Where you belong!"

It's a tactic many cities employ to attract people to their downtowns, but some experts say it's a mistake. If you distract potential buyers with pennants and hanging baskets, that means they're not looking in shop windows.

The car as an accomplice in downtown-killing came into even greater focus when we arrived in Moncton. We were greeted by Deputy Mayor Joan McAlpine who took me on a tour in Doug Steeves' 1956 Chevy Bel-Air two-door hardtop. The city, which caters to 100,000 people, has worked hard to revive its downtown and maintain what was historic. "We only got our heritage bylaw passed recently," McAlpine explained. "We lost a lot of heritage buildings in the 13 years we worked on it. The old train station—that was a real heritage building—they replaced it with an awful-looking shoebox. Another heritage building is now a parking lot adjacent to the Moncton Development Bank."

And there are ongoing controversies. "When the heritage bylaw was close to getting passed, a developer demolished some beautiful old houses on Botsford. Now the Province of New Brunswick wants to tear down the Wallace warehouse building on Church Street to make a parking lot for schoolbuses. At the school there's no place for kids to stand for buses. And then there's the sway-roofed house near Bore Park, the oldest house in town. It can be maintained. It was a house of ill-repute. If the walls could talk, they'd tell you the torrid history of Moncton."

The city's history is one of fighting setbacks. One hundred and forty years before, it was the decline of its wooden shipbuilding industry; in the last decade it has been the departure of Eaton's mail order, Swift's meatpackers, CN shops, Marvin's Biscuits. "They were all major blows," said McAlpine. "But our motto is *Resurgo:* We rise again. We have the Maritimes' largest shopping centre on the edge of town. The downtown died but we've spent a lot of time edging it back to the focal point of the city with sidewalk cafés." The problem, said Doug Steeves, is that people go to malls instead of downtown because they don't want to pay for parking.

In 1912, Haney had no trouble finding parking. He and Wilby arrived at 7 p.m. in Moncton, headquarters of the Intercolonial Railway. His worship Mayor F.C. Robinson handed Mr. Wilby a pennant with Moncton on it. More importantly to Wilby, Mayor Robinson was a Good Roads enthusiast and an ardent lover of automobiling. Wilby, like a communist, enjoyed meeting "fellow travellers," and already he could see a growing interest in the trip. The "duet of throats" he heard cheer him in Truro had "swelled to a chorus" by Moncton. In *The Car* he equated the crescendo of support that grew across Canada to that of the hubbub that grew across France when Napoleon made his way from Elba to Antibes and on through the countryside to be reunited with his army in Paris. Wilby, who claimed he was five-foot-eight but looked shorter, may have had a Napoleon complex himself.

Wilby told a reporter from the *Transcript* that Nova Scotia roads were wonderful as far as scenery was concerned but were very poorly kept. It should be

> the people's highway, and built by the people. What I mean by this is that in the United States they have formed associations among the farmers who guarantee to keep their section of the road in the best of shape by constant grading where there are earth roads. I do not suppose a heavier test could be offered than the present rainy season, but if it is going to take four or five hours to go from Halifax to Truro, what time will it take for a motor car to travel from Halifax to Vancouver? I am looking forward with great interest to my trip to St. John to find out what New Brunswick has in the way of roads.

The sign in Wilby's hotel said Moncton's tidal bore would arrive at 10:10 p.m. The "bore" was a tourist attraction of the day, a rush of water up the Petitcodiac River from Bay of Fundy tides. When the tide is out the river trickles, exposing long banks of red mud and the hulls of boats tied to the wharves. When the tide comes in, especially in the spring under a full moon, it could be a wave more than three metres high, announcing its arrival with a low, rumbling roar. Observers compare it with a wall of the divided Red Sea in old Bible pictures. Other times, the wave was but half a metre high, which it must have been the night Wilby walked a mile to the viewing post to see it. He spent four pages in his book humorously maligning the "Moncton Miracle," scoffing that he had nightmares of sleeping through the arrival of the tidal bore.

Deputy Mayor Martin handing British writer Thomas Wilby a letter for the Mayor of Vancouver..

Fonce Val (Jack) Haney, the Reo's top mechanic, overlooking a curve in the Saint John River.

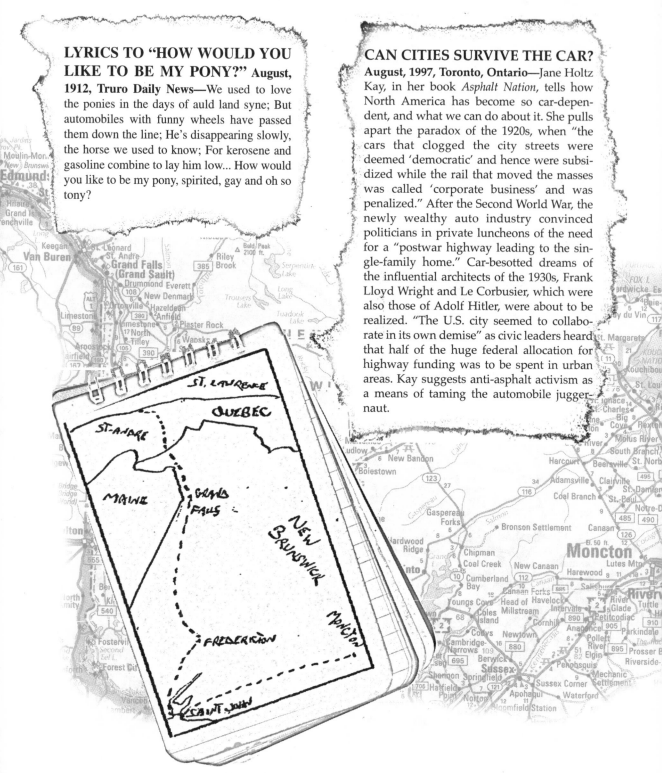

LYRICS TO "HOW WOULD YOU LIKE TO BE MY PONY?" August, 1912, Truro Daily News—

We used to love the ponies in the days of auld land syne; But automobiles with funny wheels have passed them down the line; He's disappearing slowly, the horse we used to know; For kerosene and gasoline combine to lay him low... How would you like to be my pony, spirited, gay and oh so tony?

CAN CITIES SURVIVE THE CAR?

August, 1997, Toronto, Ontario—Jane Holtz Kay, in her book *Asphalt Nation*, tells how North America has become so car-dependent, and what we can do about it. She pulls apart the paradox of the 1920s, when "the cars that clogged the city streets were deemed 'democratic' and hence were subsidized while the rail that moved the masses was called 'corporate business' and was penalized." After the Second World War, the newly wealthy auto industry convinced politicians in private luncheons of the need for a "postwar highway leading to the single-family home." Car-besotted dreams of the influential architects of the 1930s, Frank Lloyd Wright and Le Corbusier, which were also those of Adolf Hitler, were about to be realized. "The U.S. city seemed to collaborate in its own demise" as civic leaders heard that half of the huge federal allocation for highway funding was to be spent in urban areas. Kay suggests anti-asphalt activism as a means of taming the automobile juggernaut.

Chapter 3

New Brunswick on the Weld

August 29—Moncton

Wilby was enchanted by the names the natives had given towns. He understood the origins of some names, but he was flabbergasted by the likes of Manawagonish, Kouchibouguac and Shinimacas: "When it came to tackling Choctaw perpetrations like Toutimogouchiasiabash and the full-flavoured Pugwashsourispagdhaliouchen, I gave orders to change our course and fled."

Lorne and I both smiled at Wilby's humour as I read his book aloud daily over the hum of the motor. It was the beginning of our reassessment of the man we had learned to hate for what we knew of his pompous attitude toward North Americans and his treatment of Haney.

My morning in Moncton—a city named after the second-in-command to General James Wolfe at the Plains of Abraham, Colonel Robert Monckton—began with a chocolate-filled French toast at Victoria Bed and Breakfast. The proprietress, Sharon LeBlanc, had come in late the night before after a 144-kilometre drive from Saint John, and her daughter wasn't looking forward to her 170-kilometre drive that day to Fredericton. In Wilby's day, they could have had a stress-free ride on the train.

Doug Steeves picked me up in his blue 1958 Chev Delray to catch up to the Findlays. Steeves is related to one of the founders of Confederation, and his family is long associated with the birth of Moncton, but he was more interested in talking about his connection, on his mother's side, to the early-century Scottish singer and humourist, Harry Lauder. "As a kid I always wanted to drive a car," said the 63-year-old Steeves. "If someone parked one in our driveway, I'd have to go check it out. When you grow up in a small place like Dorchester, you didn't have much to draw your interest. I relate more to cars of the 1930s and post-war cars. The car club is almost like a fraternity. We have so much in common and it's a family-oriented thing."

The Findlays had hooked up their camper at Dave Kennedy's home, which overlooked Lake Petitcodiac. The Petitcodiac River, the route of the tidal bore that so enchanted Wilby the night before, had been dammed to create the recreational lake. The "Daily Miracle" as Wilby referred to it, still arrives twice a day, making its way up Chignecto Bay and the Petitcodiac estuary, but the creation of the lake and a causeway from Moncton to Riverview has reduced its impact and allure.

As tiresome as the trip to Saint John was for Madame LeBlanc, it was a slice of heaven for us. Led out of town by other New Brunswick Auto Club members in a '27 Ford roadster and a '64 Valiant, we found back roads devoid of yellow lines. Farmers' silos and treetops ruled the horizon. We even found roads with no hydro poles and saw houses where a couple of old dears were nurturing a garden of gladiolas. Every so often we saw a satellite dish, which must ease isolation the way an Eaton's catalogue would have done in Wilby's day. The old road, Lorne said, was worth choosing. "People drive miles out of their way to get to a freeway. We're going miles out of our way to avoid them."

We could drive an old car in the country because we had the security of the camper following us as a support vehicle; it came in handy when we ran out of gas at Intervale. On the trailer behind the camper we kept two plastic gas tanks for such occurrences. We had the benefits of better lubrication and cleaner gas, even though it was also non-leaded in 1912 (they didn't begin to add lead to gasoline until the late 1920s, when it was thought to be a means of getting more wallop from the tank). But there was nothing we could do about improving fuel efficiency. The engine dictated that, and it was still the original 30-horsepower with external valves so you could see them lifting to allow gasoline into the cylinders for the mini-explosion which drove the car forward. For a non-car buff or someone as mechanically disinclined as myself, the engine was like a schoolroom display. Unfortunately, it only allowed us to get up to 13 miles to the gallon (5 kilometres to the litre), just as in Wilby's day.

Not only was the camper a help in breakdowns, it also allowed us to carry our luggage on it and whatever tools we needed, making our Reo so much lighter. Our Reo only had to carry a few cameras, newspapers and writing pads; Haney had trunks of tools on each running board, but his most important aid was haywire. In 1912 haywire was like a credit card—most motorists didn't leave home without it. We were dependent on duct tape and bungee cords, stuff that would have made Haney drool. They came in handy when the hinge on our windshield cracked. The 85-year-old windshield couldn't handle the force of the wind created by our cruising speed of 60 kilometres an hour. Maybe Haney faced the same problem. It's probably why he did most of his driving with his roof and windshield folded down.

Lorne fixed up a means of keeping the windshield from flying off and decapitating us, but I was a bit nervous about it, especially when we passed a church whose sign out front said "Prepare to meet thy God."

Just past Roachville and the Salmon River covered bridge where we stopped for a photo, we came upon another stunning valley, the type you'd expect to find in a calendar photo. Wide-winged birds glided in an ecstasy we could only imagine from the ground. Although we saw many dairy farms along the way, the scenery wasn't much different than what Wilby described as the "picturesque wilderness" of forests and streams, "unexplored rivers teeming with fish, and the wild free air of mountain and lonely valley." We didn't see any ox-teams as he did, closing in on Saint John, but we saw an old motel by the side of the road that could have been used for the Bates Motel in the movie *Psycho.*

Upon closing the Wilby book for the day, I trapped a fly inside. Without missing a beat, Lorne asked, "It wasn't on the flyleaf was it?"

After an hour's stop for lunch in Hampton—then a resort town 40 kilometres from Saint John—Haney and Wilby were met at 2:30 p.m. on the Marsh Road outside of Saint John by Mayor Frink (whom Wilby called Mayor Fink in his booklet for the Reo company), Reo dealer J.A. Pugsley, R.D. Paterson, chairman of the Good Roads committee, and President T.P. Regan, Maurice Coll, W. Walter Emerson and Harry Ervin of the New Brunswick Automobile Association. They were all in a giant 90-horsepower Olds Limited, and for a car enthusiast like Haney, it would have been eye candy. The Olds was so huge it had two running boards just to climb into it. At three metres off the ground, it was an ideal snob car.

Saint John, one of the country's oldest cities, was named by Samuel de Champlain when he visited there on Saint John the Baptist day, June 24, 1604. In 1912 it was commonly known as the City of Loyalists, but Wilby didn't know why. After negotiating its steep hills, they spent an hour at Pugsley's Canterbury Street dealership, and then took some photos on King Street. There they saw a monument which humbled Wilby—no easy task. The walking John Bull spied a memorial to the 10,000 United Empire Loyalists (UELs) who landed at the market slip. Wilby was embarrassed not to have known about the Loyalists who made their way north from the 13 colonies after the American Revolution ended in 1783. Included was General Benedict Arnold, who had a business in Saint John from 1786 to 1791. Knowing about that Revolution without knowing about these men and women is like the

> French Revolution without Robespiere or Roman history without Julius Caesar, or slavery without Wilberforce or Abraham Lincoln. I ought to have been mobbed for my ignorance, for not to know what a UEL is, is not to know the most glorious historical fact in Canada—is to be excluded from even a bowing acquaintance with its best stock, its truest patriots, its finest citizens, its staunchest British bulwarks.

It appears Wilby went by the library—what Haney called "some fool doings" in his journal—to get information about the UELs. He dug up a book by Beckles Wilson called *Romance of Empire*. In his jingoistic mode, Wilby said someone of Longfellow's abilities should write a melancholic poem to counter *Evangeline*, to explain the pathos and misery of the UELs who left everything behind in the United States because of their dedication to King and country.

Despite its exquisite setting at the mouth of the Saint John River overlooking three bays and Saint John Harbour, the city didn't feel welcoming. It had undergone a dreadful renewal after the Second World War, and was allowed to spread to become one of the largest cities in area because of the construction in the 1970s of a thruway system. Its downtown waterfront had been renovated, but we never got near it. We made an appearance at a Speedy Muffler—servants of the car are often relegated to, and contribute to, the ugliness of unfashionable parts of town. Then I got marooned at the newspaper offices in a vain attempt to see their microfilm. When I left the *Saint John Times-Globe* to catch a taxi, I realized, from the car that nearly clipped my heels, that the city was not made for walking.

The taxi counteracts the auto's tendency to isolate people and prevent interaction. There is a driver, who to ease the boredom is looking to be loquacious, and then there's you, the passenger, the captive audience, able to talk to a stranger. In Halifax one taxi driver told me about his days in the Korean War, strafing the shoreline trains from a destroyer offshore. In Saint John, facing noon time traffic and more road construction, I was safely in the hands of Edwina Roberts, who was born in Toronto's Cabbagetown and grew up in Calgary, Whitehorse, Fort Williams, Inuvik, Tumbler Ridge and Hay River. "I'm a bartender and cook by trade. I cooked for railroad camps," she said. "Tumbler Ridge six months, then Mexico and back to Prince George. Then I met this Swedish guy and I went back into the bush. Then I broke. I had a breakdown." Her bubbliness dissipated. She didn't talk any more.

She dropped me off at Larry's Welding, where Lorne was getting his brass windshield hinge welded. Larry was Larry Albert, so I went inside the office looking for an Albert. When I asked the secretary where I could find an Albert, five pint-sized girls, who looked between the ages of three and seven, said they were Alberts. I eventually found Larry, an Acadian who once owned monster trucks, but the hobby got a bit expensive. Four tires and four rims cost $20,000.

"Since 1960 I owned my own welding shop. Myself I been clear to Victoria and California, me and wife on a bike. Saint John is still nice to come home to. It's one man's town, an Irving town. He has a lot of money but I have one daughter and son and seven grandchildren. Seven girls, no boys. My son has been working for me since he was 16, when he left school. He drives a crane." When we went to pay, he said he doesn't like to charge for breakdowns on the road. "A lot of people who travel don't have a lot of money."

The gas stations of the Irvings, whose patriarch Kenneth Colin or K.C. Irving started his empire by running a Model T Ford dealership and gas station after the First World War, can be seen across the Maritimes. After nearly a century of running the province and reaping gazillions from it, K.C. died in 1992. His will said his children could only inherit his fortune if they left Canada.

Our escort out of town was a man who could only be lovingly described as Herman, the character in the Garry Trudeau cartoon. He had a sad-sack expression, the same meaty nose and face, the same pear-shaped body. When he got out of his light blue '51 Pontiac, with its 350 Chev engine, he moved as slowly as his car had been cruising. He drove us by the Reversing Falls, the work of the Bay of Fundy throwing the river northwards. It was reversing as we drove north, although it didn't for Wilby and Haney. Wilby explained that the river is five metres deep and the tide of the Bay of Fundy raises the water level in the harbour by eight metres, thus creating the perception of the river going backwards.

Wilby, who was always quick to give encouragement to locals about their roads, perhaps as a means of ingratiating himself, said the New Brunswick roads were better than Nova Scotia's. One of the merry men in the Olds Limited, who escorted them out of town for 24 kilometres to Westfield, told him, "Don't. Don't ever let anyone about these parts hear you say that. We kick like thunder at our roads. We want better ones."

The Pathfinders briefly stopped at Hoyt, as did we, because Lorne sensed the Reo wasn't firing on all cylinders. He felt the spark plugs and, sure enough, one was cold. While he replaced it, we discovered that the big news in Hoyt, 50 kilometres from Saint John and 50 kilometres from Fredericton, were the new 911 emergency service numbers. So said an old woman in a large red shirt and shorts who came out to talk to us. She also confided that the town could boast "a ball diamond done with lights." Wilby also talked to a woman in Hoyt—the postmistress—who told him to carry on to Fredericton Junction, where he would find an inn. They had hoped to make it to Fredericton, the capital of New Brunswick, 37 kilometres further, but the hills interfered with their speed and they settled on a little inn.

On the way there they may have passed Mrs. A. Connolly of New York, who was in the midst of a three-day walk from Saint John to Fredericton. Described as "young, healthy and vigorous," her story made the newspaper probably because she was a woman who would accept the challenges of walking the old post road alone.

In 1912 Fredericton Junction boasted two inns, The Canadian Hotel and American House. They catered to travellers changing at the junction of trains to and from Boston, or the Halifax- and Montreal-bound engines. Ray Harris, a former railwayman who checks out life on the main street from his front porch, said it was about 9 a.m. when the No. 40 from Montreal arrived, 11 a.m. for the slower train from Montreal, and 11:30 a.m. for the train from Boston. "Once upon a time you didn't need a car," said Ray's wife Helen. "All you had to do to shop was just step on the train to go into Saint John or Fredericton." Wilby and Haney stayed at the American House, maybe because it had a telephone, and more importantly for Wilby, a bar attached to it. When they stopped, their odometer read exactly 150 miles (240 kilometres). The building was now a white-sided family home, but it no longer had an attached bar or verandah. The present owner, Eric Russell, took pride in the changes he'd made. "The hallways are six feet wide—it's a big house. It takes all of an old guy like me to keep it going."

In the days of the Pathfinders, it had seven rooms, with four for steady boarders, and one dining room that could sit 12 to 14 people on two tables. They were set with white linen tablecloths and napkins, silver utensils, silver salt-and-pepper shakers and silver cream and sugar bowls. It was known for Aunt Hannah's baking that finished off each dinner, but Aunt Hannah might have been young Hannah when Wilby described her as a "pleasant-looking" young woman who

> divided her attention between an exacting baby and her guests at supper, which was served in a small back room, where a big stove strove vainly to counteract the chilly effect of the linoleum-covered floor. Tea and Canadian steak, of doubtful cut, but usually served under the imposing name of "tenderloin" or "sirloin," followed by cake and canned fruit, proved to be the staples of the meal. There was a little guest parlour in the front of the house, where the assistant waitress and a lady caller passed the time exchanging light and cheap badinage with a gentleman visitor from the adjoining bar. The floor was of hardwood and uncarpeted, while a tiny jet of acetylene gave niggardly of its light. In one corner stood a cradle, in another a what-not littered with hoary literature.

As we neared Fredericton we saw a roadside sign announcing "Grading/Terrassement; Paving/Pavage. New Brunswick Building Better Roads." Votes must go to good-roads enthusiasts in 1997 just as they would have in 1912.

We were met at Brentwood by a '39 Cadillac with dual side-mounted spares and fenders over them, and escorted into the capital. I ended up at the Carriage House Inn, a bed and breakfast within walking distance of downtown and the promenade along the Saint John River which, to my pleasure, led to a statue of Robert Burns. The town was appealing with its outdoor cafés and growing numbers of students gathering for the school year, but it had one of those downtown malls that make little or no connection to the street. Then again, better downtown than on the outskirts. One sad realization, though, was summer's demise—dusk arrived too quickly on the banks of the tranquil Saint John River.

August 30—Fredericton Junction/Fredericton

Around the large Carriage House breakfast table was a small United Nations, where Japanese, French and English were spoken. One man and a woman from Sydney, Nova Scotia, were in town to drop their son off at university. They talked of moving the woman's mother to Prince Edward Island.

"My mother moved from Welland (Ontario), where she lived for 48 years in the same house, to PEI, where she was born," said the woman. "She is 85 now, and her 88-year-old sister is there."

"But there's not the same shopping on the island," piped in the husband.

"Yeah, but she calls her sister," said the wife, "and they go for walks."

It was the first of many anecdotes that depicted the marooning of young and old by the single-purpose neighbourhoods cars create. Seniors too old to drive can't live in their old neighbourhoods, so they end up in homes for the aged, and rarely in a place where they can partake in meaningful daily walks. Children are restricted by fearful parents, either to their street or sometimes their homes, because of heavy traffic and hostile four-lane roads. They can't go anywhere without their parents driving. What seniors and children need are neighbourhoods where they can walk for life's simple pleasures.

The Findlays' stay at the Wandlyn Inn was more fire station than United Nations. Irene had taken the toaster in from the camper to make toast for breakfast. The alarm in their no-smoking room went off, and they tried everything to get it to stop. They were worried they'd have to pay a $50 fine because no one would believe that only the toaster was smoking.

Lorne had worked on the car and found a piece of felt he was looking for, and two washers. He lowered the float in the carburetor, which controls the amount of gas getting to the engine. "If you lower it, it might run a little leaner." I nodded, but it meant nothing to me. I was wondering if I could lower the float on my own body. I was worried that, by sitting in the passenger seat all day, and just moving my arse to allow them to get at the gas tank underneath my seat, that I might have a problem with weight gain. I too would like to run a little leaner.

Haney and Wilby had about as rough a day as we would have, but Wilby would have been more upset if he knew about the publicity another motorist would receive on his visit this day to Saint John. While Wilby achieved moderate publicity, much ado was given the arrival of Dr. Benton Young of New Jersey, who was attempting to cross the continent and back in a Columbia car to win a $10,000 bet. In an argument with a hardware dealer in Trenton, New Jersey, Dr. Young vowed that he could do the trip across the United States within six months without any money. In return he would get a dollar a mile and he would give the car away at trip's end. Anyone who helped Dr. Young along the way would be eligible for a draw to win the rebuilt and repainted Columbia car after the trip.

After what Wilby called a rushed breakfast, they left at 7:45 a.m., taking more than two hours to make it 37 kilometres along a muddy, rut-filled road to Fredericton. On the way they picked up a tall, deaf, 88-year-old who was legging it to the city with the aid of a stick. Wilby said the man, who clambered in after throwing his stick in the tonneau, was as proud as a child about his first ride in an automobile. Born in 1824, the old guy, grandson of a United Empire Loyalist, had to hang on for dear life. Wilby heard him murmur, "Never seed such roads in all my life. They've never been so bad since I can remember."

In Fredericton, Haney bought gas and fixed a hole in his radiator with something he called "semental." Wilby did his bit speaking to the editor of *The Gleaner* before they headed up the valley on the west side of the river to Woodstock, where Haney bought a box camera. They probably stopped for lunch on the banks of the river at a summer hotel. From the side of the road a young man called out "Hey Jack." Haney didn't know who he was at first, but realized it was "the student from Woodstock." Perhaps it was an apprentice he had taught at the Reo factory, or someone who stayed at his boarding house in St. Catharines.

Armed with photos of the 1912 trip, where both Haney and Wilby are captured surveying an alluring bend in the Saint John, we tried to find the same point along the river, but we were flummoxed, as were several locals, as to where it could be. The world has changed so much in 85 years, there could be subdivisions or a forest where once there were farms, or farms where once there were forests. And the Saint John River, a wide, lazy waterway buffered by meadows that give way to wooded hills, has a few bends in its 673-kilometre run. We stopped to try to duplicate a photo, and found the river was just as dreamy in daytime as it was at dusk, its shoreline trees casting shadows that blended greens and blues. Nothing indicated this would be the trip's most stressful day, a day when we wondered whether we'd be able to complete our journey or not.

With Lorne's son Peter giving him a breather at the Reo wheel, we were making good time firing on four cylinders up the east side of the river (the Trans-Canada consumed the west). When Lorne was in the camper he often stopped to snap his own set of trip memories, so when Peter and I lost them, we weren't too concerned. We found a muddy junkyard entrance to use as a backdrop for photos, and then continued on, always looking over our shoulder for signs of the camper.

At Hartland, home of the world's longest covered bridge at 391 metres, we wondered whether the camper had passed us during our photo session, or whether Lorne and Irene had had an accident. While waiting, we took some photos as though we had found the location Haney and Wilby had used. We ventured across the bridge to a park, where wedding photos were being shot. On the day that the Pathfinders picked up a man at the end of his life, Peter drove the new couple, 21-year-olds Toby and Tamara Bodechon, around the parking lot at the beginning of their life together. The father of the groom was extremely pleased, as if the Reo had bestowed a blessing on the marriage. It was either that or he was smiling at the thought of starting his own Who's-on-first? routine. Instead of Abbott and Costello having Today pitching to Tomorrow, he had Toby pitching to Tamara.

It made me wonder why cars have become so important on wedding days. Is it that they give the image of wealth, in weddings that are more about image than meaning, or is the pursuit of old cars to bring the bride to the chapel an attempt to tip the hat to the days when their parents were married? Marriages and old cars have become so intertwined that the guy in Halifax seemed normal driving around town with a mannequin attired in a wedding dress.

To occupy the time waiting by the side of the road, Peter talked about the 1913 Henderson motorbike he owns. The first trip around the world by motorbike was in a 1913 Henderson. If we survived this trip, he half-jokingly thought he'd consider taking on the world. Then I wandered over to the local garage sale. Because it was a weekend, garage sales dotted the road, but Hartland's was particularly appealing. I was tempted to buy a convex car mirror, one thing the 1912 Reo didn't have, but I didn't know if Lorne would appreciate me ruining its historical authenticity, or gluing it to his nicely painted door. The sale offered *Penthouses* and *Playboys*, even well-thumbed copies from 1980, and film videos to die for, literally—the greatest artistic achievement amongst the lot was *Honey We Shrunk Ourselves*. Used shoes, country music cassettes, four ceiling fans in their original boxes, broiler ovens that looked like someone left the toast in too long—and for a mere $40 you could get a Smith-Corona typewriter, complete with used Liquid Paper, Taperaser and Taperaser refill. Among the high-end electronic equipment was a black-and-white TV, a beat-up Realistic record player and stereo, and the all-important stereo-cassette adapter for your eight-track player. Although it seems as if eight-tracks were around in 1912, they weren't. I left without making a purchase.

Haney, with his new camera, had taken photos in Hartland and Florenceville, and stopped for supper in Andover, at another summer hotel on the river's edge. Haney said in his diary that for 35 cents they didn't have enough food to feed a chicken, while Wilby's command of the English language allowed him to say they ate supper of "a vegetarian kind." As twilight neared, they were still 40 kilometres from their day's destination of Grand Falls, and they only had 35 kilometres' worth of petrol. Their first obstacle was an 8-kilometre-long swamp which the locals had tried to make passable with felled tree stumps—the first corduroy roads they encountered. Not only were they bumpy rides, but they were always in poor shape. After crossing the swamp and its smelly growth, the Reo ran out of gas on an incline. Because they were in the middle of nowhere on a narrow road, and retracing their steps was not an option, their predicament was daunting. Wilby moved to the back seat, if he wasn't there already, allowing Haney to remove the seat next to him and peer into the nearly empty gas tank. To gain pressure, Haney blew into the gas tank and started the car, and with more cheeky work, managed to surmount two big hills before using the downgrade to arrive in Grand Falls.

Wilby called the arrival a miracle, as he did the realization that

> the unfortunate chauffeur did not burst his cheeks or succumb to asphyxia, for it fell to his lot to blow into the petrol tank every few moments of the remaining journey....How tremblingly we scanned each succeeding rise in the ground! How joyously we hailed every descent, every slight declivity, until swamp and hills were past and the small hotel of Grand Falls stood before us.

Haney was a bit more sanguine about it all. His diary said the hills were bad, "so in order to feed the gas tank I blew into the tank and then plugged the vent hole with a piece of match." They arrived just before 10 p.m., having covered 256 kilometres. Haney noted that he only had to fill the motor once with oil. He felt the car was running "pretty fair." He tightened up the bolts, spring clips and the left front wheel before he set out in the morning, and took off the remaining spring rebound strap at night, because it was doing no good. Before going to bed—which he was relieved to do—he would write A.G., his girlfriend Annie Glendenning Swan, who would later become his wife. He had lost his water pail, which was valuable to keep topping up his radiator. Maybe that 88-year-old, in search of a souvenir, hooked it with his cane as he disembarked from his first horseless carriage ride.

Just about where Haney and Wilby must have struggled on an upgrade, Peter stopped the Reo to check our water and spark plugs. From across the street came a man and woman on a motorcycle, two Acadian men and a native woman on foot. For some reason the situation became intimidating, as if we'd stopped at a biker gang hideout. We had a pleasant conversation, and I offered to keep things jovial by taking a picture of the crew. One man backed away and the woman balked. Peter and I couldn't help but think they feared the police would get their hands on the photo. They told us that we were about 13 kilometres from Grand Falls. Peter, trying to be lighthearted, asked if Grand Falls was bigger than the place we were in. The woman shot back, "What's wrong with our little place?"

Peter and I had reached Grand Falls and found no trace of Lorne. Getting more worried by the minute, we waited prominently in the parking lot of a Metro gas/convenience store, a place where the essentials of life are held: gas, cigarettes, lottery tickets and videos. The owners were helpful, probably because the look on our faces suggested something bad had happened. I called the RCMP, who are responsible for policing the Maritimes, but the dispatcher hadn't heard of any accidents. Still, I called several hospitals. No accident victims had been treated.

We became a curiosity, sitting at the side of the road fielding questions about the Reo. One man, who was impressed by the car, had the penchant for putting *la* on the end of all English words, such as "Unfrigginbelievable-la!" Our motorcycle friends drove up in a car and offered us a place for the night at their friend's house across the street. We politely declined, but it showed how quickly we pigeonhole people, especially with a motorcycle involved. They didn't look intimidating sitting side-by-side in the car. The man said he and the other guy cut wood for a living at Près-du-Lac. "We even drag the trees out with horses, just like old days. We also have machines. We do whatever the owner wants. We select cut."

Whereas Haney was quick to use his acetylene gas headlights and drive at night, assured of meeting few other vehicles, our car would be run off the road. By today's standards our taillights and headlights were as good as toy flashlights. Besides, we didn't have any acetylene gas. Just when the anxiety was building around 6 p.m., a guy named Hermel drove up and said Lorne was looking for us at the Falls. We breezed down to discover he had needed a welder again, this time for the trailer hitch. He promised to tell me the story tomorrow, so we raced around looking for accommodation. There was a big Labour Day weekend mud run the next day—an event we should have entered with our high clearance and 85-year history of tackling mud. But this posed a problem for finding bed and breakfast rooms. When the Findlays had found a campsite, I ended up getting a room in Mont Assumption, an old school run by the Catholic church that had been converted into a hotel.

Hermel, a jovial chap and a stranger to the phrase "politically correct," said: "It's no problem to stay at Mont Assumption. You have to sleep with either a priest or a nun, but that's all right."

August 31—Grand Falls

Mont Assumption was large and stark—an old school where noises echoed, preventing a sound sleep. If there was a priest and a nun in the next room, they were committing every sin in the Bible. I had breakfast with the erstwhile love-makers—a thin truck driver and a long-legged parking ticket collector for the city of Montreal. It made me wonder how Wilby made it through his trip with no conjugal visits to his wife in the United States.

The woman who ran Mont Assumption asked if we had taken Highway 108, the old logging road which cuts across the province east to west. There's nothing but forest on both sides, because the road was built for lumberjacks. I said "No," realizing that we were about to leave the Maritimes having explored so little of it.

On the front steps of the Mont, where there's a dramatic view of the Saint John River and the state of Maine on its west bank, Lorne told me we had no choice but to take the Trans-Canada Highway. Other motorists did not treat us as slowpokes—instead they honked their horns in encouragement. The car was running on all four cylinders so we were doing close to 70 kilometres an hour, creating a coolness at the back of the head from the draft. I thought for a minute we should have done the mud run, just to show that we could compete, but there was too much excitement about heading to a new province, and all the angst about speaking French.

Nine kilometres this side of Ste-Anne, the provincial and federal governments were driving a new route for the Trans-Canada through a forest, and were proud of it. At Ste-Anne-de-Madawaska, a highway-side cemetery boasted flowers at each upright headstone. Lorne said the gravestones in B.C. are mostly flat, but this cemetery was as striking as it was foreboding for what we'd learn at St-Jacques. To make the morning even more morbid, a cross at the side of the road prompted Lorne to ask, "Do people in Ontario put crosses at the side of the road when someone dies in an accident?" I said that some do, and he related his trip going across Montana. "It was a nice straight road. We saw multiple crosses, sets of three, four and five. We saw two with seven—a whole family must have been wiped out."

Lorne finally got around to his welder story. When he noticed his hitch had busted off his camper, he jerry-built a substitute and then, coincidentally, stopped at the same junkyard where we had taken the photo, to look for a welder. "The guy said 'We could weld it, but not professionally. We have a friend who can, but he'll probably preach at you.' In the kind of mood I'm in, I told them, I can handle some preaching." When Lorne arrived at the welder's home, he saw a bandstand covered in Biblical murals and scripts on a trailer in his yard. "He set to the welding without preaching," said Lorne. "He was a really nice guy with a Southern accent from the States. He never preached at me, so I asked him to tell me about it. Then he started."

The man became a born-again Christian while he was in jail. He had a vision in prison that God would send him his wife. It took 10 years, but she came. With his wife he now has three teenaged daughters, and he returns to jail to preach. Lorne interjected that this beats jail. The man misunderstood at first, but then said, "I'll never be back there again." While he worked, his two younger daughters tried to out-talk Irene. A vain attempt. The older one practised her gospel singing for her father's preachings. It was New Gospel music, which Lorne said was too far out for an old duffer like him. He wanted ear plugs.

The guy actually builds trailers, and wanted to build 40 of them so he could get enough chairs for his trailer/ministry. He asked Lorne for $30 for his job, but Lorne gave him $50, saying he wanted to buy some chairs.

While Lorne was telling this story we were passing Edmunston, N.B. There Wilby had run into his own preacher, a Dr. Ridder, "Millionaire Tramp" and theosophist lecturer. Dr. Ridder was wearing a Norfolk suit (Wilby was from County Norfolk) of thick tweeds and "a flaring red tie accentuated his social creed." Ridder walked from lecture to lecture. He preached that, ideally, a man should never cause another man a moment's pain or bitterness. Such preaching allowed Wilby to express his belief that Britain's poor should go to North America. "What life and hope awaits in these kindly sunny valleys for the ignorant and wretched."

The 1912 Reo started out at 8 a.m., after Haney filled up with gas and greased the transmission and axle. He bought a funnel and was carrying 34 litres in a reserve tank. They crossed the bridge over the falls at Grand Falls. Wilby wished he could have been there in the spring when thousands of spruce logs go over the brink. While facing rough and sodden roads, they still made good time, especially when they picked up an hour with the time change at Edmunston. At Temiscouata Lake they ate crackers and cheese for lunch. In the Malecite Indian language, *Temiscouata* means "deep all over." The British used to come from Halifax by water until they reached the end of this lake—Fort Ingalls is just up the road—and then they'd portage to Rivière-du-Loup on the St. Lawrence. The portage route was fine for feet, but not for cars. Poor roads prevented them from reaching Rivière-du-Loup until 4:30.

Before leaving New Brunswick we bought gas at the village of St-Jacques. I went inside to buy a newspaper but was struck dumb by the headlines of the French tabloids. *Le Devoir* said Princess Diana was in a bad accident, while her boyfriend Dodi was dead. The other one said: *"Lady Di est tuée."* I checked with the woman at the counter, who confirmed my pathetic translation: Lady Di died in a car accident. I bore the bad news to the rest, but they didn't seem that fazed. The Reo has no radio, so we hadn't heard the news. When we climbed back into the car, the news had finally sunk in. Lorne said: "I thought you said a lady died in a car accident. I could see the horror in your face and I wondered why. Ladies get killed every day in car accidents." Then he shook his head. "People look upon them as the luckiest people in the world, the fairy tale wedding, all that. The older I get the more I appreciate being born into a poor family and having nothing when I was growing up."

Upon entering Quebec, Lorne said, "Two down, six to go." Unfortunately, we weren't going to do all 10 provinces because we clung to the original itinerary. It was only as of 1997 that a bridge connected Prince Edward Island to the mainland, and in 1912, Newfoundland wasn't part of Canada. Quebec, in those days, was Canada's most prosperous province. It grew 50 million bushels of oats, sold 4 million British pounds of pulp and paper, 6 thousand tons of maple syrup and was known for its fishing and hunting, whether the prey was salmon, bass, pike, whitefish, Caribou, moose, red deer, mink, beaver or yellow fox.

In a vain attempt to discover where Wilby and Haney might have alit at Temiscouata, we pulled over by the lake in Cabano. The car drew its usual crowd, but this one included a man who could relate to our transcontinental goal—Phil Latulippe, who made a name for himself running across Canada three times for charity. The 78-year-old lives in Loretteville, north of Quebec City, but he grew up in Cabano. A house trailer by the lake draws him there each summer, but not to relax. "This summer I will have ridden my bike 5,000 kilometres from the end of May," said the white-bearded man with endless energy. "And fast walking I'll have done 2,000 kilometres by the end of September." Before I could ask him when he relaxes, he said, "I'll be ice skating and skiing when I go home."

His fitness kick began in the Canadian military. He started running at Base Petawawa where he set the world record for the fastest 300 miles (480 kilometres): 77 hours, 30 minutes and 30 seconds. In 1971 he ran from St. John's, Newfoundland, to Port Hardy on Vancouver Island in 140 days, averaging 62 kilometres a day. In 1984 he went from Anchorage, Alaska, to Quebec City, averaging 55 kilometres a day, and five years later, at age 70, he went from Vancouver to Halifax in 140 days with same daily average. He was blasé about his feats, but he got more excited relating the story about the diver who went down 71 metres into Temiscouata without any breathing apparatus. He spoke fondly of the lake. Just then a float plane cut across the bulge of Mount Lennox over the way and landed on the placid water. It was as if the lake was a personal reservoir of strength for him—at least that would go some way to explain his endurance.

He was a bit envious of our undertaking, saying his own jaunts were the most interesting parts of his life. "The scenery! At times you must stop and look around and take it in. And the people. They are so kind, so nice to me. In the Prairies, my wife would pull in at a farm. As long as they know what you're doing and you're doing it for charity, they would welcome us in." His experiences crossing the country convinced him that the best way to solve Canada's separation anxiety is to put all the separatists on planes to the west for two weeks. "They'd come back and we'd never hear another word about separation."

When Wilby and Haney departed from Temiscouata, an old man gasped at their goal of reaching Vancouver. In 1997 Latulippe, old only on his birth certificate, sighed at the Halifax to Vancouver sign and pointed to his sweatshirt. It promoted a plan to create a Trans Canada Trail: "I'm just waiting for this to do it again."

I was impressed by Lorne's stamina and agility at 70, but Latulippe was twice my age and had twice my spirit. What he did, he did for charity, and he did it in a healthy, environmentally friendly way. Although we were spewing out our share of greenhouse gases for 53 days, we at least knew "Waaaaah" we were doin' it, and we felt good about our cause.

We had lunch in the camper and set off for the St. Lawrence, past barns that seemed to sink into the ground. It turns out they're potato houses, part of a huge empire of frozen french fries and potato chips for McCain's foods. *"Jesus Sauvé"* (Jesus Saves) was spray-painted on a rock. Farther down the road I expected to see the French equivalent of "But Beliveau taps in the rebound," in honour of *Le Gros Bill*, Jean Beliveau, the famed captain of ice hockey's Montreal Canadiens.

Wilby's book gave me the impression he exaggerated his observations, but having duplicated his route, I have more respect for *A Motor Tour*, even if he does go overboard sometimes. Approaching the St. Lawrence, the river was

> visible in the sky—in the peculiar broad spaces of light that filled the world to the north—long before its shores at Rivière-du-Loup came into view. The afternoon had been divertingly full of the minor incidents of the road—a Gallic lunch at a Temiscouata village inn, a running of the ordeal of scores of rampant dogs, and encounters with scared drivers who had frantically endeavored to blindfold or hide away their perfectly docile steeds. But the bigness and grandeur, the majesty and beauty of the St. Lawrence were such as to sweep away all other memories, while the mind dwelt upon all the wonders before it in mountain and sky, in water and in air.

We didn't drive into Rivière but chose to get off the Trans-Canada as soon as we could, thus coming down to the shore along a hill with a 10 percent grade. We could smell the brakes as we happened upon Notre-Dame-du-Portage, but that soon gave way to the smell of the sea, for the broad sweep of the St. Lawrence is like an invitation to the ocean, enticing its viewers outwards. The shore is marshy; blue herons scoot along the water and cormorants perch on rocks waiting for some unwitting fish. We had driven nearly 1,000 kilometres, yet we were at the sea again.

Our joy at reaching the St. Lawrence—as Wilby suggested, sweeping away all other memories—was heightened by a visit by Rolland Thivièrge, a Montrealer who came to greet us from his cottage, Stella Maris, across the street. Thivièrge, 70, explained about The Five Islands: The Big One, The Middle One, The Garden One, The Long One, The Small One. "Across here is 12 miles," he says, with an excellent command of English. "When the Indians used to get to Lac-St-Jean, they stopped on the islands to take a rest before crossing the St. Lawrence and going up the Saguenay River. In Notre-Dame-du-Portage there's a monument to Indians with a canoe. You see the boats travel on the other side of the island. This side is too shallow. Ducks Unlimited take care of the island. It's a bird sanctuary. No people are allowed."

The retiree had only given us a small taste of the St. Lawrence. He ran across the street and came back with a stunning set of sunset photos. Sometimes the fire of night bounced off his windows; other images included an orange sun leaking scarlet across the water. "I've been retired for 10 years but we've been here for 12," he said. "We have the best view. I sit here and watch the sunset. You cannot miss it each night." We asked him what he was trying to say with his flagpole, which has the Quebec and Canadian flags sewn together. "Some people don't like it. We're both federalists. We spend the winter in Florida. We even left Florida to come vote *No* in the referendum."

As we began to leave, he gave Irene a kiss goodbye on both cheeks. She said, "Oh! A French kiss."

"Oh no," said Rolland. "I won't give you a French kiss."

Now Irene, whose facility with the English language is incessant, realized her mistake and tried to motormouth her way out of it. After more than a minute of nonstop talk, Lorne finally told her not to dig herself any deeper.

Haney and Wilby had found a boulevard for 5 kilometres leaving Rivière-du-Loup, and then went about 40 kilometres an hour along a river trail. The successor to that trail now led us, in the glorious sunshine, a few kilometres to St-Andre-de-Kamouraska, where the Pathfinders spent the night in a summer boarding house.

Before going to bed, Wilby was enchanted by a crimson sunset painting "impressionistic pictures on the broad bosom of the placid river."

Although Lorne and I had never discussed it, we entered Quebec with an uninvited hitchhiker in the back seat whom neither of us had seen climbing into the car. The figure had grown out of our fears, fears that our stay in Quebec would be hostile, that we would have trouble communicating, that we would leave the province feeling discouraged about Canada's future. So far, the stops in Cabano and Notre-Dame-du-Portage prompted Lorne to say, "All you hear is the bad stuff about Quebec. Not all about these wonderful people. It makes you annoyed." But it was nothing like what awaited us in St-Andre.

In this town founded in 1791 I found an exquisite B & B called *Auberge La Solaillerie*, an old mansion built in 1848 for a family of a man who sold agricultural implements. While I checked in, Lorne and the family were just about to head to the campground when they were waved over by a group of revelers who pleaded to take one photo with the broad-shouldered Reo. The group was celebrating a 60th birthday, so they mugged for photos around the car and stopped traffic to sing "*Bonne anniversaire*." After almost a half hour of kibitzing, Lorne told the group what he had just told me: "When I'm in British Columbia we only hear the bad stuff about Quebec, yet today there is a whole different story we have to tell."

A woman replied, "We only hear the bad stuff too. You tell everyone when you get back home about us." When he cranked the car back to life, the crowd sent him on his way singing "For He's a Jolly Good Fellow"—in English.

Our expectation of a hostile reception was wrong. It made us question the picture given by the media, and our own insecurities of survival in a land where English doesn't predominate. The disturbing thing is that it took an antique car to get conversations going, to toss that gloomy hitchhiker out of our back seat, to break down barriers. But that was the Reo for you; since Halifax, the beguiling hulk had turned heads, raised thumbs and slackened jaws. It was nicknamed the Pathfinder in 1912. That night, I thought we should call it the Smilemaker or the Icebreaker. It made me wonder how I could take another trip without it.

RULES FOR CROSSING ROADS,

September, 1912, Vienna, Austria—A notice has been issued to the effect that pedestrians who wish to cross a road, must do so in a direct line, taking the shortest path. Those who do not obey this rule, thus endangering their lives, will be reprimanded by the police and if they do not then comply with directions, will be subject to fines. The purpose is to permit the smooth flow of automobile traffic.

COUNTIES DON'T WANT HIGHWAY HASSLE, September, 1997,

Ottawa, Ontario —A delegation from Eastern Ontario went to Queen's Park last week to discourage the Harris government from handing over the provincial highway system to municipalities. The province has announced it wants to hand over the responsibility for 244 kilometres of Highways 37 and 41 to four county governments, including Renfrew, by Jan. 1, 1998. In all, about 6,000 kilometres are to fall from the provincial grid. That would leave the counties in charge of maintenance, repairs and snow-plowing on roads, which would lead to patchwork levels for each, depending on which county was fastidious or not. It's estimated that each kilometre of provincial highway costs between $7,000 and $10,000 a year to maintain, and they must be maintained in perpetuity.

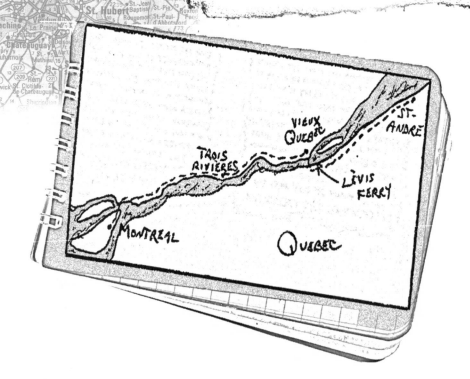

Chapter 4

A Song in La Belle Province

September 1—St-Andre-de-Kamouraska

At 4:45 a.m., my groggy eyes wondered what century I was in. The wooden floors and the antique bed made me think of Haney, tossing aside his slumber and getting dressed on creaking boards for another day of trying to choose the right fork in the road. Then again, my world was too pretty, too comfortable. I was able to run the wide mud flats of the marshy shore, where nets hung to catch eels riding the ebbing tide, and then come back for an elaborate breakfast and a long, warm shower. It was one thing to play at being in 1912—I had the best of both worlds.

At breakfast I chatted with an English-speaking Montrealer, who seemed paranoid the surroundings. He was tentative in his chat with the waitress, as if the next indignity would convince him to leave Quebec. He spoke in low tones, almost conspiratorially, that this was definitely separatist country. "It's a different world in the rural areas. Montreal is federalist, and the rural areas are separatist." He looked beleaguered, on edge, an us-and-them demeanour. It seems a self-fulfilling prophesy, though, that all the media hype would lead to more distancing. We could hardly make a judgment with our cursory exposure to the province, but I was definitely less jaundiced. When checking out the proprietor reminded me that it was September: *"C'est le fin d'été."*

Haney and Wilby set out at 7:30 a.m. along a grassy trail with wagon wheel ruts and faint markings of horses' hooves down the middle, yet they made good time. Wilby thought of the early French pioneers, and don't forget those UELs, who carved a living from these lands. But his preoccupation was with the French. He had a snooty, belittling approach to the French farmers he saw, a view common in his day.

His words show how much the image of Quebec has changed. They also reflect the fall in Britain's status as a world power. His insights stemmed from the preconceived views in the novel *The Golden Dog*, by William Kirby, distinguished by its pathetic view of French history through the eyes of a 19th-century English Canadian. No wonder Wilby had such a belittling attitude.

Wilby gave them backhanded compliments, saying that along the primitive road he was constantly reminded that the people in the shabby houses were

> direct descendants of those who had penetrated the Pays d'Haut, the West, with sublime courage and inspiration. If anybody deserves Canada, surely it is this old-fashioned, English-language-murdering, tobacco-growing, semi-illiterate, easy-going, badly dressed 'antique' —the French Canadian....It is years since France abandoned her child of the wilderness. But with a loyalty that must touch even an Englishman's heart, the child has remained faithful in spirit to its Latin parentage.

Haney was frustrated by his inability to speak the language, which led to his annoyance with Quebeckers and the predominance of their religion. In his diary, he wrote the "country was all out to Church, in fact the church is everything here. People live mostly in poor squalid looking huts. The churches and the priest homes are fine."

It was a Sunday in 1912, so Wilby spoke of seeing the buggies and traps of the French Canadians going to church in their Sunday best. In 1997, it was a Monday, Labour Day, but we couldn't miss the churches he had seen. High above the road, the monastery and church were still there, "easily the most striking features of the shores," as was another church built in 1768 at L'Islet-sur-mer, where in 1912 horses were tied up in long rows to its iron railings. A crowned virgin "clothed with the stars" looked benignly down from above on "chattering groups of simple peasant folk." Wilby made reference to clapboard houses and well-built churches of brick, stone and copper. The hamlet was ignoble, the church

> noble. It soared while the hovels grovelled. Few of those gay and irresponsible Habitants beneath the shadow would murmur, would question the right of the church to be rich and beautiful, to be adorned with jewels of rare price, while Progress, Modernity, the practical application of the Arts and Sciences, and even Sanitation,

remained outside upon the steps. With about eight miles between parishes, the church was not only his spiritual mentor, but it provided him his entertainment, his common rallying-point, his concerts, his theatres, his picture galleries, and his point of view.

Villages were still long and straggling. The narrow seigneurial lots still existed, as did the roadside shrines, crosses where families could come to pray. We even saw a roadside oven that must have enchanted Wilby and Haney.

The housing stock had obviously improved since Wilby's day because we saw several homes wrapped in tidy verandahs. If the south shore was once a poorer part of Quebec, it was no more. The age of the buildings continued to impress us, especially Lorne the Westerner. A sign said Kamouraska was founded in 1764—it was also the birthplace of "O Canada" lyricist Adolphe Basile Routhier. In Anguille, we saw the 1834 home of Jean Charles Chapais, a Father of Confederation. The red roof and double spires of Eglise de St-Jean-Port-Joli were built in 1779. At Cap-Saint-Ignace, 325 years old and the second oldest town on the south shore of the St. Lawrence, the remains of a windmill built in 1675 sit off the road as you enter town.

Lorne started the day saying, "We've had a wedding, a birthday, next thing we'll have is a funeral." Sure enough, at St-Roch-des-Aulnaies a hearse waited outside the stone chapel. We didn't participate in the cortege, but we had our own line of traffic to deal with. Cars fell in behind us when they couldn't pass on the two-lane road, but Lorne courteously pulled over to let everyone get around us. The source of the jam—other than cottagers returning home at summer's end—was a student driver. Then a motorcyclist in a colourful helmet came alongside and revved his engine. After admiring the Reo, he pulled in front and did a wheely, like a horse raising its front legs to say goodbye. "I guess," said Lorne, "it's his way of saluting."

Actually, horses did rear on this stretch when confronted by the Reo in 1912. Haney had noted in his diary that "horses are very much afraid of mobiles." Had we more time, and wanted to tip our hat to the days when horses were the prime source of transportation, we should have stopped in at the *Musée des voitures à chevaux* in Saint-Vallier, which houses a collection of 65 carriages and other items, "testifying to centuries of devotion between man and horse."

It sprinkled rain at Cap-Saint-Ignace, spoiling our record of perfect weather and threatening to ruin *les ventes de débarras* (garage sales)—hey, if the politicians don't find an alternative, garage sales could be a great source of Canadian unity. At Montmagny, which we learned plays host to the world's best accordion players, the St. Lawrence is totally fresh water. The sea goes no farther. At nearby Kamouraska, the water still retreats two kilometres from shore twice daily.

Talk of receding water prompted Lorne to explain why he was bald. He had *alopecia universal*. At age 55 he lost all his body hair within eight weeks. "It has something to do with your immune system. I went to a dermatologist. It was quite upsetting at first. I wore a toupee for a couple of years. Then on a trip with friends to Peace River, it was getting hot so I decided I wasn't going to wear it anymore. It shocked them a bit, but they were good enough friends it didn't matter. It also shocked everybody when I got to work."

I listened intently, knowing my head was on the same slow, determined march.

Just outside our destination we stopped at a roadside oven. A woman baking bread said ovens were placed there because of the fear of houses burning down and so that more than one family could use them. Wilby had met a woman, 85 years before, baking bread in an open-air oven made of dried earth and stone with a hood to shelter the baker from the elements. It had reminded him of outdoor ovens he had seen among American natives the year before, and in the Orient "where they have been an institution from time immemorial."

A well-kept Edsel went by, signalling an upcoming reception from *Les Belles Auto D'hier* club. Ahead lay a burgundy and beige '31 Chevy Special Sedan, with dual side-mounted spares, an eagle hood ornament and a valise on the luggage rack; there was a '33 Cadillac Lasalle with dual side-mounted spares, back and side blinds, a flower holder behind the driver's ear, a greenish matching chest on the luggage rack at back, and three sets of windows with the last set folding outwards vertically. The Caddy also had trumpet horns, original wooden ruts on the running board, wooden ashtrays with metal cigarette containers and a V8 engine with hydraulic valve lifters. Its owner is Jacques Boutin, whose house we were going to for tea and beer.

In Boutin's yard were his '29 Chrysler roadster, '29 blue Ford with parking lights, '56 Chevy, '56 Cadillac Coupe de Ville with missiles coming from the front bumpers, a '55 Dodge DeSoto and a '55 T-bird. Club members showed off a '57 red Chevrolet Bel-Air, a '61 Pontiac Laurentian, a '60 Lincoln Continental Mark V and a '69 yellow Cadillac, an original shade in models that also came out in pink and baby blue. "Some guys buy the No. 1 wood for $800, we buy car parts," said the owner of the yellow Caddy, Daniel O'Connor. "You see a lot of old cars now. The baby boomers are going back to their roots. They want to see cars from the fifties and sixties and they're the only ones who can afford to do it." Their club started two years ago and now has more than 300 members.

I tactlessly joked that I had to do this trip while Canada was still a country. O'Connor, a 49-year-old of Irish- and French-Canadian blood, responded by saying: "If you feel the pulse, you won't find a big separatist movement. There's a few idiots speaking loudly, and they're all in government. They've got a helluva problem. The Hull area doesn't want to separate, West Islanders don't want to, the Indians don't want to separate. It's not like it's going to be easy. You've got your nuts up there and we've got ours down here. When it's something good, you don't hear about it."

In an exchange of speeches, Lorne couldn't help but get emotional about the reception he had just received in Quebec. It was one of those moments when nobody had to say anything.

The Lévis ferry, which Haney and Wilby had used, was still in operation, but club president Daniel René, who organized our stop, offered to drive me to Old Quebec. Charles Dickens had once described "its giddy heights, its citadel suspended, as it were, in air; its picturesque streets and frowning gateways." On the way along the river to *Vieux Quebec*, just beneath the Plains of Abraham—site of the 1759 battle where France lost Quebec to the British under General Wolfe—was another battle. One of the cars had stopped at the lights and another had pulled over to the side of the road. One man tried to walk away from the argument, but the guy behind kept baiting him, which led to the fisticuffs. I asked what one of the phrases meant in English, but the Renés looked uneasy with their 14-year-old daughter in the back seat. Evidently, it was another case of road rage.

The Lévis ferry had been needed in 1912 because the Quebec bridge had collapsed a few years before while under construction, with a loss of nearly 100 workers. As Haney and Wilby took the ferry, they could have read about the upcoming International Congress for Testing Materials in New York that would discuss how to avoid a disaster like the Quebec bridge. Upon disembarking, the Pathfinders tried to make it up one of the narrow, granite-blocked streets of the Old Town, Mountain Hill, that is now known as Côte de la Montagne. The Reo backfired a few times, as if to announce its arrival, and then stalled halfway up, threatening to run down the zig-zag street. Wilby leaped out in embarrassment. The Reo came to a full stop

> athwart the line of traffic, while all Gaul collected on the side walks. The situation was ludicrously humiliating. The delighted crowd did not scruple to point sarcastically to the inscription on the tire drum which flauntingly announced the Pacific as our destination. The lettering of the inscription, too, had grown to five times its normal size. I sprang out to lighten the load. "Turn her round and back her up! Quick!" I cried, and ingloriously sought self-effacement among the onlookers. Here we were undertaking the longest road tour ever attempted in Canada, and yet we were unable to climb a paved hill!

Because of his touring experience, Wilby may have told Haney how to get up the hill, but Haney knew better than anyone that reverse had a lower gear ratio than any of the three forward gears. He probably had told Wilby to get out to lighten the load. Arriving at 12:45 p.m., Haney spent the rest of the afternoon going over nuts and bolts, greasing the cups and pumping the tires for the first time since Halifax. The left rear tire had a bad cut from a large nail, but it hadn't been punctured.

Haney stayed at a rooming house next to the Campbell garage, which is where General Montcalm supposedly died after being injured on the Plains, while Wilby stayed at the Chateau Frontenac. He gave his address as Belvedere Road when he wrote his report to the U.S. Office of Public Roads that spring, but he wrote it on Chateau letterhead. The Chateau is a superb vantage point from which to explore old Quebec. From the summit Wilby could see "the blue Laurentians, a dent in the shore that must have marked Montmorency Falls, the island of Orleans that Cartier dubbed the Isle of Bacchus because of the wild grapes he found there." The Citadel prompted him to compare Quebec and Halifax, a comparison just as apt today "One, open to the sea, welcomes all external influence; the other, inland, surrounds itself with a rampart of insularity, prejudice and conservatism. One is sure of its goal and its future; the other is at cross purposes with itself and its destiny."

While Haney worked on the car, Wilby went with Frank Carrel, owner of the Quebec *Daily Telegraph* newspaper, on a 45-kilometre jaunt to Ste-Anne-de-Beaupre, a shrine where pilgrims came to be freed of their lameness, blindness or any such ill, a place advertised as being "where miraculous cures for helpless ills have been performed." Wilby had arrived as church was coming out and was impressed by the scene of so many bad singers continuing their song across the square.

The Findlays left the Reo at the campground and checked out Old Quebec in their camper, with Peter taking special delight in finding references to General Wolfe, the name of the school he taught at in Vancouver. I strolled around, unable to strike up any conversations with Les Habitants. Although Paris is called the City of Lights, Quebec City at night is mesmerizing. The streetlights with five globes that had been introduced to the city just before the pair went through 85 years before, still adorn the streets. Lanterns hang from the walls, fancy teardrop lights illuminate boutique signs, arc TV lights shine for the taping of street musicians, and the headlights of cars cruise down Rue Saint-Jean, with the red glow of brakelights heading the other way. It was evidently the place to be, as cars cruised in a well-established ritual. I ducked into a newspaper shop only to see evidence of a car that wasn't cruising, the world's most famous car crash in Paris.

Newspapers like *The New York Times, International Herald Tribune* and the *Globe and Mail* were full of it. Some of the local papers hadn't time to do it up as big as they would have liked. The Sunday edition of the *Progres-Dimanche* newspaper, whose motto is *Pour "vivre" Le Saguenay, Lac-Saint-Jean,* was all about *"mourir"* in Le Saguenay. To live in that area meant to die in horrendous auto accidents. The headline over a picture of twisted wreckage was *La Route de la peur et le Parc frappent encore. Two Morts* in large letters. At the bottom was a last hour story, *Lady Diana meurt dans un accident.* Page 3 had two pictures and two stories of accidents. The rest of the thick newspaper was full of car ads. It appeared that *Progres-Dimanche* survived on the sales and crashes of automobiles.

At the Chateau Frontenac, CNN gave details of Diana's death and "Larry King Live" interviewed a reporter from *Time.* The magazine man stumbled across the accident scene on the way home from his family vacation. He saw the hubbub of police, but he didn't think twice about it—he took his family home. "In Paris you'll always find police making a big deal out of a car accident."

September 2—Quebec City

Wilby's fraternizing with Frank Carrel had two outcomes: a long story in his English-language daily and a place in the Labour Day parade. Not only was Carrel a newspaper baron and head of the automobile association, he also organized the parade automobiles. Wilby told the *Daily Telegraph* it was his ambition to be the first to cross Canada and to find a route for a national highway. "Not necessarily the most direct route," he said, "but the most picturesque and historic, as there is a question whether the route under contemplation will run via Sherbrooke or Quebec." He found the scenery a "continuous panorama of matchless beauty," including the perfect natural setting of the St. Lawrence and the unique features of habitant life, but the road's attempt to take advantage of the beauty was "inadequate. The roads were fair to wretched in Nova Scotia, and from good to bad in New Brunswick as a consequence of seven weeks of constant rain which turned the streets into a veritable quagmire. Chains, however, were never once used."

Because they didn't have an early morning start, Haney played tourist in the city of 75,000. He was shown around town by an employee of the Campbell garage (Haney had an affinity for the garage—his first job was at a Campbell's garage when he moved to North Baltimore, Ohio). He got to see inside three of the city's more famous churches—he wasn't into religion, but he did the tourist thing, likely taking in Notre-Dame-de-Quebec Basilica Cathedral, the oldest North American church north of Mexico, the Anglican Cathedral of the Holy Trinity, and Chapelle des Ursulines, where Montcalm is entombed. Haney also went down Mountain Hill, the oldest street in Quebec City, which he said "was as crooked as a dog's hind leg and about 10 feet (three metres) wide." As Haney saw the sights, Wilby went down to the immigrant wharves to do some mental belittling of the non-Brit immigrants.

While those 1912 guys loafed, I had an early-morning run through old town, looking to find a plaque on the wall that might have indicated where Montcalm died. I ran up to the citadel, where a soldier from the famous Van Doos (*vingt-deux*) battalion refused to let me in. I ended up taking a rear-guard action and ran through the sergeant's entrance. What a view of the St. Lawrence heading off to sea between the old city and Lévis. Then I ran along the terrace de Chateau Frontenac and met Valentine, a French researcher who has been in Quebec for 18 months working for a drug firm.

The chat moved around to what she thought, as an outsider, of separatism. She chose her words carefully. It might benefit her workwise if there was a closer arrangement with France, but she didn't feel strongly about it. And how did her

Quebec colleagues feel? Were they *séparatistes*? "Oh yes," she said, making me wonder if our recent view of the issue was distorted by talking to only older Quebeckers who the polls say are more closely tied to Canada.

With the Findlays staying in campgrounds, I had to take long cab rides trying to catch up to them. On the morning of September 2, I had an Egyptian taxi driver, who I'm sure Wilby would have delighted in meeting because of his time spent as a special correspondent in Cairo. The driver and I got along well until he revealed his lack of knowledge on how to get to Camping à L'Aeroport, and his apparent unconcern for getting me there on time. To be fair, he didn't want to speed and lose his licence. He had immigrated after meeting a *Québécoise*. He spent time in Montreal, Toronto and Vancouver, and wished he had stayed in Toronto. When he slowly climbed a hill past an old monastery, I also wished he had stayed in Toronto.

I didn't know what was planned for the morning, but for the car buff it was as close as you could get to paradise—the home of Jean-Marie Paradis. Instead of making a pilgrimage east to Ste-Anne-de-Beaupre, the pilgrimage for car buffs was at Chez Paradis west of Quebec in St-Augustine. A visit left me in a daze, incapable of deciphering what day or decade it was. The entrance to Paradis's office has a Pabst Blue Ribbon sign in the window with some hub caps. Inside, above the window, is an old picture of Christ with the words *Ne me blasphémez pas* (no swearing). The wall was decorated with old *Shell* signs, a big round *Approved Packard Service* sign, *Buvez Coca-Cola* and *Molson Bière* and *Pneus Général* signs, a *Packard* clock and a *Grads Cigarettes* thermostat. His garbage can had a touring car on it, and under the glass on top of his desk were old postcards with cars on them. To boot, he has a 1949 engine for a Villières motorcycle mounted on some wood.

Then we entered a 10-bay shed and he turned on the lights. The lights between each of the bay doors were the old circular domes that sat atop gas pumps. Signs from *Imperial Gasoline, Packard Imperial, White Rose No Knock, Bengal Green, Gulf, +70 Champlain, Texaco* and *Premium Richfield* shed light on a fantasy world of cars and car paraphernalia. The cars included a white '14 Model T—the ones where speed was adjusted by hand while using three pedals to propel the car forward—a '40 Plymouth, '31 Ford Woody station wagon, '26 Franklin, '51 Mercury Monarch with lion hood ornament, and a '30 Packard with a hood ornament of what looks like a goddess holding a tire. His *truc cher*, a '32 Cadillac Limousine once owned by Quebec premier Alexandre Taschereau, was one of five made in Oshawa. It has a window dividing occupants from chauffeur, dual side-mounted tires, trumpet horns and safety glass.

Asked if he had any doubts he had Taschereau's car, he said, "Not everyone could afford to have a Cadillac in the Depression. I can be sure it was not a blacksmith who bought it." Two decades before purchasing his Caddy, Taschereau was one of the dignitaries who escorted Haney and Wilby to Crown Street, or De La Couronne, on their way to Trois Rivières.

Paradis, 71, started his collection in 1956, when old garages were disappearing. Jean-Marie had to go out late at night though to collect the stuff. "My wife didn't want me bringing this junk home during the day time." He worked in the used car business and thought it would be fun to have an old car. He bought a 1921 Chev Touring Car, and then thought it would be fun to buy a Ford. "When you have two, you want five, when you have five, you want 10 and so on," he said. "In my dreams, I wonder what they were like in the showroom. They must have been beautiful."

Pointing at the '32 Cadillac, he said, "Look at the horns, the hood ornaments. That's really something. It's part of my life. I've had the Cadillac for 35 years. I had the Franklin for 37 years. It has a wooden frame just like new."

He built his garage in 1969, and not only filled it with autos, but also with miniature cars built as toys for rich kids, cans of grease, about 200 signs, old coffee tins, metal cigarette containers and even the old racks for the quarts of oil that used to be stored in large glass bottles. He had an IOKA oil rack, and he wondered if it stood for Irving Oil, Kerosene and Alcohol, or Irving Oil, Kenneth (the old man) and Arthur (the oldest son). The collection of oil racks is rare and priceless, but Jean-Marie says if he gave the IOKA one to his neighbour, it wouldn't mean anything. Asked how much his collection is worth, or how much he spent on it, he retorted, "Just like a guy who drinks—I don't know how much I've spent."

The navy blue, wood-framed '26 Franklin had seat covers over the leather, and an ad on the back wheel cover: *New Bath House, Walled Lake Amusement Park, Pearce Management* in small letters, and in smaller letters, a copyright from some firm in Chicago. "The first advertising," declared Jean-Marie, who was smoking one Belvedere after another. Aficionados from all over the world come to see his cars. He just sold two cars to a man in France.

Paradis pointed to a Packard Service sign with his cigarette hand. The sign is shaped like a radiator. "I saw it in 1962. I finally bought it in 1993," he says, telling a familiar story for people who buy old cars. "The guy died. I got it from the estate." All across the Maritimes we heard from car buffs who tried to buy cars from old guys who didn't want to part with them. The only way they got the car was to outlive the person. They clung to their piece of the past. Whether the car was in an immaculate garage, or under cobwebs and hayseeds in a barn, they didn't want to give them up.

Jean-Marie's wife Claire says that although her father-in-law couldn't change a flat tire, Jean-Marie was always into cars. He married his love of cars with his love for everything that's old. "He has enough books to read for the next 100 years."

Jean-Marie, the father of two boys and three girls, said he'd like to know everything, "what Quebec was like when the pioneers first came here, how the old mills worked, the history for each car. I've seen the cars as a young boy. There's a story on the Plymouth hood ornament, the hood ornament on the Ford, there's a story in everything. I read quite a bit in the winter, but there's never enough time to do it all."

Lorne has seen exceptional collections, and once worked at the B.C. auto museum, but he was impressed. So too was Peter: "Our whole culture is wrapped up in the car. Look at all the kids' toys, the miniature cars, the picnic basket."

Out back, believe it or not, was another large shed that had become a rabbits' warren because of all the parts. Lorne, like Jean-Marie, doesn't believe in putting new parts on old cars. "You have to be correct, have the right wheel sizes, colour, upholstery material and mechanized parts to be the same," said Lorne. "If I want a car to run well, go fast and have good brakes, then I'll buy a car like that."

Lorne and Jean-Marie walked through the parts shed picking up pieces of metal, saying how great the part was and where it came from. Lorne had met his doppelganger in the heart of separatist country. They both harboured a desire to go back in time, to days when cars were designed better, when buildings weren't put up to be knocked down, when all the furniture wasn't made at Ikea. We got back in the Reo and waved goodbye. Jean-Marie lit up another Belvedere...make that doppelganger minus the smoking.

I returned to Wilby's book and their day. They didn't leave Quebec City until 4 p.m., so we were way ahead of them. Over the hum of the motor, I read aloud

Most of the people who crowded the sheds and siding were going out to the prairies for which we were bound. The majority were of British stock, and it formed a fascinating occupation to contrast the finely alert Anglo-Saxon with the groups of brutish-looking peasantry from the Continent of Europe. One came across men and women in whose eyes the light of intelligence had never shone. By the side of a fair-haired, laughing English girl stood a Roumanian peasant woman and her husband, who suggested the advanced guard of a horse of Huns on a new invasion of the civilized world. One wondered what Canada contemplated doing with such hopelessly raw material...

"We made a nation out of them, Wilby," said Lorne, punching the sky.

Wilby was often pompous and jingoistic, but Lorne and I continued to be impressed by his observations of the land, his comparison of Halifax and Quebec. Even in 1997 the two cities remain similar. They represent the two invading nations, England and France; they are two of Canada's oldest cities and they both have citadels. Their downtowns are both very walkable and tight-knit, but their outskirts spread like other modern cities.

The north shore along the Chemin du Roy, which has existed since 1743, was patched with cornfields, but it wasn't as quaint as the south shore. Maybe, because of the preponderance of modern homes set back further from the road, I felt no connection to the communities we drove through. And for someone looking for good anecdotes to take home, the absence of Canadian flags and the prevalence of fleurs-de-lis was mildly disturbing. Then there was our first real rain of the trip, and to add to the gloom, the road sign warning *La Vitesse Tuée*: Speed kills. I needed reminders like that while crossing the country with no seatbelts.

Haney and Wilby, with their late start, didn't arrive in Trois Rivières until 10 p.m., partly because they got stuck on a hill just after Pointe aux Trembles, 32 kilometres west of Quebec City. Haney said it was too steep for gas to feed without a full tank so he tried backing up. About 32 metres from the top he could not get any traction. "There were four French peasants standing along the hill," wrote Haney in his diary. "I got them in the rear seat to hold her down and was able to back up and over it. I will put pressure in the tank when I get to Montreal."

Wilby, of course, was caught up with the grand scheme of following in the foot-steps of La Salle, Marquette, La Verendrye and the Jesuit martyrs Brébeuf and Lalemant, although he admits they didn't have much of a trail or path to guide them, no hotels or the up-to-date comforts of modern civilization.

> Compared with their horses and canoes and moccasined feet, the instrument to my hand was clumsy and ineffective, demanding its wayshowers and advance men and a thousand and one other evidences of preparation, before it could prove effective. And after all was said and done, there were to be stretches where my machine could not follow in their wake—spots where man is still hermit, symbolizing Tragedy, Solitude, Desolation.

He found the homes of the Quebeckers desolate, and when they stopped at an inn in Sainte-Anne-de-la-Perade for supper, he attacked the locals for not having the culinary skills of their French forefathers. He had a sorry meal in which the flies had reached the food first, and then fell dead in his cup of tea. They travelled in darkness to Trois Rivières, never really knowing their way. They stopped and honked their bulb horn when they were lost, and beckoned advice which they only half-under-stood from residents who emerged from their homes into the gloom of a trail shad-owed by full-foliaged trees.

Haney was frustrated at being unable to speak the language. He wrote that he "will be glad when I get out of the cussed country, for I can't understand anything they say, everybody is French." He also was upset that the only garage in a town of 15,000 was a kilometre and a half from the hotel. He took some comfort in writing to his "girlie" and then to bed. In Haney's magazine piece, the balm of time and his lighthearted style makes light of how exhausted he was each day on this early stretch of the trip. "It was simply a case of get up early, plow through mud and water all day and go to bed as soon as possible. I was pretty good at getting to bed." Wilby looked down his nose at Haney's desire to go to bed, oblivious of the work Haney was doing early in the morning to prepare the car for the road. He took the opportunity in his book to say that work should be only another name for play. In his rustling around the hotel, he found a stray volume of William Drummond and sat up reading.

Trois Rivières has a confusing one-way street system but we found railway tracks and the Rue Champfleur. Wilby and Haney ignored the motor league tip to stay at the Sanotorium de Doctor Blois; perhaps they were afraid their lack of French would have condemned them to doctor's care instead of a room. They stopped at the 34-year-old Hotel Canada, which had just received a fresh coat of paint and furnishings. Wilby said the rooms were mere cubicles with fanlights above the doors that let in bright corridor lights, "shockingly oblivious to the common rights of sleep." The hotel burned down in 1972, and the only hotel-like structure across from the tracks was now a strip joint. I didn't think my wife would have wanted me to scare up a room, even if they rented them, so I carried on to a bed and breakfast with a view of another old-time transportation route—the St. Lawrence River.

September 3/4 — Trois Rivières/Montreal/Oka

With Wilby's head filled with the bedtime reading about Johnnie Courteau, he and Haney left Three Rivers at 8 a.m. Courteau was a character who spoke franglais

> "Victoriaw she have beeg war, Egyp's de nam' de place —
> An neeger peep dat's leev'im dere, got very black de face,
> An' so she's write Joseph Mercier, he's stop on Trois Riviere —
> 'Plees come right off, an' bring wit you, t'ree honder voyageurs."

Drummond would have appealed to Wilby because Drummond's descriptions of the lives and characters of French Canadians would have affirmed his own misconceptions. Quoting from an unnamed source, Wilby said "it took but little talent to set the foibles of a people to metre, but it calls for genius in touch with the lowly and the divine to make a man a poet by the Grace of God. Truly Drummond's salient quality is overflowing sympathy with the people of his adopted Habitant world." Wilby was sympathetic, as one could only be while looking down the nose he is holding. He called Drummond's depiction of the habitant country between Three Rivers and Montreal a fascinating study in patriarchal simplicity, "its primitive methods of life marred only by the apparently unnecessary poverty and squalor of so many of the people—a poverty and inertia which were to stand out in vivid, startling contrast to the ways of the men who are making a new-fangled Canada to the west of the Great Lakes."

About 13 kilometres west of Trois Rivières, at Pointe du Lac, they ran into a fork in the road. It had a sign with a hand pointing and words that read something like "Dtr" or "Dir. Automobile," meaning the car should go around and not continue ahead. They did not realize their error until they had gone down a gully and tried to get out the other side. They were in the dried-up sand bed of a feeder to the St. Lawrence. Wilby said the wise thing to do would have been to backtrack, but he felt they could manufacture some adventure by plowing ahead. An audience of school-children watched as they made about a dozen attempts to get up out of the gully. They tried to follow their ruts in a direct line over the top, but the car kept spinning rainbows in the sand. Instead, they retreated and rerouted. At Louiseville, where Wilby stopped to buy films, they watched with half the town as river loggers tried to unfurl a bad log jam up against the town bridge. Wilby took some satisfaction watching someone else's mishap.

Their day was unbelievably dull and chilly, and then became unbelievably warm; coincidentally, ours did too, though not as hot. They stopped at St-Sulpice for lunch, managing to get some sustenance after scouring back alleys for hidden bakeries and a delicatessen shop.

The 1997 newspapers were full of the car's most famous victim. By September 3, this much was clear: the chauffeur of the car speeding Princess Diana away from the paparazzi was drunk, or *"ivre"* as *Le Soleil* announced; the speedometer, it was reported wrongly, was stuck at 196 kilometres per hour, and the only occupant to be wearing a seatbelt, the bodyguard Trevor Rees-Jones, survived the crash. As well, the mother of all funeral processions was being planned to honour the princess. Meanwhile, the paper announced that 11 people died on Quebec highways on Labour Day weekend, a holiday that has developed a macabre reputation for being a killer. The 11 were two more than the number who died on Labour Day weekend, 1996. Meanwhile, *Le Soleil* was doing a puff piece on the Nissan Maxima, not only noting how quiet it is inside, but also how great a sound system it had. The *Montreal Gazette* advised its readers to set limits when teenagers learn to drive, making sure to evaluate the child's maturity level, supervise them long enough, take them out at night and in adverse conditions to see how they cope; set an example by obeying traffic laws and using a safety belt; make sure they have a destination in mind when they get behind the wheel; make it clear inappropriate driving will not be tolerated; and discuss drinking and driving. That was in an eight-page section totally devoted to car sales and advertisements.

Wilby wrote that all the majesty and glory had disappeared from the scenery of the St. Lawrence, and we agreed. He wrote about tall skeleton trellis work of iron and wood which did duty as lighthouse to guide the steamer traffic across the river flats (we found none). But we both found the banks were low and monotonous all the way to Montreal. The singular common sight along the way was the *balançoire*, a swing with two benches facing each other. Lorne, 70 years young, joked that he would have to get one for his retirement.

Both Reos arrived in Montreal at 3 p.m. but whereas Wilby and Haney had a lovely tree-lined entrance to the city, ours was a long line of drive-through joints, strip malls and towering signs—car-inspired—inviting us to shop at this box or eat fast food out of that one. The cars, one looking like the other, whizzed along the six lanes, except when they slowed down to our speed to get around a twisted bicycle. It seemed harsh—when you saw the police officer propping up a cyclist's head above a pool of blood—to go on. It was like a battle scene where medics tend to the injured, and all the soldiers trudge on in the attack. No time for emotions or concern. The cyclist was a victim of a war. Carry on, carry on. The war must go on.

Downtown Montreal was a nightmare of epic proportions. Because of one wrong move we were left stuck in traffic for 15 minutes trying to go back one block to our turning point. I felt like Wilby must have felt in Quebec City; it was pathetic to have that sign "Halifax To Vancouver" on our back while we were heading nowhere. People passing us by seemed to laugh, if they paid any attention at all. I just wanted to get out and abandon the car. We were late for a date with Speedy, and when Lorne, now driving the camper, took the wrong fork in the road, like Haney and Wilby had done earlier in the day, we were even later. When a motorist is late, the roads seem busier and narrower and longer, and anxiety builds. To make matters worse, an antique, open-air car isn't very good in traffic jams. The air is choked with exhaust fumes from the Reo, never mind the other 40 cars surrounding us. The heat intensifies and we could see everyone trying to cut us off. It became more precarious farther away from the core, where roads were wider and speed limits higher.

Although we were far from where the Canadian Open golf tournament was being played, the story in the *Montreal Gazette* about the potential traffic chaos was understandable. It had been many years since Royal Montreal Golf Course was moved from near Mont Royal to Ile Bizard, but the Open was a testament to the folly of moving something away from public transit. Tournament director Bill Paul, in announcing a bus shuttle service for golf fans, said, "To permit everyone to drive their own cars would have caused major problems and concerns for residents of the area as well as for the club."

While *The Gazette* seemed to discourage use of the car, in 1912 the newspaper *La Patrie* seemed to be supporting the arrival of Haney and Wilby. At Montreal the pair received the radiator emblem of the Automobile Club of Canada, and the city pennant, presented by Eugene Tarte of *La Patrie*. Wilby, with so many pennants on board, got the feeling the trip had taken on the nature of a royal tour, "so kindly were the attentions of the motoring and good roads public." A crowd assembled and *La Patrie*'s photographer had to part the crowd to get a photo of the Pathfinders.

Wilby took the time to explain to *Le Devoir* his history of making the circular tour of the U.S. and his trips in Egypt and across Europe. Mr. Frank Girdwood, the Reo representative in Montreal, accompanied Wilby and Haney and Mr. Houte of *La Patrie* to see Monsieur Lavallée, the mayor, who encouraged them on their enterprise. A local automobile club made Wilby an honorary member at a reception held that night, and booked him into the Hotel Windsor, a "lordly" hotel where Wilby had afternoon tea and listened to music before heading out to explore the city.

Montreal grew out of Ville Marie in 1642. It became a commercial trading centre because of the confluence of the Ottawa, Richelieu and St. Lawrence Rivers, and was later a major centre for the fur trade and the railway. Wilby followed amber lights to the top of Mount Royal, where he surveyed the city of 900,000, Canada's largest, and recalled the words of Voltaire when Montreal capitulated in 1760: "France and England are at war for several acres of snow and are spending on the fight more than the whole of Canada is worth....The country is covered with snow and ice for eight months of the year and is inhabited by barbarians, bears and beavers."

He had heard of the Laurentian Mountains, and how their lure as a tourist destination would improve roads in and around Montreal. But he made a point then that is even more appropriate now: "The tremendous stretch of new suburbs across the Montreal plains has made sad havoc of the fine farming land and the rural thoroughfares. . . ."

Haney wasn't much for fussing with dignitaries, especially when he had to listen to Wilby take all the credit and not make mention of the Reo. In his diary Haney said they spent from three til six o'clock "getting our names up in the papers and fussing around with the nabobs of Montreal." It was his first sign of testiness in his diary, which might have been prompted by his own letter to the woman he called his "wife" or "the girlie" in his diary, Annie. When he wrote in his diary that night, he began with: "Got a letter from the wife, most acceptable of anything I have had since leaving St. Kitts." Because of the cost of phone calls, Haney was left to depend on getting mail at pre-arranged locations with his fiancé. Maybe he had a trying day with Wilby, but his pent-up feelings about Wilby were about to explode over the next few days. He would have preferred to continue on the road to Ottawa, for he said "Ottawa to-morrow or bust," in his diary.

Our Montreal experience would have pushed us on toward Ottawa, but darkness descended as the Findlays found a campground in Oka. We had crossed "a tremendous stretch of new suburbs" only to find that no bed and breakfasts existed. Instead, I ended up in St-Eustache which, when the Pathfinders went through, was being sued $300 for having bad roads that caused damage to a Montreal man's car and forced him and his family to return to Montreal by rail. St-Eustache had great roads in 1997, wide and paved and with the requisite desolate motel that could have been in any town. The motel was without charm, without context, and it had probably wiped out some older hotel nearby. That night I wasn't fond of the car—engine of the economy, killer of farmland, advertiser in newspapers, vehicle of destruction, hearse of the beloved.

Parishioners gathering outside a Catholic Church in Quebec.

The Pathfinders glide by Chateau de Ramezay, built in 1705, in Montreal. It is now a museum.

Meeting some curious Quebecois children along the streets of Quebec.

FLEECING AUTOISTS, September, 1912, Hartford, Connecticut—One of the fine automobile rides of New England is from Boston to Portsmouth, thence on to Poland Springs or up to the White Mountains. Scores and hundreds of machines spin daily over the excellent road, and dozens and scores of their drivers damn the law of New Hampshire and the bunch of grafters in the little hamlet of Seabrook, who arbitrarily hold up defenceless travelers and rob them in broad daylight. The New Hampshire statute says that traveling at 25 miles an hour for a distance of a quarter-mile is conclusive proof of violation of the law. Machines with New Hampshire and Massachusetts markers roll gaily and undisturbed through the little settlement 20 miles or so east of the border line. But Connecticut or New York cars are evidently on journeys where delay is serious. Travelers who approach the place are warned by children who cry out "Trap, trap."

SETTING LIMITS WHEN YOUR CHILD LEARNS TO DRIVE, September, 1997, Montreal, Quebec—If you've got a teenager who is champing at the bit to drive, here are a few pointers that may mean the difference between life and death truthfully evaluate your child's maturity level; pay attention and observe your child's driving skills; teach them how to handle emergency situations, either at night or in adverse conditions; set an example by obeying traffic laws and using your safety belt; make sure they have a destination — aimless joyriding can lead to trouble; reinforce that drinking and driving is unacceptable; make it clear that inappropriate driving will not be tolerated. Driving courses in Quebec, unfortunately, are no longer obligatory.

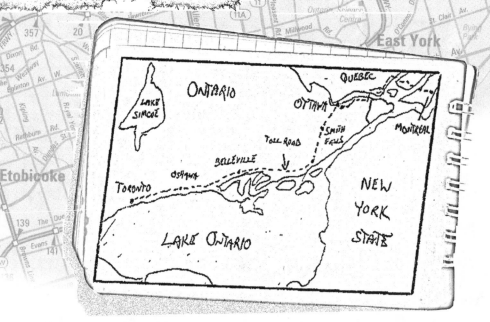

Chapter 5

Ontario—Halfway Across to Halfway House

September 4—Montreal

Montreal didn't have much to offer Haney other than mail and a good bath. He put it succinctly, "Montreal is bum." Ever mindful of his expenses, he paid the most so far for a hotel, $4, and he had to pay an extra $1 for storage of the car in what amounted to an open carport. With a Model T Ford leading the way, they got away from Montreal about 10 a.m., launching themselves into a sea of rain and bad roads. When there were any roads at all, it was a toll road, said Haney.

It was a day in which both Reos passed the 1,000-mile (1,600-kilometre) mark, but our crew had sunny weather while we rambled along a lovely drive in Quebec, past fields of sunflowers and undulating roads. Wilby saw double-decked barns with a sloping gangway for cows leading to the second floor. There was a photo of such in his book—the cows wearing the same contemplative, I've-got-more-stomachs-than-I-need look as today. Actually, the black-and-white pattern on the Holsteins matched the patchwork of clouds in the sky, casting shadows on the hills rippling the horizon. The road wound gently along, allowing us to interact with roadside bystanders, who gave us the thumbs-up, or simply a smile.

Lorne was pumped because we'd be met by a 1925 Maxwell. He had a '25 Maxwell roadster at home, along with a '35 Packard, a '26 Auburn and a '26 Model T coupe. Jonathan Maxwell and Benjamin Briscoe, who both worked for Olds, built the first Maxwell in 1904. They designed a thermo-syphon system which heated the gas up in the carburetor, but during the First World War they nearly went broke. Chrysler moved in and helped them out, which prompted a story from Lorne about Walter Chrysler. He rescued Willys-Overland, then Maxwell and Chalmers. The first car with Chrysler's name on it came out in 1924, and in 1925 the Maxwell Corporation became the Chrysler Corporation. Walt invested at a good time because most car companies were hurt by the First World War and the 1921 Depression.

Lorne said the best early cars to collect are the three Ps: Packard, Peerless and Pierce Arrow. "They were expensive, chauffeur-driven cars, but really wealthy people had Deusenbergs," he said. "The Deusenberg Brothers built great racing engines, but they started building their own car in 1922. Of all the cars built, only 500 are missing. They were well-built cars. The word 'Deusy' comes from Deusenberg."

Haney and Wilby crossed the Ottawa River from Carillon to Pointe Fortune on a ferry trip that cost them a dollar. It was manned, wrote Wilby,

> by a contemplative, beetle-browed Scotchman with such deep-sunken shrewd blue eyes as to convey the alarming impression that he was doing the thinking for the entire country. After ripping the silence of the sleepy world with a shrill blast of the whistle, he put off leisurely into the current, head on to the distant rapids. Imminent and unavoidable destruction stared us in the face, but still the skipper thought on, his hoary begrimed head sticking motionless out of the stoke-hole. One had the assurance that he was steering the ship by hard thinking, and that when the right moment came he would think a little harder in order to bring her round and swing her inshore on the strong current.

That ferry now costs five dollars, but Lorne and I went by the ferry landing without thinking it still existed. Just north were the Carillon rapids Champlain visited by canoe in 1613, now altered by a hydro-electric dam. Champlain arrived at the rapids to disprove the account of one of his lieutenants who claims he took the river to the northern seas. We went on to Hawkesbury, where a bridge (they were working on a new one) carried us across. I didn't dislike Quebec, like Haney, but I was still glad to see the familiar Ontario licence plates and to feel at home.

No sooner had we arrived than we heard a screech on the road. Thankfully, it was *almost* an accident. "Ears" Findlay noted, "The guy had one brake working."

The original Reo nearly caused a bad accident. A woman with three kids came along in a horse and buggy. The kids got out in case the big-boned, bad-tempered horse reared at the sound of the motor car, but the woman refused to, even though

Haney offered to lead the horse by. The woman insisted she could get her horse by the car, but it got away from her and threw her out onto the ground, where she hit her head on a rock. Wilby said she "lay against a big boulder in the grassy ditch with wild beseeching eyes and blanched cheeks. For a moment we had visions of a tragedy of the road for which we might be held responsible by the men who hurried to the scene from nearby fields."

The woman recovered and exonerated the Pathfinders. However, Wilby said a chicken "was rendered speechless" when it sought shelter in the wrong wheel rut. The Reo also encountered a hen that came away from the collision with "a sidelong lurch," a Collie dog that hurled itself at the Reo's wooden-spoked wheels, and two other dogs who yelped or rolled away after colliding with the Reo. It was as if the province's animals went kamikaze to stop the Reo's intrusion into Ontario. Eighty-five years later, it appeared the animal kingdom had learned to avoid automobiles; we did not collide with one our entire trip.

Besides canines, the Reo was dogged that day by a sporty Model T Ford that Wilby referred to as a "bob-tailed motor car." The occupants were hatless, coatless and "were having a hilarious time" thanks to the contents of a "mysterious flask of handy proportions"—no doubt an early case of drinking and driving. From the ferry, the car had sped ahead of them, but the Reo passed the imbibers picnicking on impromptu tables made from the tonneau cushion and a suitcase. Later, both Haney and Wilby were miffed to find the car had caught up to them at a crossroads.

One of the occupants said, "By the way, was you the fellers that run down the woman back there on the road?" The Pathfinders were stunned into silence. Haney asked why? "Becoz if you was, they tried to put the thing on to us and have our scalps. So we quit, and we're quitting still." Mortified that they might have injured the woman, the Pathfinders vowed to pull over, preferably behind a screening hedge, to avoid endangering the occupants of horse-drawn carts.

The Ontario side, on old Highway 17, was unremarkable, so a great morning drive turned disappointing. A woman pushing two kids in a stroller along the highway showed the predicament those without cars sometimes face—you may end up risking life and limb taking pathways forged for cars.

In 1912, while many men had taken to cars, women were still using horse and buggies. Besides the economic and societal stigmas, said Lorne, the cranking of cars kept women from behind the wheel. The 1912 Cadillac changed that. It had the first self-starter, based on the use of a battery. The Cadillac also cured another problem associated with driving—it provided electric lights. To use headlights on most cars at the time, including the Reo, the driver had to walk to the front of the car, open the headlight, turn on the compressed acetylene gas connection and strike a match. Another method stemmed from a chemical reaction between water and carbide. Such a primitive system was time-consuming, not only servicing the carbide generator, but in cleaning up the inside of the headlights after use.

We met the Maxwell at Cumberland. Dave Gurney took us by way of a beautiful and evidently expensive entrance to Ottawa. It harked back to the idea of building a road for its scenic beauty. Besides the '25 Maxwell we ended with an entourage of a '28 Chevrolet and a '47 Ford truck guiding us to Parliament Hill.

Ottawa, chosen by Queen Victoria as the capital of Upper and Lower Canada in 1856, is a city of contradictions. It is noted for its hiking and biking trails and its canal that turns into a long winter skating rink. But it also allowed its railway station to be placed on the edge of town, along with its baseball stadium, and it permitted its hockey team to build a rink 20 kilometres outside of town so everyone has to get there by car. It cut off a couple of roads downtown and turned them into a pedestrian precinct, but there is rarely a warmth or feeling of a city, except in its downtown mall. Canada's capital, unfortunately, is not a city to emulate.

An Ottawa resident named Susan Gardner, who treats victims of car crashes at a physiotherapy clinic, said she is always amused at people being afraid to fly. "They're told 'You have a 1,000 times greater chance of getting killed in a car accident than in a plane,' and they're unfazed. They almost expect to get killed by cars, but they wouldn't want to die in a plane."

When the original Reo chugged into Ottawa at 6 p.m., it was bespattered with mud and streamers hung from almost every part of the car. The *Ottawa Citizen* described Wilby as an "author, journalist, globe trotter, idealist and adventure hunter." He said he was travelling at his own expense "under the auspices of the Canadian Highway Association" to show "the supreme advantage and need of a coast to coast highway as an invaluable artery for vehicular traffic of all kinds."

During the early part of the trip, Wilby was often referred to as being from Quebec City. *The Citizen* said Wilby came to Canada "about five years ago," which may have been true, but he had been based in New York City off and on since 1905. The only evidence of Wilby living in Quebec was during the early months of 1912. Who knows whether he was trying to suggest a Canadian connection: however, he admitted to being a special correspondent for the London *Morning Post* in Vienna and later for the *London Express* in Cairo. He also told *The Citizen* the run from Montreal to Ottawa,

> is usually made I believe, in eight hours, but it took us longer owing to the bad state of the roads which were very heavy after the rains. It was a surprise to find that the highway between two cities was so poor except within about eight miles of this city. The road from Montreal to Ottawa will form an integral part of the future Canadian Highway and it seems to me the Dominion government could very well set an example to the rest of the country by getting these 118 miles in shape and thus providing a model for the west.

Wilby told the paper he was keeping a log of his trip which should be of value to geography students or anyone interested in a coast-to-coast road. Also, he would describe little-known Canadian scenery in magazine articles and in a novel, like the successful romance he wove around his circular tour of the States. Although unimpressed with this capital city, he commented that the new hotel, the $2-million, 350-room Chateau Laurier, "seemed to proclaim that the Canada of today would be the nation of tomorrow."

If Wilby was thinking of another romance novel it was the last thing on Haney's mind. He finally let loose in his diary, admitting, "I am heartily sick of my companion and will be mighty glad when the trip is over. He is too damn selfish."

Our drive had taken us past Rideau Hall, the Governor General's home on Sussex Drive, but in Wilby's day the country estate was detached from the city. The Hall typified all that is great about England to Wilby, but he took the opportunity in his book to slam the concentration of land under the British aristocracy. For a brief moment, Wilby and I are of like minds: Canada wouldn't have such English-driven success if England hadn't "driven her disinherited, disillusionized, pauper sons to the city from the land that was theirs by the right of God, that the property of the Many may be held by the Few, and become the playground of the unproductive Rich." But Wilby is on his own when he says Canada was God-sent to perpetuate the

English race. Now that the feudal system of the French Canadian has been swept away, he adds, "a never-ending army of men is sweeping through the wide-open portals of freedom back to the land of their inalienable birthright."

Wilby spent time with Harry Ketchum, driving by Rideau Hall and checking out the shores of Chaudière Falls where a huge lumbermill buzzed night and day. Wilby was fascinated by lumberjacks who drove the logs down river, risking their lives to pull out key logs in a jam with their cant hooks. He was amazed the logs climbed "to their death" up a chute. "The eye was riveted with horror by that deadly gang-saw. In it was concentrated the evil genius of the place. It was the ultimate expression of the civilization which had invaded and doomed the forest."

Late in the afternoon he returned to the Chateau. Parliament wasn't sitting, so it wasn't filled with cigar-smoking politicians debating reciprocity or Borden's Imperial Policy. He ordered tea, but when it didn't taste like tea he ordered coffee. When it didn't taste like coffee he asked if they ran a drugstore out of the kitchen or whether they boiled fish in the teakettles. He felt he had been given an imitation of cod-liver oil. He went to the restaurant for water, then soup, with the same result. Outside he stopped a policeman to ask what was wrong with the Ottawa water. The officer told him he could get free treatment at the city's expense until he was cured. Wilby had been drinking water treated with chloride of lime. The Brit may have fictionalized his experience—he said the cop wanted to take him to city hall, where he'd have to pledge "not to say anything of what has happened to you in Ottawa." As it turns out, Ottawa's water had been scrutinized for months; the day Wilby left they announced that a new water line had been improperly installed. The steel pipe had gaping joints, allowing sewage from a 12-inch sewer line to "percolate in." The medical health officer had issued warnings of contamination between May and July, but a public warning was only issued July 9. A fever outbreak began the following day.

The Findlays stayed on a wooded property near Richmond. In the interest of getting an early start, I avoided the Chateau Laurier in favour of a bed and breakfast in Stittsville. I imagined a small farming community and an old farmhouse, but ended up at a new home just off a four-lane main drag. Suburbia was taking over small towns, all because of the freedom afforded by those horseless carriages.

September 5—Ottawa

In his book *A Motor Tour Through Canada*, Wilby rarely mentions his chauffeur and never refers to him by name, but he begins his seventh chapter with an old school ditty that Haney hummed as they made their way to Lake Ontario at Kingston. In a drive "festooned by the plume-like Lombardy poplars," cornflower and goldenrod, he quoted his driver, who liked to sing while he drove, humming

> "The golden rod is yellow,
> The corn is turning brown;
> The trees in apple orchards
> With fruit are bending down."

The reference suggests a camaraderie on the day of the biggest clash between the Pathfinders. According to Haney it started when Wilby complained about the Reo running over a chicken the day before; it made Wilby sick. Furthermore, he did not like going 40 kilometres an hour, and the bumpy corduroy roads made it impossible for him to take notes. In his diary, Haney said he "had a warm argument with the Captain today." His complaints made him "rather a soft outfit for the Captain of a transcontinental automobile trip." I'd like to blame their cantankerous moods on the Ottawa water, but Haney probably had more justification for being upset. He did all the dirty work for the trip, and would have expected to, but he didn't expect to be treated like a servant, compelled to respond to Wilby's whims. On the night of the 4th he sent two telegrams, informing the Reo Motor Car Company of his problems with Wilby. On the 5th, when he was ready to go at 6:30 a.m., according to Wilby's prompting, Wilby slept in until 7:30. To make matters worse, it rained all day and ended with a thunderstorm. The roads were so rotten, Wilby said "they broadly hinted at the timeliness of the airplane." They had to ford two creeks because the bridges were out, and nearly got stuck in one of the creeks. Haney put the mud hooks on and pulled them to safety.

"One poor devil does all the work 'that's me'," he wrote in his diary. "I am hooked up with about the worst companion that possibly could be. The work is going to be hard after leaving Toronto, and not having a MAN with me, I don't know how I'll make out." For starters, their situation was ripe for confrontation. They were two weeks into being thrown into close quarters for two months. They had to put up with the weather, the bumps, the struggles of the road for eight to ten hours a day, getting to bed late and getting up early to do it all over again. Never mind that they had two different attitudes toward their jobs—they were men from different cultures and generations. It's surprising tensions didn't boil over earlier.

Our trip along the backroads of Eastern Ontario, past farms of dairy cattle, pigs and sheep, went through Richmond, which was named after the Duke of Richmond who lived there in the mid-19th century. Local lore has it that he had been bitten by a rabid fox and chained himself to a tree so that he could die without affecting anyone else. At Smith Falls, we stopped to see the falls and ended up becoming preoccupied by an egret which makes its home in the river.

Haney had bought another five gallons of gasoline in Smith Falls, and probably heard the town's big news that the three sons of Mrs. W.H. Frost had bought their mother a 90-horsepower Oldsmobile with metre-high wheels as a birthday gift. While the Pathfinders made their way to Belleville they would have passed the Olds heading to Smith Falls.

We made good time into Kingston, giving us a chance to lounge between Fort Henry and the lake for lunch. I grabbed a ride into town to go to the library and then met up with the Reo at Automotion, the Automotive Evolution Center and Museum. It was most aptly in a strip mall next to a busy four-lane street far from the soul of the city—you know, one of those arterial roads that extends its arm out to the freeway like a drug-pusher rolling up his sleeve for a hit. Inside the museum, which was supposed to be educational, was an enlightening photo exhibition that, unintentionally, said it all about the impact of the car with before and after shots. Once, the old photos told us, there were human-scale streets, with human-scale buildings. Now they've given way to four-lane thoroughfares devoid of humanity and civility. The museum's cars, mind you, were phenomenal, including a 1917 Briscoe, the car with a single headlight in the middle. It was owned and on loan from a Mrs. Briscoe, who was no relation to the original.

After breaking away, we had a two-hour drive to Belleville, where I stayed at The Clarion Inn—the same hotel Wilby and Haney found, although it was known as the Hotel Quinte in their day. The news said Athens got the Summer Olympics in 2004 by promising to clean up the city's legendary air pollution and traffic problems.

Had the Pathfinders read the day's newspaper, they might have been wary about entering the elevator at the Hotel Quinte. At the Windsor Hotel, which they had left the morning before in Montreal, a businessman named Roddy Ryan of Brockville fell five floors down the shaft of the service elevator. He fell head first through the roof of the elevator, not landing on but knocking over the elevator boy and a waiter who was picking up a breakfast in the basement to deliver to a room. Ryan's body was badly broken, including his back, and he was dead when picked up. He had been a guest at the hotel for a week, and had his shoes shined in the basement not more than three minutes before he was picked up for dead. That's the way I'd like to go, I thought, with my shoes just-a-shining.

September 6—Belleville

The anticipation about finally getting a chance to see my family woke me early, but most of North America was already awake to watch the funeral of Diana, Princess of Wales. A TV commentator named Tom said it was the same month in 1982 that Diana represented the Queen at the funeral for beloved Princess Grace, who also died in a car accident. "Little did I know 15 years later I'd be watching a simple coffin containing the Princess of Wales, also bearing the royal standard, who also died in a car accident," said Tom as the coffin arrived at Westminster Abbey.

Millions were watching, yet how many would make sure they used seatbelts, stopped speeding, or made sure they would never drink and drive again? When a famous person dies in such circumstances, there is a chance for more people to learn a good lesson, but the moment was mostly lost because the focus remained on the pursuing paparazzi and the harassment of celebrities. Should we think again about how the car fits into our society? Mercedes-Benz spent literally billions making its car one of the safest in the world, but if you don't wear seatbelts, you'll end up prone in another vehicle with three straight-faced blokes crowding the front seat of a hearse, moving slowly down Whitehall to Westminster Abbey.

At breakfast, many faces were tear-stained. At the help-yourself grapefruit slices, I asked a woman if she had watched the funeral. She nodded, holding back even more tears. On the way back up to my room I asked another teary-eyed woman in the elevator the same thing. She said "No." She was called to town because a close relative had suffered a heart attack. That put full throttle to the reality meter.

Lorne had done his own reality check on an unshaven, scruffy guy who reluctantly answered the door of the campground office.

The man said, "Did you watch the funeral story of my girlfriend?"

"Mother Teresa?" Lorne slyly suggested, in reference to the famous nun who died the same week.

"No, Diana. She was a wonderful person. She loved people."

"And Mother Teresa didn't?" Lorne asked.

Wilby, perhaps in deference to the Ontario Deaf Mute Asylum he passed outside Belleville, mentions little about his trip to Toronto. "In heat and sunshine," they took famous historical highways, associated more or less with the incidents of the War of 1812. Maybe Wilby lost his notepad, or lost interest in the scenery, for he doesn't refer to this stretch in his book or any magazine articles. He wanted to wax on about Toronto, which Haney said they reached at 3 p.m.

We, too, had a sunny day, but it was a bit more complicated. The modern world infringes upon old Highway 2, but it is still an appealing drive, especially with the Bay of Quinte on the horizon. Places like Cobourg, with a vibrant downtown, have stopped shopping centres from killing their cores. Thus, there's an economic advantage to cities that control the impact of the car, but that rarely dawns on town councillors or planning directors who act like facilitators for developers instead of servants of the taxpayer. The result is that every town looks alike, so people drive hundreds of miles to visit towns that look the way towns used to look.

Our daily road construction met us at Port Hope, another town with a positive image, and then we went north of Highway 401 to be met by a '47 Cadillac driven by Jil McIntosh, a car buff/journalist who was leading us into Oshawa. The conversation turned to the economic advantage of being handy with cars, not only to fix your own, but to know which models were good cars and which ones weren't. Chrysler, Lorne said, had horrible cars in the late fifties, and then started making good cars again in the sixties. Olds had good cars until '57, and then they put in a new automatic transmission. It was terrible, but they made a comeback.

The first car Lorne drove was a '26 Model T Ford. On his paper route lived an old man with his two spinster sisters. When the old man died the sisters were left with a '26 Model T two-door they couldn't drive. Lorne, 16, asked his father if he could buy it. He was told to forget it. "I told this Doukhobor guy about it at the orchard where I worked at the beginning of the war," said Lorne. "In those days you couldn't get any gas without a ration card. He bought it and we concocted a home brew—some coal oil, high test gasoline and regular gasoline. It gave us something to do for the evening. You'd go swimming at a cottage on the lake. In those days you didn't do anything bad when you went out. You just had fun. We'd take a couple of girls out we were keen on from the high school."

Near Oshawa they obviously hadn't learned anything from Port Hope or Cobourg. Two big malls were going up, but it was appropriate for the city. Oshawa was the home of Sam McLaughlin, whose family carriage business was one of the Empire's largest at the turn of the century. In 1907 he started making cars—a McLaughlin Buick, and then it became Canada's Detroit, as the McLaughlin company was bought out by General Motors, leaving Sam as head of GM Canada. If any cities should acquiesce to the allure of the car, you'd expect places like Oshawa, St. Catharines, Oakville and Windsor, major car producing cities, to be poorly planned cities that will do anything for cars. Sure enough, that's the case.

And at Oshawa's Canadian Automotive Museum, the city's dynamic mayor, Nancy Diamond, didn't see anything wrong with letting the marketplace dictate what went where. In her lonely downtown, where you could have ridden the Reo along the sidewalk Saturday afternoon and not hit anyone, there were murals to Old Sam and one of his Buicks. It was a common site across the country: tips of the hat to old cars, seemingly oblivious to the fact they had to paint the walls to try to attract people downtown because the car has enabled them to go anywhere but. *No free parking? I'm going to the mall.*

We arrived in Toronto closer to 5 p.m., but Haney and Wilby arrived two hours earlier, even though they missed the people they were supposed to meet at Halfway House on the Kingston Road 10 miles out of town. The Pathfinders' instructions were to climb the big hill after Highland Creek and follow the winding and undulating gravel road, with a calm level stretch of three miles, to Halfway House. It would have been difficult for them to miss the inn, a two-storey wooden structure that since the 1860s had been a place to stop halfway between Dunbarton and Toronto, get a drink and a bite to eat, change the horses or grab a room for the night. It would have been easy for us to miss Halfway House because it has been picked up from the corner of Midland and Kingston roads on the eastern outskirts of Toronto and moved to Black Creek Pioneer Village at Jane and Steeles in northwest Toronto. That's the way to preserve the past— pick it up and move it someplace where kids can clamber off a schoolbus to see history.

However, they did miss Halfway House, veering north of it. When the Pathfinders realized they must have taken a wrong turn, Haney got on the phone, knowing his bosses would be looking for him. He doubled back to greet what one paper called "a large party of the representative automobile men of Toronto," who gathered to "do honor to the tourists." The Reo executives there made sure the Reo name made it into the newspapers. Haney told them that Wilby had done little to promote the car, and Haney could do little because reporters rushed to hear Wilby's words like bugs to a windshield. Not so in Toronto. *The News*'s coverage had a wonderful opening: "Looming through the dust of Kingston road late yesterday afternoon, two dusty and travel-stained motorists in a mud-splashed Reo car reeled off the last few stages of a 1,360-mile jaunt from Halifax to Toronto. Steadily for nine days and a half they had pounded along through mud and rain with minds bent on the ambition of establishing an all-red motor route." *The News* quotes Haney extolling the virtues of the Maritimes. "No roads in the world," he said, "are more beautiful." He was ignored by *The Globe*, but the *Toronto World* must have been satisfying. The paper quoted Haney saying the Reo had no tire or engine troubles since leaving Halifax, and they referred to his passenger as J. Thomas W. Wimble.

Mr. Wimble, ahem, Wilby, checked into the nine-year-old King Edward Hotel, Toronto's finest at the time, where the Ontario Motor League put on an informal dinner that night. "It is on account of his pioneer work in the good roads, or, rather, road-locating movement that he is receiving the support of the various motor clubs," said one newspaper. Wilby told them that Ontario roads—surprise, surprise—were the best they had taken so far, but he didn't like having to pay for them. "Whenever a good Ontario road is reached or a good bridge, a heavy toll is charged." He preferred instead the European idea of toll abolition and a gasoline tax to pay for good roads. "Although Quebec spends a great deal more money in this way, one cannot appreciate it in the roads." Probably in reference to the railway conference going on in the city at the time, he countered with his well-honed argument: "The railroad has made Canada, but not unified it. This is left to the motor route."

Haney left after dinner to entrain to St. Catharines to see his "girlie" Annie and take care of the Reo. Wilby was introduced to the nearby Arts and Letters Club, in what was the old York County Court House. It is a safe bet he had trouble making his way down the spiral staircase after more than a few drinks pontificating to fellow *artistes*. Both Pathfinders would have been greatly relieved this night, and it probably had little to do with their conquest of eastern Canada.

September 7 — Toronto/Niagara

If this was an off day, it wasn't so for the Reo's drivers and mechanics. Haney, after a visit with his girlfriend, had to get back to Toronto with new parts and to clean, grease and oil his belaboured car. Lorne, meanwhile, had pulled the Reo down to St. Catharines behind his camper so he could attend a Sunday reception at the St. Catharines Museum. The museum had a full display on Haney, thanks to the diligent efforts of the museum's Arden Phair. His work in accumulating artifacts of the original trip encouraged me to write a newspaper feature on Haney for *The Standard* in St. Catharines. That led to the involvement of Lou Cahill, a long-time public relations guru, getting the Canadian Automobile Association to honour Jack posthumously, and to Fitzhenry & Whiteside agreeing to publish my small book, *Jack Haney*, for its *Canadians* series. To write the book I tracked down Lorne so he could explain how the Reo worked. So here we were, having come full circle.

A good number of antique car enthusiasts and some of Jack's distant relatives, gathered at the site of the old Reo factory that lured Haney to St. Catharines. The factory started as a grist mill in 1882 at Race and Geneva Streets. Oldsmobiles were made there by the Packard Motor Company from 1905 to 1907, and then Reo took it over to assemble cars in 1909. In 1910, Reo began building four-cylinder cars. In 1914, auto production gave way to munitions manufacturing, and cars were never built there again. Reo kept its headquarters in the city but moved its production line to Toronto. It marketed cars, taxicabs, and Speedwagon trucks until 1922, when they moved headquarters to Windsor. That year the company also built what was undoubtedly the first Canadian camper—a six-cylinder open Reo with a special rear section holding a double spring bed, tent, and camping supplies. The factory was torn down to make way for two 20-storey condominiums.

From there the entourage went to Haney's gravesite in Victoria Lawn Cemetery, and then on to a museum reception at the edge of the Welland Canal, which connects Lake Ontario to Lake Erie. Jack used to service the machinery that dug this route of the canal, which was completed in 1932.

Speeches were exchanged, and a few people jumped on the Reo for quick rides or to get their photos taken. Lorne, in a great leap of faith, what with the canal so close by, actually let me take my wife Ann, daughters Emma and Annika, and son Alexander for a ride. Like Haney, I had an Annie waiting for me—my 83-year-old mother. When she came to Canada in 1951 she could get by train from Niagara Falls to Niagara-on-the-Lake. My mother never learned to drive a car, and 46 years after she emigrated, she has less mobility. She'd like nothing better than to pop down on a train to see her grandchildren, but she is trapped by progress.

The display inside the museum includes a reproduction of a noted 1912 ad for the Reo. Ransom Olds was the first automaker to use a professional advertising firm, R.M. Owen, but like other pioneers, he felt the best way to advertise a car was to have it win a race or complete some endurance test or long-distance haul. A Reo had been one of the first cars to cross the United States in 1905—the Percy Megargel trip. In 1911, the Canadian Reo company boasted that one of its cars had made the 40-kilo-metre climb up nearby Hamilton mountain in an hour and five minutes, that another Reo had completed an 8-kilometre race in Ottawa at 85 kilometres per hour, and that a Reo was the first car to drive from Saint John, New Brunswick, to Halifax and back. But Olds knew the power of good advertising. R.M. Owen had given him catchy slo-gans such as "Nothing to watch but the road," "The car that did is the car that will," "Just your style," and the saucy "You can do it with a Reo." The 1912 attempt to find an All-Red Route was a grand adventure for the Canadian company, but its publici-ty campaign was aided by Olds' ad entitled "My Farewell Car." It proclaimed the 1912 Reo was Olds' last and best design. Olds, 48 years young, objected to the idea of a "Farewell," but his advertising guru, Claude Hopkins, reminded him that the actress Sarah Bernhardt retired seven times. The ads were credited with restoring the company to financial health.

St. Catharines, which once lured factories because of its proximity to the canal and cheap hydro-electric power, became a General Motors city, although most of the auto business in Canada went to the Toronto-Windsor corridor. But the impact of the car lingers. When I think of the city, I think of the use of a car by murderers Paul Bernardo and Karla Homolka to abduct 15-year-old Kristen French in broad daylight, on a stretch of city road left desolate by the car's influence—the street was so wide and the houses so far apart, there were no "eyes on the street," the natural policing that social planner Jane Jacobs says comes with a well-designed, tight neighbour-hood. I also think of the lovely YMCA, erected with citizens' donations in the early part of the century, that was demolished for a parking lot downtown, the old Russell Hotel that met the same fate, as did a turn-of-the-century home that had the double-car whammy of becoming a parking lot and host to signs for speed-reading drivers, the billboard. My experience, writing a column and watching how disjointed and detached government is from its people, gave me insights into how developers take advantage of every weakness in the democratic system to finagle the power to do whatever they wanted with their land, which was rarely in the public interest, and never catered to any other form of transportation other than the car. To top it all off, cars came into focus when I interviewed a high school class in 1996 about part-time jobs. One student fell asleep because he was up to 2 a.m. working on a school night. He said he worked to support his car so it could get him to work.

The canal next to the museum virtually marks the border between St. Catharines and Niagara-on-the-Lake, a town of 13,000 which owes much of its allure to the fact it hasn't been destroyed by the car. It takes in the old villages of Queenston, St. Davids, Virgil and the Old Town of Niagara, where I lived at the time. It is also the site of a great debate about how we should plan our towns and cities, and what role the car should play. The Old Town lures tourists wanting to explore its vantage point at the mouth of the Niagara River. There is a white-man history that goes back 240 years, native trails that go back thousands of years, and great 19th-century housing stock that is built on the old-fashioned grid system—the type that allows you to choose more than one route coming-and-going, thus reducing the need for wide col-lector or arterial roads. The Old Town, for the most part, had escaped the detritus of the car culture—strip malls and big parking lots. But tourists loved the place so much they were swamping the town with cars. What's more, developers want to cater to the influx.

It led to two large projects: one brought in New Urbanist architect Andres Duany from Florida to plan the neighbourhood with the residents, while another development paid lip service to the idea of community by developing land near the Queen Elizabeth Way highway. The Duany-inspired plan, on the edge of the Old Town, already feels like it belongs, although it threatens to steal some downtown cor-nerstones, like the bank and the library, for itself. The development near the highway is just a catalyst for the growth of strip malls and a cluster of houses totally dependent on the car. Right next to it is the new campus for Niagara College. It was placed at a highway exit ramp in the misguided belief a college should be equidistant to different cities, even if that meant putting it in the middle of nowhere, far from any public transit or community. When it opened, it had to cancel some of its English as a Second Language courses—foreign students who needed the course couldn't get there conveniently.

Unfortunately for Haney, he couldn't dawdle. He had to get back to Toronto, which had already experienced the teething pains of having 5,300 car owners. In May alone of that year, $1,365 in fines were taken from 100 drivers. Half the fines were for speeding, and the rest of the offences had to do with disobeying rules such as not giving way to horses. Speeding was such a problem that Kennedy Road north of Danforth Road was constructed with bumps to make speeding uncomfortable.

Wilby, meanwhile, settled into what he heard was "The Boston of Canada"—Toronto—a place some still considered a western city. He said the city's advantages arise mainly out of an accident of topography, placing it "where it catches every breeze that blows out of the intellectual world, every prima donna who sings in New York or Chicago, every impresario and piano prodigy, and all the tourist hordes of Niagara and the Lakes. English theatrical companies, starring in America, find it easy to give in Toronto a one-night stand or a week's repertory from Buffalo, while European lecturers can no more escape Toronto than Toronto can escape Lake Ontario."

An architect at Wilby's new "Club," where he had an excellent home-cooked luncheon that Saturday, told him the city should never have been built close to the lake, for it encourages rheumatism. "It lies too low," said the man. "It's wonderful what a few days in the country will do for a Toronter, however. The wilderness is so close that we can easily get out into that world of freedom and the sunshine of the hilltops. Even England may envy us a dog, a gun and a canoe in the primitive wild."

Wilby didn't envy the plight of the English immigrant, whom he found "working as porter, serving me my cigars, my newspapers, selling me my cravats, cleaning out the stores, driving the motor cars and doing the clerical work." The British women, however, had carved their own identity. He found

> a white-shirt waisted, bargain-counter haunting, street-car patroniz-
> ing, hurrying, well-developed non-sentimentalizing Anglo-Canadian

blend of womanhood. Well-dressed, with some of the English-woman's colouring and little of her tender voice, placing emphasis rather on good taste and good manners rather than delicate shades of refinement, there she was, not a creature of fine bouquet, not a devotee of outdoor life, but well-set-up and with so much gained to compensate her for the little she had lost.

Haney was trying to make sure the Reo was well set-up, preparing the car for its first huge hurdle in northern Ontario. He had his photos developed when he arrived, and found the ones that Wilby had taken were all blurred—either Wilby was a bad photographer, or he intentionally ruined Haney's photos. Haney, in the midst of a war with Wilby, was inclined to believe the latter.

Wilby, of course, was oblivious to it all at the Arts and Letters Club, the original site of which has now been turned into a swish Court House Market Grille, but has retained its circular staircase that is likely to give a drinker vertigo, whether the drinker tipples as much as Wilby or not. Besides an architect, it's unknown what part of the cream of Toronto's artistic society Wilby would have met there. Vincent Massey, future Governor General of Canada, joined in 1911. Ophthalmologist J.E. MacCallum, future patron of Tom Thomson and the Group of Seven, joined in 1912. Frederick H. Varley and A.Y. Jackson were not yet members, but he might have run into other Group of Seven artists such as Frank Carmichael, Arthur Lismer, Lawren Harris, Franz Johnston or J.E.H. MacDonald. It was the type of place that drew visits from composers like Sergei Rachmaninoff or Maurice Ravel, when they were in town, or that other writer-explorer, who was the first to reach the south pole 10 months before Wilby reached Toronto, the Norwegian Roald Amundsen.

ABUSE OF THE AUTO, September, 1912, Toronto, Ontario

Driving a high power car at full speed is a pleasurable form of intoxication, but like all intoxication it has its penalties, and they are heavy. If not sensibly used, there is danger to those in and out of the car in the case of an accident. Physicians have also learned that a driver's eyes and nervous system may suffer seriously. The tax on the eyes is enormous, for they are kept at constant strain looking for obstacles and inequalities in the road. The wind and dust, in spite of the goggles, often causes troublesome inflammation that yields only to rest in a darkened room and appropriate medical treatment. Another ailment that may also affect the passengers is a painful stiff neck caused by unconscious muscular tension. But the most serious penalty that follows abuse of the automobile is neurasthenia or nervous breakdown. A man cannot with safety substitute another form of mental strain for the needed relaxation.

DAIMLER-BENZ UNVEILS FUEL CELL PASSENGER CAR, September, 1997, Frankfurt, Germany

German auto maker Daimler-Benz AG today unveiled what it says is the first fuel cell passenger car to be powered by liquid methanol. Fuel cell technology is an alternative to the standard internal combustion engine of cars today. The fuel cells convert natural gas, methanol or hydrogen fuel into electricity without combustion. The only byproduct is harmless water-vapour exhaust. In the case of the new Daimler-Benz car, methanol fuel is converted into hydrogen, then fed into the fuel cells to produce electrical energy that powers the vehicle. At a time when regulators are demanding cleaner cars, its technology will revolutionize the auto industry because of its lack of polluting emissions.

Chapter 6

In Search of Scotia Junction

September 8 — Toronto

Haney worked on the car until noon, which allowed the Pathfinders to head up Yonge Street by 2:30 p.m., past Mount Pleasant Cemetery to Davisville, the villages of Eglinton, Bedford Park and York Mills and on up to Aurora, where they were instructed to turn left at the Poor House and cautioned to drive slowly so as not to irritate the locals. Davisville, Eglinton and York Mills are now subway stops within Toronto. It is safe to say the Pathfinders left a much different city than we did. Whereas we had to slice our way through the towers of the financial district on Bay Street and then up Yonge Street, one of the longest streets in the world, their skyline was marred by an abundance of hydro poles and overhead tram wires. Visitors at the time from Europe, where hydro wires were quickly buried, said that once Canada grew up, the skyscape wouldn't be so marred by the posts. Little did they know that almost 90 years later, hydro poles and wires still blight Canada's landscape.

Toronto traffic was not as claustrophobic for us as Montreal's, but maybe that was because we weren't in a hurry when we left at 1:30 p.m. As we made the slow uphill trot away from Lake Ontario to the land of lakes, we were firing on only three cylinders, a constant source of concern. Lorne would change a plug and it would work for a while, then it became sparkless. As we passed a go-kart track in Innisfil, I was tempted to take one for a spin—just to get in a vehicle with a little pep.

The number of cemeteries we passed told us we were on an old road; in fact, Yonge Street, from Lake Ontario to Lake Simcoe, was built by the Queen's Rangers for military reasons in 1796. But other than seeing the odd farm as we neared Holland Marsh, the scenery was too modern, too common, too familiarly Ontario. Fortunately,

Lorne could transport me to another world with his knowledge of cars. The '39 Buick Opera Coupe, he said, "had a little wee bit of a back seat. A woman sat in the back with the front seat folded forward. She had a vanity in the back." Lorne has a '26 Auburn Wanderer, with two clips on the door that allow you to fold the front and back seats down into a little bed, with matching pillows. "The guy I got it from only used it once on a trip from Vancouver to Portland. Late in the day he had a flat tire, so he made the bed and spent the night there. They were *Pullmanized,* after the Pullman sleeper train. Nash did it. They were famous for it."

The scenery of strip malls leading north from Toronto put me to sleep sitting up in the Reo—I didn't need a Pullmanized Auburn. Then the rolling hills north of Toronto and our first flaming red leaves of autumn led to fields of corn. The city of Barrie, unfortunately, was more four-lane and one-way madness.

Wilby was pleased by the farmhouses and villas by placid Lake Simcoe, and a road which "slowly transformed itself from a landscape dotted with manufacturing towns, and threaded by fine roads, to a pastoral and rocky one." He told reporters the road was the best of his trip. "Houses were of brick and were surrounded by flower gardens and lawns. There were fine school houses, clean, healthy-looking school children and fine bridges." Wilby was a great believer that good roads would lead to better lives for people next to the roads. The roads themselves would act as a catalyst for people to pull themselves up by their bootstraps and strive for economic well-being. The U.S. government, said Wilby, theorizes that a "bad road means bad living conditions for everybody in the vicinity. A road without culverts and with bad bridges, means a shabby insanitary schoolhouse, untidy fences, poor, tumbledown barns, dilapidated farm houses, absence of churches and gardens. And the U.S. government is right." It probably didn't occur to Wilby that better roads were near places where the residents were better off, or if it did occur to him, his good-roads-improve-society line was too good a piece of pro-roads propaganda not to use and re-use. At century's end the opposite is true. Better homes are not next to improved and widened roads. No one wants to live on a busy thoroughfare. The rich often retreat to areas with few roads.

North of Barrie, Wilby went to Oro Station, Shanty Bay, Hawkestone and East Ora, passing the Ontario Asylum for Idiots and on to Rugby and Orillia. We cut through old farm roads, finding one barn with a large mural of the actor Raymond

Burr, but we couldn't figure out whether it was a likeness of Perry Mason or Detective Ironside, the two TV characters he portrayed.

In Orillia we'd be getting pulled over by the Kopps—Ben and Delma, friends of the Findlays who used to live out west. When he moved to Vancouver Lorne stayed with Delma's mother and a houseful of Children's Aid Society kids. "The Kopps had a beautiful six-year-old girl," Lorne said. "She was crossing the street one day when her shoe came off. She bent over to pick it up and a car struck her."

"Did she die?"

"Yeah." The girl has not been forgotten by the Kopps and their friends, and the streets and byways of the country continue to take six-year-olds each day. It is probably no different than the days when horses would buck and kill their mounts, but car accidents happen more frequently, and with more cars on the road, take a higher toll. Yet it has almost become an accepted part of life. Everyone knows someone who died in a car accident. And life goes on.

The old hotels around Gravenhurst are long gone. One, the Muskoka Sands, had been around at the turn-of-the-century, but was now a luxury resort for the rich folk to escape Toronto and grab a piece of calm by the lake. The waiter in the dining room, where a huge orange sun could be seen setting over the idyllic lake, was from St. Catharines. I had interviewed his girlfriend for a story on that city's comeback—how do you rescue a dying downtown that wasn't built for cars but for people? The sun, which was too bright to look at, eventually made it below the horizon, leaving a rustic painting for the eyes.

Wilby and Haney, who would later take his own family up to the Muskokas each year, also found a backroom restaurant that night, but I'm sure they didn't have the same view. Their route from Barrie was along a road that could only

> force its way by sinuous twists and turns between the barren, rugged hillsides. Snappy, hilarious work to penetrate the lanes of bush and hemlock and tender birch! All but impossible to dodge the huge boulders which formed an integral part of the road—the heralds of the country of the Great Lakes, sending out skirmishers of muskeg and primeval forest and towering cliff.

They arrived in Gravenhurst by the light of the moon, a moon that now enchanted me from the balcony of my room. What it would have been like in those days, before the rich blocked the poor from gaining access to such beauty, when lower-middle-class guys like Haney could take advantage of the ruggedness if he could get there? Now a guardhouse greets you as you come to Muskoka Sands, giving off a snobbish image that is perpetuated by many of the resort staff. "It was supposed to be a greeter, a place for someone to welcome you," explained the girl at the desk, obviously omitting its image as a means of keeping out the riff-raff. "But the person just sat there for eight hours not doing anything."

I said I thought it looked hostile. Then she admitted "It's like a penitentiary."

The car, in a way, succeeded in separating the classes as Wilby so desired. Gated communities, where guardhouses prevent unwanted cars from entering, are the epitome of the car-induced separation. The idea of living together, of being part of society, is forsaken. The rich don't want to see the poor, and the best way to do that is to escape by car down the right streets away from the poverty and misery of the human condition.

September 9—Gravenhurst

The morning by the water's edge, where chipmunks happily cavorted, was glorious, helping me pass the time as I waited for the car to come by. Instead of enjoying the moments, however, I felt stranded, so it was a relief to be back in the Reo; the fresh air, the sights and its hum soothed the soul. We also had a newly paved road, which didn't hurt. As we headed north a blue '52 Chrysler went by. "He's going to the Barrie swap meet," said Lorne in reference to the previous weekend's antique car get-together, "but he's slow."

We passed the 45 degrees north latitude sign outside Bracebridge. "Halfway to the pole again," said Lorne, "but we never seem to get there." At a gas station I had a $1.60 Dutchie doughnut, the honey-glazed kind that must have had diamond-studded raisins in it. When I picked up Wilby's book to read it again, we were 136 kilometres from North Bay, the same distance Wilby referred to in the book. We passed the Highway 117 turnoff, where the local paper told us a 33-year-old man had been killed the week before. A car struck him while he walked along the highway in heavy fog. At least this motorist stayed on the scene and notified police right away.

Before they left Gravenhurst at 9 a.m., Wilby found the town dominated by a huge, ugly water tower and a church spire, and brick rather than wooden façades, bringing it "a thousand miles nearer civilization." The town had also discovered advertising: the tree outside the watchmaker's held a gigantic watch which always said it was five o'clock; the hardware store had a huge circular saw and barbed wire outside; the bank had flowerboxes and gay awnings outside. Even outside town, where a forest fire had left blackened stumps, one enterprising entrepreneur had put up many-coloured posters announcing "Jones Emporium for Fashionable Goods" and "Splendid display of natty Ladies' Hosiery." Wilby wrote: "How insolent seemed this puny self-importance of the merchant of small wares." These were the early days of the plague of roadside billboards.

Haney nipped into the hardware store to buy a shovel, hammer, axe, tackle,and a pump which he attached to the gas tank by soldering on a valve. With his challenges expected to grow, Haney didn't want to have to keep blowing in the gas tank every time the Reo had to climb a hill or they found themselves short on fuel.

Autumn was approaching as the Reo duo left town, pestered by blue-bottle flies under blue skies. While we could smell pine, they found alder and maple trees fringed in crimson against a backdrop of poplars, young birch and fir. On what would be a troublesome day, they missed a turning and ended up under a tree for their packed lunch. Surprisingly, a sturdy-looking woman from a nearby farm gave them unfresh milk. Haney had rustled up some raisin and honey cakes—which made me wonder if they were a precursor to the Dutchie doughnut I had just eaten.

When they embarked again they made it over a railway crossing and then got stuck on a sandhill. After backing up, letting Wilby out and then making another run, Haney's car dropped axle-deep in sand at right-angles to the hill. Wilby said:

> This storming of a sand redoubt by a thing of steel and horse-power is something to wonder at and admire. The creature charges joyously, terrible to behold, shattering the great silences of the wilderness with its battery of guns, raging and storming, groaning, moaning, then roaring and whirling again. The sand flies from her rear as from the mighty back kick of an ostrich leg. But her spirit is broken at last. The wheels spin on the same spot in frantic, static dynamics. A tremor only runs through her frame and she ceases to roar impotent defiance. She admits defeat. The silence is piteous, primitive. Only horses can now bring life to the useless, motionless mechanism.

Manufactured contraptions commonly got stuck on this hill, and reliable horses had to pull them out. The situation would have jollied the locals who despised these new-fangled inventions and preferred the quiet clip-clop of horses to the gunning of an engine, and they would have been knee-slapping happy when they found out the horses pulled so hard they twisted the transmission shaft, consigning the Pathfinders to a two-day delay. Haney describes it in *Motoring* magazine:

> After nearly burying the car in our efforts to get over, we would need the help of our friend the horse. I started out to find him and about a mile up the road I found a farmer who was putting in hay. He had a team that looked good to me and we soon had them hitched to the car, but they could not budge her. Finally, with the use of block and tackle, we got out. As I was getting ready to start again I discovered, as a result of the terrible jerking, the car was in need of a little fixing.

In Wilby's book is a photo of the horses pulling the Reo out of the sand. Two farmers are standing beside the Reo while Haney's arms can be seen behind one of the farmers. Haney is headless, which makes me suspect it was the first attempt by Wilby to remove any evidence of him from his book. In trying to duplicate the photo—without the horses—we searched for the spot on the road where the car must have faltered. It became the most enchanting afternoon of the trip. We knew it was just north of town, near a railway track. What we had to do first was find the railways' tracks that made it a junction—the Toronto-to-North Bay and the Parry Sound-to-Ottawa lines. The latter was found underneath a bridge, hiding mysteriously under a canopy of trees, as if the vegetation wanted to hide the shame of the route shorn of its ties and its rails. It was constructed at a time that access to Lake Huron was more important; its demise meant that Scotia was no longer a junction, but just "Scotia" like the small sign on Highway 11 indicated.

We found a level crossing over railway tracks, but trees hugged the road on both sides, whereas the original photo included trees on one side, with a farmhouse and barn dominating the horizon to the left. Lorne ventured that it was the exact spot, but I played the doubting Thomas. Lorne then pointed to a large boulder at the side of the road. It was the same boulder in the photo, so we took numerous photos with the car astride the road. Still I wasn't satisfied. While Irene and Lorne went off to make sandwiches, Peter and I took the Reo and found a farmhouse up the hill, a place

The re-enactment of the August 27 launch. In Halifax, Jack Haney watched Thomas Wilby scoop up water from the Atlantic to carry to the Pacific. In Eastern Passage, across Halifax Harbour, Lorne Findlay has his Reo pointed west, while John Nicol follows Wilby's lead.

The 1997 crew outside Ottawa House, built in 1775, which overlooks the Bay of Fundy: Nicol, Lorne, Irene and Peter Findlay. Many 19th-century bridges were covered, like this one in New Brunswick, to protect the wooden floorboards.

Burchell Fulmore's yellow '34 Chevy Master cabriolet with a rumble seat. Cross-Canada runner Phil Latulippe, with Lorne, on the shore of his beloved Lake Temiscouata: wishing he was crossing the country again.

In 1997, the roadside ovens still existed, but more as a tourist attraction. In 1912, Wilby joked that in Quebec, "sometimes the kitchen had revolted and escaped into the road."

Horses were needed to pull the Reo out of sand in Scotia Junction, Ontario, south of North Bay. The struggle to free the Reo bent the crankshaft, forcing them to spend two days there. After scouring the countryside, and some deliberation, the exact same location was found 85 years later on an empty road in this forgotten hamlet. It is now known as Scotia because only one train line cuts through.

Left: Tommy Fraser, 83, and the car he raced 50 years before.

Ike Clarkson's "cousin" Marguerite Ablett, 93, and his sister Gussy, almost 91, at the seniors' home.

Below: Bill Dennstedt, 80, on the right, and friends, and his rebuilt McLaughlin.

When downtowns become ghost towns because of the proliferation of malls on the edge of a city, old cars are often painted on the sides of buildings—ironically, the guilty party to the abandonment of downtowns is painted benignly, like this one in Moose Jaw, Saskatchewan. A Reo welcome in Macleod, Alberta.

Haney, in 1912, standing on one of the rocks that crushed the town of Frank, Alberta, six years earlier. In 1997, when Findlay re-enacted the photo, the scene of the mountain's whimsical devastation remains eerie.

called Bill's Hill, that had the same windows in the same location as the original photo. Still I wasn't sure. We went up and down another road and found another railway crossing, but it bore no resemblance to the photo. Then someone told us we could find the town on Station Road. We found it—a dirt road with several shacks—but it hardly looked like it was once a town. At the end of the road it turned left and up a hill, which was so steep Peter decided to go up backwards.

As I jumped out to lighten the load, a man in workclothes and work boots emerged from the adjacent ramshackle house. The grizzled face belonged to Paul Durand, a 69-year-old former bushman who smiled at our predicament. "That reminds me when we were way up in Cobalt, rocks sticking up all over the place," he said. "We old-timers, we had to back them up the Goddam hill."

I told him about our challenge to find the hill where the car got stuck. He said, "Come into the house, this warehouse or whore house or some fucking thing." He had a way with words, but he was trying to find his photos of old Scotia Junction. "The station used to be in front of the house," he said, pointing at some photos of an old station and a lovely house with a porch that he claims was the same as the one now clad in fake-brick siding. The water tank in the photo, he claimed, was outside in pieces—a mind with a vivid imagination could decipher it. When shown the photo in Wilby's book, the Montreal-born man with a hint of a French accent said, "It's not right here, for sure. I'm a bushman. You have to go more by the lay of the land and the shapes. I seen scenery here between Sudbury and Timmins as the crow flies. I know how to identify the land." He had prospected all over northern Ontario and had done some packing, going into the bush for nine months, moving gear from locale to locale ahead of "high mucks" who were looking for traces of Eric the Great. "We figure he went up the Albany River. On that trip he made, they used to go to shore with rope tied to shoes. By hand drills and hammer they'd drop a pin in to fix rope on it." As a bushman he explained that the lumberjack is the guy who cut trees down, but the bushman marks the trails for him to cut. "I blazed a trail, 19 miles of a zig-zag road through the rock between Shining Tree and West Ree."

Calling himself the mayor of Scotia Junction—which was only fitting because he was descended from a seigneur, an upper-class Durand from Normandy in the 1600s—he took out a 1906 plan of the Village of Scotia Junction, Township of Pusey. Station Road was really Edgar Street and Alice Street until the emergency 911 system was set up and wiped out the historical names in favour of efficiency. He said it was a town at one time, with the junction of two railways, a boarding house and a hotel.

When we went outside, he pointed to where he found "square-by-12s," and over yonder, evidence of a corduroy road that used to guide travellers around the swamp. Where there is now a wild collection of marshy weeds, the hotel Haney and Wilby stayed in sat on stilts with a cat walk from porch to road. "When I came here in 1965 I found telephone poles in ground—the old stilts. Up the street was a school." Next to his house he showed me an old school bus he was rebuilding: "It's going to take me to the Yukon some day. I'll go for two months of summer. I want to sell everything here and get the hell out. I want to be a gypsy."

The sale wouldn't be your everyday garage sale, or maybe it would. Across the street was another shack he owned. "The Scotia Mall" was guarded by five goats, including a milking one he called "My Sheba. She's my queen. She's half deer. Her mother was bred with a deer. She took off for two-and-a-half days in the bush. I was taking an old fence apart when I heard snorting behind my back. The bastard had big horns. He must have been coming back for some nookie...Sheba was so wild. Until she had her babies I couldn't touch her. She was mild then. She stood up in her manger when I came to see her. Then she started snuggling up to me." Inside the shack was a scene that resembled a discount clothier after a Boxing Day sale—a jumble of clothes for kids and adults, and odd knick-knacks, crayons and then a counter where he dug up some more old photos of Scotia Junction.

Meeting Paul Durand made me feel awfully sentimental—not the sentiment, though, that would make me call a milking goat "My Sheba." In a brief conversation Durand had given a history of the land, from Eric the Red on down to the seigneurs, the wonderful wilderness, trudging into the unknown looking to make a living, and then looking for a way out. Paul Durand, bushman, self-made man, descendant of the upper crust, lover of the land, entrepreneur, grizzly enough, offside enough, alive enough to strive to be a gypsy again. I even identified with his love of history, his desire to resurrect what had been trampled by so-called progress. Sure, time marches on, and world history is inundated with towns that come and go once their use has been exhausted, but why lose track of what we once had. What bothered me was not so much losing the hotel and the name of the street, but we abandoned a whole way of life in abandoning the train—the desire to live close together near a station, the ability to congregate at the Scotia Junction hotel and meet people from around the world. And why not choose the train to get from node to node, instead of driving 12 to 16 hours as northern Ontarians do? Why not overnight on the train and let the rumble rock you to sleep? Gaze out at the branches under the moonlight. Wake up to ponds before they give birth to shadows...

> Scotia Junction for me was a place of wonderment. For Wilby it was a geographical expression set down promiscuously and irrelevantly in a swamp in the heart of Ontario, a station at which two railroads, crossing at right angles, pointed to the four points of the compass, a little wooden hotel, a scattered farm or two, and a great ghost of an abandoned wooden boarding house whose skeleton frame, looming through the gloomy silence, hinted at the strange futility of certain badly calculated human hopes. Scotia Junction was the end of the world.

Haney said they ran into problems about 4 p.m. in Scotia Junction. A team of horses, owned by a taciturn Irishman named Murphy, pulled his car out but twisted his transmission shaft in the process. The shaft goes the length of the car from the engine, working like a crank to turn the back wheels and propel the car forward. The shaft is too soft, Haney wrote, so they'd have to wait a day to get a new one, and he didn't expect to get away until September 11. He also came to understand how much help Wilby would be, for he wrote in his journal that he's "trying to figure out some sort of rig to pull the car out with one man. Can't do it with the block and tackle. About everything that has tried that hill has had to be pulled out."

After Irene fixed lunch, we had no problem pulling out of town. Buoyed by an afternoon of straddling the century on two boulders, we decided to head to North Bay. Because Haney and Wilby scooted across much of northern Ontario by boat and train, we had to speed on where they stopped to match schedules again by Manitoba. Just before Katrine, a road construction crew gave us one of our bigger compliments —they told us to slow down. Fiscally conservative Ontario is making the highway to North Bay four lanes, which will come at an enormous cost, now and in the future. Through this stretch we saw our first wild animal, a red fox, and our first "Beware of Moose" signs. It prompted Lorne's story about a bear by the roadside and a nearby rock covered in blood. "I thought it was two bears. It was only one. A truck hit it at night and cut it in two. The bear's heart was in the middle of the road."

Besides the frequent evidence of roadkills of smaller breeds of animal, the roadside always had cheery things for the imaginative eye. Lorne, inspired by a cow clearing the grass between the fence and the road, deadpanned, "The grass is always greener on the other side of the fence." I spotted a sign, "Yard sale inside," which made me think Paul Durand had a cousin with his own Scotia Mall.

September 10 — Scotia Junction/North Bay

After the hectic pace of Toronto, trying to get the car fixed on what should have been a day of rest, Haney had a fairly leisurely day. He had breakfast at 8 a.m. and went up the hill to the Murphy farm to take out the transmission. He hung around Hotel Scotia Junction, and was at the train station at 8:30 p.m. when the new transmission arrived. It was too dark to change it, so he kept working on his one-man windlass idea until he figured it out. He hoped to get one made in North Bay. He went to bed at 9:30 p.m., knowing he'd have to get up early to make his switch.

Lorne was also playing mechanical wizard. Sensing a problem, he took out his exhaust valves for a look—the spacer which keeps the valves fitting properly had vanished. Ever economical, he put a nickel in to contain it; it didn't work so he sprung for a dime. "I don't know how long it will last," he said, "but I'll get my 10 cents worth. This dime might be a bit soft and the valve could pinch a hole through it. If it does I'll put another one in, but I don't know how the mint will feel about that." Peter took the car to Tweedsmuir School. The car and Peter's teaching skills kept the Grades 3 to 6 students captivated for 40 minutes. The kids had some astute questions; one kid asked if the digital camera Peter used to put photos on the Internet was the same kind the paparazzi who chased Diana used. Peter told them the story of Scotia Junction—the hamlet has become so bypassed by history that even the reporter who covered Peter's visit had never heard of it. The school was named after a British author, but it wasn't Wilby—it was John Buchan, who as Baron Tweedsmuir was Governor General of Canada from 1935 to 1940.

Wilby was getting a bit worried by the delay. Not only did the car seem like it was not up to the task, but he also had heard from enough people in Toronto to convince him he had no other route around Lake Superior than by boat or train.

Ahead lay only dismal prospects of watching life drag slowly on in this forsaken spot for the next few days, while the surgical operation was performed which would replace the old and useless organ of the unfortunate car. It was a fitting spot in which to effectively hide the ignominy of disaster; but one would have preferred companionship in congested ways, or the enchantment of the broad St. Lawrence, or the roar of belligerent seas—anything but this Sybil silence of dreary flats, a hush broken only by the raucous grinding of metallic wheels and the wheezy cough of aggressive locomotives. Some day one will dress for dinner in the future city by the swamp. But now the moose takes a look at the railroad from the tamaracks on the high slopes. The beaver persists in building his dam as if the Indian were still lord of the waste places and hunter of pelt. He and the moose, the chokeberry and the wild raspberry, seem as permanent as the hills.

He was bored staring at a thin line of tamaracks and glistening lines of steel disappearing in four directions, while his "chauffeur" wandered "moodily seeking his kind and moaning inwardly for a taste of civilization and its dissipations." If he meant "alcohol" when he said "dissipations" he was probably referring to himself, for Haney didn't drink and Wilby eventually died of cirrhosis of the liver.

Haney's distaste for drink began when he was a child playing along the banks of the Wabash Canal near his home in Huntington, Indiana. Each spring he and a friend would tie a knife to a hoe handle and head out in search of the dark grey venomous snakes known as Mississippi moccasins. These snakes made their way up the canal each spring and lay coiled at the water's edge sunning themselves. After a day of chopping their heads off, Haney headed home for supper and decided to take a shortcut over a fence. When he hopped up to clear it, the makeshift knife slipped from his hands and his bare feet landed on the blade. Blood spurted out of Haney's foot. His friend dashed for Haney's father. Joseph Haney stopped the bleeding, but he took Jack to a river man who also caught the snakes and sold them to a zoo for a living. When the river man got bitten by the snakes, he drank a bottle of whiskey as an antidote against the venom. So by the light of an oil lamp, Mr. Haney held his son's head and guided a bottle of liquor down his throat. Fonce, as he was then known before he picked up the nickname Jack at the Reo factory, awoke the next day thinking his head was on the Huntington train tracks as a Chicago freight train rumbled by. After that day, Jack never went near alcohol.

On September 10th, Wilby met the female version of Paul Durand. She, too, lived next to the railway station, but her abode was a white caravan. She also knew the town's history and what went on in the village, which amounted to the coming and going of trains and people who stayed at her husband's hotel. Wilby went up to see the Murphy family in action—the family of 12 living off the land to make sure its table was full: sons pulled out stumps from the field with their team of horses; "young and pretty daughters" took care of the household chores. "Here," he wrote, "in the hottest place of summer, the coldest of winter, the loneliest place always, a family of twelve lived in a shack of a house, prosperous and happy, and figuratively pitched the Doomsday Book on to the waste pile....The Murphys were their own rulers and their own subjects!" His comments were in line with his belief that the unfortunate poor of Britain, and for that matter Ireland, should stop burdening the King and make their new life in Canada.

September 11 — Scotia Junction/North Bay

Haney woke up at 5:30 a.m. to get to work on the new driveshaft, but he had more helpers than he bargained for. Eight young Murphys came out to the barn, his hastily improvised car hospital, to gawk at Haney's work. Haney designated the 10-year-old his chief engineer and assistant. This lad was so taken by his position, he rode the running board when they finally re-embarked at 8:30 a.m. Haney gave Mr. Murphy a $10 bill for all his troubles, which included pulling them out of the sand, storing the car, helping him pick up the new transmission and returning the old shaft to the station after Haney had boxed it up. Wilby says they had some difficulty spilling the young Murphy off among the bushes, and "dissipating his new-born dreams of the tempting world beyond the limits of the farm."

Yet the day of the bent transmission shaft would pale in comparison to their struggle northward, a struggle that was so bad that Wilby contemplated quitting the trip, although he fails to mention that in his book. First they blew a tire, which Haney fixed so quickly he didn't refer to it in his diary. They made South River, a lumber town that showed off its products in its house siding and wooden sidewalks. For Wilby, a town without bricks wasn't much of a town at all.

It was sunny and warm, and the road tree-lined and undulating. When they got about 43 kilometres from Scotia, Haney said "the fun began." Wilby said it was somewhere beyond South River that an eager search was made for anything other than sand or swamp or mud or "oleaginous pools" which now began to mark their progress. He wished the sand from the hills had filled up the swamps, or that the swamps had been up on the hills for airing. They heard rumours of an unavoidable and menacing hill in their path, and Wilby took details of its latitude and longitude,

> as a captain might in searching for a reported Atlantic derelict. Fifteen miles were wasted in endeavoring to discover the fork which would lead to the hill. When a hill came in sight, we would say: "Ah, there it is," and when we had managed to surmount it, we would add: "Thank God, we're over it and now we can cut along to North Bay." Then came another hill and still another. But the real hill did at last appear. Ideally situated miles from anywhere, it was approached through a "corduroy" path lined by swamps, and it was edged all the way up by thickets nicely mingled with a choice selection of rocks. Rushing the hill was out of the question; for the "corduroy" or log road at the foot would have broken our springs and landed us upside down in the thicket before we reached the incline.

Haney said they got to "a high hill with about a 40 percent grade and a ruddy slippery surface." Considering the 1997 desire to have cars tackle nothing more than a 5 percent grade, the hill must have been imposing. The Reo stopped halfway up and then began to slide backward without waiting for the brakes. When it rested momentarily on a hummock, they jumped out and blocked the wheels. They tried twice more to climb it, and then decided to rely on the car's better judgment, and headed off in search of another route. Haney later said, "If this was a hill, I had never seen one before; it looked more like a patent fire escape."

Wilby described a "sailor's knot" of paths, a steep, 200-metre-tall hill, getting stuck on corduroy stairs and putting Haney's new invention to good use.

> For an hour or more we wrenched away like draught horses at the block and tackle, standing on a huge boulder that crowned the fiendish elevation. The sun cast chromatic reflections upon the lichen coatings of the vari-colored stones and rock, and at last it sank behind

the barren poles of the fire-blasted trees beyond the summit. Still we dragged wearily on the long wire tackle, staggering groggily, out of breath, cheered only by the buzzing vicious flies which refused to be stampeded. The car performed spectacularly. It split the welkin with its roar, jerking forward with violent wrenches and jerking as suddenly back-wards, in order to catapult one of us into the radiator. We multiplied human energy with a new-fangled windlass arrangement born of chauffeur genius and deftly constructed by axe and fallen birch stumps.

It's a toss-up who the "one of us" was who catapulted into the radiator. For the first time, in the middle of nowhere with the fate of the trip on the line, Wilby would have been compelled to help. Haney put the car on cruise control—used the hand-throttle to give it gas—while both of them pulled on the taut "wire lasso." At times their stubbing post for their windlass bent the branches that held it, and came flying out of its socket toward them. While the Reo clung to the hill like a cat, or as Wilby said "hung like a lobster with its claws," Haney pumped up the petrol tank, filled in the hollows between the rotten or missing logs of the corduroy stairs with stones and even jacked up the wheels one by one to get them over. They inched their way up, getting hung up again on rocks before finally letting the rubber-clad claws of the Reo land in some stones, and then the soft mud of the hill's crest. Before they went any further, Haney raised the floorboard to see what he didn't want to see—they had already twisted the new driveshaft. They were perched on a hill with not a soul, never mind a hotel, in sight. Haney managed to put the car in low gear to cover the remaining 24 kilometres to the nearest town at Trout Creek.

On this day in 1997 we too backtracked—to pick up a new computer being delivered, not by train from Niagara, but by courier from Niagara. With dime in place, Lorne reckoned the car hadn't run so smoothly since 1914. Even though we had the same car, we felt guilty having an easy time with the roads, while Haney and Wilby struggled on hills to the south. If we could have backtracked in time to help them climb those corduroy stairs, we would have been there.

Although we didn't have such steep grades, we had the same pathetic brakes. Lorne said the brakes are next to useless when wet. I said if it's raining in B.C., he could go down the mountains on his own. He said if the brakes are warm they'll be dry enough to work, but one modification made the Reo less of a death trap—Lorne put in a bypass for the car's awkward braking system. The Reo's brakes were more dangerous than they needed to be. The brake pedal was really the parking brake. The clutch pedal, if fully depressed, became the working brake, so if you were going uphill, and you pushed down too far to change gears, you could actually stop the car. Conversely, if you were going downhill, and you geared down to second to slow the car, you would lose that advantage by applying the brakes. It would be: Flimsy brakes versus Newton's Laws on Momentum. Instead, Lorne drilled a hole in the floor and attached a socket to the brakes. By constructing a fulcrum, he could apply the brakes by sticking a pipe into a socket and pulling on it. Lorne could match Haney's ingenuity. Then again, given half a chance, I would have figured it out. Sure.

Night was descending as Haney directed the car forward in low gear toward a long bridge with a gaping hole. A kilometre away, though, they found a farmhouse where a shabbily dressed woman came to the door with her children hanging to her skirt. The Pathfinders explained their predicament, but she told them there were no men folk about—her husband and sons had gone west to make some money on the Prairie harvest. She told them they could "rummage around," so Haney gave her a dollar and found some planks. Within an hour, he built what Wilby called a "crazy bridge" and the Reo crept across it. With Wilby ready to cash in the trip if the car did not make it, Haney guided it to safety. By 8 p.m. they saw Trout Creek. They had driven 100 kilometres, but only 48 kilometres closer to North Bay. They found a place to eat, but hadn't booked a bed yet when Haney wrote in his diary that "Wilby is pretty sore about the delay, is almost ready to give up. The trip is a farce anyway."

From Haney's perspective, such pathfinding required two men able to block-and-tackle obstacles as they arose. From Wilby's perch, his experience could guide a capable car across. He felt the Reo showed tremendous courage making its way up the hills, but for the second time in three days the driveshaft bent under strain. In his circular tour of the United States, his Ohio Mudhen never let him down, nor did his chauffeur, Fred D. Clark. Wilby was impressed with Haney's ingenuity, but he wanted him to be more deferential to the world traveller in his passenger seat.

On our entrance into Sudbury we were greeted by a *Road Kills* traffic sign, and it wasn't varmints they were talking about. Sure enough, that day's paper included a story about a Highway 400 accident in which a couple in their forties and a 17-year-old boy, all from Sudbury, had died. With great distances being travelled by Northerners who cover that ground quickly, the North has more than its share of accidents.

Sudbury, under grey skies, was every bit as grey as expected. Downtown there are outcroppings of the shattered rock on which the city is built, Sudbury Breccia, which was produced some 1.8 billion years ago from a big shock, probably a volcanic reaction or a meteor. Surrounding the city are scatterings of small trees. Scientists realized years ago that the emissions from the city's smelter were killing trees and turning the area into a moonscape. Now an even taller smokestack shoots its emissions into the low-lying clouds, sending the pollution God knows where.

At the Big Nickel we learned that rock becomes ore when enough minerals are found in it to mine. Peter suggested the nickel on the original Pathfinder Reo could have come from here. From the Big Nickel you could see a huge ridge of blackness across the way, where five railway cars from the mines backed slowly along its summit. In the greyness it looked other-worldly or forbidden, a world not for humans but only machines. As if on cue, a V-shaped flock of honkers fled south.

Despite a light rain that spit at us through a new crack in our windshield, the joys of the North were upon us. The enormous rocks the road had blasted through showed off a jagged edge that revealed not gold or silver but colours and textures that must have drawn the Group of Seven northward. The rain did not bother us; the car had a do-it-yourself windshield wiper we never used. Unlike new cars, where rain drips inside when you open the door, the broad roof of the Reo kept most of the rain out of the seating compartment. We passed stunning stark beauty, the trees sloping down to the edge of the Vermilion River; the rocks, when they weren't dazzling us like thousands of colours coming out of fibre-optic ends, displayed the graffiti talents of youngsters just begging to tell the world of their undying love for "Katya," or their campaign to "Legalize pot now."

In discussing the Sudbury human-roadkill sign, Peter said they weren't uncommon out west. He saw on TV the night before what happened when they took away speed limits in Montana. The first year there was a slight decline in road deaths. The second year accidents and deaths were up 30 percent. As Peter discussed this, he kept veering off to the road's shoulder to allow faster cars to whiz by. Seatbeltless, in a Reo from an era when cars regularly tipped over, I started devising escape routes should the car follow in the path of its peers. Peter, sensing my paranoia, said, "The oxygen masks will descend from the ceiling when cabin pressure..." I interrupted him to say, "And your flight attendant will be the first to jump out." I figured the structure to support the mohair roof would not suffice as a roll bar, so my plan was to leap clear, depending on which way the car rolled.

We finally pulled over in Massey, 85 years minus two days behind the Pathfinders. Before I checked into either of the two unappealing motels on the Trans-Canada Highway, I stopped at the Massey museum to see if any 1912 hotels still existed. Carolyn Hein of the museum said the Balmoral Hotel, Clifton House and Massey House had all been wooden and had burned down. She showed me pictures of the first car in Massey, which arrived in 1907, and gave two explanations for the names Spanish River and the town called Espanola. "Some say there were some Spanish coins found on the shore there," said Hein. "The other theory, passed on by Sarah Owl, is that in the mid-18th century her great, great grandfather went on a raiding party to the south and brought back a woman captive who spoke Spanish."

The town was named after James Massey, a surveyor for Canadian Pacific Railway, a company that often dictated where northern towns would grow. Hein remembers seeing Governor General Vincent Massey waving from the back of the train, but she doesn't know whether Massey, whom Wilby might have met at the Toronto club, knew the town wasn't named after his distinguished family.

The museum showed just how different the North is from the rest of Ontario. It had a collection of lumber stamps—an insignia that would be sledge-hammered into the end of logs so the sorting lumberjack could identify which lumbermill they belonged to. If someone tried to saw off the end of the logs to steal them, the stamp of the lumberjack would show through. The museum had a schoolroom with books that must have enchanted students earlier in the century: Samuel Hearne's *Journey from Hudson Bay to the Northern Ocean in the Years 1769-1772*; Alexander Henry's *Travels and Adventures in Canada and the Indian Territories, 1760-1776*; Sir Alexander Mackenzie's *Voyages from Montreal through the Continent of North America to the Frozen North and Pacific Oceans in 1789 and 1793*; and *Pathfinders of North America*. It included stories of the "Coming of Norse Sea Rovers," "The Cabots Gain a Foothold for England," "Cartier Enters the St. Lawrence," "Samuel de Champlain Explores the Interior," "Radisson and des Groseilliers." The book, written in 1939, made no mention of Thomas William Wilby, intrepid motor explorer.

Hein told me I could learn more about Massey if I visited Isabel Hobbs on the edge of town. Before I left for Hobbs's home, I turned on the news at the motel. The station showed its static camera on Highway 401 in Toronto, with the cars bumper-to-bumper. The next story was about a puppy being dragged for two miles by a van.

Isabel, age 80, had stories that predated the Pathfinders' arrival in Massey. She conjured up the survival-of-the-fittest era when people alit in the North in search of wealth. Because money was involved, they just as often found betrayals as they did riches. She told the story of her father's two cousins who ran a lumbermill. One ran the business and one did the accounting, until the accountant upped and left with all the money. Her father bought the mill from the remaining brother. Because it virtually ran itself, he had spare time to go prospecting, and once, when he and two friends thought they had found a vein of gold, they staked a claim to the property—or at least his friends did. They left her father's name off the claim. "My father still couldn't believe it. 'They wouldn't do that, they're my friends,' he'd say."

In her haphazard files, she had arrowheads and celts that dated from 3,000 B.C.— "They were so nice and smooth, you wonder how the Indians had the patience to do that." She had newspaper clippings saying broomball was born in Massey. In May of 1912, four months before the Reo's arrival, a men's soccer team saw a child swatting a ball with a toy broom, found their own brooms, set up rules and played a historic, injury-filled encounter. She also had a clipping about the 1910 train wreck at the new railway bridge over the Spanish River—the engine made it across, but not the passenger cars: 43 men, women and children died in 40-below-zero weather.

A lot of her collection juxtaposed the train and the car. She had a photo of the last station agent shutting down the telegraph equipment when the railway station closed August 20, 1970. "The train used to be big," she said. "When the train came, you went up to see who got on and who got off. In those days you could send the mail down to Sudbury in the morning and you could get a reply back at night. Now it takes a week." In one of her boxes she also had an X-ray from the time she dislocated her ankle in a car accident. She loves the car, even though she doesn't want a four-lane highway. "The first highway had a bridge with just enough room for one car to go on." With a forlorn look, she added, "It didn't go where the highway goes now." Moving the road, she says, cost the life of her son Robert (she also lost her daughter Velma Jane, 7, to polio just a year before they discovered the vaccine). He was on leave from the army when he went out, not realizing the highway had moved closer to the train tracks. "They drove over the tracks and stopped," she said. "I think they thought the train lights were car lights."

Haney's car lights were only on for an hour or two this day in 1912. He sat down for a meal of fried eggs and fried potatoes in Trout Creek, likely at the Evers Hotel (now a hard-core drinking establishment) quite satisfied for overcoming the day's obstacles. Wilby, however, expected more out of the "dingy wooden inn, thick with the tobacco smoke of sleepy lumber-men and an argumentative array of boarders." One of the boarders was a "facetious old man of the 'sly dig' variety," whose wit I'd expect Wilby to enjoy. Wilby must have been the victim of one of his digs, or maybe the elderly clerk from Sheffield didn't show him enough respect. He said the man "diffused an airy freedom eloquent of New World democracy," which means Wilby didn't like him. For Wilby it was OK for lower-class Brits to emigrate to Canada to avoid starvation and homelessness in Britain, as long as they kept their forelock-tugging ways to the upper crust. When someone had absconded with his writing implements, the old man said, "My pen! My pen! My kingdom for a pen!" By the way he wrote it, Wilby didn't appreciate the Shakespearean paraphrase.

An equally loquacious parrot presided over the writing table, where a commercial traveller used flypaper to secure the edges of his paper from "furtive gusts of wind." The walls boasted colour prints, including what Wilby called "the glorious charge of Balaclava." (Sixty years after 600 Brits charged into the "valley of death," it was still considered a noble act of obedience toward less-than-intelligent superiors.) In the dingy smoke room, the shabby wash-house, the dining room and even upstairs, there were more prints of the world's nobility, and Wilby seemed shocked that Sir Wilfrid Laurier would be included among such a group. "One hardly knew," wrote Wilby, "whether this formidable display of blue blood was to teach the advantages or the disadvantages of democracy."

AUTOMOBILE POLO, September, 1912, Wichita, Kansas—The Black Demon automobile polo team defeated Grey Ghosts 3-2 in a game marked by several thrilling incidents. In the second period Carl Evans of the Black Demons drove his car between the goal posts at top speed to block a drive for goal and swerved so short that his car completely overturned. In the third period Frank Garrety of Grey Ghosts missed a swing at the ball going top speed and tumbled down from his car. Evans was unable to avoid him and the car passed over the calf of Garrety's leg, only bruising him however.

DEALERSHIP MOVING TO CITY'S EDGE, September, 1997, Sudbury, Ontario—Canada's oldest Chrysler dealership is abandoning downtown Sudbury because of a lack of parking and a desire to combine its new and used car lots. "We're not leaving the downtown with any bad feelings, but in this particular type of industry, land is the biggest thing," said Mike Doyle, whose dealership first opened in 1921 and has been a fixture on Elm Street since 1926. "You have to have parking for customers. It just doesn't exist here—parking for customers, for inventory. And people with time restraints, they just aren't receptive to going to two locations. It's 20 minutes across the city to look at used vehicles."

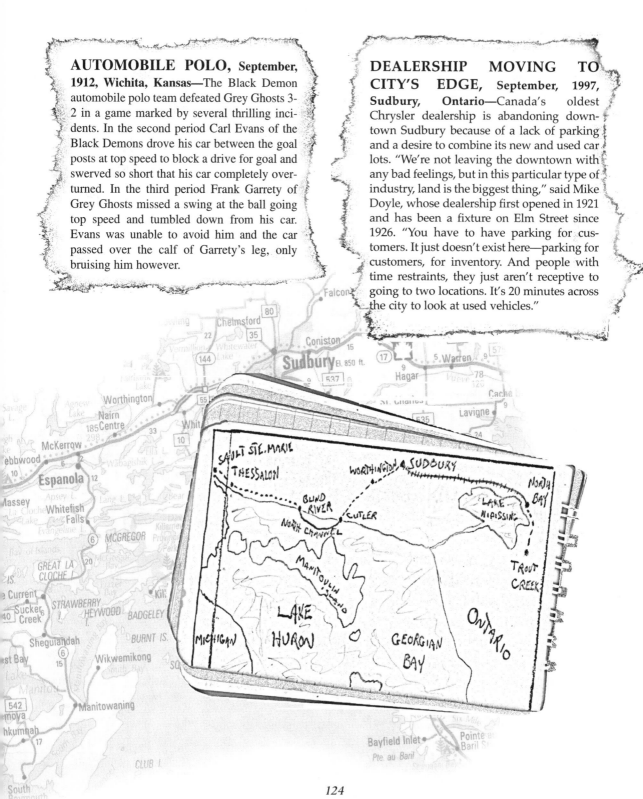

Chapter 7

Finally Heading West

September 12 — Trout Creek/Massey

Democracy, and the way Canadians clung to it, seemed to occupy Wilby's thoughts every day, perhaps as his means of addressing his disgust at Haney wanting to be treated as an equal. Haney, on the other hand, wanted respect and someone to work with to make the journey a success. He realized the enormity of the task, and his value in making the trip a success—without his ingenuity and industry, Wilby's chit-chat wouldn't have got them out of Nova Scotia.

For the second day in a row, Haney got up just after 5 a.m. to remove the drive-shaft. Instead of taking it to a welder, as we did with our windshield hinge, he took it to the Trout Creek blacksmith shop to be straightened and reinforced. Wilby, mean-while, went into the post office next door, where a white-bloused woman pushed his mail through a protective wicket and a tall, lean postmaster poked a rusty stove with a wood shingle and sized Wilby up. Trout Creek had one gravel road—where the grass was doing its best to sprout between the pebbles—with telegraph poles and a wooden sidewalk running alongside. Wilby also checked out the white-painted fences edging gardens of sunflowers and morning glories on the west side of town, and found a solitary cow grazing in the graveless churchyard.

Outside the hotel, where hundreds of matches and cigarette butts littered the road, the mended Reo pulled up before noon. In his book Wilby emphasized that dinner was "sharp at twelve." The reader could interpret it as an order from a bad-tempered waitress. Haney's diary suggests Wilby was making a dig at his chauffeur. After working for so long to fix the car, Haney wanted to eat before departing. Wilby was impatient. Haney's diary says "Had a little spat with Captain at noon. He wanted me to go without dinner after working on car for six hours. I let him down hard."

Wilby, to his credit, never mentions any spats with Haney in his book, but he dissed the New World democracy Haney cherished, using the stoop-shouldered, prosaic waitress as his target.

> She had the air of one who said: "This is really not my job. I don't care whether you like me in this capacity or not. This work is only temporary. I hate it any way. It's beneath me, and I am not aiming at giving you satisfaction. I'm just as good as you are." In the small communities of this new world, I had often seen the man who only on request came to take the suitcases from the car and the landlord who left me to find my own room in the hotel. I had heard, too, of the woodman or coalman who would not deliver his wares to the house from the pavement without extra payment, the dustman who would not remove the garbage until another man had been paid to fetch it from the backyard to the street, and the servant who dictated the terms of her reluctant service. And I wondered whether they could in reality satisfactorily compare with the "downtrodden" equivalents of Europe, who have learned to take pride in their humble tasks and perform a service obligingly and artistically, with evident satisfaction in duty well done. Only in the land of the Habitant did I find that grace in the service of others—a reminiscence of rose and lavender—that belongs to a settled civilization.

While they ate lunch the Reo drew a "dingy" crowd of people who had heard about its day-old heroics. Wilby was proud that the Reo's exploits would tantalize Trout Creek, but he had doubts whether the car was able to achieve success for him. Getting out of town even became complicated. To find petrol they took a shortcut to a nearby chemical plant, which necessitated building up the ground to get up and over the railway tracks. When that failed, they took a run at the tracks from the opposite direction and slid off the sand embankment into a hollow. Workmen passing by helped the pair out of their predicament. Instead of wasting what little petrol they had left, they set out on the 80-kilometre trip to North Bay with a pilot. In his diary, Haney is sanguine about the car's misfortune in the hollow. All he said was "had a deuce of a time getting gasoline."

At the Chutes Provincial Park campground where the Findlays stayed, the Reo came to the rescue of the camper, whose radio had drained its battery. The Reo jump-started it; another case of the old helping the new. While there, the Findlays met a man who had covered some of the same territory as we had, and more. The widower from Edmonton drove to Montreal to see golfer Tiger Woods play in the Canadian Open. Woods didn't make the cut to play on the weekend, so his long trip was for naught. Lorne was telling me this as he veered onto the shoulder of the road to let Trans-Canada drivers pass us. I continued to devise ways to dive off the Reo and roll in order to sustain minimal head injuries.

At Blind River, where the original Pathfinders arrived by tugboat from Cutler because of impassable roads, there was a stretch of swamp where the road was built up several metres—in Northern Ontario it becomes abundantly clear that road-building must have cost a small fortune. Farther along, at the horseshoe pits of Iron Bridge, I was reminded of its English namesake where there's an industrial-age museum. That age seems so archaic now. One day there will be a monument to the car age, with a similar look back to a world that was so crude and dirty...

For lunch we stopped at Thessalon, where Wilby and Haney spent the night of the 15th. Michael Heintzman of *The North Shore Sentinel* said we were just one of many transcontinentalists who stop in, be it runners or cyclists or people on a mission. Wheelchair-bound Dave Shannon had just gone through to raise money for paraplegics, but the most unusual tourists were the Grants from Scotland, said Heintzman. David and Kate Grant, in their forties, sold their home on the Orkney Islands to embark on a seven-year trek around the world with their three children—son Torcuil, 17, and daughters Eilidh, 15, and Fionn, 12—and an 800-kilogram Belgian workhorse to pull their red caravan. As Heintzman spoke, we realized we had passed them on the south St. Lawrence shore. It looked like a gypsy wagon with the father walking alongside.

The Grants got the idea of using a horse and caravan from an Irish tourism magazine, and reasoned it was less complicated than a motorized vehicle. "I am not particularly fond of the internal combustion engine," said David when he stopped in Thessalon. "The thought of breaking down somewhere without parts just didn't do it for me." (It was a thought that didn't intimidate Haney, but David Grant just wasn't born early enough in the century.) Since the Grants began they had gone through Slovenia after it had declared independence; David had been arrested for defending his caravan from drunken Mongolians with a slingshot; they were almost denied entry into China; their first horse had died in Japan, and the cost of getting their caravan and horse to North America had almost ended the trip until an American company heard their story and shipped it for them. Even though their trip would set a record for a family vacation, the Grants were not in it for records, but only to travel along the world's roads, meeting new people and experiencing new cultures.

By comparison our trip seemed small, but we carried on—the Findlays to Sault Ste. Marie and me to the Thessalon library (Heintzman agreed to drop me off in The Soo). Wilby's book and Haney's diary didn't reveal much about their stay in Thessalon; the library coughed up even less. The Pathfinders could have stayed at the Moorehouse Hotel or the Queen's Royal Hotel. The library didn't have anything on the trip, but there were photos of lumberjacks with brag loads—seeing how high they could pile logs of white pine on top of a horse-drawn cart.

My introduction to Sault Ste. Marie was negative, which I blame on its one-way streets. Between downtown and the water is a one-way, four-lane road with a fifth added for turning. As I tried to make it across, one driver almost clipped my heel. The city seemed to be saying, "Have a car or else." The first person I met could not afford a car, or even his next meal. Reg, a fifty-ish man with a sheepish grin, approached me asking for a dollar so he could buy two hot dogs. When I said I left my money at the B & B, he confessed to why he was in such a predicament. "I been drinking. Five years I never drank. You know how it is. I don't know if you do or not." I thought that Wilby, the guy with the bad liver, might have understood this man from Antigonish, Nova Scotia. Reg said he had had a bad day, and while we walked he picked up a Dairy Queen Blizzard cup someone had left on the sidewalk and finished it off. "You get up in the morning and have to look at yourself. Today's got to be Friday or Saturday, I have no idea." He threw away the Blizzard cup, but not before acknowledging how good it was. "Wish I could straighten out," he said. "Been in detox program for five years. Bang. I don't even know what I do half the time. I got no friends because I have no money. The more money you have, the more friends you have. The less money you have, the less friends you have. But it doesn't mean I can't win this war."

I had to go back and get my wallet anyway, so I also grabbed some cookies at the B & B and looked for Reg. When I found him there was no question about his hunger. He was so desperate to eat, the cookies became crumbs on his lips. He told me he had been divorced for three years and been drunk for three years. "She's a gambler, and I'm a drunk. You can't fault her for leaving me." He would like to help her out of her addiction, "but I can't help people when I'm drunk." We went into a local diner and Reg asked for lots of onions with his hot dogs. "Make it miserable (with onions)," he told the waitress. He asked me for a cigarette, which I didn't have, and he realized I wasn't going to buy him a pack. He even tried to weasel money out of me by telling a story of a saintly girl who gave him $30 and didn't ask for any back. I just nodded and kept on eating. His desire to converse ebbed, and after he had demolished his food, he went out to talk to a woman who was much younger than him. Before I could say "bye" he was gone, thus proving the adage he had passed on to me: "The more money you have, the more friends you have. The less money you have, the less friends you have."

The waitress, a weathered woman in her early fifties, was scornful of Reg and his ilk: "They drink their money and they come in here looking for food, or some sucker will buy it for them."

"Does that mean I'm a sucker?" I asked.

She just looked at me. She didn't have to speak. "That woman's a bum, too," she continued. "She'll come through here again looking for you. She's a prostitute!" She said it with such venom I expected a bolt of lightning to strike the pavement in front of Mary's Restaurant. The clientele didn't seem to faze Eddie the owner who, sitting in a booth, looked like the cook from the Beetle Bailey cartoon. On his plate were the spoils of his work—all the spare pieces of pork and beef piled high on top of french fries and carrots. The *pièce de résistance* came when Eddie poured honey over every inch of his plate. He had been running Mary's Restaurant for 45 years; it was his place and he could die of hardening of the arteries if he wanted.

Eddie and his buddy, an older guy in a baseball cap, said the downtown wasn't always so quiet. In the sixties they made the main street a one-way. "I think it helped it die," said the man in the hat. The mall finished it off. The downtown was once surrounded in residences, but they were torn down for parking lots, which the main street backs onto. Eddie and his friend didn't know how people parked before those parking lots came along. Out on the streets people were going from one lottery kiosk to another, looking for one that might have a machine that works in a city that has the headquarters for Ontario's lotteries. The jackpot was close to $20 million. I felt like passing on to them Reg's adage about money and friends.

Haney and Wilby arrived in North Bay at 5 p.m. only to learn there was no road to Sudbury. Having spent the last four days going nowhere, they decided not to take any chances—they booked a place for the Reo on the Sudbury train. Wilby did not waste much time there, preferring to head west, but he was surprised to meet what he called a successful "Old Timer" businessman.

> The man who was the first to dicker with the Indians, who turned the first sod, made the first clearing, battled in the van for the communities of men who would one day follow him into the wilderness, is usually worn and spent before the day of his material rewards comes...The up-to-date successful-Old-Timer is quite another thing. He rides in a big touring car, wears kid gloves, has the finest house, the finest clothes, and the finest office, does more work than a dozen others, goes to Europe or California for his recreation, and morning noon and night booms the town for all it is worth. He is well-mannered, always has a smile and an imperturbable temper. But you will notice these features of the man after you have observed the most salient characteristic of all—that successful business air.

This man whisked Wilby off to see the mayor, hotel, town clerk and president of the local board of trade. The man boasted that he helped to make the town what it is. He stuffed Wilby's pockets with promotional brochures and pencils, matchboxes, patent lighters, office rulers and pocket clips. North Bay was surrounded by national parks like Algonquin and Temagami and great beauty, he told Wilby. When the Georgian Bay Canal was built, connecting Lake Nipissing to the Ottawa River and then the St. Lawrence, it would become a great hub. All it needed was a road. The area was accessible only by train or canoe, which Wilby equated to a doctor without instruments, or a student without books. "As well might the astronomer be blind and man headless, as a town exist without the Road—that outlet for the swelling forces within, that harbinger of civilization and progress, without which man remains but a tragedy in the universe."

The railroad journey to Sudbury still "rankled" Wilby when he wrote his book. Haney wrote in his diary that Wilby took the 9:30 p.m. train from North Bay, which must have given him some joy to be in separate towns from his travelling partner, for he writes that he is feeling good. Haney also wrote a letter to Reo headquarters and six postcards. "How's the girlie anyway?" he signed off in his diary. "Wish I could see her for an hour. Good Night."

September 13—North Bay/Sault Ste. Marie

With the Reo thrust into a closed railroad car for a 128-kilometre, $18 ride, Haney could relax before taking the 10:30 a.m. train. In Sudbury, he arranged to have a self-styled winch made and shipped to meet him in the Soo for a mere $3, and he met Billy McLeod whom the Reo company had paid to help them on the new government road to the Soo. Wilby, meanwhile, was not in the best of moods. Never mind the absence of a road north of Superior, he had already been stymied between North Bay and Sudbury. On his train ride he talked about the crowd of settlers heading west, squatting in the pale green, plush seats of what is known as a "first class day coach," but which at night is converted into a stuffy, uncomfortable, bedroom. For Wilby's upwardly turned nose, the settlers were "of a desirable class—not needy immigrants, and their cheeks wore a flush of health that promised well for the valiant fight with the wilderness." Out the window he could see railroad camps, the "plain wooden towns" that begged for a road to improve the

> dismal little places! How it would rouse them to renewed hope and activity! And what a change would come over the neglected little roads, not much more than paths, which ran in and out, playing hide and seek with the bushland until they ended somewhere in a tangle and gave up the foolish game! They bore a pathetic resemblance to the human settlements around them, which they were vainly trying to reach. They bore the same look of dilatoriness, the same air of being shelved and pushed aside from life's joyous activities.

Wilby repeated his "good roads lead to social improvement" schtick with the *Sault Ste. Marie Daily Star*. "It seems to me that the citizens of North Bay, Sudbury and the Soo," he pontificated, "would be performing a public service by working together under one association for a good highway from Montreal to the Soo."

Because we had scooted ahead of Wilby and Haney, we spent a non-travel day in the Soo. I went to the library which had not only a map of where Lake Superior had swallowed 350 ships, but it revealed that the Pathfinders had taken the freighter *A.E. Ames* to Port Arthur. They missed the scheduled ferry by getting stuck in mud. I asked the librarian about the emptiness created by the one-way system, and how everything seemed to be cut off from the main street by parking lots. She said this harbour area was full of rats and old warehouses, a no-man's land for the public. Whatever was done, she said, was an improvement. I wasn't so sure. Outside it looked like the Soo was in an intercity tarmac competition, and it won. One no-man's land had been replaced by another. The night before, when I went back to get my wallet, I cut across a nearly vacant parking lot toward two men who looked nervously at me as I approached. And it was still light out! Even the next morning, cutting across the asphalt moat that surrounded the mall, I was eyed suspiciously by a family in a van, obviously waiting for mom to buy something in the mall. Tundras of tarmac immediately create hostile environments where you expect bad things to happen, so the family cowers behind its locked doors, and I feel like an intruder. They obviously buy into the mentality that pedestrians are not welcome at malls—they're for people who can afford cars and afford to shop there.

The shopping mall itself is a no-man's land if you are homeless or down on your luck. By default, old downtowns become the habitat for the homeless and the beggars. Yet it is on the main street where you're more likely to find the city's history, its government, its banks, its architecture. At Queen and East streets is the clock tower, which dominates the thoroughfare and is now part of the Sault Ste. Marie museum. It was a post office when the duo came through, and it had just been crowned with the clock. Wilby hung out at the Soo Club House, an exclusive men's club that was situated just around the corner in a brick home, but it no longer exists—the club is now the New Algo Club; the original building was demolished for a senior's residence. Toward city hall a plaque on a bank building honoured the early natives of the Soo. "Legend says they came from the northeast before 1600." The city hall itself—where you'd expect a monument paying homage to some great day in the city's history, or to those who fell in the Boer, Korean or World Wars—had nothing but a sign offering Free Doggie Doo disposal bags.

Amidst this dysfunctional downtown, at the corner of the big parking lot, was the main attraction this Saturday morning—a train trip up Agawa Canyon. The train had already left, filled with passengers looking for a way to check out the fall colours without the stress of driving. The passenger train doesn't stop in the Soo anymore. The car relegated the train to tourism, another attraction at a theme park.

My goal this day was to get to a campground on the edge of town, where the Findlays were staying, so we could make the big jump north the next morning. On my stroll down a major road out of town—there was no public transit to aid me in my quest—I ended up asking a woman for directions. June Goddard told the story of driving down to see the southern part of Ontario and getting lost. She took seven hours to get from Niagara Falls to Barrie, a drive which can normally be done in under three hours. "My girlfriend said 'I'm glad you weren't going across Canada.'"

The Findlays, meanwhile, had their cracked windshield repaired, took some photos near the International Bridge to the United States, went to the Soo locks, which raises ships from Lake Huron to Lake Superior and vice versa, and to Place Roberta Bondar, a pavilion and park named after the Soo's female astronaut. There they met a bunch of kids who climbed all over the Reo as if they owned it. Peter, in an attempt to persuade them to be concerned about the car, took their photo and told them he'd put their picture on the web if their teacher e-mailed him. When I met the Findlays that night at the campground, Peter was dutifully trying to file his updates for the Internet. The campground also had cabins, and more importantly a place to wash your clothes. It made me wonder how Wilby and Haney got by with clothes washing, and the absence of dryers?

Haney, Wilby and Billy McLeod didn't leave Sudbury until 6 p.m. They were aiming for Cutler, but Haney in his diary said they only "got to Massey, 25 miles." Actually, they did cover 40 kilometres all right, during a rambling, two-hour ride, but they got lost and made it only as far as the Selwood Hotel in Worthington, a town of 400 built to tap the Canadian Shield for its nickel and copper. The town collapsed soon after its mine did in 1927, and was not on the map we had as we ventured west. McLeod hadn't proven himself as a pilot, but Haney needed an ally like McLeod, a "nice chap" who could distract him from thoughts of Wilby. Haney noted he was having a winch made in Sudbury to be shipped to the Soo. "Good-night!" he signed off. "Captain is getting worse."

September 14—Worthington/Sault Ste. Marie
On this morning Haney and Wilby crossed the Spanish River, incidentally, at the same time that Tom Thomson, one of the Arts and Letters Club artists, was coming down the river after a long canoe trip. Thomson probably never met the Pathfinders

because they were in the midst of a 90-kilometre run to Cutler. After lunch, the lack of a road with a bridge forced them to put the Reo on a tug boat, 56 kilometres in the North Channel, along the northern shore of Manitoulin Island. Haney tells his diary it was "great sport" getting the Reo on the tug. When they reached Blind River at 6 p.m., they bought 10 gallons of gas for $3.50 and made it another 51 kilometres to Thessalon by nightfall. Five kilometres into their quest they got stuck in the mud, but McLeod helped Haney liberate the Reo.

The 1997 crew shot up north the next morning, heading for the big statue of the Canada goose at Wawa. The car gave us the chance to pursue isolation, to leave cities behind and be at one with nature. It wasn't the thrill of total departure from modernity, to use Wilby's line, but a taste of the North, and what Canada must have looked like to the early voyageurs, if one can ignore the two-lane highway which, wastefully, became a four-lane highway at times. There was much to beckon the visitor to return at the other end of summer, the empty picnic tables along the Superior shore, the undented sand that must wait another eight or nine months for bathers. On the shore of this ocean disguised as a lake were several cottages, obviously owned by those who were let in on the secret—the freshness of the air, the clarity of the streams, the clumsiness of timbers nature had scattered against a rocky waterfall. As friendly as the people were in the Soo, I was glad to be away from a world where each car demands seven parking spots. Here was the best use of a car—to cross the Batchawana River and feel the glory of remoteness.

Folk in southern Ontario kept telling me the drive would be boring until the Rockies, but boredom never managed to hitch a ride in the Reo. There was always something to see, especially at our speed—if we missed it, all we had to do was turn our heads slightly and it'd still be there. And Lorne always had stories. He said the first guy to build an internal combustion engine got his idea from a gun. He thought if the explosion was controlled and repeated, it could be applied to a motor. The first man to apply the internal combustion engine to a car was Belgian Etienne Lenoir, who in 1862 propelled a vehicle 10 kilometres. In 1885–86, when Daimler and Benz played with a new car, Lenoir put his engine on a boat, creating the first motorboat.

In the Reo, of course, there was no radio to distract us—radios were not a common item in 1912. That didn't stop others from hearing us on their radios. By this point, we had done enough radio interviews that people knew who we were when they happened upon us. We'd see a car drive ahead of us and pull over to take a photo, except they couldn't ready their cameras fast enough as we flew by at 60 kilometres an hour, so they'd get back in their cars and drive farther ahead, hoping to be ready the next time—even we had to put up with paparazzi. Others would roll down their windows as they passed and yell that they just heard us on the radio. It also gave people a chance to look for us, or in the case of 23-year-old Jon Upton of Goulais River, a chance to chase us down the road and ask us to pull over.

Upton was a devotee of ALPCA, the 3,000-member American Licence Plate Collectors' Association. I'm not joking. After seeing our photo in the *Toronto Star* he chased us down on the premise of seeing our 1912 licence plate—he didn't realize it was a replica. His interest in licence plates began when he was about 11 years old. "We bought a cottage near Searchmont, Ontario, in the mid-eighties. The previous owners left a lot of junk behind, so every so often we'd collect some of it and go to the junkyard. While we were there I saw a licence plate on the front of a station wagon and I wanted it. It grew from there." Now he has Ontario plates from 1918 onwards, although he's missing a few years. He admits that living up in Goulais River is a bit slow, so he feels it's a good way to pass the time, while he takes a year off between getting his bachelor's degree and master's. His licence plate is PMPKN.

In the morning we passed the Trans-Canada Highway halfway mark, but that is only if we had started from St. John's. It was a jaunty, basking-in-the-sun day, especially with the Reo firing on all four cylinders. "When you've got four of them banging, it pulls like a charm," said Lorne. "Hills are us." The lack of slopes reminded Lorne of being stationed in Saskatoon during the war. "There was a place called Pleasant Hill. I wrote home saying it's so steep you could coast a bicycle up it."

The huge outcroppings of rocks, while they posed problems for road and railway builders, formed wonderfully textured, salmon and grey walls for the road, then revealed vistas of red and yellow trees sprayed amid the green valleys. To the east were tourists on a train going up the Agawa Canyon, but this drive was stress-free. Part of the joy was keeping company with Lorne, a genuine and unpretentious person who only had kind words to say as he drove along wearing a grey mac, his old green busdriver's jacket, and brown slacks. He wasn't in the trip to become famous or make money. He was simply trying to complete a personal goal and publicize the story of the original Pathfinders, especially Haney, a man he admired.

Haney and Lorne would have got along just fine had their deeds not been separated by 85 years.

> Wilby described this "New Ontario," where we were headed, as be-
> longing to lumber-men, to occasional skippers of coasting schooners,
> lonely railway station agents, a few idle fishermen, fast disappearing
> trappers or Indians. It cuts the world of Canada in two. It divides the
> comparatively quiescent East from the vibrant, virile West, as a sur-
> geon's knife cleaves limb from limb, hampering national existence.
> For hundreds of miles along the lake, and for hundreds of miles to
> the east and west of it, civilization has left a No-Man's Land from
> Superior to Hudson Bay. It remains almost precisely as the French
> found it in the days of Louis XIV.

Under hazy skies we had lunch at Acona Bay, not far from the Montreal River, where the Group of Seven used to come up and paint. While in the parking lot over-looking the bay, we ran into a Ranger Smith character named Klaas Oswald. Oswald said the stretch of highway we were heading towards, between Montreal River and Wawa, was the last stretch of the Superior portion of Trans-Canada Highway to be built. That's why Wawa has a big goose overlooking the highway, to mark its com-pletion. He said we should expect to see remnants of old roads that went over the rocks, instead of through rock cuttings. As a publicity stunt in the late 1950s, to get Ottawa to finish the Trans-Canada, Wawa men walked all the way to Montreal River. It was the most expensive part of highway to finish, and that's why the government was reluctant—it didn't have any money, just like today.

While he talked, standing there in his brown Stetson with a gold Ontario pin on it, brown tie on a shirt that had a brown crest trimmed in green and gold on his epaulets, he used binoculars to make sure some men in a boat offshore were not over-fishing. Completing his uniform was an HNK, .40-calibre handgun. Asked if he needed it to fend off bears, Oswald said, "No. People." He said there were some bears and moose around, but you didn't have to look far for moose, which we found hard to believe. The upcoming stretch has the highest moose kill per road mile going, mostly at night. "There's hardly a stretch where a moose hasn't been killed. They don't have to worry about hunters from the U.S.," he said. "They have to worry more about the cars." I suggested that we build tunnels under the highways to give the moose a chance. He said trying to direct a moose to do anything is like trying to load a pig in the back of a pick-up. "The moose will run along the roadside and you don't know whether they're going to go off in the bush or cut in front of your car." Cutting off the Reo Special Touring Car would be a crime, said Oswald. He had a 1920s era book called *The Boy Mechanic.* It featured stories about how to turn WWI trench helmets into flowerpots, and ones on how to convert a car into a touring car and have a picnic on the running board. I had never heard of *The Boy Mechanic*, but I imagined Lorne as its poster boy.

Peter took over the controls for the afternoon run to Wawa, which in Ojibwa means "wild goose." We ran into neither goose nor moose, but there were several roadkills. The first had nearly every bit of meat picked off by scavengers. Later, we saw two crows picking at a dead porcupine. We were happy not to see any moose in similar circumstances; obviously, lessons on how to safely cross roads have not made it into their genetic makeup. When we saw sign after sign warning us to look out for moose, especially at night, Peter reasoned that they were all hiding in the bush saying, "Gee, I haven't seen a 1912 Reo for years." A big lumbertruck roared by with its modern version of a brag load, nearly making us a part of the scenery, but Peter held tight until we made it to the Montreal River pictographs, which included a tricky walk down to the water's edge. Some early natives (or some astute tour operators) drew 35 red ochre-and-grease pictures on the side of sheer rockface at the edge of the lake. Located in 1959 by Selwyn Dewdney, they're known as the Agawa Rock pictographs. The serpents, bear, caribou, canoes and a panther were thought to celebrate safe journeys across the lake, or the war victory of a great chief. Peter was stunned by the surroundings, especially the colour of the trees. "You don't see views like this in B.C. You don't see ferns and this is richer in colour because there are so many deciduous trees here, as opposed to mostly evergreens. Back home the seasons melt into each other, whereas they're more abrupt in Ontario."

The last stretch north meant more rivers and clean-looking lakes, so many that it felt like we were in the midst of a beer commercial. I was reading a magazine story on Mary Pickford, a Canadian female movie star when Haney and Wilby were gallivanting across the country, which kept my mind in the early half of the century. Then a fog descended, and the car seemed to be driving into heaven...that is, until we saw the sign "Wawa Hometown of NHL stars Chris Simon and Denny Lambert.

Population 4,600." Looming above us was the big 2,000-kilogram Canada goose, erected to mark the 1962 completion of the Trans-Canada Highway. Thomas Wilby, who predicted the highway could be completed by 1917, was only off by 45 years.

September 15 — Thessalon/Wawa

Despite a 7:30 start on a 50-kilometre jaunt to the Soo, where they had to catch the 1:30 ferry to Port Arthur, the Pathfinders still missed the boat. The problem: pouring rain. They had a good road until they were about 16 kilometres from the Soo, just west of Echo Bay, where the new government road was washed out and the rear wheels of the Reo got stuck in a wallow of mud nearly a metre deep. Even with the help of McLeod, it took them nearly three hours to get pulled out by a team of horses, which cost them $6. They also had to change a tire because they had run over a broken bottle. The trio stopped for lunch at a construction camp, and had what Haney called "a good feed," but that meant they arrived in the Soo at 2:30 p.m. Having missed the ferry, they decided to wait for the steamer *Ames* which was expected through the Soo locks sometime that evening.

In the meantime, Wilby railed at the absence of roads which had already undermined his goal of a true transcontinental tour. "For instance," he harangued to the *Sault Daily Star*, "there is no continuous highway between North Bay and the Soo, and much to my disgust I was compelled to twice ship the car in that short distance. The Soo is shut off from the east and the west alike. It seems almost beyond belief that Canada has gone so long in its forward strides towards nationality and allowed itself to be cut in two by the No Man's Land of Northwestern Ontario. I am motoring across Canada to help spread this propaganda of a unified Canada, because the modern maker of roads is surely the automobile."

Wawa in the morning was like a dream, with the early morning sun bouncing off the lake and creating an other-worldly glow on the wooden ceiling of my B & B by the water. We were heading west now; no detours north until British Columbia. On our way we saw new pavement being laid at the city's airport, an all-important part of northern life for tourists as well as residents trying to get anywhere in a hurry, especially to hospitals in the south. Despite the car, distances are still too vast. Other northern facts of life included the forest fire hazard indicator, which can either be low, moderate, high or extreme, and the local gun club. I was tempted to run into the

Michipicoten Rod and Gun Club and express my urban-influenced support for gun control legislation, that gun owners should have licences for their guns the way we must have dog licences, but I also wanted to make it to the Pacific in one piece—the Reo wasn't a good getaway car.

Lorne had two concerns when he started out—wondering if he could cope with the language in Quebec and the roads north of Lake Superior. The roads, he reasoned, can't be in good shape because of pressure from local voters, but they were smooth. Where they weren't smooth, they were being re-paved. We hardly had a day without road construction: "Highway Improvements next 33 kilometres. Completion Fall 1998." At the campsite the night before, the Findlays met three Michigan couples who were interested in the car because it was built in Lansing. They waved and honked as they passed us by, pulling their little camper-trailers.

Going across the top of Lake Superior turned out to be the ultimate in Sunday drives, a far cry from 1912. When Wilby learned their passenger ferry was gone, he spent the evening in the comfortable chairs of the Soo Club House where he was told any hope of crossing north of Superior by car was like picking every winner at Epsom Downs racetrack—for a month. His new friends said the wilderness north of the lake "belonged to the locomotive alone. They pictured gloomy rock masses, outcropping stone ledges, unbridged torrents, forests and tangle alternating with tracts of sparse timber and scrub, and vast wastes of burned tree stumps. But they all affirmed positively that roads were conspicuous by their absence, and that if I must have roads, I must motor through the United States."

That route would have followed the southern shore of Lake Superior to Marquette and Duluth, over to the Red River in Minnesota, and then follow it north through Fargo and Grand Forks to the Manitoba border at Emerson. The road would be bad to Winnipeg, but at least it would be straight. But at this point in the trip, Wilby refused to succumb to the easier trip state-side, where a larger population had generated roads sooner than in Canada. And because they were sooner, there was no need for Canadians to build a road to connect to Manitoba, if they could always get there through the States. A Soo Club House member told him

> No automobile has ever been north of Lake Superior. There's no road, and we motorists are entirely shut out, when there are wild beautiful places of theatric beauty up there to renew our spirits and give us

back—ourselves. If you wish to save the car and to arrive at the Pacific with a few pieces of its mechanism still clinging together, keep out of the wilderness of New Ontario. The machine will immolate itself on the first tree stump that blocks the path, or grind itself to junk on the rocks, or drown itself in the swamps and bridgeless rivers. The lumbermen go there only in winter and make a roadway in the deep frozen snows for log-hauling. But not even with snow on the ground could you get through with an automobile.

Wilby writes this in his book as if he fully intended to give the land route a go. But he had been told by Halifax that such a journey would be impossible. *Maclean's* magazine did a feature on the need for a national highway the previous winter, stating that the overland route from the Soo to Port Arthur is "a good four hundred miles of rocks and woods—chiefly rocks. Heartbreaking country to build a road, and...with no towns and settlements worth mentioning to be linked up with one another." If he was still thinking of going boldly where no man had gone before, surely he would have been cured of such braggadocio at Scotia Junction or Trout Creek. And we know from Haney's diary that they tried to make it to the Soo on time for the passenger ferry, so maybe he hid this from the reader on purpose. This was the place to break it to the reader that carrying out his original goal was doomed by reality, but that the endeavour was still worthwhile.

Upon passing Magpie River, Lorne said he didn't see any magpies just like he didn't see any moose at Moose River. The moose we didn't see continued to occupy us, forcing us to compete on who could see one first. It also led to a story about "Moose," the Findlays' first camper. It was a one-tonne dairy milk truck, a '55 Chev that Lorne converted into the family camper. It was so big for the five little Findlays that it earned the nickname "Moose." "The kids were all little gaffers then. Later I found an Easter Seals bus. I thought it'd make a great camper. I really did a job on that one." Lorne said buying older vehicles was cheaper and it was what he knew. He joked that he'd probably fail his mechanic's licence now. "I can still do work on brake work, but there's so much run by computers. I guess I could figure out a new car with $40,000 or $50,000 worth of equipment."

We encountered a different type of roadkill—shredded tires—and the forests boasted more evergreens, a few birch and less fall foliage. When trucks with low trailers and a funnel in the middle passed, we were struck by the smell of trees. It happened to be wood chips—the funnel allows them to be dumped onto a conveyor belt at the pulp mill. We often saw beaver lodges in the middle of a marsh-edged pond, but we rarely saw a beaver. The most contented man in the world seemed to be the lone fisherman in the lone boat on Hammer Lake. The most popular line for the spray-painting on roadside rocks was *Ave Maria*, and the most popular items sold at roadside stores were Ice, Bait, Licences, Liquor, Beer. As well, we found no fungi in Fungus Lake, and we wondered whether one could dance the obatanga in Obatanga Provincial Park.

Wilby, quite naturally for an Englishman whose recent history had been one of conquering foreign lands and populating nearly barren territories, portrayed New Ontario as a Sleeping Beauty of virgin forest, lakes, muskellunge and rocks that had been rolled or shoved into place by glaciers of a million years ago. It was a place of rivers "that rose to where the foot of man has never trod, of huge inland waters that never hear the echo of the human voice, or the myriad flashing jewels of lakes only fleetingly visible to the train traveler." It was a place waiting for a Prince to "step boldly along the narrow portages and the snowshoe trails of the by-gone French trappers and voyageurs, over rocky ridges and through the silent forests of pine and spruce, balsam and birch, to wake Nature to the life of man."

If Nature had to be wakened, it certainly was in White River. Here, Nature met Walt Disney. White River, once known as the coldest place in Canada, partially because of a recording of 57-below in 1936, and partially because winds coming from the south or the west can pick up the cold from Lake Superior and hang around for three weeks at a time. But now you can expect to see the Disney trademark on the Canadian Shield, all because of a bear nicknamed Winnie. "On August 24, 1914, Lt. Harry Colebourn of the 34th Fort Garry Horse and the Canadian Army Veterinarian corps, while en route to London for the war, purchased a black bear while in White River," said a sign at the tourism office. Colebourn placed the bear in the London Zoo, where A.A. Milne often took his son Christopher, thus inspiring the storybook characters Winnie-the-Pooh and Christopher Robin. A tourism clerk said the town preferred to be known as Winnie-the-Pooh's birthplace rather than the coldest spot in Canada. The Pooh connection, though, is not without its cost. Disney has bought the rights to the Milne character, so your 50-cent postcard, if you want Winnie on it, now costs $1.15. A few pennies for the store, and a few pennies for Uncle Walt.

Signs continued to jump out at us from the wilderness. "Our future depends on forests. Don't destroy it with fire," or "Carelessness costs," evidently a reference to drunk driving. Another sign with a telephone on it prompted Peter to deadpan, "That's where the hunters go to make their moose calls."

A sign for Terrace Bay, with two moose on it, told us the town was the "Gem of the North." The moose come to town to drink from the pulp mill's effluent canal. Terrace Bay has such a nice-sounding name and such nice views, but its pulp mill is one of the bigger polluters in Canada. It was obviously a company town by the slickness of the homes and streets. Instead of stopping as planned, we continued on to the Aguasabon River Gorge, where we took photos of the car on a dirt road. Then it was on to Schreiber, home of the Canadian boxing champ Dominic Filane. Peter said he read that the town of 2,000 has 28 sets of twins, and lots of Filanes, such as Filane Variety and Filane's Fallen Rock Motel. At Rossport, where we planned to stay for the night, the Reo ran out of gas right next to the entrance to Nicol Island. I ended up at a bed and breakfast where I met two Quaker women who were visiting isolated Quakers on their way to Yellowknife. One of the women lived there, while the other, Dorothy, is a 67-year-old nurse a few months away from leaving her job at Toronto's notorious Don Jail.

At the Serendipity Café next door, we had a cheery conversation about jail. "The Don Jail is as bad as it gets. The young good-looking inmates are raped. It's part of the initiation." The cells are in sets of 36, 18 back to back, the plumbing being behind the walls separating them. As a nurse Dorothy doesn't tend people in beds. She gives out drugs and tends cuts from fights, which are fairly common and lead to lock ups for 24 hours. Unfortunately, she doesn't see the good guys in jail, the ones who behave and don't want to get back. She sees the guys who keep coming back and think they're beating the system by accessing health services. She was last there in July and when she goes back in October she expects to see the same men who have been out and back again since the last time. "They are fearless. Then there are some guys in there who are scared to death."

It was with some joy that I realized the serendipity of my situation: I was free, far from jail even though I had crossed half the country without seat belts, I had a loving family waiting for me back in Niagara-on-the-Lake, and I had the luxury of a slow car to the Pacific. A magnificent sunset descended beyond Nicol Island. I felt I didn't need to own that island to feel like a rich man.

While Wilby enjoyed the Soo Club House, Haney waited down at the docks for the steamer *Ames*. He waited until midnight. When it didn't arrive, he booked rooms for the night and planned to hitch a ride with some boat in the morning.

Finding a road through Ontario's north was next to impossible.

SNOW NO BARRIER TO AUTOMOBILE OF CANADIAN MAKE,

September, 1912, Woodstock, N.B.— Adolphus McLean, an electrical expert of this city, has just completed the invention of an automobile which is stated to be equally useful at any season of the year. New Brunswick is the land of deep snows and cold, long winters, but Mr. McLean's invention is said to rise superior to the obstacles imposed in this regard, and although not quite completed patents will be shortly filed in Canada and the United States to protect its manufacture, if successful. The working model of the machine combines utility with beauty and plows through a foot of mud with as much unconcern as if working on a paved street.

RUSSIANS DREAM OF BUYING LUXURY CARS,

September, 1997, Moscow, Russia—While many Russian car lovers spent hours making themselves comfortable behind the wheels of Volgas and Volvos and Volkswagens at the third annual Moscow auto show, a 19-year-old Russian was caressing those streamlined bodies, as well as Mercedes-Benzes, Audis and BMWs, with the lens of his camcorder, insuring he could have a lasting memory of the world's finest automobiles. "If I could I would buy this one," said Kostya Bagaturov, zeroing in on a BMW Z3 M roadster as it gently rotated on a platform with crowds watching its every move. The fascination of Russians with cars is seen as a product of long-repressed desires set free by capitalism. Although owning one remains just a dream for most Russians, the ability to chase such a goal has become as essential as life and liberty, and is often equated with the pursuit of happiness.

Chapter 8

Sailing Across Superior

September 16—Sault Ste. Marie/Rossport

The steamer *A.E. Ames*, a steel package freighter that normally carried grain and general cargo, did arrive overnight, and the Transcontinentalists were ready to embark at 10 a.m. The Reo ended up down in the hold, where Haney discovered it had a cracked spring seat—the casting where the spring fits into the frame—which he would have to fix in Fort William. Haney remained there for the voyage, maybe for some quiet, maybe to get away from Captain Wilby. Having Billy McLeod along for three days made him realize how much he detested being alone with Wilby. Haney's dedication was to the Reo company, and the car. He wasn't there to make history, but he also didn't want the pig-headed demands of a non-mechanic to ruin the reputation of the Reo. He wrote that he's "getting more sick than ever of the Captain," with "the Captain" underlined darkly in his diary.

Wilby wrote on four different occasions that taking the steamer across Lake Superior made him taste "the bitter wormwood and gall of my disappointment," whether he did that as he "restlessly paced the steamer's deck," which he said in three pieces, or whether he was doing that as he "restlessly paced the grassy lawn at Port Arthur which overlooks the magnificent panorama of Thunder Bay," as he wrote in his book. Nevertheless, he would make time on the lake, instead of struggling to make bridges and to breach rock outcroppings on shore. If he had any intention of crossing the country in 35 days as he estimated, he needed the advantage of crossing 700 kilometres by boat in 24 hours.

All his estimates might have derived from naïveté or his relatively easy trek across the United States the year before. People had been driving across the States since 1903, when Dr. Horatio Nelson Jackson became the first to do it. Jackson was followed by professional racers and mechanics from car companies seeking publicity. Percy Megargel's Reo held the record in 1905 for the fastest trip from the Atlantic to the Pacific, but Wilby said his round-trip was tainted because the car was shipped from Portland to San Francisco. The only genuine round-trip, Wilby told reporters along the way, was by the Mead brothers of Connecticut who drove and camped for 60 days. Wilby admitted that even "a quartette of ladies, and next a pair, drove across from east to west, apparently without male help, making rather better time than the men. The familiar 'hero' type of transcontinentalist—he of the gun, the overloaded car looking like a junk shop, and the twenty-day-old beard who had been figuring gloriously in the local sheet as a veritable Beowulf of adventure and daring—began to look just a little ridiculous." By the end of the decade even families dared to cross the country by car. Trails had been blazed and some of the roads had been paved by the time Wilby embarked with his chauffeur, Fred D. Clark of the Ohio Motor Car Company of Cincinnati, who had crossed from Atlanta to Los Angeles the year before with a Mudhen. Also along was Wilby's wife of three years, Agnes.

The trio left New York City on August 31, 1911, with three goals to take the longest round trip on record; to log the middle west route to the Pacific; and to prove they could embark on America's finest sightseeing route in the most comfortable fashion. For the most part, they succeeded. They completed a 16,000-kilometre, 105-day circular tour with no camping equipment other than a picnic basket. They intended to sleep in hotels each night, which they did save one night when they slept in the car in Utah; another night in Arizona they were forced to walk seven kilometres to sleep in a ranch after their Mudhen got stuck in dry quicksand.

The return trip was along the Sante Fe Trail to St. Louis, where Wilby wrote a letter to Washington, D.C.: "We should feel proud of the honor if it could be so arranged that President Taft give us a handshake—we feel that this would be a fitting climax to our trip." The reply from a bureaucrat was discouraging, but when they arrived in Washington, Wilby met with President William Taft to report on his adventure. The Wilbys made it back to New York by December 13. The actual driving took 85 days. The obstacles were so few they only used two sets of tires, changed two spring leaves and the chuck on the driving wheel. His report to the Office of Public Roads included photos he took with a large box camera.

For Agnes, the trip would have special meaning. Her father, Sidney Andrews, was a larger-than-life character who in 1869 made his own pioneering trip across the U.S. He wrote descriptive and engaging letters back to his home newspaper. Wilby's preoccupation with visiting Arizona and New Mexico may have something to do with Andrews' stories. Agnes, of course, could not avoid being stereotyped. The Emporia, Kansas, *Gazette* said that Wilby's job, aside from finding a road on "soil peculiarly conducive to automobile purposes," is seeking the best aesthetic and historical route for tourists. "That is where Mrs. Wilby gets in. A woman cannot have much to say about the details of the log—even should she care for it—but when it comes to matters of taste and discrimination, her judgment goes far. Mrs. Wilby, by the way, is a pioneer in auto travel, claiming to be the only woman who has crossed and recrossed the continent in a car."

If Wilby could not find a way west in 1911, it was easy for him to go north or south and find a route. In Canada, so-called New Ontario was jammed between Lake Superior and James Bay, so there was no escaping this broad, rocky corridor. No one had dared to direct a car over this stretch. Save for a few railway outposts and scattered logging or mining operations, it was largely uninhabited. And the obstacles which took the Canadian Pacific Railway 10 years to ford, where the CPR's William Van Horne said they found "200 miles of engineering impossibilities," were not about to part like the Red Sea for Wilby to find his All-Red Route.

The Findlays filled up the Reo and two spare gas containers for what would include a momentous stop at the Terry Fox Memorial outside Thunder Bay. There had been coast-to-coast runners and walkers long before Fox, but no one's story had so gripped the nation. After making it halfway across the country running a marathon a day on one leg, Terry succumbed to cancer. We couldn't go by without paying homage to the man who raised awareness and money for cancer.

After breakfast with a couple from Minneapolis, who were making the circular tour of Lake Superior by car, and Don Jail Dorothy (even though she lives in Toronto, which has the best public transit system in the country, she said she couldn't live without her car because it gives her so much security in the city), we set out on our journey by filling up the overheated radiator with water. Although I was a bit spooked by the radiator boiling over so early in the morning, Peter told me not to worry. "We had an old Auburn that used to boil over half the time. In Grade 2, I drew a picture of the car with steam pouring out of it like a whale spouting water. That's what it was like growing up in the Findlay family."

We hadn't driven far when we had the misfortune of seeing our first moose. It was a roadkill, and its carcass, with horns still attached, lay at the side of the road. It had been nearly picked clean by scavenger birds. We had longed to see one in its majesty, yet all we found was a travesty.

A motorcyclist drove by and gave us the thumbs up. Peter pointed out that truckers wave with their right hand while motorcyclists wave with their left (because the throttle is on their right). Peter is a motorcycle enthusiast. "You can see the mechanics of it and get at things." Because of Canadian winters, motorcycles are useful only eight to nine months a year. We agreed they're dangerous. We get so used to looking for two headlights, the shape of cars and their ability to cover ground, that motorcycles too often catch us by surprise.

The red granite walls we drove through continued to enchant us. When we emerged from the man-made corridors for another glimpse of Superior, we realized the steamer duo were much the poorer, a sentiment Wilby would have shared. In a magazine story, he says speed on a long-distance touring

> is out of place. The man who wants to get from New York to San Francisco in the least number of minutes possible will patronize railroads for many a year. It would please such a passenger if it were possible to make the journey in one night, or better yet, one hour. Scenery, enjoyment and pleasure have no part in such a journey and in an automobile tour from coast to coast and return, there should be nothing but enjoyment.

Lorne subscribes to the belief that long-distance driving should be enjoyed and that there is even an art to it. He described his older brother Ray, a longtime trucker, as "a beautiful driver." If the trip taught me one thing, it is that there is more to driving than I had thought (probably like most people who toddle along in the passing lane oblivious to the anger they are igniting). I never thought of driving as something that could be "beautiful," or an art. I knew about fast drivers like the Villeneuves, but hadn't paid much attention to institutional drivers, the truck or bus drivers, that take pride in never being a threat to other drivers, or parking their vehicles just right, or taking curves at a seamless speed, making trips as easy as possible on their human or inert cargo. Lorne said there was a real fraternity of truckers in the fifties when they were working for wages and they had the luxury of stopping for chats and frivolity at roadside diners. They all knew each other, he said wistfully, telling the story of truckers climbing a long hill at less than 30 kilometres an hour, and having one trucker jump on the trailer of another and climb over the top of the cab to press his face on the front windshield and say "Hi!" Lorne said, "The guy in the truck nearly keeled over."

The statue of Terry Fox used to be at the side of the highway, but it created such congestion they moved it to a hill overlooking the highway. Besides a chat with a cop in his Camaro cruiser, our visit was so quiet it was reverential, reading the testimonial to Terry, and gazing off the ridge with him to the ships lying in Thunder Bay. Lorne summed up the visit by saying, "We're all smaller than him."

Thunder Bay still seemed uneasy with the long-ago amalgamation of Fort William and Port Arthur. The city seemed too spread out, especially when I was trying to find a bed and breakfast. I did make it to the library, where I found the great headline in the *Fort William Daily Times*, which must have been written with a smirk on the headline writer's face: "Autoist comes in boat, goes west in train." I ended up at the bed and breakfast of Sonja Isaksen-Sitch, a 47-year-old widow who lost her oldest daughter in a car accident. Sonja was a child of Danish immigrants who listened to the CPR ads and came to Pass Lake. Along with Dixon (Alberta), and New Denmark (New Brunswick), Pass Lake was a Danish settlement. Sonja said all the residents of Pass Lake got their citizenship in 1966. "We were proud to become Canadians. The adults didn't have to, but we had to answer all the questions. We sang 'God Save the Queen,' swore allegiance to the flag, and sang 'O Canada.'"

Because she lived on a farm she had to get up at 6 a.m. to catch the schoolbus, unless she got a ride in her uncle's Model A Ford. Its floorboards were so rotten she had to watch where she put her feet. "There was also a hole in the cloth roof, so if it rained I had to hold a piece of cardboard over the roof. I remember I was only six years old. We had no electricity until I was 13, and our first automatic washing machine we had to swing back and forth like a baseball bat. It was a hard life, but a great life. When you went out to have fun it was community activities. We've got a good country, but we need something to complain about or we wouldn't be happy."

Her other guest was Stan Daniel, a 59-year-old salesman who was born in the small farming community of Lashburn, Saskatchewan. "In those days your pregnant mother went to hospital on the train and you came home on the train. My dad thought I was the greatest thing. He ran down the street telling everybody. When I was 13, 14, 15, he didn't think the same way." Stan felt just as strongly about the country. "Canada, for anybody who wants to participate, is a fantastic opportunity."

Port Arthur was bursting with opportunity in 1912 as Haney and Wilby made their way there. While they slept on the steamer they covered one-twelfth of the journey across a country that was still welcoming immigrants to nearly vacant land.

September 17—On Lake Superior/Thunder Bay

We hadn't lived until that morning we woke up in Thunder Bay and met Ab Carroll, an 83-year-old codger who was quick with a quip and a bawdy tale. We met him at a Speedy reception. Ab, who sold Chryslers, Dodge DeSotos and Reos, was the first person in northern Ontario to sell a Reo schoolbus. It was made in Leaside, now part of Toronto, in 1946 and it cost $7,521, said Ab, who seemed like he was still holding the receipt. He also happened to have some photos, including one of him riding a bike backwards toward a blonde woman. "When you're after a blonde you can do anything," said Ab, who must have been in his seventies in the photo. "You see I'm keeping an eye on my wife," he added, explaining why he was facing backwards. He also had a photo of his wife and a car the year he married her in 1940. In those days, before car production was halted to help the country wage war, Fort William folk could go down to Toronto to pick up a car, but they had to drive it back through the States by way of Duluth, Minnesota, to the Pigeon River boundary. U.S. Customs gave drivers 24 hours to get it in and out of the country without being charged.

Ab remembers the day he told a new hiree at the car dealership to go to the back of the lot and pick up the light black car. Then he put the fear of God into the boy by saying, "Whatever you do, I don't want the dark black car." Ab eventually rescued the boy who couldn't distinguish black from black, and couldn't figure out when his leg was being pulled.

With Ab was 83-year-old Roy Eves. Both Roy and Ab worked on the Trans-Canada Highway around Thunder Bay as part of a relief measure during the Great Depression. They didn't have machines in those days, only horses and shovels. "We grouted out the stumps with a grout, which was like a pick-axe, and we dug ditches along the side of the highway," said Roy. "It was tough work, but it was a living."

They got $5 a month building roads, and in the winter of 1935–36, they'd cut birch, dry and split it and draw it into logs and get $4.50 a cord. "Those were tough days," Ab added, "but it never hurt anybody."

Tough days, they all say, but everyone seemed to long for them. Or maybe they just longed for their youth. Just then a propeller plane flew overhead toward the airport. It looked like a scene from the film *Casablanca*.

Roy ended up as a milkman from 1938 to 1979. He started out delivering milk with a horse and carriage, getting up at 4 a.m. for his route. "I'd have no one to talk to except that horse for three or four hours. I worked seven days a week. Then in '47 we got trucks in Port Arthur, one of those Divco trucks where you had to stand up to drive them. He retired when the trucks were retired in '79, victims of a car culture that traded the familiar clinking and clanking of the milkman in the morning for the opportunity of driving to the corner store. "No wonder a lot of people are out of work," said Roy. "The milkman is gone, the breadman is gone. You get everything at a convenience store."

The youngster in the crowd was Gordon Cameron "Scotty" Bell, a 72-year-old who continues to race cars—on ice. Since 1972 he had been racing on frozen lakes in La Crosse and Chippewa Falls, Wisconsin, and in Minneapolis, Mankato and Duluth, Minnesota. A snowplow clears the snow off the lake to create a track 15 to 20 metres wide and 2 to 3 kilometres long, with hairpins and sweepers and straightaways. They're not oval, and Scotty says they're not particularly dangerous.

"Anything is dangerous," said Bell, who was chief forester with the local pulp mill now owned by Avenor. "It's dangerous out here on the street. On ice there are very few injuries. No one has been killed in the last 30 years. We get to speeds of 130 miles per hour on the straightaways." They get traction by scuffing the original tread off their tires and recapping them with studs right in the mould. He drives a yellow Saab Sonett, but he says Rabbits are the most popular car in competition.

Scotty got into cars because his father used to sell farm machinery, so he was always "up to my ass in grease trying to help him fix farm machinery." He marvels at how much cars have changed, but he says they're still four wheels, a motor and a steering wheel. The next big improvement, says someone who has spent his life replanting a renewable resource like trees, is to find a substitute for gasoline-fed engines. "When you get the Chinese driving cars, you wonder how long the gas will last. I think man would figure out something else, but the world would virtually stop if all the gas was cut off. I won't be here to worry about it, but maybe your grandchildren will." I suggested that people in the North eat up a lot of gas driving long distances, that they should have a system to put the cars on trains. "But there wouldn't be any fun!" countered the man who has also participated in high-speed car rallies, going through the woods at 145 km/h. "That's the name of the game."

Fun is certainly what Ab was having, holding court with the remaining car enthusiasts. As we were leaving, he told the other codgers that, "What was once Clark Gable is now hardly able, but I wish I was 70 again. At the doctor's the other day I saw this 72-year-old woman..."

While we put Thunder Bay behind us, Wilby and Haney were just arriving. The steamer *A.E. Ames*, named after the head of the Toronto Stock Exchange, docked about 11 a.m. That afternoon Wilby spoke to the Good Roads Commission in the Board of Trade rooms. The Board of Trade presented him with a Port Arthur pennant and yet another letter which he had to deliver to the Governor General who was on tour in western Canada. Wilby also visited the old Dawson Trail, which had been used by General Garnet Wolseley and his troops as they went west on their Red River Expedition, after the uprising of Louis Riel in 1870. Wilby would have heard of Wolseley's exploits as a lad growing up, because they both came from Norwich. Wolseley and 1,200 men left Toronto in May, when Wilby was nearly three. The supposedly peaceful force of 400 British regulars and 800 militiamen from Ontario and Quebec crossed the No-Man's Land by hopscotching across from one lake and river to another, arriving in Fort Garry on August 24. Wilby saw where the trail left off, because the scows and tugs from the expedition lay rotting in the water. He could not have ignored the parallel between the two sons of Norwich. Just as Wolseley's slow journey to keep peace in Manitoba convinced Canadians of the urgency in linking the country by railway, Wilby wanted his journey to convince Canadians about the urgency of linking the country by road.

Wilby also met several enthusiastic citizens and reconstructed their dialogue, which is not too different from conversations we had in 1997.

"Motored from Halifax, eh? Well, well," exclaimed one. "That's a stunt. Shipped your car across the lake? Yes, of course, you'd have to do that. Here, Mr. So-and-So, shake hands with this gentleman from

Halifax!" Another citizen "Going west? And you've come all that way from my old city? How are the Haligonians? As slow as ever? Here's our Deputy-Mayor and the President of the Board of Trade. That's the car, is it?" "Glad to meet you!" from another townsman. "Here's our M.P. Thinks he's going West, Jim. But he hasn't seen Port Arthur yet. Why not give us a long stay? You can't find a better place in Canada."

Wilby seemed intrigued by Port Arthur and Fort William, because they were so different from what he knew. For starters, two sets of railways tracks come down a street to the waterfront, crossing in front of hotels and several pedestrian walkways, and nothing bewildered Wilby more than tracks that were not elevated or separated from humans, which he found to be the case not only in Quebec but also across Ontario. The huge bells of the trains clanged and freight cars shunted back and forth, but the pedestrians took little notice as they crossed the tracks, including one man who emerged from a small kiosk wearing knickerbockers and a Norfolk jacket—a single-breasted, belted jacket with a box pleat down the back. The port, which had just undergone $4 million in renovations, including dredging and the construction of a huge grain elevator which Wilby marvelled at, had its own publicity bureau, and the man in the duck-shooting jacket from Wilby's home county was quick to hand out pamphlets extolling the area's merits for big game hunting, fishing or canoeing. The area was in the midst of a boom, with the Canadian Pacific, Grand Trunk Pacific and Canadian Northern railways all having terminals there. A coach and freight car manufacturing company had just promised to employ 1,000 men, so housing prices soared. The pamphlets also suggested visitors could avoid hayfever by living there, because the ragweed and goldenrod seeds couldn't make it across Lake Superior. "Try Port Arthur and get the habit of living there!" said another pamphlet, and the one that was used in newspaper ads across the country: "See Naples and die. See Port Arthur and live." But Wilby was most impressed with the grain elevator, the largest in North America. Rising as it did out of a "chaotic litter of piles and planks, rails and footbridges, dirty wharves and a confusion of water basins," he called it "a skyscraper, a Francois Premier Chateau and a Bastille rolled into one. It had nobility, tragedy, destiny, stamped all over it. It dwarfed men to pigmies, it soared with Babylonian majesty. It breathed force and power, and it challenged the hills and the capes whose fit companion it was." It was alive with huge revolving belts, wooden chutes and frames that acted like weavers' looms, with arms and openings through which the "wheat and oats poured like molten gold." Huge trays jiggled back and forth to cleanse it of impurities. "Standing there, hushed and awed by that strange vibrant life around me, I felt that, for the first time, I grasped the key to the might and dominion of the Canadian New World."

While Wilby was cheerful with the townsfolk, he was making life miserable for Haney. He was upset with the pennants Haney had placed on the car before disembarking in Port Arthur. Just as we were given pins by civic officials along the way, the Pathfinders were given pennants. If they received no pennant, as in Ottawa, Haney bought one for 25 cents. Maybe Wilby found the pennants undignified, something Simon Fraser or David Thompson would not have done. So, on the way to the post office, they argued, with Wilby saying he would get another man if Haney wasn't prepared to take his orders. Haney wrote in his diary: "Hurrah! Watch him walk to Vancouver."

Bucking a westerly wind we headed toward Manitoba. Lorne had his foot to the floor and he couldn't get the car close to 60 kilometres an hour. Before we got to Kakabeka Falls, Lorne's roadside eye spotted a 1958 Edsel at a flea market. It was the Edsel's first model, with sculptured lines down the side and an oval horse collar grill. Lorne said it was the ugliest one they made.

Kakabeka didn't live up to its billing as the "Niagara of the North." However, its lookout point was striking and its information displays prompted reverie of bygone days. There was David Thompson's map of the Northwest Territories and another scene of "The Great Rendezvous: For two weeks during the summer, Grand Portage came alive with the shouting and laughter of some 2,000 carousing voyageurs. The North West Company came down in 11-metre canoes, its cargo wrapped in 90-pound (41-kilogram) bales. They brought tea, cloth blankets, glass beads, silver trinkets, tobacco and lead shot. The furs would arrive from the west and north in 8-metre canoes..." When the border was determined with the United States, Grand Portage ended up on American soil, so the portage route for the North West Company shifted to the Kaministiquia River at Fort William, leaving the voyageurs with a more difficult portage at Kakabeka Falls and a long rising trek to the Savanne River.

Back in the Reo, the conversation got steered to one of Lorne's former jobs as a historian/researcher at the British Columbia Museum of Transportation. The museum was a going concern until the Minister of Heritage, Bill Reid, moved it to his riding—a few short years later, the museum collapsed. When it left town, Lorne left it: "I was heartbroken. They had an auction to sell everything off ten years after, and I couldn't bear to go and see what happened." It was his first close-up look at the worst of politics, and it wasn't pretty. A few months later Lorne, now working as a tour bus driver, took a busload to a ceremony officiated by Reid. In his speech, Reid told the crowd that the museum had moved, but people like Lorne still volunteered there. Lorne had lost his job and his pension, and he was shocked the minister expected him to drive an hour or so to volunteer. "It made me so sick. I didn't want to think of it for years. He cost me...he cost me. He cost me the museum I loved. And then he had the nerve to say that Lorne over there is one of our volunteers."

One of those 12- to 15-seater vans went by, and Lorne says they're popular with Europeans, who put their camping equipment in a box on the roof. I told him he was a font of information. Lorne replied, "Yeah, I ought to write a book. Life is tough for left-handed bald guys. You know those earphones that have a nob on the top to keep it in place? They're pretty rough on bald guys."

When we pulled over for lunch, we heard Lorne being interviewed on the radio. He was asked about stopping at the Terry Fox memorial, and Lorne backed off any comparison: "My trip is frivolous compared to his. We're doing this sort of for fun and a bit of history." While we were stopped, a 1966 GMC truck pulled up. We were being followed, again, this time by a painter from Quebec.

Robert Beaulieu, 43, said he is known in Quebec for painting antique cars and ships. He had been sailing since he was 18, and in the winter he works as a shipkeeper, looking after a ship at drydock. The officer's lounge is his studio, and he calls the creaking cold ship his "winter condo" with a good machine shop. "It's the closest I'll get to being master of ship." He said he had been following us for days and would like to do a painting of the Reo. He was going to follow us as far as Winnipeg. When he learned the Reo had only a 30-horsepower engine, he said his Harley motorbike had twice as much. Lorne says the Harley horsepower came from "Shetland ponies. In the Reo, they are Clydesdales."

By now we had slipped into another time zone, and although time zones are a fact of life—we were now two-and-a-half hours behind Newfoundland—it means more on a cross-country trip. Every day we were chasing the sun, and the time zone changes made it seem like we were getting somewhere. And the beauty of going east to west was that our interior clocks had us up when the sun rises, which is the best time to see a new land, before the machinations of everyday life distract us.

Because we were covering territory the Pathfinders covered by train, we had no set destination, no town or old hotel to seek out. We were crossing through a wide cut in the forest. On our right were the railway tracks that had the old county designation signs alongside them. Peter, like his dad, could amuse himself by finding rare cars at the side of the road, like a Ford Anglia. He had a great appreciation for history and the design of old cars. A new Thunderbird would go by, and he'd say, "In the old days the design would have stood out. Nowadays it's just another car. All the romance has gone out of them."

While the Findlays hunted for old cars, I had my eyes peeled for wildlife, and the elusive moose. At one point I felt it would have been easier to believe in Rudolf the Red Nosed Reindeer than in the existence of moose, but it was a good thing. Maybe they had learned to avoid the tarmac and these horseless carriages.

At Ignace it was time for my nightly portage, where I carried my worldly belongings, my clothes and my computer, to another bed. The lonely trudge to another night spot is better thought of as a portage, or at least the romanticized version of one. It must have been exhilarating crossing the country under your own power, sweeping the oars, heaving the canoe on your shoulders, feeling relief as you reached another body of water. Work one set of muscles, then another, enjoy the sense of accomplishment when you finally lay your head down at night.

This night I ended up at the Lone Pine Motel, which is about a kilometre or so off the Trans-Canada Highway next to a small lake. It had several empty rooms, but getting one wasn't so easy. The man who owned the place, a Ukrainian Canadian named Mike Shyska, vetted potential customers. When he saw Peter and me at the door, he was worried about young men breaking up their rooms and partying. Shyska had built his motel by hand, nail by nail, and he didn't want it ruined by some lager louts. When we told him Peter was just dropping me off, I passed the test and was allowed a second-floor room overlooking the lake, and he even took me over to the main street to get some food. On the way he had some Second World War stories and some sage advice: "Follow the right guy." His own roundabout story was about choosing between the devil and the "right guy."

On the balcony that night I watched the sun go down with a bit of sadness. Even though we had gained an hour, it seemed like the sun was setting awfully early. I felt the coolness that day, sweeping around the back of our necks in the Reo, and the aspen leaves fluttering like flowers beneath a canopy of tall evergreens. Even they seemed to be waving at us. We were halfway across the country, fall was fast approaching, and I needed a scarf. Popularized by early motorists, scarves were made infamous in 1927 by the American dancer Isadora Duncan. Her scarf got caught in the rear wheel of a car she was riding in near Nice on the French Riviera, strangling her at age 50.

While Wilby fussed around Port and the Fort, Haney went over to Fort William and had lunch. He found a machine shop just outside of town and fixed the spring seat and then loaded the Reo for Selkirk, Manitoba. He had supper, went to a picture show, sent wires to the Reo Company, then took a bath at his lodgings before going to bed. Whatever Wilby had said to drag him down, he knew at least he was doing a good job keeping the Reo running. He, too, knew he was halfway across the country on the most difficult challenge of his life.

September 18—Fort William/Ignace

Wilby spent the night in Fort William, despite what the *Fort William Daily Times* wrote. The morning paper said Wilby left the night of the 17th on the express train to Selkirk. The *Port Arthur Daily News*, an afternoon paper, said Wilby left on the 18th for Selkirk. The *Daily Times* might have known the Reo car departed on its $43 ride to Selkirk, and assumed the Pathfinders had also parted. Haney notes in his diary that he spent the night in Fort William, and then waited until 4 p.m. on the 18th for the 9:10 a.m. train, which was more than six hours late. He left at 4:30 p.m. for Kenora, arriving there after midnight. Wilby arrived in Winnipeg at 5 a.m. the morning of the 19th, when no train was scheduled to arrive, so he must have continued on the same train that Haney was on, instead of disembarking in Kenora. The men were also separated when Haney arrived in Selkirk on the 19th.

Regardless, Wilby had lots of time this day to pontificate. The people who had tried to find him a land route to Winnipeg kept talking about the road to Duluth which would soon be finished. Wilby tried to get their goat by asking, "But why Duluth? Does not charity begin at home? Why not a road to Winnipeg? Why get tourists into Canada if you cannot get them through Canada? Must they stop on the spot where they land, for want of those arteries of communication which are the life blood of a nation?" Wilby was disappointed that Canada was quick to connect with an American highway leading from Montreal to New York, and the Meridian Road that would connect Winnipeg with Kansas, without first enhancing its own Canadian connections, such as a road from Winnipeg to Port Arthur.

> One suspects that this particular form of road building is intimately bound up with the question of dollars and cents; that Canada is throwing a sop to catch the American capitalist. As yet Canada has not enough money to go round. Today British capitalists are invested up to the hilt in Canada, and the road is a potent medium by which the Dominion can attract the rich Yankee investor. The wealthy American farmer is another important asset whom the Canadian Government cannot afford to overlook. Next to the Ontarian farmer, he is the best settler of the West. He has experience, grit, science, shrewdness and industry. He is almost bound to "make good," and he almost always comes by road over the border, with horses and cattle and wagons. Canada is practical, first and foremost, and even a transcontinental motorist must finally admit the wisdom of these north and south roads.

On this morning we had more interest in non-road travel. The Reo had its photo taken with a Beech float plane that was instrumental in opening up Ontario's north, not only for tourism, but for exploration. At the campground, the Findlays met two couples from Toronto. One man was a retired schoolteacher who felt he knew more about Reos and Oldsmobiles than Lorne, insisting that the Reo was a General Motors car. Even though Lorne patiently reviewed the entire history of Ransom E. Olds, with suggested readings and all, the man refused to believe him, saying he would do his own research. The two women had come up with their husbands to shoot moose with a camera, or otherwise sit in the camper and knit. The men had come up to hunt, and just to prove they meant business, they had an all-terrain-vehicle with them. Supposedly an ATV makes the chase easier, and it can carry the carcass of the animal out of the bush. But the big-wheeled machines hardly seem sporting. And, to me, it would ruin the whole idea of enjoying nature's solitude, the fresh air and the exercise, but what do I know? I don't like guns or internal combustion engines.

It was one day we were cheering for the moose to remain scarce. Lorne said if the moose are anything like the deer in B.C., they clear out away from roads when hunting season begins. "It's like they sense the danger." We didn't see any moose roadkills; rather, a more depressing kind—four wreaths denoting a fatal car crash.

The landscape seemed to be so full of lakes and marshes that we wondered why the land hadn't sunk. We were heading toward Lake of the Woods, where there are 14,000 islands tucked away in coves and inlets on the edge of the Manitoba border. The islands create so many connections between land and water that the Lake of the Woods has more than 100,000 kilometres of coastline, which is more than Lake Superior, the largest lake in the world. When Lorne was a child, he always knew where Lake of the Woods was, because his father left his home inside the Manitoba border to work in the bush around the lake.

The Findlays and I continued to amass stories of people passing on to us their most private anecdotes, often of sadness. I often felt like an Albert Camus character, waiting on a bridge for someone to tell me his or her life story. Lorne's most memorable case had been the time he dropped a busload off at a shopping mall. He filled out his log and then decided to go in for a bite to eat. On his way in, he was stopped by a woman who asked where the bus was from. For 20 minutes she told Lorne what a bad husband she had. The mall was her daily refuge away from him.

What I gleaned from all those conversations is that there are thousands of people out there who want to connect with other humans. We must not have enough meetings in our daily lives and the car doesn't escape blame. With so many trips beginning and ending in cars, we don't run into people as often as we would if we walked through our neighbourhoods. I once rented a house in Florida where I had no idea if anyone else lived on the street until garbage day when bins sat at the end of their driveways. No one in the neighbourhood walked. Any evidence of neighbours quickly disappeared up those driveways and into their double-car garages, where the doors automatically opened and shut to make sure the occupants of the cars didn't have to leave the safety of their garages. Urban planning theorist Jane Jacobs says that in some American cities people are encouraged to remain in their cars for safety, just like tourists visiting big-game parks are encouraged to remain in their cars until they reach the safety of the lodge. The ripple effect of the inability "to meet people in a place where contact can become meaningful," says William Michelson in his 1970 sociological work, *Man and His Urban Environment*, leads to "an increased incidence of reported medical problems."

By lunchtime we reached downtown Dryden, "Where the West begins." The local newspaper and cable TV show swarmed the Findlays. In the afternoon we went by a llama farm, which prompted Peter to suggest we could put antlers on them and say we found moose. Peter also wondered whether the moose might have migrated to the Northwest Territories. He had been listening to the CBC and heard a story about the correspondent who was late for an on-air assignment. Hunting season had started so the correspondent stopped to shoot a moose along the way, making a priority of bagging his winter's meat.

The preponderance of water meant we'd soon forego what one French writer called "this melancholic and marshy land," the forests that had guided us for the last week, the black spruce in the swampy areas, the white spruce on the hills, the poplar, birch, Jack pine and balsam. We'd be leaving the rocks, those hardened icebergs that jutted into our midst, revealing one of the oldest layers on the earth's crust. Most of all we'd be leaving the people who had come to the North and carved out lives for themselves, the miners, the lumberjacks and all those other prospectors who had come to find something precious. We certainly had.

In mid-afternoon we reached a place that once had so many muskrats in the lake they called it Rat Portage. Since 1905 it has been known as Kenora, and there we would join again with Haney, who got off the train this night shortly after midnight. Five years before Haney's arrival, and before the National Hockey League was founded, the Kenora Thistles hockey team won the Stanley Cup.

While Haney loafed around all day before boarding the train, Wilby wrapped up his thoughts on Ontario and half the country. Perhaps on the train he saw the waves of farmer-type immigrants, with their tickets and the promise of a roof over their heads in Winnipeg, and decided he would like a better class of immigrant for this prominent member of the Empire. He said Canada had many things going for it, but it should not just be asking for farmers and harvesters to come to its shores for $3 a day plus room and board. Wilby said they should make a plea for the Rudyard Kiplings, the George Bernard Shaws, the Maurice Maeterlincks of the world. He felt

Canada should be scouting Berlin, Paris and London for budding playwrights, poets, philosophers and scholars, many of whom are restricted financially in the "over-crowded old world." He felt Canada should send such notices across the world:

Wanted for Canada! 300 brainy authors! 150 philosophers! first-class passage and good living guaranteed to the right men! Also new ideas, plots and scenes; quiet surroundings with unlimited nature! Secure your passage early!!

The original Pathfinders missed out on a colourful jaunt along Lake Superior, near Terrace Bay in Northern Ontario.

AUTO HAS PASSED BURLESQUE STAGE, September, 1912, Detroit, Michigan

—The time was when artists of the comic supplements delighted to picture the automobile as an absurdly cumbersome piece of machinery, propelled for the most part by farm and truck horses rather than by power generated by gas food. However, that stage has long since passed, and, now, the motor car might be compared to a swallow for grace and so fully able to care for itself that not even a passing glance is given its fast disappearing old-time friend. And, one need not be a Sampson, a locomotive engineer nor an expert mechanic in order to throw the levers or know how to operate the mechanism of the modern automobile.

DEALER GIVES AWAY CARS TO HELP UNEMPLOYED, September, 1997, Sanford, Florida

—Dot Frost burst into tears and jumped up and down when she saw the 11-year-old, gold Ford Tempo parked on the dusty lot of Charity Cars. "At last," she said. "Thank you, Jesus. I am too happy." For Frost, who has a temporary job after spending a decade on welfare, being given a free car may be a ticket to a better life, to finding permanent employment. Social workers say transportation is the biggest obstacle to training welfare recipients and finding them work. Many jobs are in the suburbs, while welfare recipients are concentrated in urban areas. And many of them must work nights or weekends, when public transportation is limited. Said Phyllis Busansky, who oversees Florida's welfare program: "You can teach a person to fish and feed him a lifetime, but if you can't get to the river, you're not going to fish at all."

Chapter 9

Waylaid in Winnipeg

September 19—Kenora

Haney may have gotten off in Kenora because he didn't have a berth on the train, or to get away from Wilby, who continued on because he had a berth, or he was anxious to get to Winnipeg, a larger city where he could get news of the world and enjoy big city comforts. With the train being seven hours late, Wilby might have said, "Carry on. Enough of the delays." His early morning observations from the train, gazing out into the darkness, found the rocks less in the foreground, and then

> a vast level plain stretched itself before my eyes, and the rich black earth of wheat-growing lands was before me. There was an occasional shadowy school-house and farm, a dim shape that was a narrow wheat wagon, some pin-points of light that represented a small prairie town dominated by a grain elevator, a blur that was a tent or a shack or a prairie "windmill," on its tall Eiffel-tower stand—and then the darkness of returning sleep.

When Wilby arrived in Winnipeg at 5 a.m., he knew the Fort Garry Hotel across from the railway station was still a year away from completion, so there was a dearth of good hotel rooms. The top hotel was the six-year-old Royal Alexandra, where he hastened without a reservation. The front desk clerk told him there were no rooms. "The hotel's always full." By a strange coincidence, I was told later the same day that the Fort Garry was fully booked, but we both managed to get a room.

Our day started at 7:45 a.m., the same time that Haney embarked for East Selkirk. Because of problems filing with our computers, we didn't get away from Kenora until 10 a.m. Of course, we passed another in our collection of oversized symbols— the nickel, the goose, and now Husky the Muskie, a 13-metre-high symbol that says you have arrived in fishing country. Around Kenora it is clear why it took so long to drive a road through to Port Arthur, for the road is built up 10 metres above the marsh below. As railway engineers discovered, it is not enough to put a foundation into the marsh, but to build one, have it sink, build one, have it sink, and build one again. It must have taken acres of fill, probably from the rock they carved through, to build a road. The cost today to build a completely new road through the marsh would be as prohibitive in 2000 as it was to those bureaucrats Wilby berated in 1912.

The Findlays that night stayed at one of the world's worst motels—it was noisy and had mattresses Haney may have slept on—which had Lorne wistfully telling stories of campsites they had stayed at. In campgrounds, whether it's because everyone is doing the same thing—trying to see the country in a lazy or economical fashion—there is a built-in camaraderie. Not that the Findlays needed any help igniting chat with Irene and the Reo along. Irene was a magnificent conversationalist who could talk to anyone and everyone, whether she knew their language or not. The Reo, though, usually drew a swarm, and so enchanted campground proprietors that the Findlays sometimes stayed for free. Almost nightly the Findlays had a fond tale to relate from the campsite. Lorne was always pleased to hear campers say they passed the Reo that day, and they were impressed at Lorne's ability to sense people coming up behind him and courteously move off to the shoulder to let them by. Of course, everyone had a story to tell about an old car that meant something to them.

Before we left Ontario, in the spirit of emulating Haney's tendency to sing as he drove, the Reo was overwhelmed by two voices that seemed like they crawled out of the swamp to croak:

> Land of the silver birch
> Home of the Beaver
> Where still the mighty moose
> Wanders at will.
> Blue Lake and rocky shore,
> I will return once more,
> Boom diddy boom boom
> Boom diddy boom boom
> Boom diddy boom boom boom.

It's difficult to say which set of Pathfinders would have been more thrilled with the coming of Manitoba. For the Findlays, it was that much closer to home. For Haney and Wilby they would have been given a reprieve from tackling huge and unknown obstacles. As for which 1912 Reo would have sighed or tooted its bulb horn the loudest, the long-gone Reo would have honked its way to East Selkirk in joy. Lorne's Reo was just purring along, waiting for the next challenge.

The Manitoba Welcome Centre couldn't have been more friendly, and it set a buoyant tone for our introduction to this province that entered Confederation in 1870. We found an old highway, Highway 15, that eased us out of the forest and into the plains. Along the way we stopped at Bear Lake Park for lunch. While Irene did her noontime magic, I strolled into the solitude of the bush—it ranks as one of the more glorious moments of the trip. The name of the lake kept my nerves poised and on the lookout for not-so-gentle bears. The alertness awakened the senses. I inhaled the smell of the birchbark, felt the breeze that swayed the treetops, saw the shafts of light dabble at a masterpiece with ambers and crimsons, and most of all I heard . . . nothing. Silence. No motor, no chatter, no notebook, no questions, no answers. Nature's balm was massaging the psyche. No wonder the moose were hanging out in the bush. Given the choice, I'd be there too.

Peter steered us into Winnipeg against a prairie wind that necessitated the use of the Reo's blanket to fend off the cold. What was disturbing, besides the similar hotel experience as Wilby, was how our first impressions ended up the same.

In Wilby's day Winnipeg was Canada's third largest city, Queen of the Prairies and geographical centre of the Dominion, which Wilby naively thought would one day become Canada's capital. Founded as the Red River Colony exactly one hundred years before by Scottish settlers, its layout emulated Paris's Champs Elysées, or London's Mall, with broad boulevarded streets and rows of trees on either side. Main Street itself, following the lines of the old Hudson Bay Company's trail, was 40 metres wide, and the rest fell into proportion. "Apparently, there was no such thing as a narrow thoroughfare, and very shortly there would be no such thing as a shack or a shanty, since the rude buildings of the city's infancy are being rapidly swept away to give place to imposing structures of brick and stone." Wilby, again, was retreating to his good-roads-mean-good-houses schtick, a variation of which he gave to a reporter of the *Winnipeg Telegram* that day.

My first impression of Winnipeg, though, was marred by exploration. On the way to a Winnipeg Blue Bomber game that night, I walked through mostly empty downtown streets in the shadows of tall buildings. The pedestrians I encountered were down on their luck, and the traffic—it whizzed by as only it can on one-way streets—seemed to tell us that the world had passed us by. Again, Wilby encountered similarly idle people, of which he was quick to form his opinion.

> Yet as I walked these noble streets, fashioned after the spaciousness of the neighbouring prairies, I was struck with the fact that at every step I rubbed against crowds of the unemployed and the out-of-elbows. What were they doing here at the gateway to the enormous possibilities of the west and the north—these out-of-work men, labourers of foreign nationality, the overflow of peasant Europe? Were they waiting for the ensuing spring to commence operations in the wheat fields? Were they recovering strength from illness, seeking employment in a city which had nothing but the shovel and the snow-removal of winter to offer them, or returning from the harvest to fritter away the winter in the small and unhealthy sleeping accommodations of the purlieus? Winnipeg, as yet, has scarcely any factories, and a farming region where all the eggs are in one basket can offer little more than six months' employment each year to unskilled labourers.

To get to Winnipeg Stadium, I had to catch the No. 11 bus on Portage Avenue to the Polo Park mall, walk through the mall and past the Winnipeg Arena to Bomberville. Portage was a bit busier than the wasteland I had crossed, and someone on the bus assured me that the two downtown malls, Eaton's and Portage Place, breathe some life into the city core. "However," the woman said, "people like coming here to Polo Park because you can park your car." Bomberville was packed. The passionate crowd oozed a sense of community. Everyone cheered the Bombers, the mascot, the Bomber History True or False, the fake field goal attempt, the kicking of a rouge attempt by the receiver just before halftime, the winner of the "Dirtiest car in the parking lot" prize. (Had I only had my own car with me...) The experience thrilled me so much I even bought a Blue Bomber scarf, which was a bit shorter than Isadora Duncan's.

The sense of community that didn't exist downtown might have been because the city had been evacuated to the Bomber game. Or it could have been the tendency that Wilby had touched upon, that the wide streets were fashioned after the expanse of the prairies. With so much land, there was little interest or need in building tight-knit neighbourhoods.

Haney had a more adventurous day. He got off in the depot of East Selkirk, expecting to find the Reo there, and then had to walk the seven kilometres to Selkirk. He saw no sign of Wilby or any of the Reos that were supposed to escort him into town (the rains had been too heavy for them to fulfil their obligation) so he rowed across the Red River, had lunch and then took a tram into Winnipeg. He found the house of Syffers, the man who was supposed to give him his expense money, but he wasn't in. Then he found Leo Andrus, the Reo factory man in Winnipeg who went with him that night to Selkirk to retrieve the Reo.

September 20—Winnipeg

The Reo had not yet set its rubber-soled feet in Winnipeg, but that didn't stop Wilby from hobnobbing. On this Friday morning he called upon Mayor Waugh, and then he went to the Industrial Bureau at noon, where he was the guest of the local automobile club for lunch. He gave a short address on the subject of good roads, obviously lamenting the absence of a road from Winnipeg to Port Arthur which left him car-less in speaking about his car trip. That afternoon's paper announced, though, that the Reo had arrived in Selkirk and that Haney would be bringing it to Winnipeg with the help of Andrus and A.R.M. Wright, assistant secretary of the Board of Trade at 1:30 p.m. In his diary Haney said he was able to unload the car at 10 a.m. Driving through what he described as "a deluge of rain," he didn't arrive until 5 p.m. If Haney had thoughts of an easy drive across the Prairies, they were quickly dashed. His phrase for his troubles this day was "fierce roads." What really stopped the Reo was something they'd become all too familiar with—gumbo, a fine black soil that becomes a suckingly muddy surface when wet. "It is a rich, argillaceous mould or loam," wrote Wilby, "formed by the lake deposits and forest growth of ages, and resting upon a clay sub-soil. Its dark colour is due in part to the long accumulation of the charred grasses left by annual prairie fires and the collection of decayed vegetable and animal matter."

Wilby said his driver and car arrived amid drenching showers, "covered from head to foot in mud, and in a spirit of covert mutiny." It had taken them the greater part of the day to navigate the seas of mud which they encountered. "As I could get no drivers to continue further west with me under prevailing climatic conditions, there was nothing to do but wait in Winnipeg for the return of the sun to its wonted 'orbit.'" If Haney put his foot down and refused to take on the gumbo, Wilby should have known better. He knew full well what a menace gumbo could be. A year earlier, in an American newspaper, he advised transcontinentalists stuck on the Prairies during a rainfall to wait for clear weather to avoid the gumbo.

The theme of the speeches at the Industrial Good Roads League was the great need for trunk roads in Canada, and the part Winnipeg will play as the hub of a network of roads designed to improve commerce, attract tourists to Canada's beautiful scenery, help the farmers get their products to market and improve intercourse among Canadians.

President Belcher of the Winnipeg Auto Club—founded in 1904, it was the first of its kind in Canada—said it is the only means of "bringing the provinces into the relations that they ought to have with each other. We do not know each other in Canada as well as we should, and the lack of highways is the cause of it. I can't think of a pleasanter way of bringing the provinces to know each other than by the use of highways that will pass through some of the most beautiful scenery on the continent. From a standpoint of pleasure alone the country cannot be seen from the railway car to full advantage. Automobiling is the only method of obtaining an accurate picture of the country through which you pass."

Wilby, never one to miss an opportunity to ingratiate himself with his hosts, said he felt Winnipeg was the future capital of Canada. He felt beauty alone was justification for building the road, but added that the nature of road-building was that it was not enough to build one—roads had to be maintained. Poor roads had made Wilby six days late on his trip, and he doubted whether he could reach Vancouver on October 1 as planned.

There was much joy at the idea of the Canadian Highway Association meetings which would begin in Winnipeg on October 9. Manitoba premier Sir Rodmond Roblin, who had already legislated the goal of a macadamized road across the province, promised to be chairman, so Wilby decided to pay the premier a visit. He showed up at the plain-looking government building (the current buildings on the Assiniboine River had not yet risen) and was surprised to find the casualness of inter- action, whether it was government ministers addressing each other by their first names, or the "comely looking lady-typist whistling a lively rag-time to the merry clicking of her machine." Wilby related the story of how Roblin and his son were held up by gumbo just outside their front door. Sitting in their car in formal evening dress, they looked at each other wondering which of them would climb under the car to release them from the "durance vile." Three years later, Roblin would be tossed out of office amid allegations he'd received kickbacks from construction firms building the new Parliament buildings.

At our Speedy pitstop this day we met students from Bonnycastle Elementary School who were following the Reo on the Internet. That night we attended the Manitoba Classic and Antique Auto Club's annual awards at a golf club where the parking lot was full of cars from the 1910s and on. The cars were all carefully parked, as I soon found out.

The group included couples anywhere from their thirties to their seventies, divided among several round tables when they weren't at the cash bar in the corner. There was a policeman, a postmaster, managers for Manitoba Hydro and Manitoba Bell, contractors, a transmission shop owner—a cross-section of the community brought together by a similar love, or maybe not. Simmering just below the level of discussion was a battle between the purist antique collectors, who want to restore a car to its original condition with its original parts, and the hot rodders, who think nothing of taking the frame of an old car and packing a more powerful motor under- neath. While the purists cringe at the idea of old parts going to waste, hot-rodding is a tradition that started in the 1930s with car enthusiasts souping up old Model Ts and As, or turning them into trucks.

Mort McKechnie, a 53-year-old hydro worker, said the trend started in the thir- ties when there wasn't enough of the car left to restore. He straddles both fields, going one weekend to an antique meet at the Minneapolis state fairgrounds where he'll have one of the 8,000 cars there, complete with a dance with fifties music and attire. The next weekend he'll go to a hot rodder meet with his 1937 Ford Sedan deliv- ery truck, which he calls "the forerunner of the station wagon." He's looking for a Chev from the fifties for the same reason many old car enthusiasts do. "It's in my blood. When I was 16 my parents had a '51 Chev. When I see one my thoughts go back to my early teens or childhood, riding in the back seat..." His voice trailed off, as if in reverie. "You can't do it until you can afford it. It becomes an expensive hobby. You spend a lot of time in the garage in the winter. We have long winters here. You build them in winter and drive them in summer."

Lesser conflicts existed between those who buy cars to fix them up and sell them to the ever-eager American investors, and those who believe you should buy a car and expect to be buried in it. Some of the members believe that once you sell a car south of the border, it becomes too expensive to import it back to Canada. Norbert Touchette, a 35-year-old owner of a transmission shop, feels they should be bought for keeps. He and two of his brothers are into cars. Even though their father wasn't into it, they had go-karts on the farm. Because of the isolation, cars meant freedom. "My dad didn't want me to, but I bought a '70 Mustang at age 17. I still have it today. I try to improve the car year after year, so it don't deteriorate. I don't own them for profit. I have them to enjoy them. You can make 40 percent selling them to collectors in the U.S., but we need to keep them in Canada."

Keeping enough cars around is important, says Wayne Howell, a 43-year-old owner of a couple of mechanical contracting companies. There's safety in numbers, and that's a reason for being part of a club. "I enjoy getting out to functions like this. It's getting more and more difficult unless you're in a group. You can't take a '56 T-bird to Wal-Mart. People pull up a few inches from you car and slam their door open. When we attend activities together, you get protection for your car. These people know what we've gone through to get the cars in this condition." Howell has been a car buff since he was 14, when he used to rebuild cars in his backyard. With his friends they used to have a competition as to who could build the ugliest car and drive it. Howell tinkered with the Morris Minor he had at the time, and still prefers what he calls "the working stiff's" cars. More people give him the thumbs up for his '51 Dodge Coronet than any of his more expensive cars because everyone can relate to Dodges, or an old Chev. He connects more to cars from the fifties, but his goal is to have one from each decade.

Although enthusiasm for old cars has grown, probably with the surge in disposable income among baby boomers, the Manitoba club has shrunk from being a club of 300 members to just under 200. The reason is the growth of specialty auto clubs. Winnipeg has an amazing 32 auto clubs, whether your taste is for Pontiacs, Studebakers or Fairlane 500s.

Then there's the traditional fight between Ford and GM buffs—Fix-Or-Repair-Daily versus Gutless Motors. To break that up, Chuck Ingram, the postmaster from the suburb of Bird's Hill, weighed in with an argument for the Sunbeam, a car whose forefather in 1924 once set a land-speed record that existed for 12 years. Although some folks at Chuck's table argued that the Sunbeam is really a vacuum cleaner, Chuck has been carefully working since 1989 with a Sunbeam parts dealer in Los Gatos, California, to reconstruct one of three prototypes for the Tiger Sunbeam that raced the 24 hours at Le Mans in 1964.

Richard Smith, a 63-year-old telephone company manager, told the story of the 1917 Reo Speedwagon truck he bought in the fall of 1960. Some hot-rodding friends ran into an old guy on Highway 59 who said he wanted to sell the Reo, but there was only one hitch—the truck was in the guy's living room. Undaunted, Smith went down to see it. "The guy said 'I want to sell it. I want $35 for it.' He had it in the house surrounded by the china cabinet, chesterfield and pictures and dining room tables. I asked him how he was going to get it out. He said 'Don't worry, come back tomorrow and I'll have it outside.' Sure enough, it was there, but I never asked him how he got it out. I drove it into a shed in '62 and it's still there. I gave it to my son. I've told the story a hundred times and no one believes me. I should have taken a picture."

In the midst of the awards and door prizes, I did my Wilby routine and gave a short speech. I said I was new to the car world, and I was amazed at how many women were involved in car clubs, thinking that it was mostly a guy-thing. That elicited a few hisses and boos. Then I expressed my confusion about what swap meets were all about. All these car couples go in their antique cars to swap meets, spend a few days, and then come home in the same cars. "If you weren't swapping cars, what exactly were you swapping?" I asked to nearly dead silence. Was the attempt at humour too close to the truth? I quickly retreated to my seat.

Some guy named Harry won two door prizes, and another member of the club yelled "Watch your back?" suggesting he might get rolled in the parking lot for his gifts. Overall, besides all the esoteric talk about straight sixes, undersized bearings and camshafts, there was lots of frivolity. Here was an example that cars don't necessarily have to isolate people; they can also bring people together.

The Reo was out late this night, and because Lorne had declined to light its headlights, it went home to the campground sandwiched between the camper and another car. I started to walk back to the centre of town, looking for a bus. As good as the Winnipeg transit system is, the city is too spread out to make the bus trips frequent enough.

September 21—Winnipeg

The Pathfinders had probably heard the line: If you like Winnipeg you'll like the west. It was named Manitoba's capital when the province joined Confederation in 1870, and officially became a city three years later, with about 3,700 residents. In 1878 it had a rail link with St. Paul, Minnesota, and in 1881 it had a Canadian link—the greatest factor in settling the prairies. By 1883 Winnipeg had 30,000 people, and when Haney and Wilby arrived it had grown to a city of 140,000. The pair must have seen the government's free hotel for immigrants and the line-ups at land offices; they must have run into adventurous Easterners who planned to use their money from harvest work to start new lives. In a city, wrote Wilby, of such democratic growth,

> everything has been proved possible—it is perhaps not strange that there should be a more or less general acceptation of the democratic theory that Jack is as good as his master—and often a good deal better. In London, one who asserted that axiom would have to prove it, and when he had done so it would be believed—not before. In Winnipeg, its truth is assumed, and there is no necessity of proof. Your man may smoke in the same hotel lounge where you smoke. He may dine at the same restaurant, and if he chance on the same table and you have any regard for the minor graces of life, it requires infinite tact to remind him of your point of view. He is easily offended at, and quickly resentful of, any definition or distinction of quality. This mental attitude is common in the New World among those who toil with their hands and not with their brains. Its explanation is to be found in the fact that, there, working people pass rapidly from low wages to comparative wealth, and that, not having had the time nor power to intellectually adapt themselves to their new environment, they do not often change associates while speech, habits, tastes, remain the same.

Wilby uses "Jack" to refer to someone who thinks he is as good as his master, which could have been a direct shot at Haney. "Jack" was an everyman term, a "John Doe" of its day. Still, the timing and context of his comments could not be more appropriate. Haney did want to use his Reo expertise to dictate when the car did and didn't move.

On this Sunday the Findlays went to Broadway First Baptist Church and toured the capital city. I went to the library and also chatted with Randy Rostecki, 46, who trained as an architectural historian but works as a historical consultant. He said 1912 was the end of one of Winnipeg's boom cycles, where both immigration and wheat production slowed. "It reached the end of a natural cycle. It was the last great year of growth in the city." The real estate industry suffered a lull in 1913, reflecting a national recession, and the Panama Canal opened that year, which meant all commerce didn't have to cross the country to reach Europe. When Winnipeg tried to get things going in the spring of '14, the First World War broke out, and Canada had more important things on its mind. The war, says Rostecki, also was the dividing line between good and bad urban planning. After the war the city continued to spread, as did its network of wide roads.

Gumbo had an influence on road widths, said Rostecki. "In pre-city days, the trails were wide because of mud holes. The mud is very tenacious, and there would be slews in the middle of the trails, so the carters would go around them instead of getting stuck. The trails widened out, and sometimes the horse and carts travelled abreast each other. There were plans to cut down the size of Portage and Main in 1886 or '87, and the issue recently popped up again."

The city is still rich in architecture, he said, but it would be richer had they not lost the old city hall and other buildings, like the Royal Alexandra, the hotel where Wilby stayed. All the bank buildings that sprung up to propel the business of the West tried to outdo each other with ornate edifices. There have been several suggestions as to why Winnipeg never reached its potential as a great city—some have suggested the General Strike of 1919 discouraged new businesses from setting up—but Rostecki says no one has put into perspective the impact of the car. Winnipeg got its first car in 1899, but the first one on the streets arrived in 1901. By 1910 it had a pretty good fleet of trucks that started an interprovincial service to Regina in 1913. "Donald Street was considered the most beautiful street in Winnipeg. Now it's anything but. Houses got old, went to seed in the thirties and forties. Somebody got the bright idea in the forties that these big healthy trees, 50 years old, spread disease. They wanted to have parking on the street and run more cars. In about a three-year period they cut down 950 trees. We've learned a lot from what cars have done to cities, but it doesn't have to keep happening."

The city had angular parking once upon a time, which helps downtown businesses to have parking next to their stores, but now the emphasis is on three- and four-lane one-way streets to move the cars quickly through the city, which many experts say is the worst thing for downtown businesses. In 1972 Winnipeg absorbed the surrounding towns which had been connected to it through a suburban street car system. That had been ripped up in 1955. In the new Unicity, the old town cores have been blurred. The detachment from neighbourhoods, combined with the growth of shopping malls, has had a deadening effect on the small to moderate-sized business in those areas. Because the city is so vast, and there's no way a transit system can run efficiently with close to 700,000 people spread over such a large area, people feel they need a car even more, which accentuates the problems all the more. "We used to have a pretty good city," said Rostecki. "We've had a long history of development, and a long history of undevelopment. Tear something down for no good reason, and end up with a vacant site. What we have now isn't what our forefathers planned for us."

At the library, it wasn't difficult finding a parallel between 1912 and 1997. The current papers were full of the Diana tragedy, and of Elton John, whose song in her honour, "Good-bye England's Rose," was about to sell millions of copies. On the same weekend in 1912 were stories of Sarah Flower Adams who, 50 years before, wrote the hymn "Nearer My God to Thee," which was

> consecrated for all time to the memory of those who went down with the *Titanic*. Since that dreadful night, nearly four months ago, the hymn has sold far and wide. In London alone the street sales amounted to hundreds of thousands. Little is known of the writer. We are told, however, that she was a woman of great sympathy, charm and beauty, extremely musical, and as her poems show, deeply religious; that her wit was brilliant and her gaiety a delight to all who knew her; and that she fell into corresponding periods of deep melancholy. She loved the sea intensely.

On the same page was an article on the world's most eligible bachelor: "Who will marry the Prince of Wales; Only a limited number of princesses from which a choice can be made."

Haney and Wilby didn't have the best of days. Haney must have returned to Selkirk the night before to sleep. That would explain the $4 he paid for cleaning the car and storing it, and the first notation in his diary, "Got out at 8 a.m." Using both a bus and a streetcar, he met his fellow traveller, writing later: "Had big fight with Wilby. He was going to leave at 1:30 p.m. today. I said No, owing to condition of car and roads. Expect to leave the 23rd. Worked on car all afternoon. Found Syffers tonight. Went to show and am now going to bed." Syffers, or a name similar to that, had his $300 in expense money. Haney would have been just as keen as Wilby to leave town and do the Reo Company proud. In the paper that day was a large ad for "The 'All Red Route' Reo, mapping out the Natural Highway Across Canada, from Halifax to Vancouver." The ad was sponsored by Reo Sales, the Reo Motor Car Co. of Canada Ltd. and Percy Plews of the Plews Automobile Company, agents for Reos in Winnipeg, who "looked after the interests of the tourists while in town," said the magazine *Gas Power Age*. The magazine also said arrangements were being made to give the driver of the ocean-to-ocean trip, F.V. Haney, "a little reception" when the car arrived around Sept. 26 or 27th, and on the same page it mentions their arrival and Wilby being "head of the party since leaving Halifax."

The Royal Alexandra Hotel, where Wilby stayed, was less than three weeks away from hosting the second annual convention of the Canadian Highway Association. At the convention they would show lantern slides of the Pathfinders' trip in a lecture titled "Across Canada over the Road," and no doubt some of the delegates had already seen the duo along the way, including Frank Mutton of Toronto, G.A. Simard of Montreal and W.A. Anderson of Saint John (in the next week Mayor Fleming of Brandon and George Thompson of Indian Head, Saskatchewan, would meet the pair). Some of the other papers presented included "The Evils of the Patronage System as Applied to Road Building," and "Convict Labor on Roads." Wilby probably influenced the speech of L. McMeans, the MPP for Winnipeg, who at the convention said that good roads "were the crying need of the day. Good roads expedited business and enhanced the values of the land they served." Robert Forke of Pipestone, who would represent the Union of Manitoba Municipalities at the conference, would go one step further: "Roads were good for morals and business and were avenues of progress. Education was also affected, as bad roads would not be used to send children to school."

That night at Winnipeg's Forks, the hub of nightspots down at the fork of the Red and Assiniboine rivers, I would forget about Robert Forke and morals and make like Wilby: I had too many beers celebrating the halfway point of the trip.

September 22 — Winnipeg

In his book, Wilby is much more enlightened about gumbo, and lighthearted in telling stories about it, than in his discussions with Haney. While Haney insisted it was impossible to make any headway in the rain across a muddy land, Wilby was itching to leave town, partly because he had preached to the newspapers about being king of the highways. To the reporters, Wilby had not even driven across town, never mind been seen in the car. Wilby said the steadily falling glass of rain was the subject of conversations in hotel lobbies, in government and municipal offices, in restaurants and newspapers offices.

> No one could say enough in condemnation of the wanton pranks the climate had played that year in Manitoba. Rain had fallen all summer and throughout the autumn. The crops could not be harvested and the motorist could not motor. If he were rash enough to take his car outside the city limits, the chances were that he would never return with it. Reports had come in of automobiles stranded everywhere across the Province.

Wilby had the benefit of hindsight when he wrote that, but Haney was wise to refuse to proceed. The car had taken a beating going 45 kilometres from Selkirk to Winnipeg. It meant that Haney spent the entire day working on the car, to grind its valves, take out the clutch to oil and clean, yet it was still "chattering pretty bad," he wrote. Haney sent wires to the Reo company to resolve two issues—whether he could put the pennants on the car to show what the Reo had accomplished, and whether he was in charge of when the car went anywhere. His obstinance this day may have saved the trip, for the roads were not fit to drive on. Had he said "Ready Aye Ready," as Wilby demanded, the trip would have been delayed even longer, if it would have been completed at all.

The rain was another parallel, for earlier in 1997 the rains led to the century's worst flood, where more than 256,000 hectares were under water across southern Manitoba and the Dakotas, forcing 75,000 people to flee their homes. When we ran into people affected by the flood, they had that never-again look in their eyes. The adults we spoke to had already sold their homes, to get away from the lowlands on the banks of the Red River. The kids from Bonnycastle School, though, had another opinion. One Grade 5 student wrote for our web page: "We do have crazy things happening with the weather. We had the flood of the century but we had a great time babysitting plants and raising money for relief and the whole province really was right out there (helping each other)."

The 1997 Reo made it on national television this day, appearing on CBC-TV's *Midday* program with Lorne in his usual eloquent mode and the writer on the trip with a Wilbyesque hangover. Peter drove by Bonnycastle School with the Reo, which prompted another submission to the web page. The class had fun learning about Canada as they followed the Reo on the Internet, and they wrote that "it was so exciting to finally talk to Peter Findlay in person instead of just by e-mail. He came back to our neighbourhood where he could get onto the Internet and there was lots of excitement when he arrived at the school on Monday and lots of noise as we honked the old-fashioned Reo horn. The experience was so exciting we don't think anyone in the class will ever forget it."

Later, I talked to Neil Einerson of Manitoba's Historical Resources office. He painted a picture of the city's history more benign than Rostecki's. Sure, the great land boom of 1882 didn't turn Winnipeg into the Chicago of the north, but its architecture rivals some of that in Chicago, especially in the warehouse district, which he said was very much like what existed in 1912. Despite the removal of trees and the boulevards on some of the city's streets, Winnipeg still had the largest urban elm forest in the country, and there was a program in place to maintain the trees. The spread-out nature of the city is "more of a prairie approach to housing, not as much terraced housing. Cities do spread more. There are very large lots and there were a number of municipalities that came together to form Winnipeg." He says there remains an approach to neighbourhood planning; different sectors within are still noted for their character. As for the number of people living in cities as opposed to the country, he said that came about as a result of better transportation.

The need for cars and trucks to end the isolation of the farmer, and bring produce to market, was a huge issue in 1912. The newspapers contained stories about "Farmers on the Prairies feel the want of time-saving appliances. More automobiles will be introduced." One farmer, W. Harrison, said the "dearth of automobiles in the prairie provinces will be a heavy detriment in securing adequate means of transportation for the heavy grain crops. Year by year the prairie farmer is growing to depend more and more on the auto as a means of getting his grain to market, and so great has been the demand for the machines that dealers are literally swamped with orders." The farmers reasoned that the motor car is far superior to the horse because there is no expensive feed bill or delicate regard for health. "Besides," said Harrison, who must have had a car dealership on the side, "the auto cannot be overworked, morning and evening, one or twenty-four each and every day, it makes no difference for the great creation of man which is made to serve man alone. Not only have automobiles found their way into practical farming methods in the middle west, but the farmers have in many cases purchased runabouts and touring cars for the use of the family. These cars prove to be a feature at fall fairs when exhibitions and contests for wheel supremacy are held." In other words, the propaganda about the economic viability and dependability of cars had already been propagated.

The other issue of concern to farmers was the price of gasoline, for Western Canada had more gas-propelled engines in use per capita (including farm machinery) than anywhere else in the world. The price of gas fluctuated, supposedly because of supply and demand, came the standard line from Standard Oil Company, the most hated corporation in America. The issue being debated in motoring magazines was whether Canada should regulate the price and quality of gasoline.

While Manitoba was mired in mud, making motor car travel impossible for Wilby and Haney, *Maclean's* magazine ran a piece on "The Auto Driver" that seemed a bit ironic.

> With my motors a-drumming, you can hear me coming, coming,
> Till in smoke and dust and vapour I go swirling madly by,
> While the wheel my hands are gripping, as around the turns we're whipping,
> And I toss the miles behind me as the vivid seconds fly;
> For I know the others follow, swooping over hill and hollow,
> With their motors' sharp staccato keeping rhythm with the race,

And my racer leaps and lurches as I fling past towns and churches,
Where a blur of trees and fences marks the swiftness of the pace!

Every nerve and muscle's straining as in speed I'm gaining, gaining,
And the wind that rushes by me makes a roaring in my ear,
And the car is rocking, jolting, in its frenzied thunderbolting,
And I pray my lucky angel that the course is free and clear;
For the slightest break or faulting sends a racer somersaulting,
Turns the snapping snorting engine to a heap of smoking scrap,
And although I take my chances under any circumstances
I am not exactly yearning for my everlasting nap!

Yet it's great to have the making of a record record-breaking
And to feel the car responding as you "throw 'er open wide,"
With the motor singing cheerful, though the pace is something fearful,
And you're running like a cyclone that is roaring as you ride;
If you lose, or if you win, you feel the fever throbbing in you,
And you never will recover from the motor-racing thrall,
With its chance—glad or tragic—with its glamor and its magic,
With its stress and strain and danger and the glory of it all!

The Reo hopped a ride on the steamer *A.E. Ames*, pictured here in Haney's photo as it approached the Soo Locks.

ENGLAND LEADING THE BAN ON BILLBOARDS, September, 1912, London England—The English are showing an excellent example to Americans in refusing to allow scenery to be ruined by horrible blotches of advertisement spread over everything. The Kent county council has adopted a bylaw prohibiting the erection of unsightly advertisements, hoardings and boards in the county. A penalty of 25 pounds is provided for infractions and a further fine of five pounds a day for every day the offense is continued after conviction. The bylaw prohibits any person from exhibiting an advertisement visible from any public highway, whether a carriageway, footway or bridgeway, or from a railway or from open land or water open to the public and so placed as to disfigure the natural beauty of the landscape.

LIVING THE WAY DISNEY INTENDED, September, 1997, Celebration, Florida—Compared to the 18th- and 19th-century towns it emulates, Celebration is an instant-town, without the layers of social, political, architectural and landscape history that give communities depth and texture. Ten years in the planning and three years in the building, the new town is a celebration of architecture, of public space, of color, of nature. There are no slums, no boarded-up businesses, no junker cars rusting away in back yards. Looking at what made communities great in the past, walking is emphasized through raised wooden walkways trisecting a wetland park, as are sidewalks, back alleys for cars, and both a school and a downtown commercial district within walking distance. Three square blocks of shops, with free parking hidden in the landscaped interiors of blocks, makes the town both pedestrian-friendly and car-friendly.

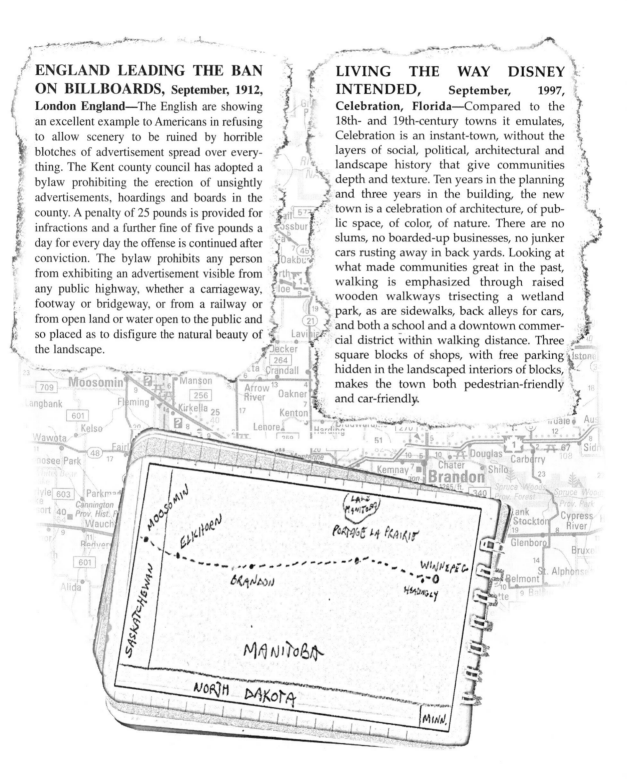

Chapter 10

The Manitoba Mystery

September 23 — Winnipeg

The wires from St. Catharines hadn't been received, but there was no doubt Wilby would get his way. His departure was already two days later than he said it would be. To make matters worse, he had arranged for a sendoff from the mayor's wife. (The mayor soon announced he would not seek re-election, citing the loss of a dear friend on the *Titanic* as the reason.) There is a photo of Mrs. R.D. Waugh at city hall pinning a Winnipeg pennant on the Reo, uncharacteristically with its roof up. The Reo then drove by the government buildings "to take leave" of Premier Roblin, Wilby's pal, and then headed north to park in front of the CPR depot for another photo with the locomotive, *The Countess of Dufferin*. Like the Reo, the CPR steam engine was the first to cross the continent to Western Canada. At 3:30 p.m., the Reo finally left the *Manitoba Free Press* building where the Pathfinders received a route map from automobile editor A.C. "Ace" Emmett, a pillar in the development of Manitoba roads and the man who came up with the idea of numbering highways—an example now followed by countries around the world.

We got off a bit earlier and had a jaunty ride west along Portage Avenue. A pedestrian yelled to us, saying she had heard us on radio that morning. Lorne said he liked Winnipeg because the streets go everywhere, and the city also had a ring road, which Lorne felt was important. In Vancouver they decided in the early 1970s not to allow thruways to cut through the city. "It takes so long to get anywhere. They don't understand the pollution of 100 cars at the stoplight, instead of a thruway to move people through the city." It was such a joyful day I didn't want to start the debate that public transit should have been Vancouver's first priority, or that the absence of thruways is why Vancouver has seen a resurgence in families moving downtown—thruways have just as many bumper-to-bumper problems, and the off-ramps of thruways usually kill the older neighbourhoods they enter. Anyway, we went by Assiniboine Park, established in 1904, when the town's planning seemed to be at its peak. Unfortunately, Portage Avenue was like other arteries leaving Canada's big cities—with little charm. At one point we were on the Yellowhead Trail, which is dubbed the "New Trans-Canada" as it makes its way to Prince Rupert via Edmonton. Along the way we passed a tractor with three wheels abreast on each side, evidently to get the tractor out of mud. Haney could have used such an advantage, because he was forced to slog through mud for 20 kilometres from Winnipeg to Headingly.

For a while we followed a row of poplars that Lorne says are used as a windbreak all along the Trans-Canada. We were headed toward the crossroads of St. Francois Xavier, where we had been invited to lunch at the Tin Lizzie Car Barn.

The museum was run by businesswoman Marg Kentner, who has a degree in political science and a penchant for making businesses viable. Among the more intriguing exhibits was a 1917 Ford 12-passenger bus that transported fishermen and picnickers from the streetcar stop at Highway 9 to the Red River locks. Kentner explained that she owned the store next door, an old convent school that was a designated historical site. "There was not much for the men to do while the women were shopping," said Kentner. "They'd sit in their cars and read the newspaper. To make it a complete entertainment destination, I thought of the museum. I had an antique London taxicab that delivered gifts for my old store for 13 years, and a red Jag roadster. I like old things and gorgeous things. Old cars represent something really good, a different era than we live in. I was always cleaning it. I'd see other old cars going by, so the idea for a museum had a long gestation period."

She also did her research. Per capita, Winnipeg had more car collectors than any Canadian city. She learned about swap meets, and cruise-bys, and knew that the enthusiasm for cars would only grow as the baby boom generation retired. Besides, car buffs always needed a place to store their cars, so what better place than to have her take care of them while they were exhibited to the world?

The collection included the 1951 Cadillac convertible car that drove Princess Elizabeth and Prince Philip when they came to Winnipeg and stayed at the Royal Alexandra Hotel. (When Princess Anne opened the Pan Am Games in Winnipeg in

1999, she used that same car.) It was owned by Jack Smith, a Hudson fanatic, whom we were told we should visit. "He has a great collection," someone said, "but you'd need earmuffs. Every third word is a swear word." Lorne quipped, "That comes from trying to keep Hudsons on the road." Lorne's museum had rescued a 1926 Hudson hearse that was being used by a tree doctor. In the glassed-in back was a rotten piece of wood with a sign 'Don't let this happen to your tree.' Lorne said they were happy to get it away from such a bad life.

The museum had a book called *America on Wheels*, the companion to the PBS television series that seemed to be pro-car. It talked of how the in-breeding of small communities was reduced because the car encouraged people to travel. It had graphic photos of how polluted and horrible cities were because of horses. Not only did horses have the gall to defecate on the streets, but they died with their horseshoes on in the line of duty: fifteen thousand horse carcasses had to be removed from the streets of New York in one year. In winter the streets were never cleaned properly, so kids died of asthma as a result. One page showed a typical street (c. 1900) "featuring uncollected garbage, unshovelled manure and rampant disease. The advent of the automobile age actually improved conditions, making the horse obsolete and the removal of garbage more efficient." In an I-told-you-so mode, Lorne said "The saviours of the earth wanted to go back to that." Kentner, not one to mince words, replied, "Extremes on each side are bad. Pollution lessened with the first coming of the car, then it went overboard."

At the convent school, Irene found a place to browse and enough people to start 20 conversations. One involved a San Diego woman who had moved away 40 years ago. During a pleasant conversation about San Diego, I attempted a joke by saying that she must come back for the snow. She replied, "I used to come back every year until 1993. My brother and his wife were killed in a head-on collision. My dad died five weeks later so there's not as much of a reason to come back."

Our trip to Portage was like an ad for cross-country trekkers seeking flatness. They got it. Outside our destination we met members of the local automobile club at Fort La Reine, where remnants of Canadian history lay haphazardly on the property, looking abandoned after the tourists had left for the summer. Besides a few colonial houses, including a school house, there was William Van Horne's private railway car—all reduced to a makeshift tourist joint at the side of the road. The people we met told us that Portage had flourished when the military was nearby. The Southport military base, which employed 2,000, had been shut down five years before. It is now used for helicopter training; Bombardier tests its planes there. Macdonald, another air base 22 kilometres to the north, had closed in '59. Portage's best selling point, besides the giant Coca-Cola can on the other side of town, was the natural habitat known as the Delta Marshes. Like other towns trying to claim "the best of," the folk at this phony fort said the delta marsh had the biggest variety of birds anywhere in North America.

Downtown, I stayed at the same hotel as Haney and Wilby. However, it had seen better times. Some young entrepreneurs had taken over the building and ran a thriving bar on the main floor. Upstairs, the rooms were the domain of denizens on welfare or those whom Wilby described as "out of elbows." My door looked as though it had been jimmied so many times there didn't seem to be any sense in locking it. The hotel was still standing because it was made of brick from the city's brickyards; thus it was less susceptible to fires than many of its contemporaries.

For local history I was told to contact Les Green, 71. He told me the history begins with melting glaciers that formed Lake Agassiz. When the lake receded it left a bed of soil almost two metres thick—the reason the Portage plains have never had a crop failure. The town got its name from white fur traders who found Indians making a portage from the Assiniboine to Lake Manitoba. "La Verendrye built Fort La Reine in 1738, then they all went away and left it. Some years later Hudson's Bay came and built it up again. Later they built a department store. My mother said it had quality everything until it burnt down in 1913. We're not a French town. It was a pivotal place in the fur trade, right from the start. With portages, Indians could canoe as far as they wanted from Edmonton to Lake Winnipeg to Hudson Bay. All of western Canada drains into Manitoba. That's why we have all the hydro power."

Les's great grandfather had come to the Red River settlement in 1871, "the year after Louis Riel was kicking up a fuss. Winnipeg wasn't much of a place, so they came out and squatted in the early 1880s. In 1884, his great-grandfather and grandfather started Portage La Prairie Mutual Insurance, because Eastern insurance companies were reluctant to sell homesteaders insurance. The company spread from coast to coast, and Les worked there for 43 years in public relations. "When the railway came, the population in five years grew from 500 to 3,500. Up until then the main modes of transportation were river boats on the Assiniboine and oxcarts." He pulled out a photo of the last oxcart to leave Portage. "They made them with wood and tied them together with leather. They didn't put any grease on the wheels so the wheels always squeaked. You could hear ox-trains coming for miles."

His connection to the 1912 Reo trip was slim—his father, a printer, worked on the *Weekly* and *Daily Reviews*, two Tory papers then published out of Portage. The city's member of parliament was Arthur Meighen, future prime minister of Canada, while Charles D. MacPherson, whom Wilby mentioned, was the Liberal provincial member. *The History of Portage* by Anne Collier noted that Adam Brown, Sr., introduced cars to the city by picking up two Studebakers in South Bend, Indiana, in 1902. D.S. Lyon opened the first garage in 1908. Collier wrote that when cars first made their appearance on the streets of Portage,

> they were considered "things of the devil" by many. Horses shied and ran away, tethered ones reared up (as high as possible) and their whinnying, snorting and galloping caused quite an uproar when mingled with the racket of the pioneer models. Mystified people gathered in crowds whenever they saw an approaching car, and only the most daring of women would drive in one.

Les, a quiet man, lived with his wife in a modest house decorated with photos of children and grandchildren. Before he dropped me off at my hotel, he told me his wife was once his sister-in-law. When both their spouses died two years earlier, her house needed taking care of and he needed someone to do the cooking, so they got married.

The hotel had lost its Roman-columned verandah and its architectural charm. No longer did the second floor boast a ladies' parlour with mirrored walls, "soft chairs and divans and an Edison Talking Machine." Its bar was still finished in oak, but it was bereft of "elaborate fixings, the equal of anything in Winnipeg." Its floor was still of fine maple, and there was evidence of the four large fireplaces that kept it warm in winter. It had become little more than a doss house. As I lay in bed that night, listening to the shouts of drunken hotel mates, I didn't realize we had already surpassed where Wilby and Haney had landed that night. On this day the Reo could only make it to Headingly, which Wilby described as "a huddle of two or three crazy-looking houses apparently far past reform."

> From the tiny window of my inn, I could see the broad black highway lined by wire fences but otherwise open to the world like a great staring lidless eye. It was my first intimate contact with the prairies. For weeks I had looked forward to them, dreamed of them. Yet, now that I stood face to face with them, I was as unmoved and emotionless as they. I was disappointed in them.

Haney was not so disappointed in the Prairies as he was in being forced to leave Winnipeg just to satisfy Wilby's whims. After arriving in Headingly, he returned to Winnipeg by electric car, where he finally picked up the expense money he needed. On this part of the trip he would have a co-pilot—the Reo mechanic Andrus—but his best friend was still the car, and he didn't like the idea of sending it into a sea of mud unnecessarily. Like Lorne 85 years later, he identified with the Reo. It would have initiated conversations with people where he kept it, just like in 1997, and those people he met compensated for his sufferance of Wilby.

September 24—Headingly/Portage la Prairie

The Portage Hotel didn't have much but it had a remote for the cable TV. A flick of channels tripped across Country Music Television and the video "Dancin', shaggin' on the boulevard," by Alabama. In it youngsters were driving around in nice cars with skimpily clad women. It was in many ways an old-fashioned vision of the car, an image of the car as power, freedom, a tool to attract women. Most of the TV ads concentrated more on freedom, the ability to go off the road and across land—attributes Haney would have appreciated.

Haney spent the night in Winnipeg, for he made several purchases which he marked down on the 24th. He bought a compass, which would come in handy on a prairie with few landmarks, a funnel, a pail, a nozzle, a cork, some gloves, shoes and a rope, all for $13.20. They wouldn't get away from Headingly until 1 p.m., which gave Wilby some time to moan about their predicament.

> The cold grey light of the next morning revealed a great untimbered, level, dried-up sea of land, as cheerless as on the night before. The broad field-fringed highway leaped straight as an arrow across the illimitable plain in the direction of Portage-la-Prairie. On either side of the road-ditches were other trails or ruts, so that the highway had a probably

total width of about one hundred and fifty feet. The fields were comparatively small, and almost all of the little wheat grown had been cut. Now and again a modest farmhouse came into view, with its accompanying herds of cows, reedy sloughs of water and flocks of crows. Thistles mingled with the feathery grasses, and small yellow flowers occasionally speckled the roadside with tiny points of gold. Crossroads —"road allowances" as they are called—led off to right and left, but their straight lines were broken by clumps of trees which marked the winding course of the Assiniboine and hid the country beyond. Wheat stood in sheaves, but only a few binders were at work.

The weather had been so wet that threshing machines had been idle. A threshing outfit works best when grain is dry. Grain stalks go in one side and all the seeds are threshed off, with the stalks going one way and the seeds the other. Farmers also complained about the scarcity of labour. They were willing to pay as a high as $3.50 a day, but could not get enough hands.

There weren't many hands about as we left downtown Portage. A mall on the city's edge had drawn away business. Then the highway department had finished it off. In exchange for looking after the main street, it had asked the town to get rid of angled parking. Not only did this increase the road's design speed—discouraging potential shoppers from slowing down—but also shoppers now had to parallel park on a busy thoroughfare. On the way out of town a Wal-Mart sign read "We sell for less: Satisfaction guaranteed." The sign didn't say anything about killing downtowns, but it didn't have to. Before we left we saw the city's claim to fame—the country's largest Coca-Cola can, which was erected in 1905 as the town's water tower. Until Las Vegas built a monstrous Coke can, it was the largest in the world. Nearby, an old drive-in theatre was decaying on the side of the road.

We passed one landmark the original Pathfinders must have seen, the 1890 Burnside Cemetery along the Trans-Canada. However, there was no wheat left standing as we made our way west. I told Lorne the story of Les marrying his sister-in-law, but he was unfazed. "That's very scriptural. In the Bible you were required to take care of your brother's wife if something happened to him."

Lorne then embarked on a story that—at the time—bore no connection to the idea of prairie relationships. He talked of stopping in Elkhorn, Manitoba, the next day, where a bachelor farmer named Ike had collected old cars before it came into fashion. Lorne went up twice back in the sixties to look at his cars, and he'd find Ike on his farm, still using steam tractors to run the farm. He had so many cars that he offered them to the Manitoba government. "It's one of the best collection of cars around, and it's in this out-of-the-way town near the Saskatchewan border. He had a Briscoe with a single headlight in the middle of the radiator. There's other treasures, but the Elkhorn museum can only do so much with what it has to work with."

Lorne had driven this way to pick up a GMC schoolbus whose top speed was 65 mph. He was bucking a headwind across the prairies so he couldn't make time. Birch, cottonwood and poplar trees try to protect drivers along the Trans-Canada from the wind. In Wilby's day, he had waxed on about the poplars he'd seen, but he failed to make mention of one of the Prairies' more enchanting sights—the Northern Lights. Perhaps Wilby couldn't see the lights from inside the bars he frequented.

For a while the Trans-Canada follows the same route as the Yellowhead Highway, which eventually heads north through Edmonton toward Prince Rupert in Northern B.C. It got its name from a half-white, half-Iroquois trapper who had light-coloured hair. The French voyageurs called him *Tête Jaune*, or Yellowhead.

The Reo hummed along the two bland strips of Trans-Canada pavement cutting across the Prairies on what was a big-sky day. Lorne had a quick glimpse in the distance of a '49 or '50 Chev, and then he heard our fourth cylinder trying to cut in. "It's burning off the soot." He tried to educate me on how some parts of the car worked. The gasoline explodes forcing the pistons to move. The pistons turn the crankshaft which turn the drive shaft at the rear wheels. The camshaft is connected to the crankshaft via gears. The camshaft lets the gas into the piston and lets the exhaust out of another valve. As for tips on buying used cars, he told me to look behind the radiator to see if it's been in any collisions, look down the side of the car for ripples from body work. "You should try the steering, see if the tires are wearing evenly, check the oil to see if it is black or dirty or watery."

With nothing cozy about the Trans-Canada, and the alternatives far out of our way, we stayed on the highway as long as we could and then veered south. We found a road allowance to stage a photo, like the ones of Haney and Wilby crossing the prairies alongside the telegraph poles, and then passed a bog with water still in it—whenever the Pathfinders found a low spot they'd drive in the field around it. When it looked like we were nowhere near where they had gone, we'd see a pond and remnants of old roads and farmhouses that Wilby and Haney must have discovered. The roadkills were consistently skunks, rabbits and a raccoon which was either dead or playing possum. At Carberry we saw R.J. Waugh Elementary School, which prompted the question Waaaah?

Lorne's father came from Manitoba. "They lived away from anywhere until the branch line came through. One by one everyone would move to the rail line. They'd move their entire house. They'd do it in the winter so they could slide the house on a sled. They stayed in the house while it was moved—with the fire going and everything."

A hawk soared overhead and Lorne switched to hand throttle—"my cruise control"—and took his foot off the pedal as the car shot through fields of picked sunflowers. In the distance, grey-white smoke signified the rejuvenation of the soil with nitrogen. Farmers cut the grain down to eight inches and then burn the rest. The burn-off drew complaints that Winnipeg kids were suffering from asthma because of it, giving the rural and townsfolk something else to argue about. Lorne, or at least his stomach, had fond memories of being in the area at Canadian Forces Base Shilo during the Second World War. "Did they ever feed us during the war! At the base in Saskatchewan it wasn't that good. In Shilo they killed us with food." On the other side of the Trans-Canada was a cropduster, which Lorne described as "an engine, a wing and nothing else. They can fly down to the ground and up." Momentarily it was something to marvel at, and then you realized it was spraying chemicals on a field not far from grazing cows. Let's face it, ever since a cropduster chased Cary Grant across a field in *North by Northwest*, they have had a bad name.

Members of the Western Manitoba Pioneer Auto Club met us in Brandon at a Ukrainian restaurant, the kind where paper placemats have local trivia on them to keep you occupied while waiting for dinner. It noted Brandon had 2,000 hours of sunshine a year, which prompted someone to add: "And an equal amount of minus-40 degrees, but they didn't tell you that." Gerry Dyck, one of our hosts, had his own trivia about why railway tracks were four-foot, eight-inches wide, as were wagon ruts and Roman roads. "It was the width of a two-horse chariot. In other words, the width of two horses' asses." We had just missed their club's pitchfork fondue, which was probably a good thing for our arteries—they stick rib-eye steaks on a pitchfork and put them in a pot of oil and marbelize them.

I commandeered a '65 Mustang to a bed and breakfast named Casa Maley, where I dropped off my bags and changed clothes. The day was a scorcher. We had a brief ceremony at city hall, which involved going up to the mayor's office. That night there was a runoff of nine candidates for the mayoralty. An alderman goaded Lorne into sitting in the vacant mayor's chair, as if it was a big deal, but Lorne looked uncomfortable. He didn't identify with politicians as much as he did with the common man.

The Pathfinders had a windy day, such that it "played a tattoo on the leather top of the car and fanned the blood to a disagreeable chill." As we had on our way to Portage, they also veered off the main road. They ended up mowing down barberry-like bushes, and happened upon deserted small towns, each built around a railway station, a post office and a store. While the road was spongy and wet, remnants of a trail through the grass proved a better surface. They happened upon a car whose occupants told them the mayor of Brandon had come past Portage to look for them.

> They point ominously backward, to where they declared there was another car, with a lady passenger and two men, which have been hauled out of the mud twice that morning. With that they waved us a farewell, and their car, stripped to racing lightness, ploughed its way into the thicket again.

Andrus and Haney put down wheat sheaves to get over depressions in their way, but they had to drive in second gear until they found smoother roads and lighter soil. While they drove, "black curly clouds formed side curtains and fringes to the windows of blue in the heavens, and in the far west, light lovingly lingered when the sun was no longer visible," wrote Wilby, "a rainbow promise of what was awaiting us in the higher and drier plateaus." He mentioned that Lake Manitoba, about 20 kilometres to the north, had the best duck and goose shooting in Canada.

Haney was able to run the car over hardened prairie at a clip of 50 kilometres an hour for the last 16 kilometres into Portage la Prairie, which they reached at 5:30 p.m. The town with a French name gave Wilby a chance to laud the early explorers.

> Radisson and de Groseilliers in 1666 penetrated along the Winnipeg River to Lake Winnipeg and from there to Hudson Bay. They later returned to France, and not meeting with encouragement, they went to London, where their tales of great inland seas, big navigable rivers and limitless plains filled with big and small game, aroused such

interest that in 1669 a company was formed and chartered by Charles II. Thus was born the Hudson's Bay Company...

Portage stood on the Saskatchewan Trail, as the Company called it, and its main street was so wide, as it is today, that Wilby, from his vantage point at the Portage Hotel, wanted a telescope just to see what was in the store window across the street. He suggested the roadsides were "so far apart that a man at one front door could not cover, with any chance of good target practice, a man facing him in the opposite doorway," and "a herd of buffalo might have stampeded along its entire length without doing any harm." The street reflected its past, when "bullocks were saddled like horses to the springless Red River ox-carts to convey supplies." Oddly enough, Wilby asked to see a Red River oxcart and someone gave him a collection of postcards which included a photograph from 1880 of the last ox-train pulling out of Portage (the locomotive made them obsolete). It may have been the same photo Les Green showed me 85 years on.

While Wilby, Haney and Andrus were firmly tucked into the Portage, a hotel that would later house prime ministers and Ernest Hemingway, it dawned on me that we were ahead of schedule by one day. My visits to the Brandon library and university exposed the error. We should have been in Portage with Wilby and Haney. Nevertheless, the different town, the different weather—they had a chilly day, while the warm, July-like sun still hung over Brandon as I walked from the university to Casa Maley—didn't dissuade me from the belief we were in their tire tracks. I was intoxicated by the fresh air and being ensconced in the Prairies, where the amber and green fields do not look much different from 85 years ago. For some reason it all made me feel closer to those men of 1912.

September 25/26—Portage la Prairie/Brandon/Moosomin

Bill Shwoluk, my host at Casa Maley, seemed to be having the time of his life. The stocky proprietor had raised six children singlehandedly since 1975 when his wife had died. Four children became doctors, and the other two were also in health care. Casa Maley was a rambling 1913 structure that had oak everywhere—staircases, ceiling beams and supports, wainscoting, window casings, door lintels—all built by Hugh Pearson, a woodworker from the Orkney Islands who used only hand tools to achieve his intricate woodwork. It would have been a stately home in its day, and still is, if you could ignore Bill's renovations to the basement, where his talent is on display. In the old billiard room hangs a brewery sign that Bill the artist reproduced—it was the brewery owned by former owners of Casa Maley. As well, Bill the handyman has put in a dance floor, where Bill the dance teacher teaches ballroom dancing, and in the corner is a massage table, where Bill the masseur kneads the bodies of anyone who needs his services. Upstairs, in his labyrinth of rooms, Bill the landlord is host to young women from the university: one who entertains him with her flirtatious banter and a nursing student who entertains at night on the piano. To make the mix even more eclectic, he was putting up two visiting Malawi students for 35 days. "I'll rent a movie and we'll all sit around and watch it," said Bill the waiter as he served breakfast made by Bill the chef. Bill the raconteur talked about growing up on a farm doing chores morning and night, being envious of the city boys who didn't have to work during summer holidays.

A Portage history book contains a photo of a gathering of cars outside the Portage Hotel. The caption suggests the photo is from 1913, but it really is the send-off for the Pathfinders. Although cars had been around Portage for 10 years, Wilby regarded the collection of cars as progress—just as ox-trains overtook the canoe and the dog sleds of yore, so too would the oxcarts be left behind by trains and then cars.

It is safe to say the conversations they had in 1912 differed greatly from ours. They would be happy to find a road; we took roads for granted. Wilby and Haney were preoccupied by local flora and fauna; we rarely saw animals that were still alive. Wilby wrote about huckleberry bushes on each side of the road, and someone told him to look for Prairie chickens under the silvery berry plant; the Prairie chickens, or grouse, were scarce. He'd see 50 or so kingbirds chasing their natural enemy, the hawk, through the sky; if we saw a hawk, it was a rare occasion. Animals were such a common feature of their trip, we could only surmise there were more of them 85 years before. Maybe the lack of fauna had something to do with the improvement of roads, or as Wilby argued,

> Do not highways mark the rate of human progress? Have not nations risen from obscurity to greatness and world power along their trodden ways, to vanish again into obscurity while their roads endured? The roads of Caesar and Napoleon still seam the Old World, though ancient Rome and the "Little Corporal" are gone. The Red River carts

have made way for the automobile, but the trail across the prairies westward remains.

He waxed on about roads because his chauffeurs—besides Haney, Andrus went with them as far as Brandon—"wore an air of grim disgust" after learning from Portage garages what the road ahead would be like, and expressed their disdain for prairie mud and highways and the "idiots" who built the road. "A chauffeur's point of view is intimately associated with intake valves, timing gears and tyres, and one is not surprised that he should detest a bad road with easy profanity and a suggestion of brimstone." Haney was not one to curse and swear in his later years. Maybe as a 23-year-old he was more emotional, or maybe it was Andrus who was doing all the yelling. On what became Haney's worst day of the trip, he is fairly calm that night in his diary.

Lorne remembered little of Brandon, even though that was the town the armed forces hit on a Saturday night to let off steam during the Second World War. Lorne said there was nothing on one side of the Assiniboine, but now it was all built up because of the presence of the Trans-Canada Highway on that side of the river.

Because we had been bucking a wind for two days, the car had used more fuel than the camper, which was purring along at 50 km/h while the Reo was working as hard as it could to go 50. September 25th, though, was a windless day, which made the smoke from the burn-off hover over the prairies, and gave Lorne a chance to make Vancouver look good. "It looks like everybody's burning. It's as bad as Vancouver smog." Just then we saw a man walking down the grassy corridor between the east and west lanes of the Trans-Canada. Lorne waved and honked, and the sound created instant joy for both the man and us. We reacted the same way when engineers on passing trains blasted their horn.

Even though we were still in Manitoba, we saw the first sign of oil wells—the familiar ducking heads nodding up and down. That, combined with the number of roads that were still gravel or dirt, gave us the impression of being a long way from Ontario. The lack of paved roads was a common complaint on the prairies, especially among car club members. Often they were restricted to touring on the Trans-Canada because it would be too easy to pick up stone chips on the sideroads.

Our destination this day was Moosomin, Saskatchewan, with a lunch stop in Elkhorn, home of Ike's car museum, or should I say, a testimony to the foresight of

Richard Isaac (Ike) Clarkson. The bachelor farmer started buying old cars when everyone was looking for a place to junk them—they were taking up too much space in barns. Ike made room, even though he was just farming land for a spinster named Marguerite Abblett. Eventually he had so many cars he had to create a museum.

Inside the front door is a tribute to local history, including native artifacts, a 1946 photo of Siamese calves and a pig embryo in a bottle, split at the belly to form two sets of hind legs. Take a few steps further, and be prepared for a car collectors' Nirvana. Up one aisle and down the other, the history of cars lay before us. We were drawn to the red-and-black 1908 Reo runabout, trimmed in brass, but there was so much more, like the 1917 McLaughlin, known as the Whiskey 6 because bootlegging gangsters could outrun police cars with it. Someone pointed out a fat-man steering wheel—a wheel designed to be moved aside as you entered the driver's seat. An EMF, which depending on your luck or your temperament, was known as an Everett-Metzger-Flanders or an Every Morning Fix-it. A 1909, green-and-black, four-cylinder Hupmobile touring car had a nameplate that read: "Guaranteed for life." "That was Ike's first collector car," said Ted Stremel, curator of the car museum since 1989, and an old farming friend of Ike's. A 1916 Overland motor-drive hearse sat near a 1930 American Austin—a puny thing known as "a teacher's car."

The museum had a licence plate collection that would have made that kid outside Sault Ste. Marie drool. "Sunny Manitoba" became "Friendly Manitoba," which irritated the francophone community that September for the absence of a French translation. They also had a plate from the Canadian Army base in Germany and an old Michigan plate that said "Water Wonderland." The plates were next to a stuffed two-headed calf that was born on the farm of Carl Anderson. "It lived three days with its two identical heads," said Marilyn Stremel, Ted's wife. "It had four eyes and two ears. That's the extent of our oddities, other than the people around here." She enjoys meeting the world's car fanatics who migrate to this town next to the Saskatchewan border, but she feels the cars are the biggest characters in the place. "I have a hard time remembering one name from another, but each one's so individual. I dust them once a week. They seem like people. My uncle had an old Buick. I thought it was the best car in the world. It purred along when I took farm goods back and forth. I got to drive it on the gravel roads. Out in the country they are all gravel roads. Just the main highway is paved."

194

Ted described Ike as "a big Irishman with large hands and an awful temper. This was his life. He was a poor farmer. He got a lot of the cars for free. All the old ones here were his. He had close to 100 cars. Some guy offered him $100,000 for them all, but he wouldn't take it. He died in '71 with cancer of the spine. He laid on the couch out front and suffered for a couple of years. Then the cancer moved into his neck. This museum started in '61. Eventually the town put a building up in '67."

Ike was pretty handy, so people would take things to him to fix, but it was not a good idea to get on his wrong side, said Ted. "He'd tell you where to go in short order. He had a truck somebody said was piece of junk. He'd lift his little finger that was the size of your thumb, and he'd wag that finger in your face and say: 'That's not junk.' If only everybody had his foresight." Although he was only six-foot-one or six-foot-two, Ted said Ike was larger-than-life. He had two spinster sisters. One was still alive, as was his "cousin," the woman Ike farmed six quarter-sections for. "For her Ike grew a little grain, but they had mostly cows. He lived there with her. They weren't chummy chummy. He just lived there. Before he came she had some bad managers. He'd take care of her, take her into town with the car."

Ike's sister, Marion "Gussy" Clarkson, and "cousin" Marguerite Abblett, were both in their nineties and living at the Elkwood Manor Personal Care Home, which was near the museum.

"The first time anybody ever farmed that land, my father farmed it," said Marguerite, 93, who came to the foyer first. "He got there in very late 1880s. We had cattle, grain and milk cows. When my father passed away, Ike was the first one we hired. Ike Clarkson had several cars before I knew he was in the business. He was a splendid character, smart and kind, very efficient at everything he did. The last of his family is his sister. She's in for repairs here. Sick people come in for repairs. She lived by herself. Ike Clarkson had his cars in a farm building next to us. It wasn't a vast number. Not very many, but they were very good cars."

I told her I heard Ike was a big man.

"No, he was normal in every way," she said. "He wasn't much bigger than me. He was smarter than most. He was naturally intelligent. What he read and heard he kept in his mind." When I suggested he could have made a lot of money from selling his cars, she responded: "He liked money but cars were like jewels to him. There was no sense giving them away after you got them. A car that couldn't run wasn't worth much in those days. He could make them run, bring them back to life." Just then, Gussy arrived.

Gussy, a month shy of 91, started by saying her brother "was always interested in machines and things like that," a phrase she repeated a dozen times. "If he had more education, he would have liked to have flown an airplane. He was born five miles east of Elkhorn, 4-12-27," which in prairie parlance is the lot, concession and quadrant. "It was No. 1 Highway in those days. Now it's old No. 1 Highway. Ike was always interested in machinery..."

Ike also liked animals, Marguerite said. He even fed a wolf on the Stoneham farm. Gussy, whose dentures slacked out of her mouth when she wasn't speaking, said he was coming home from Elkhorn with groceries when a wolf jumped up and took a loaf of bread from him. Instead of being an animal lover, she remembers him trapping animals to eat or to sell their fur. Marguerite said he "was very kind." Gussy countered, "He was quick-tempered. He was interested in airplanes too."

Marguerite interrupted. "He wasn't out of proportion," discounting the earlier insinuation he was big. "I remember being at a dance one time. Something was wrong with a musical instrument. I was dancing with him. He played the mouth organ, but that's all. When the instrument broke, the fellows went outside to have a little drink—the ones who were supposed to be playing. They were amazed Ike picked up the instrument, fixed it and then played it. It was some square-box deal."

"A violin," said Gussy.

"It wasn't," said Marguerite. "It was a square box. He hadn't played it before."

"He played the violin," said Gussy.

Marguerite, by now getting fed up with Gussy, said: "I was there. He was 19 years old...I wish he was here." Marguerite would smile every so often, as if in another world with her reminiscences. The dance story was either news to Gussy, or she had forgotten that her brother might have been close to Marguerite. "He was good company," Marguerite allowed. "We built a granary together. That was to put the cars in when he brought them home."

"What he's done with that museum is due to Marguerite's mother and her," said Gussy, getting emotional, with tears sliding down her cheeks and her dentures sliding out of her mouth. "And you let him ride that nice horse. The horse he'd ride to go trapping and hunting." Gussy said Ike's grandparents were the first settlers in these parts. "My mother played piano. Ike made the violin he used to play. He taught himself to play. Everything he tried he would accomplish."

"We were at a dance at the Victor one time," said Marguerite, without missing a beat. "We were having a good time. You don't have to put in that I was Ike's partner at the time when the music stopped..."

Ike was 58 when he died in 1971. May he rest in peace, whatever the real story is on him. Maybe Ike didn't marry Marguerite because she was nine years older. She was obviously protective of her man, as though she was closer to Ike than his sister. Marguerite evidently felt more lucid than his sister. Before I left, she said: "You'll do wonderfully well if you can make anything out of that."

Outside of Elkhorn the Reo suffered its first 1997 breakdown: a small brass waterline broke, causing the car to overheat. Lorne didn't take long to fix it, and we were on our way to Moosomin, where General Andrew McNaughton of Second World War fame was born in 1887. Moosomin was also the site of the big surprise—the Findlays' 49th wedding anniversary. When we arrived at the Moosomin post office, the postmaster was keen to see Lorne and Irene Findlay, who had 44 pieces of general delivery mail. They even got cards from folks we met in New Brunswick, Nova Scotia and Quebec City. It was all orchestrated by Lorne's sister Babs, with the help of Peter, who would later decorate the car with streamers and wedding bell balloons to chauffeur his parents down Moosomin's main street.

The *Moosomin World Spectator* newspaper offices had back issues. An item in one said the National Highway Pathfinder attending a Board of Trade meeting: "Mr. Wilby gave an intensely interesting and practical address on the advantages of good roads, and was very favourably impressed with the idea of Broadway Avenue becoming a part of the Canadian National Highway."

Broadway Avenue still existed, but it was no longer part of the Trans-Canada. Pearl Jamieson, a local historian, took Broadway on her way back to her Gertie Street home. She has 5 kids, 9 grandchildren and 11 great-grandchildren. "Had a bunch of them this weekend, nearly killed me," said the 73-year-old. "They make me happy twice—when they come and when they go." In her shed she had a sign with a red square on it that designated the Red Route. The sign was hung up on the side of buildings, showing motorists the best way across the country. While we leafed through old newspaper clippings, she said sarcastically, "They were the good old days, I don't remember anything good about them." The first car she remembers is an old Model T with brass. "Cralley Hyslop had it. He left it at home and took his horse and buggy into town. He would polish it every day. During the Depression they turned the Model T into the Bennett buggy [after Prime Minister R.B. Bennett]. The horses pulled the Model Ts when they couldn't afford gas."

She, too, knew Ike, who was a friend of her husband John. "He was the type of guy who found a horn and built a car around it. When he died, he left it to the government. There wasn't a thing to say it belonged to Ike. He was a good old stick. Marguerite was always hovering when we went to visit. She was a quiet woman; Ike was very vocal. She was his 'housekeeper.' That's the way they called it in those days. Ike rued the day he didn't get married. He'd tell my husband 'You have heirs. I don't.' He always brought that up. It was kind of sad."

This day would also be sad for Haney. He began by taking the wrong fork in the road, which led them through a wheat field and into a swamp, and after pulling out of that, they went through a grassy field until the Reo sank into a slough up to its hubs and axles. Again, in *Motoring Magazine*, Haney is more jocular about it all, describing Andrus as "built on a very generous scale; he has a goodly share of muscle, and we found him very useful in many ways—such as building corduroy roads out of alkali sloughs, wading into holes to see how deep they are, and so forth." They managed to raise the car with a jack and then fed the hole with sheaves of wheat, boulders and whatever they could lay their hands on. They put on the Reo's anti-skid chains and constructed a road so it could return to safety. When they found the correct route, Wilby's description could have come from our Reo:

> At first the land flung itself up into great barren hills sprinkled with various stunted growths, and then it gently rose and fell in solid waves. Tiny lakes lay in the hollows of the bluffs, full of reeds which gave shelter to moor hens. Then came homely, pastoral scenes— fields of golden grain, cows browsing on rich pasture, and farmhouses embowered within plantations of sheltering trees.

But it was after they arrived in Brandon at 5:30 p.m. that Haney received his worst news—he finally got a reply from the Winnipeg wires, in which he listed his rows with Wilby. "Received telegrams from Fifield saying that signs are not needed, and from Lazelle saying that Wilby is Captain," he wrote in his diary, with Captain heavily underlined. "Come Damn near bidding the Reo 'a trip to Hell' and I would get another job, but have concluded to stick it out till I got across or fired."

Wilby, meanwhile, had an audience in Brandon, and he didn't waste it. He told the *Brandon Sun* reporter they missed two pilot cars sent out to greet them, but they had the best trail yet between Portage and Brandon, better than ones he found in the United States. He was met by President Schwartz of the Auto Club, W.A. Elliott and other prominent citizens. Wilby was impressed that Mayor Fleming of Brandon was so concerned about the trip, calling him by telephone in Winnipeg and wiring him in Portage. "Nothing can exceed the experience of riding over the undulating trails between Sewell and Douglas where the scenery on either side is very delightful." For some reason, Wilby began using "the need of women" pitch to make sure the national highway is built. "If the Daughters of the Empire and other such organizations would lend their assistance he thought the great coast to coast highway would be an established fact much sooner than otherwise," said *The Sun*.

They stayed at the Prince Edward, a Canadian Northern railway hotel that was opened three months before by a gala featuring an abundance of satin, lace, chiffon and Charmeuse gowns. The hotel was overambitious for its day, but it prompted Wilby to say it was up to the standard of anything he had seen in Canada "outside the great capital cities. I would like to find such hotels all along the route." The Prince Eddie, like many other hotels of its day, was demolished in the 1970s.

At Brandon city hall the morning after Haney learned by telegraph that "Wilby is Captain." He wrote in his diary: "Come Damn near bidding the Reo 'a trip to Hell.' "

AUTOMOBILE AS A "CURE,"

September, 1912 Berlin, Germany—The automobile now figures in medical literature as a therapeutic agent. It is said to exert a favourable effect in certain nervous disorders. At a meeting of the Berlin Society for Psychiatry and Nervous Diseases a paper was read on habitual vertigo from which it appeared that this condition is less apparent to the patient when riding in automobiles or railway trains. Another contributor stated that the patient with habitual vertigo feels in better spirits on an automobile or railway journey, and this is also true of patients with paralysis agitans. He would attribute the favourable result to the involuntary motion imparted by the vehicle, which antagonizes the sensations of vertigo and tremor. One of his patients with paralysis agitans takes several rides daily on an auto omnibus.

HEALTH DISTRICT RAISES CONCERNS ABOUT ROAD,

September, 1997, Indian Head, Saskatchewan—The Pipestone health district board has raised concerns about the safety of the TransCanada Highway. It is calling on the provincial government to twin the eastern portion of the highway as soon as possible. As health board members discussed the concerns at a recent meeting, they all seemed to have their own horror stories of their experiences traveling on Highway 1. In a letter to the Highways and Transportation Minister, the board pointed out that over the last three years, seven fatalities have occurred on the section of the TransCanada from Indian Head to the Manitoba border. Overall, fatal accidents are up 38 per cent in Saskatchewan and injuries are up 11 per cent for the first half of 1997, when compared with 1996. The first half of 1997 had close to 13,000 accidents, 51 of which resulted in one or more fatalities, and 2,370 of those accidents resulted in one or more persons injured. Only 27 per cent of fatal accidents were alcohol related, compared with a pre-1996 average of nearly 40.

Chapter 11

A Rough Ride in Saskatchewan

September 26—Moosomin

After a well-deserved rest, Wilby and Haney's morning began with a photo-shoot in front of the Prince Eddie, with the Brandon pennant proudly displayed on the Reo. Andrus headed back to Winnipeg, while automobilist W.A. Elliott agreed to pilot the pair to Elkhorn, where another pilot would meet them. At this point Wilby was saying his due date in Vancouver would be October 12, a more realistic guess after his delays in Winnipeg. A rime frost lay over Brandon, and Wilby stressed that keeping Jack Frost at bay in September and October is more important to the farmer than political change or, he mused, "the possible end of the world."

In bright, clear and milder weather than the day before, Wilby set out with Elliott—an architect in a heavy overcoat and goggles—along the "pink and purple hills of the Assiniboine." Elliott pointed out the silvery sheen of the spear grass, the tufts of sage and the red haws of the Prairie rose. "Only a month ago," said Elliott in Wilby's book, "the heavy rains made the whole countryside beautiful with a colored carpet of flowers. I never before saw the Prairies look so lovely."

They passed natives in "store clothing," wrote Wilby, disappointed not to see the "Indian in his embroidered tunic, his scalping knife and his war-whoop." But he admired the Canadian approach to allow the natives to have their land, as opposed to the American belief they should be moved to government-established reservations. The natives passed by in buggies, and would allow themselves to be photographed for a quarter. At Elkhorn there was a native school, "where the Red Man, through his children, is being tamed to modern uses." Wilby's attitude wasn't politically correct in late-20th-century eyes, but it was common at the time.

At Elkhorn, the Pathfinders said goodbye to Elliott and were piloted across the Saskatchewan border by a Mr. Flanders, "a school inspector." I ended my day at the bed and breakfast home of a school inspector. We had started the day at the home of Bill Dennstedt, who had come by the night before when we were in the motel diner, about to celebrate the 49th anniversary with a Dairy Queen cake. Bill didn't want to leave until we assured him we'd drop by. The next day he showed off his McLaughlin, the same body as a Whiskey 6, but he had jerry-built some of the car. "It had an amazing engine for its time," Bill showed us under the naked bulb in his old garage. "The circulation is the same as a modern car, with full oil pressures and a drilled crankshaft. The Chev didn't have that until '53."

One of Bill's friends was Bill Dixon, who said the car was "just a pile of nothing when Bill bought these here." His arm was withered, so he felt compelled to explain. "I got this arm caught in a grain auger, cleaning out a grain bin. I fell over the wire and fell backwards. The auger grabbed my arm and fed it in. I used to curl and play ball a lot." Another friend was Charlie Diamond, 76, who explained why part of his hand was missing. "The damned saw never stopped cutting. I was shaping a fence-post at work. I slipped on the pieces of wood. I did that in '69." Dennstedt himself was 80, and he had all of his faculties and, for that matter, body parts. "When we were boys, cars were something," he said. "The old highway went out past our farm. We used to sit and watch all the cars go by and memorize their names." Asked about his enthusiasm for rebuilding them, he added, "When you retire you like to revert back, both for physical and mental well-being. The curious mind is still there. I also bought a computer. A computer is good for a person."

Bill and the boys also knew Ike, and his friends backed up my theory for "As the Prairie Turns." Ike is like Prince Charles, and Marguerite is his Camilla, the older woman he couldn't marry.

We left town past the hotel that Wilby and Haney must have stayed in, but it was now a strip club. On the way westward, Moosomin is 221 kilometres to Regina, and the cruise across Saskatchewan gave us the feeling of being in the west. Trains full of wheat cars seem to be passing us by the hour, giving the impression the train business was healthy. The public garbage cans were shaped like grain elevators, and the real ones interrupted the flat horizons. Every so often we'd see a house protected by a row of multicoloured poplars. It wasn't that windy yet, but the windbreaks reminded us of a conversation at Bill's. In the early part of the century, motorists couldn't use their autos some days because the wind could rip the roof off or push a car over. We saw a muskrat roadkill, and Lorne said the muskrat was a little slow getting his comfy room together underground. He said they usually hibernate in late August and don't come out until late April.

One of the cars we had seen the day before was a Star, which prompted Lorne to recall its history. The Stars had such a good engine that when they got old, owners stripped the engines and adapted them for commercial fishing boats on both coasts. It had a pressure-fed oiling system, whereas most of the early cars had a scoop system to oil the bearings on the crankshaft. The Star was made by Durant Company, which was started by General Motors' founder William Durant after he got ousted from GM a second time. The Star used continental engines, whereas most of the early companies, like the Reo, built their own engines. Durant latched on to the idea that would become the hallmark of the auto industry, especially toward the end of the 20th century—outsourcing, where major automakers hire smaller companies to feed them parts.

Our destination this day was Indian Head—a guess as to where the Pathfinders ended up, albeit a wrong one. Wilby had a photo in his book of 11 grain elevators, taken from a great height, and a car circling around a road to where the photo was taken. As well, Haney in his diary said he bought gas in Indian Head, so in planning the trip we assumed they bought gas where they stayed for the night. It turns out they made the 221-kilometre trip from Moosomin to Regina in one day, but because we were ahead of them, this would be one way of making sure we would start coinciding with the 85th anniversary of their movements the next day.

Indian Head, first settled in 1882 just before the CPR came through, got its name from a disease that killed most of the local natives in 1883. On a Friday afternoon it was a sleepy town, and the lone bed and breakfast was quiet. While waiting for the owners to return, I met a man named Allen Cole, who stopped when he spotted the 1912 Reo. I showed him the photo of Indian Head from the book and he identified it as being taken from the barn at the old experimental farm, where he worked from 1952 until 1990. There's a house in the photo which he said had been moved across town, which he would show me. An Apostolic minister had the house relocated because he wanted to start a boy's school 15 years ago. They brought it over in winter right across the field when the ground was frozen, otherwise it would sink out of sight, he said. But they had trouble bringing it over the railway tracks. Not only did the house start to fall apart going over the tracks, being dragged by big "Cats" but "one guy got electrocuted by hydro wire. He didn't die but he'll be crippled the rest of his life." As we drove to the house, the country radio station in his car was playing "Time Marches On."

The entire experience of Indian Head had the feeling of time passing: Cole's story about the small grain elevator moved from the experimental farm to become a teahouse near the tracks; the front steps and deck of the relocated house remaining near the experimental farm; the winding driveway to the farm itself, where a stand of blue spruce trees were much larger than in the 1912 photo; and the vantage point where the photo was taken, a vent in the middle of a tall barn, was no longer accessible. Determined to duplicate that photo, I scaled a ladder at the side of the barn to a platform next to a circular window underneath the eaves of the barn's peak. The window was covered in years of grime, foul evidence of fowl, cobwebs and hundreds of buzzing flies. Cole, 61, scaled the ladder as if he were a kid again. He gave me a tissue to try to clean the window enough to take a photo. I snapped away but the row of spruce obliterated the background. Then again, only three of 13 grain elevators remained from the days when Indian Head was one of the largest shippers of grain in North America. In 1909, according to local sources, more grain was shipped out of Indian Head than anyplace in North America.

"Some elevators are privately owned by big farmers and others got bought out by big companies," said Cole. "They disappeared because the spouts that handle the grain are bigger, the way of moving grain is so much superior and faster, so they don't need as much space. They put through 1.5 million bushels a year. It goes mainly west to Vancouver, but once in a while goes to Thunder Bay." Those are the only trains that go through town, because VIA Rail had stopped its cross-country service on the CPR tracks. "Our station was torn down seven or eight years ago. It was a fantastic station, with marble floors. It's identical to the one in Moose Jaw."

Cole was bigger than I am and I thought he would have broken the platform, if not the ladder. Staying up among the hundreds of flies, and at the dizzying, sure-to-kill-you height, was also nerve-racking. When I finally got a chance to climb down, I did my impression of the Pope on airport tarmac. An unfazed Cole pointed back up to a steel rod that went from one end of the huge barn to the other. "When I was young and foolish I went hand over hand the length of it—twice."

The experimental farm, one of five across the country, was built in 1886. It is also one reason Indian Head was so well-protected from Prairie winds. The trees that grew from seedlings at the farm made their way around the city. The wealth of trees actually gives residents a false sense of security in the winter. A storm could be raging on the Trans-Canada and no one in town would know how severe it was until they crossed the track and hit the road. The trees added to the town's great ambience. The main street was broad, had handy angular parking and no stoplights, and only yield signs for traffic coming from sideroads. Either it is a sleepy town, or the lack of traffic suggests cars are being used as originally intended for Sunday drives and getting the farmer into town.

Before Cole dropped me off at the B & B, he told me his claim to fame was being the father of Brent Cole, the second-ranked Canadian heavyweight boxer who lost his title fight to Willie DeWit in 1984, the Olympic year. Saskatchewan is also famous for Gas Eichel who was once a punching bag for Joe Louis, when Eichel boxed out of the Lard Gym in Regina.

The real Pathfinders arrived in Moosomin at 5 p.m., intending to pick up a pilot and continue to Regina, only to find a ghost town. Most of the residents were fighting the fire at the creamery or dairy, as Wilby called it. The fire began in the chimney and spread to the upper part of the building, destroying the roof and upper storey, leaving only walls standing. The butter and cold storage stock and supplies were saved, but it would be hugely inconvenient for the farmers to the north, south and west who had delivered their cream and poultry to the local institution.

By coincidence I ended up talking about farmers' milk that night at an Indian Head bar, where the $5.95 steak special had drawn a crowd. While some people played the video lottery terminals, one woman at the next table ended a day of times-are-a-changing stories by saying only a few people keep cows to produce their own milk—"it was unpasteurised, but it never hurt us"—and even fewer fatten up cattle to chop it up themselves. Most people who raise a cow for its meat will have it sent out to a butcher.

After the hijinx of the Moosomin fire, the mayor and board of trade members assembled for Wilby's speech that night at the town hall. Wilby jokingly maligned the three-storey building because it was also the town opera house, fire station, dance hall and council chamber. But he had a fondness for places like Moosomin,

> a town hardly big enough to hold its own name, open at both ends wide to the Prairie...the Prairies would be a dull stagnant world indeed if they were not dotted with these incipient towns. Without any apparent history, these little Prairie communities are going to be the salvation of the Dominion for many decades to come.

September 27—Indian Head

I spent the night protected by a 1906 house that was protected by maple trees in the older section of Indian Head, but the rattling windows reminded me that the wind is still the dominant force on the landscape. When I arose to see a boy riding his bike one-handed past the B & B, carefree as can be, the small town became intoxicating. It felt safe—even the kids who assembled the night before strolled through the town without worrying about cars whizzing by and blasting them off the street. They were also unafraid of strangers, even polite.

The morning began with a vain attempt to find a newspaper from Indian Head that might have recalled Haney and Wilby's trip through town. Ken McCabe, editor of the *Indian Head and Wolseley News*, greeted me down at his offices, which also happened to house the rural sports hall of fame and museum in a small strip mall. They didn't have any 1912 newspapers, but I learned that hockey player Dave Karpa of the Anaheim Mighty Ducks is from Indian Head, as is Eric Petersen of the TV show *Street Legal*. Tiger Williams, the former Toronto Maple Leaf, Vancouver Canuck and all-round tough guy, is from Weyburn, 70 miles south. Gordie Howe is from Floral near Saskatoon. Howe and all five Bentley hockey-playing brothers would come here in the summer for the baseball tournament at Indian Head. Ken had tournament artifacts, including all the scorecards from July 1952 when Florida Cubans beat Baton Rouge, Louisiana, 5-3 in the final game. The museum also had an old polo stick, indicating that polo was a popular local sport when Wilby and Haney drove through.

Asked why he started the museum, McCabe explained that he grew up as the child of a single parent. "My father just upped and left when I was four or five. I had to rely on other people. I played every sport and sport meant so much to me. I had a little collection of my own so I put this together, and induct people into the hall of fame. Now I have over 300 to the induction dinner."

The early sports were influenced by immigrants from Europe. Even though baseball and hockey came to dominate, soccer and golf were big in the early days, the golf club beginning in 1903, said McCabe. "They must have lost a lot of balls in the Prairie scrub, at 30 cents a piece."

Our launch that morning was from the big Indian Head, just off the highway, where members of the Regina Antique Automobile Association congregated. Milton Rogne, who drove a quarter-ton, Model A pick-up truck, said his truck sold new for $460 in 1928. It was repossessed for $20 in 1931. In chatting about all the Indian Head elevators that are no more, Milton said, "It used to be you went into a town and there'd be an elevator, a church and a school. Now that's not always the case." He said it was lucky we came the week we did, because more farmers were free at this time of year. "It was a wet spring so we had a late gathering, but we'd normally only harvest flax this late in the year."

Once on the road, into a headwind for a sunny 136-kilometre ride into Regina, piloted by a '36 Packard 120 sedan, Lorne told the story of his repeat visitors at the campsite. While dropping me off at the library, he met a woman, her mother and her child. The woman followed the Findlays to their campsite, came back again at night and didn't want to leave. "The woman had been married to an alcoholic husband who used to beat the kids," said Lorne. "The mother said it's nice for the kids to be part of the trip. It's the biggest thing that's happened to them in six years. The girl has a journal day on Wednesday at school so she has an exclusive. She's 11. The boy is 6. They were the politest, nicest kids."

Lorne himself is the fifth of seven children, with three brothers and three sisters. His father lived until he was 100, and is mother was still alive in a Penticton nursing home at age 101. He was concerned his mother would die before the Reo could get to her. On the way into Regina his youngest sister, Marie Lofgren, her husband, children and grandchildren waved to us from the side of the road.

Before we left Indian Head, Lorne backed up the Reo in line with the large Indian Head at the side of the highway. While a hawk rode the Prairie winds above us, Lorne wanted to put the image at a distance above his radiator cap so he could turn his Reo into a Pontiac—Pontiac, the car, was named after Pontiac, the native. An

Indian head was the hood ornament on early Pontiacs. It's a detail no longer used, partly for aerodynamics but mostly because they were too easy to vandalize.

The early marketing of cars, explained Lorne, really took off with some famous ads. One of them was a picture of the Olds Limited, the one the Pathfinders saw in New Brunswick, that was so large it had two running boards. In the famous ad the Olds is racing the *Lakeshore Limited*, the famous railway train out of Chicago. In the car the driver's scarf is at a rakish angle to denote speed.

As Regina loomed in the distance, the big dilemma was trying to identify the roadkills. Lorne guessed that we had seen a red fox and a coyote, which was confirmed by our fellow antique auto drivers following us in a procession.

The Pathfinders rose early in Moosomin for the long drive into Regina, and after a breakfast at a "scrubby, little restaurant," where Wilby said they were served by "John Chinaman," they headed off with James Hart as pilot. Hart told them to expect a rough trail, a good deal of cross-country and bushland travel, and warned them to beware of alkali sloughs. For all his confidence they got lost, having missed a fork in the road, but Wilby was sympathetic, saying "a hawk would have missed it. Indeed, no guide on the Prairies had been altogether certain of his bearings, since there is either a confusing monotony in these great levels or the plough and fence obliterate or usurp the familiar trails."

Farmers' "flimsy, shabby frame" houses also irritated Wilby. They were treeless, gardenless, fenceless, set amongst the wealth of golden wheat. In the living-room, the red curtains, stretched across one corner, hid a bed. On the painted floor lay two rugs. The furniture was a table, a stove, a rocking chair and a couch. The ceiling was formed of sheet iron stamped with a decorative classical device. The walls were painted white and were hung with hard and staring family photographs. Leading from this room was the dining-room, bare of floor and ornamented by a long table and half a dozen chairs, a stove and an almanac. The kitchen stood open to the Prairie. An uncarpeted staircase led to the bedrooms. The windows were screened, the sashes being ropeless and the upper one immovable. To hold the lower half of the window open, it would be necessary to prop it up by a stick from the wood-pile.

Oh, the shame of it all. It makes you wonder whether Wilby returned to that homestead after the book was published. Would he dare? Wilby wanted to see picturesque houses with an oriel window, a gabled and vine-clad porch, or a thatched cottage bright with flowers. He reasoned that the simplicity of the Prairie home may be "following some law that was guiding Canada to paths of Spartan greatness and to national virility." But he caught himself and suggested that his Old World judgment may not be respecting the honour due a pioneer farmer settling and enriching vast stretches of what was once thought to be unproductive land.

The original Reo made its way to Qu'Appelle, and although Wilby wanted to follow the old fur-trading trails to the north, which he thought must lead to the Pole itself, they came south through Indian Head and after dusk, made it into Regina. The setting sun lit "the clouds on fire with redness." On their way, yellow gophers scampered to their holes, and the sound of the motor disturbed "a solitary coyote who slunk off to his lair." If only the coyote we had seen had made it to his lair.

We had a few receptions, one at the Speedy store, where TV cameras awaited, another at Bob and Ann Meyers' farmhouse, where there was a display of what Lorne called "cars, aircraft and related items" in what used to be a mushroom farm. Lorne wrote in his diary: "Quite a crowd was there and we all had a profitable time playing games, eating and looking at cars and stuff." One game involved putting a name to old objects on the table, and then trying to justify your explanation of what the thingamajig did. Later they went off to Russ Kelly's farm, north of town, where the club had their annual smoky barbecue until it got dark. "Lots of good food and more games along with good conversations with fine people (including my relatives) brought a fine ending to a memorable day. Still, starry and chilly night." Meanwhile, I missed the festivities to head into town to get to the library.

When Wilby and Haney arrived, the shop windows were still full of photos of the cyclone that had levelled many of the buildings. In his book Wilby used a famous photo showing the Presbyterian church, the Masonic lodge and the library with damaged roofs and devoid of windows. It is taken from the middle of Victoria Park. The church is now known as Knox Metropolitan United, the Masonic Lodge still exists and the Carnegie Library was demolished in 1960 to make way for a soulless building. If there was any doubt what the Prairie wind can do, the victims of the cyclone are buried at Broad Street and Fourth Avenue.

Councillor Vic McDougall drove me to an exquisite B & B on a semi-circular street shaded in old elms the city is consciously protecting from disease. The trees, said McDougall, are "very sacred to me" and the people of Regina, because the town, when founded in 1882, was as bald as could be. Even the lake surrounding what Wilby called the "palatial Parliament buildings" was built by hand. It reminded me of David Ben Gurion's mid-century line about "making the desert bloom."

After they found the right route, Haney and Wilby enjoyed their longest day's run since the military roads near Kingston, arriving at 7 p.m. Although the automobile club had a banquet planned for Wilby the next night, they did round up enough people to hear him give his spiel at the Assiniboia Club. He regretted, along with the club, not having a bigger crowd. For Wilby the more people he could reach in his speeches, the better were the chances of a national highway being built.

Wilby told the group he was pleased with the signposts that had been placed around Regina, "as it marked out the best and shortest road for strangers and thus freed touring of many of its worries." The club had first expected them last week, and had planned to put out more signs as they escorted the Pathfinders to Moose Jaw. Wilby was impressed to learn that Saskatchewan had the most advanced motoring legislation in the country. It required all vehicles to obey the same laws, but they were without any speed limits—an early autobahn, as it were.

"The building of a macadam road from one coast to the other would, in a very real sense, wipe out the distinction between east and west," Wilby told them. He referred to a speech by former Prime Minister Sir Wilfrid Laurier, saying that "within 25 years, there would be no east and no west but one country." Wilby also tried to boast that a road would bring a million-dollar hotel to town, but that was met with laughter from the automobile club executive.

Wilby also laughed when he heard a story at the Club about a prominent man who had been caught by the cyclone while having his bath.

> "His bathroom was instantaneously demolished, and before he could scramble out of his tub, he found himself sailing over the city on the breeze at a fifty-knot clip," said my interlocutor over a cocktail in the smoke room. "He was always a man of quick resources and ready expediency...Anyhow he never once lost his presence of mind in spite of his Lady Godiva appearance, but he seized hold of the 'hot and

cold' taps with both hands and started steering his craft. Would you believe it, he found it answered the helm like a cat-boat, and he at once turned it a point or two so as to bring him to the waterworks. There he descended, filled the tub again and calmly finished his interrupted bath! You can take it from me that he's the proudest man in Regina today!"

Wilby said they managed to get a bed at the leading hotel, which was either the King's Hotel, which was demolished in the 1980s, or the Empire Hotel, which was made famous in a song by Joni Mitchell, "Sitting in the lounge of the Empire Hotel..." While sitting in the lounge of a hotel, Wilby met an English salesman who was making his way west, and kept overtaking the Pathfinders by train. In what must have been a knee-slapper of a night, the man rushed up to Wilby and stopped him just at the instant he put a glass of water to his lips. "Don't!" exclaimed the red-cheeked Londoner. Wilby mentioned "Ottawa?" The man nodded. "Nobody drinks the water in Regina, old chap, if he's wise. Jolly bad medicine, I can tell you." The alkali kept making its way into the water table, so the man warned Wilby about drinking the water across the Prairies. "It's beastly stuff—worse than a dose of salts. Well, good luck to you. I've got to hurry off now. See you in Vancouver!"

Unbeknownst to Wilby, the reason he would make it out to Vancouver was going to occupy a seat in his Reo the next day.

September 28—Regina

Now that we were working on the same days as the Pathfinders, I wanted to fall behind, or at least get to the archives on the Monday morning. That meant I missed the trip's most dramatic day. The 1912 cyclone decided to come back this way again on the journey to Moose Jaw. The Findlays began from Kelly's farm at 10:15 a.m., driving behind a '38 Pontiac, into what Lorne called a "fierce" headwind. After taking photos at the Parliament buildings which overlook Wascana Lake, the Reo was lucky to make 32 km/h, with Lorne's foot to the floor. Lorne says his back and shoulders were stiff from keeping the car on the road, especially during the gusts. Tumbleweeds scooted across the roadway, small objects and dust flew everywhere. The wind came in gusts from the passenger side of the windshield, or from north-by-northwest, threatening to rip the roof off or toss the Reo on its side.

"We had opened up the large rear window thinking that the wind would blow right on through, but we had underestimated the determination of that wind," wrote Lorne in his diary. "Without doubt it wanted to destroy us. Happily, that nasty wind had, in turn, underestimated the strength of the Reo and we made it through, finally, to Moose Jaw." Both Lorne and Bob Meyers, who accompanied Lorne on the ordeal, were hoarse from hollering their conversation at each other over the roar of the wind. After the ordeal, Lorne said they "laughed at the exhilaration of the experience; one that Bob was familiar with, but that I had never before experienced."

The winds that day were reported at 96 km/h, with gusts up to 144 km/h. I didn't notice it so much as a pedestrian walking to Taylor Field for a Saskatchewan Roughrider game. In Ottawa, author and newspaper columnist Roy McGregor told me not to underestimate the value of the car in the Prairies, especially when it came to citizens arriving from all over the province for their hometown Roughrider games. Sure enough, as soon as I got into the parking lot, I saw a man driving in with a woman reclined on a pillow in the passenger seat. Either they had just driven halfway across the province to see the 'Riders play the Edmonton Eskimos, as many Rider fans do, or the driver had just dragged his wife out of a hospital bed to go to the game. Up on the second deck, fans had to crawl up the stairs to avoid being blown over by the winds. Anyone with beer would have to put their hand over the cup, for the wind would pick up the beer and slap someone with suds 13 seats away. To answer author W.O. Mitchell's question: We had seen the wind.

Regina was first inhabited as a buffalo hunting camp called Pile O' Bones, or at least it was so-named because of all the buffalo skeletons in the area. In the 1880s, with the coming of the CPR, it was renamed in honour of Queen Victoria. It had about 2,000 inhabitants in 1902, and grew to 30,000 by the time Haney and Wilby arrived, chiefly because of an ad campaign in the east and Europe that promised a quarter section homestead to any male over 18, providing he appeared in person at the district land agency. So many males responded that they had to advertise for groups of women to meet the pioneers. Signs like, *Please do not spit on sidewalks*, were erected to encourage men to be civil enough to catch a woman. The city's most famous landmark was the North West Mounted Police barracks. Through one window of the barracks in 1885, Louis Riel stepped out with a rope around his neck.

For the Pathfinders, it was one of those hobnobbing days Wilby loved. He met with acting Premier Calder, and the Hon. A.P. McNab, minister in charge of roads. To both he tried to impress the need for a good transprovincial road to link with other provinces. Calder maintained the province had already set aside $5 million on its good roads policy. He felt the province should look after the farmer first before the tourist. Wilby insisted that road money shouldn't be dissipated. "The road of the tourist is the road of the farmer," and the province should organize it instead of letting municipalities build and maintain roads of haphazard quality. He said that problem existed all over North America, which led to situations like Winnipeg, where car owners are virtually hostages in their own cities because of the lack of roads. Something must be done for Regina drivers. Citizens there owned more cars per capita than any other city in the Dominion. Wilby liked what he saw of Regina, whether it was the lawns and trees or the fact it was "thickly sprinkled with motor-cars" and it was within easy driving distance of the Qu'Appelle Valley and its chain of lakes made famous in the poems of Pauline Johnson.

At a ceremony in front of city hall, Wilby's reconnaissance allowed him to boast about the city's bounty. The automobile association gave Wilby an auto badge, and the mayor's wife, Mrs. Peter McAra, told him Regina was honoured by his visit, and sincerely hoped his journey from coast to coast would facilitate a permanent transcontinental highway. Before he left at 3 p.m., she pinned on a Regina pennant and one from the Portage la Prairie Auto Club which failed to give him one during his visit. The *Regina Leader Post* said prominent auto club members led them to Pense, where members of the Moose Jaw club guided the threesome onwards. Morley Wright piloted them west, said Haney in his diary, but the new third man elicited only a brief notation: "Got to Moose Jaw 6:30 p.m. with Wise along as help."

The modest reference to Earl S. Wise—the S did not stand for anything—belies his significance to the trip. The Michigan farmboy had worked for the Reo Motor Car Company in his native Lansing, and in St. Catharines briefly, before he was shipped to Regina in 1911 to work for William James Wright, an agent for agricultural implements and Reo cars and trucks. During his stay in St. Catharines he lived in the same boarding house as Haney. Like Haney he was 23 (four months older), his mother also died when he was a child, and he was the oldest, on whom the family relied to do more than his share of chores. In Wise, Haney had someone with whom to talk about cars, air his grievances, and someone with whom he could work in times of trouble. The Reo company sent Wise along to get the car across the mountains of British Columbia, but more importantly, he literally saved Haney's psyche.

Wise was shy, thoughtful six-footer with sparkling blue eyes, but he enjoyed a bit of craziness, and his antics also defused whatever edge Wilby had. Wilby might have liked him because Wise's parents came from England, and he had a dry, British sense of humour. Wilby described Wise as "young, plain, methodical," who took the seat of honour in the tonneau and "offered a dry comment or two on passing events." While the car was moving, Wise would jump out onto the running board and prop himself up against the mudguard of the right wheel to check out the valves and radiator cap. With the comic calmness reminiscent of Buster Keaton, he made his way through the tonneau to the left mudguard and perched over the motor to check out the carburetor. On the way back to his seat, he would give Haney a playful punch. He sat with his feet hanging over the side, which ruined the odd photo of Wilby's, and rolled cigarettes as if he didn't have a care in the world. Wise thought the trip was crazy, but that didn't mean he wouldn't give it his best. Haney's girl Annie said later that the presence of Wise made the 80 kilometres to Moose Jaw the most pleasant part of the trip so far for Haney.

Even Wilby enjoyed the farm country, the rich grass and the "glutinous black loam which grew some of the finest wheat in the world." To the south lay the hills of the Missouri plateau, a great pile of rock formed by glaciers, while to the north they encountered alkali, the sodium-laced soil farmers were beginning to master by continuously plowing over the sloughs and mixing the alkali with soil, turning unfit land into crop land.

Moose Jaw, whose auto club members went out in a big Chalmers car to meet the trio in Pense, ended up missing them and the Regina club took the Pathfinders right into Moose Jaw. Club leaders Dr. Irwin and his brother provided Wilby and Haney with a complimentary dinner and pamphlets, very much like Wilby had seen in Port Arthur. Instead of saying how great the city was for tourists and people with hayfever, Moose Jaw was quite clearly interested in investors. They stayed the night at the Royal George, which is now the Park Hotel.

Lorne and family were met outside of Moose Jaw by members of both the Antique Auto Club of Saskatchewan and the local historical society, who were in period costume, and by a 1911 Ford which led them into town. "Just as it left the highway a gust of wind caught its engine hood and sent it sailing up over the windshield, past the Reo and off onto the farm stubble." Bob Meyers retrieved the hood and handed it back to the owner of the Ford—the hood wasn't damaged, and all his car lost was one paint chip. The historical society put on a luncheon with speeches and presentations, and when the Regina folk returned home, Lorne ended up staying with Earl Boan, an old army buddy, on his property south of Moose Jaw. "Late at night," wrote Lorne, "the wind died and the coyotes came alive."

My day was relatively sedate after a trip to the old railway station, now a casino. A Roughrider ticket stub is worth five dollars in tokens, so people in green-and-white flooded into the casino after the game. The casino, said Vic McDougall, has been an economic saviour, even though casinos rarely have a beneficial effect on cities, especially one so far from the border. Instead, having taken over the station, it made sure the train wouldn't be coming back so fast to the capital.

On television at the B & B were a string of car ads during the Ryder Cup golf championship, and later on football games. The Volvo was portrayed as big and safe, a Pontiac Transport minivan was "built for drivers," GMC trucks were durable "365 days a year." And the luxurious Nissan Maxima was serenaded by the song "The more I see you, the more I want you..."

September 29 — Moose Jaw

Because the Regina railway station is now a casino, or, more accurately, because the train service had stopped, I had few options in trying to catch up to the Findlays. In fact, without a car, it was expensive to get around. I took a $9 taxi to get to the archives, which was near the legislature, and then because the bus service was so random, I hired a university student named Chad Jedlic to drive me the 104 kilometres up the road to Moose Jaw. That morning I heard Lorne on CBC radio, talking about how "the wind almost brought us to a standstill." He said he became interested in the trip because he has been collecting and restoring antique cars since the late fifties. The original trip, he said, was "much more difficult than mine. If there were any roads, they were dreadful roads, and of course they had no information about where to go. It was a very difficult trip. It's totally amazing they got through in that car and in those conditions. They would have loved to have had a road map. It's a real contrast in technologies."

On the trip to Moose Jaw you can't help but see a potash plant north of the Trans-Canada. It's a water mine that dissolves the potash or Kalium and then they take the water out. That morning the Reo went by Canadian Forces Base Moose Jaw, which is home to the famous Snowbirds aerobatic squadron, and visited the Sukanen Ship Pioneer Village and Museum. The museum is based around a ship built by Tom Sukanen, a Finnish immigrant who walked 960 kilometres from Minnesota to Saskatchewan a year before the Pathfinders arrived. During the drought of the 1930s, when it was difficult to make a living farming, Sukanen decided to build a boat to return to Finland. His plan was to sail it home via the Saskatchewan River and Hudson Bay. It had a removable keel that allowed the boat to sail along the rivers without it, and it could be replaced when the ship reached the ocean. He worked on it for 10 years but never launched the boat in the nearby river. He died in 1943 without ever seeing *The Dontianen* sail.

When I got to the roadside in Moose Jaw, supposedly named after the Cree word for "warm breezes"—*Moosegaw*, Lorne had gone on and Peter was fuming. It was our first run-in, and last. Peter felt his father shouldn't be driving the Reo by himself, and that he shouldn't be waiting for me. I said I couldn't ignore the importance of research, so no more was ever said.

At 9 a.m. the 1912 trio left Moose Jaw with pilot V.C. Dunning, who claimed to know the road like a book. He scorned any attempts to ask farmers along the way if they were headed in the right direction. When they violently went over a woodchuck hole in the road, he knew exactly where he was, and where the next turn in the road was. "I've been going to fill up that hole for the last two years," said Dunning. "But I never got round to it." When they made a turn toward Mortlach, at precisely the right moment, Wilby wondered how he did it. "Oh! That's easy. I counted 10 miles from that last schoolhouse. Dead easy with these sectional roads."

The land in the west was surveyed in quadrilateral townships. Each contains 36 sections of one square mile—640 acres or 256 hectares. The road allowances spanned 20 metres, running between each section north and south and every alternate section east and west. It created a checkerboard pattern which irritated Wilby, because he felt

> distances appeared to be unduly increased, while in the obliteration
> of the old, direct trails by the plough and the barbed wire fence, valu-
> able historic landmarks were being irretrievably lost, which should

be preserved by the government or marked by small stone monuments ere they are completely obliterated.

Dunning's magic left him, and he appeared lost, talking aloud as if to assure himself that his logic was sound. "I want to hit that old government trail," Dunning explained. "Any of these turns ought to lead us to it, but we'll take the one that looks the most inviting."

They abandoned the telephone wires heading west and went south and then west. Their trail faded and then came back, covered over sometimes by prairie grasses, and then marked clearly by barbed wire fencing. At times all they had was the sun to guide them, and then they'd catch sight of a railway line, and telephone poles coming from the south. Then they had to abandon the car and walk up to a brow of a hill for guidance. Dunning spotted a puff of smoke—the train—in the distance, and grain elevators which Wilby said had the "solemnity of the pyramids." All the while they ran over deeply rutted buffalo trails, taking shortcuts between sweet grasses and watering holes irrespective of the modern checkerboard. There are photos of them during this stretch, steering the Reo across a field where the wheat had been sheaved.

"The old-time trails," wrote Haney in the *Reo Echo* magazine after the trip, "are cut down six or eight inches (16 to 19 centimetres) and worn hard and smooth as boards. Some of the newer trails are merely road allowances between fences and very rough going. Further west every other section is homesteaded, and the old trails are interrupted and broken up. To get around these plowed-up sections we drove across the open Prairie, often alkali sloughs. The old buffalo trails led into each freshwater hole, and it was a trying business to get across these trails, as they were worn so deeply. I think these buffalo trails are the most disagreeable things we had to encounter. They were hard both on my associate and myself and on the car. To go over them is as bad as going over a log." The buffalo trail depressions were 19 to 67 centimetres wide, and 16 to 33 centimetres deep. "They are clear-cut as though dug out with spades. They come in like a spider web to each of the various old watering places, at intervals right across Saskatchewan and Alberta."

Finding the correct route was an issue Wilby brought up with the *Moose Jaw Evening Times*. After finding marked roads on the way to Regina, Wilby was upset he had none west of the city. "Trails and graded roads—good, bad and indifferent—stretch out in all directions, but without any mark or identification whatever. A cheap method of doing this is to use the tricolours, red, white and blue, and paint them on the telephone poles along the route. Where the poles stop, pointers could be placed to show the way to the next marked posts. In this way motoring would be made a greater pleasure than it is now when roads and directions are in doubt."

It was difficult to get lost along the Trans-Canada, which was where I finally hooked up with Lorne. He said the day before was "terrifying. I thought for sure the wind was going to flip this thing over a few times. But the Reo never missed a beat, never got hot. Boy did it work hard. Twice I had to shift down into second on a flat surface because of the wind. Don't get me wrong. I like the wind—at my back."

The wind caused a serious accident on Saturday—a semi-trailer got blown over on a curve, injuring the driver. One of the car club guys also had nothing but trouble on the weekend, but it had nothing to do with the wind. His carburetor went to pieces on Saturday, so he went home to fix it and then met up with everyone at Kelly's farm. Before the Findlays left there the next morning, he showed up in his '26 Model T. "He got into the same wind and had a flat tire," said Lorne. "He put on a spare. There was no air in the spare and he got it all changed and found it was flat. He couldn't get into a guy's barn to get some air so he had to hitchhike back to Regina. He picked up the Model T on the trailer and went home." Welcome to the world of antique car ownership.

We crossed a flat stretch and then wandered into rolling hills, with ever the big sky above us. For lunch we stopped at Lake Chaplin, a large shallow lake from which industrial salt is harvested. The salt is collected by damming off part of the lake and scraping the salt off the lake bed.

As if we didn't have enough wind, we were headed toward the windiest spot in Saskatchewan Swift Current. There we were met by part of the Swan family, who by marriage of their Aunt Annie to Jack, were nephews of the original Pathfinder, and by members of the Frontier City Antique Car Club, like Cliff Boot, 83, who remade the wooden wheels for his Model T, and Lionel Lepage, who came west with the RCMP in 1931, and got booted out for getting married.

"Them days had to be seven years in force before you got married. I didn't ask for approval. They kicked me out. Still got the same wife. She's 88 years old." Lionel also has a beef with another Canadian icon, the CPR. He worked 41 years on the railway, the last 12 as yardmaster in Swift Current. He retired 23 years ago, but retained a lifetime pass to ride the rails for free. "The crappy CP outfit. They keep sending me a free pass, even though there's no service here. I can't even ride the freight train. There's no caboose anymore. CP still operates lines in Victoria and Northern Quebec. That was part of my retirement. Now it's no good for nothing."

Showing 2,600 miles or 4,160 kilometres on the odometer, the Pathfinders arrived at 6 p.m. in Swift Current, a town of 4,300 in the midst of a construction boom and surrounded by good roads—the town's member of the legislative assembly was Premier Walter Scott, who had instituted a provincial road-building program. The Pathfinders stayed at the year-old Empress hotel, which Wilby said was comfortable and right across from "a midget town hall and fire station combined." The town hall and fire station have been replaced, and the site of The Empress, which burned down Christmas Day, 1931, is occupied by a Home Hardware store. Unlike Haney, who couldn't stand buffalo trails, Wilby told citizens of Swift Current that efforts should be made to preserve buffalo trails for posterity. If not, farmers would obliterate them with plows or chop them up with fencing.

The drive through the Prairies was often done by following hydro or telegraph poles, and hoping your way wouldn't be blocked by farmers' fences.

AUTOMOBILE OWNERS TAKE MEASURES FOR CHEAPER GAS,

September, 1912, Vancouver, B.C.—Securing a supply of cheap gasoline for the automobile owners of the city was the important question taken up recently at a well attended meeting of the Vancouver Automobile Club. This is a matter which has been bothering the automobile men considerably in the last few months, as the price of gas ascended almost daily. An agent of one of the largest independent oil and gasoline corporations stated it would be possible to lay down in Vancouver gasoline at a price of about 24 cents a gallon, and at a much superior quality to that which now costs 30 cents.

ROAD RAGE ALWAYS IN THE NEWS,

September, 1997, Lethbridge, Alberta—Road rage has been the subject of newspaper articles, TV programs and even congressional hearings although, as editor Matt DeLorenzo points out in AutoWeek magazine, there have been "angry people behind the wheel since the first traffic jam." The reason we're seeing so much emphasis on road rage, says DeLorenzo, is that "government, self-appointed safety advocates and tabloid TV" are finally beginning to focus on the human factor in the cause of highway crashes. Cars are far safer than they have ever been, both with the passive protection such as seat belts, air bags and crumple zones and active safety such as better lights, much-improved brakes, better suspension systems and better steering. The bad news is new attention has centered on road rage, as if that, and drunk driving, were the only failures of the driving part of the equation that can lead to crashes and carnage. Using the term 'road rage' too freely absolves incompetent and inattentive drivers of their part in the escalation of annoyance in other drivers.

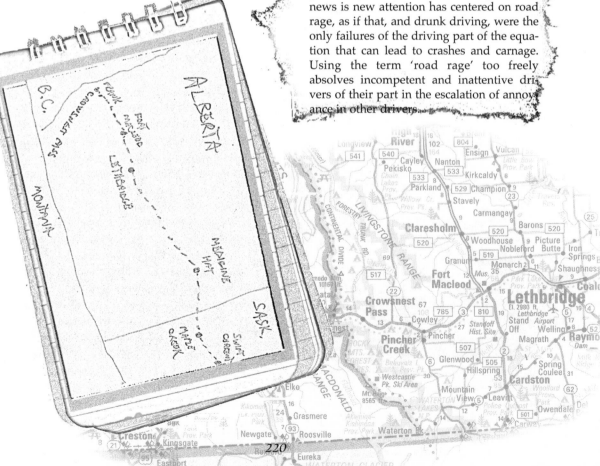

Chapter 12

Cowboy Country

September 30—Swift Current

If there was any doubt the Pathfinders were entering a west more associated with cattle and cowboys, their departure from Swift Current would have convinced them. Their pilot this day was G.K. McEwan, who led the way into open country in a bantam car that carried his wife, his dog and his gun—open season on Prairie chickens was imminent. McEwan told Wilby that every Prairie man is a sportsman when the law allows. Wilby shouldn't expect a chat, a drink or a discussion of business the next day, because everyone would be caught up with grouse fever. Wilby said the Prairie chicken is

> practically the only wild thing that has not fled before civilization and the plough. Though it can still be found in the stubble, it prefers the rolling bushland for cover and for rearing its young. Wherever there is underwood and a dip in the land, where there is coppice and brush and broken surface, there is Prairie chicken. And Prairie chicken makes every true Prairie man's mouth water.

The frequency with which Wilby refers to wildlife, and the absence of wildlife on our trip, was a mystery until a newspaper feature suggested to us that all is not well with the Prairies' ecosystem. The populations of Swainson's and ferruginous hawks, Pronghorn antelope, burrowing owls and other amphibians, reptiles and insects have dropped dramatically. Where once 2,500 sage grouse were counted in 1988 along the Saskatchewan/Montana border, only 250 were counted in the summer of 1997. Some of the populations have shifted to the south, and 4,000 hawks that flew to South America in 1995 were killed by pesticides in Argentina. Pesticides have done much to kill off the northern leopard frog population. Other amphibians have declined because of the draining of wetlands and the damming of Prairie rivers. Land use is a major factor: about 1 percent of the grasslands and 13 percent of the original Canadian Prairie is now a golf course, a subdivision or farmland, which makes the Prairies Canada's second-most endangered ecosystem next to the Carolinian forest in southern Ontario.

Biologist Joe Schmutz of Edmonton says the absence of the gopher or Richardson's ground squirrel is probably due to climatic change. Because winters are shorter and warmer, the gophers aren't getting the ground temperatures they need to trigger hibernation, and they either starve or ravage the plants they need to survive. Says Schmutz: "We've assaulted the Prairie from so many sides that we shouldn't be surprised by the changes that we're seeing. But we are. And that's because we know so little about this beautiful, dynamic landscape."

The Pathfinders didn't leave town without the requisite pennant and photo opportunity, but the photos taken this morning were different. A picture of Mayor Snider of Swift Current tying a pennant on the Reo was to become a lantern slide for the Canadian Highway Association convention in Winnipeg a few weeks later. We searched for any remnants of those slides, in Winnipeg and British Columbia where the CHA was founded, but it was futile.

With Home Hardware not offering me a place for the night, I ended up at a motel chain that had as much charm as a crankshaft. At breakfast, though, it had real people. Better yet, real farmers. One man, who turned out to be Jack Haney's nephew Ron Swan, said he had a preference for John Deere farm implements.

"I've been Massey all my life," said Nick Chavtur, announcing what make of combine he has. "We do mixed farming, everything but moonshine. Mostly grain, but we have cattle to eat the grain we throw out." He's wondering if the farm, which he works with his son Alex, has a mixed future. "The railroad is supposed to close this year. We're losing highways, they're breaking up. We don't have a highway to transport grain. It's broken all up."

The Chavtur farm is in Claydon, near the frontier with the United States. Alex told the story of a man he saw walking past the farm. He thought the guy's car had broken down, but it turns out he was walking around the continent—with two cars. Alex asked him the proverbial Waaaah? and the man replied "Just because."

"He had a Ford truck with a camper cab, and a station wagon, and both had California plates, which sort of explains things," said Alex. "He would go 30 miles a day. He'd sleep in his camper. He wasn't a big guy, but he was in shape, in his fifties, maybe closer to 60, and he was wearing shorts. He would never take a lift. He walked down to all the border crossings to check in. I don't know why. I talked to him for 10 minutes. I showed him a couple of shortcuts to take. He had already been to the east coast and Mexico." Added Nick, as if to prove an earlier point, "He said Highway 18 is the worst road he's been on in North America." Nick had a brother on the local council, but they would never do anything about the roads that were wrecked by trucks from the oil and gas industry.

"We got big tractors," said Swan. "Why don't we go chew up the politician's roads?" Alex said the government was putting in a $7-million overpass in Regina, which prompted his father to add, "I'd like to get into Regina with a tractor."

The debate went back to Masseys versus John Deeres, and the last thing I heard on the way out was: "Back in '37, my parents sold eggs for 3 cents a dozen, which didn't pay for the wear and tear on the hen..."

Our schedule was to go to a seniors' home, show up at the local mall, and then go for lunch, all of which had been organized by Ray and Islay Wiskar, members of the local antique car club. On the drive through Swift Current with George Swan, he said downtown streets were one way because the road wasn't wide enough. I felt they were too wide and no reason for there not to be two-way traffic.

At the mall, Jack Haney's niece by marriage, Alena Saxton, said Annie Haney had a sister Alena whom she was named after, and five brothers—Jim, Fred, Wes, Jack and Ed. The five went west from Huntsville, Ontario, in the autumn of 1906 and spent the first winter in an overturned wagon with snow piled around them. Sister Alena went west in 1917 to cook for bachelor Wes. When she got married and moved to Winnipeg, Annie came to cook for Wes after Jack died. Alena the niece said her uncle Wes would not have gone hungry without his sisters: "Wes could cook, but he preferred to spend his time out in the fields. Wes baked bread, played the accordion and sang, and it was something. He loved the land and every Sunday he'd sit in the pasture from five in the morning watching the calves. He'd sit there all day. We used to tease him that he had gone to church." Wes had a happy-go-lucky and mischievous nature. He'd toughen his nephews up by giving them chewing tobacco. "He got them good and sick. Cousin Herb went to town with the cart after chewing the tobacco and he got so sick he laid down in the cart. The horses found their own way home. It was that plug tobacco that came in a square tin and you had to peel the lid off with a jack-knife." Herb later became a provincial cabinet minister.

Alena also told the story of Jack Haney going out to Demaine, Saskatchewan, arriving when his brother-in-law Fred had broken the yoke for his horses. "Fred couldn't get it fixed. Jack used a hand saw and a hand lathe and made a copy of the one that broke out of a 4-by-4—in half a day. It was perfect."

At the nursing home a 103-year-old woman in a wheelchair said she was just a kitten when the original Reo came through. She said she remembers reading about it once, but couldn't recall what. Irene, ever the conversationalist, asked one old guy if he liked old cars. Emphatically, the man said "No!"

At the luncheon Lorne gave the trip's history and a quick history of the highway: "When B.C. joined Confederation the federal government promised a railway and a cart road. The Trans-Canada Highway wasn't completed until 1962." To much laughter, the Swift Current mayor added, "And it hasn't been fixed since." Not to be outdone, I said a few words to thank everyone, especially all the Swans who made it to the luncheon. I said I was glad Jack's relatives were all Swans instead of Haneys, or I would have been wondering what Jack was doing when he wasn't driving the Reo out here. No one laughed—I was two-for-two in after-dinner jokes.

Back on the road again, the car was working so hard water was pouring out of the radiator cap. Lorne said it never overheated on the windy day out of Regina because the wind blowing through the radiator kept it cool. Besides, he said, "it's all uphill west of Regina."

Gun-toting G.K. McEwan led the Pathfinders by shortcuts, wrote Wilby,
> of the most amazing description, wheeling and returning on his course
> at the most unexpected places, and darting across the rough stubble
> while his car swayed and pitched like a tiny craft caught in a heavy
> swell. We bumped through sand dust and furrows, manoeuvring in
> wide sweeps like swift-wheeling cavalry until we picked up the rail-
> road in the absence of any other recognized route. Gates had to be
> opened and shut incessantly, and it was evident that for at least half the
> time we were on no commonly recognized highway.

South of the Trans-Canada were brooding low hills, creased by shadows and intrigue, indigo in the distance just as Wilby had mentioned, though the colours he wrote about seemed like an exaggeration. Yet the sun in all its moods necessitated the full range of Laurentian coloured pencils, whether it was shadowy, treeless hills or the distant grain elevators burning orange in the late afternoon sun. The fields, in various shades of yellow and tan, were dotted with grazing black-and-white cattle.

On the rolling scrubby land between Gull Lake and Maple Creek—what was not yet the foothills—Lorne was singing, "My Love in the Rockies Is Calling to Me" by Hank Snow. The trigger for Lorne was the trains going by with an engine in the middle of all the cars; that arrangement helps trains get up and down the mountain chains of British Columbia. Lorne insisted, though, we weren't "out west until we get to the other side of Alberta." The first range we'd hit would be called, with some originality, the "Front Range" mountains.

It took me nearly until Alberta, three-quarters of the way across the country, to ask Lorne why my seat cushion was often hot. He said the car's designer put the engine exhaust under the gas tank underneath my seat because heated gasoline burned better. The other guy in the hot seat, Wilby, saw the same long ridges, which he said "began to compass us about like the Downs in an English landscape, and over them swept the stubble, spilling gold along a path bordered by the dark green of the bushland or the browns of flax."

As we passed small farmhouses, I was perusing the Swift Current paper which said we could buy a home, garage, barn and 24 acres for $69,000—it seemed inexpensive. It made us wonder if the house was the 1990 equivalent to the "rude shanties" Wilby happened upon. In a conversation Wilby had with a fellow Brit in Manitoba, the man said, "Perhaps they don't feel their deprivations as much as we feel for them. Perhaps they're not so lonely as we think. There's the railroad, you know, and five miles away a neighbor. The schoolhouse is over the brow of the hill. A day's journey by team will bring them to a big town of the plains. And by next year they will be able to install that safety-valve of Prairie life—the telephone!"

The way to prosperity, Wilby reasoned, began with a tent or a shanty, and hiring yourself out as a farmhand to get some capital to buy a team of oxen. The oxen would help you break the soil "so that it can be penetrated alike by sun and frost and transformed into a light, friable mould. It will be a couple of years before the first crop is garnered in—how much longer before the shanty will give place to a comfortable farmhouse, barn, machine shed, granaries and hog pens!"

McEwan the pilot finally put on a show for the Pathfinders at a stream that wound through the bunch grass and sage. A pair of sportsman friends of McEwan's, had joined the entourage at Thompson, crept through the grass up to the water's edge, and then a "Crack! Crack" echoed back over the sage and the bunch grass, "and the stream gave up its dead in the shape of several brace of fish-duck—long-necked, tufted and beautifully marked creatures." The area became known throughout the century, and even attracted big names like Bing Crosby, for hunting pheasant, mule- and white-tail deer and Canada Geese. Wilby noted how the hunting was much different from the hunt in England—not only had the hunter "an immense range of country in which to choose his beats, arrange his decoy birds, gather his own dead game, breed his dogs and generally look after his personal foraging. Often he cannot get back to his home until the next day, and he must find a night's lodging in a stray farmhouse or homesteader's shack, unless he prefers to make his camp in the chill darkness of the open." Wilby attests to the abundance of wildfowl, but the only ground game worth shooting were jack-rabbit and the cotton-tail.

> As dusk fell, the country grew wilder and wilder, the presence of the tufted bunch grass indicating that we were beginning to leave the Prairies of the golden wheat for the plains of the ranchman. A score of rods ahead. A little grey puff of dust, fleeing ever on and defying us to overtake it, marked the flight of the pilot car. Behind us wheat and oat stacks stood out against a rolling skyline. Above us rose and fell the grass-covered hills, dark against a background of blazing chaff fires glowing like living coals in the sunset. The path grew more tortuous, ascending the steeps only to plunge down, blindly and recklessly, into the bush. There were the usual gates to open and shut, the usual fences to dodge, while one marveled at the instinct of the men who threaded their way through the wilderness and the night, certain of their goal at Maple Creek along an apparently blind path of the Wild.

Haney said the road that day was "rough going. Had a little hunting on the way. Arrived Maple Creek 6 p.m." We, too, arrived later in the afternoon to a sign that said "Maple Creek, where past is present." It was a town that was proud of preserving its past. In fact, the Commercial Hotel, where Wilby and Haney stayed that night, was still there, and for $28 I wondered whether I might have had the same room as Haney, or that guy who shared the hot seat with me.

October 1—Maple Creek

Where past is present. On a journey like ours, Maple Creek's motto was a pleasant escape from the norm. We had often tripped across cities with no concern for their past, or cities that once had so-called leaders with a frightening attitude toward the past, as if everything that was old was bad. Winnipeg's mayor in the 1970s, Stephen Juba, comes to mind. The mayor was so quick to dismiss the old city hall, he didn't find a way to keep the magnificent building as part of the landscape.

Then again, Winnipeg never had a Rosemary Anderson, or at least a woman with as much clout as Anderson had in Maple Creek. She was the catalyst for the founding of the Jasper Cultural and Historical Centre in the old schoolhouse. "I'm going to miss running over here in my pyjamas," she said as she walked up the front steps, a week away from stepping down as head of the museum. "I'd run over to water at night during water restrictions. Some of the flowers were planted in honour of people who died." The school was built in 1910, and it was the focal point of the town for years. When they got it for the museum years ago, the school board was happy to be rid of it. It needed some loving. "The outside wasn't landscaped," said Rosemary. "I've been a gardener, a landscaper and a painter since I got involved."

The reason Rosemary got involved, and why Maple Creek must have, per capita, the best museum in the country, is due to her mother-in-law Rosa Lawrence Anderson, and eccentric landowner Irving Fleming, who willed the museum 2,500 artifacts. Rosemary says she learned about the history of Maple Creek from her mother-in-law, whose great-grandfather homesteaded a ranch on Fish Creek. "Marrying into a generation family, I heard them talk about the early days, and they talked about it all the time. When she died there was no one to pick up her torch. She'd be proud of what I and others have done to carry on her work." Her mother-in-law lived in a turreted house her Uncle Edward built in 1910 to try to coax his love Maggie from Scotland. "He said he'd build her a castle," said Rosemary. "My mother-in-law didn't like the turret because when she would stay there, Aunt Maggie kept her in the turret until her homework was done."

Rosemary raised her own son and daughter in that house after she met her husband in the navy during World War II. "I worked for the British navy. I swore I wouldn't marry a sailor and I did. And I ended up on a ranch, where I had to learn all these ways of ranching life."

The ways of the West are laid bare in the museum. In one room are the prints of the famed Montana cowboy artist Charlie M. Russell. "You never saw a horse's reins or a rope out of place," said Rosemary. "He painted the action as he lived it." The room had a collection of 100 or so cattle brands, including some registered in 1900 that are still used by the same families like the Pollocks, Lawrences, O'Hares and Perrins, and a set of horse collars and saddles from cowboys who had ridden off beyond the sunset. Another room is dedicated to the memory of The Grand Theatre, which opened in 1903. On a makeshift marquee, complete with flashing lights, is a billing for a film shot in nearby Cypress Hills called *The Canadians*, starring Robert Ryan. Even though a projector sits at the back of the old theatre seats, the stage is set with a TV and VCR for locals who want to catch a film. The Grand Theatre seats are removed, though, for the town's New Year's Ball.

The museum has an oak barber chair, a reproduction of the old railway station—it was one of the largest shipping points for cattle and was still standing until 1977—and a display on the old hospital where nine patients lost their lives in a 1945 fire that came up the dumb waiter. As soon as the town was incorporated, it became known for its sports: curling, including the Hansen brothers who won the provincial title, the hockey player Barry Dean and Canada's best bucking horse, High Chaparral. The Murraydale Stampede, the oldest continuous rodeo in all of Canada, is local, as are the generations of rodeo queens and the cowboy Edwin Perrin, who competed in saddle bronco and wild steer riding at the Imperial Rodeo in 1924 in London in front of King George V. He was still alive, down at the senior's home.

Edwin was a contemporary of Irving Fleming, who travelled across ranch lands in a Model A truck looking for bargains and nuggets of history. "He had a magnificent collection of barbed wire," said Rosemary, in awe of Fleming's diligence. "If you ever did fancy old spurs, he had them." In the same room were goat-skin chaps, which were worn for coming into town on a Saturday night, as opposed to the work chaps used to protect their legs when riding.

In a sadder story, Irving also ended up with artifacts from Chief Payepot. "When Sitting Bull settled in Cypress Hills, Chief Payepot sat on the railway tracks and tried to stop the train from coming through. The Indians were trading belongings to ranchers for food. One guy ended up with Chief Payepot's moccasins, his tobacco pouch and carry-all, in which he carried his bola rock to kill small animals, like rabbits. The village of Piapot is named after him."

Somehow, getting a town named after him wasn't much consolation.

Fleming did a lot of trading, and ended up with an entire pioneer kitchen, including a china collection with a tea rose pattern. He had old hanging lamps, little Dutch clogs he got from someone who came back from the war, a hand-powered vacuum in which one person pumped and the other held the hose—a good aerobic exercise. "He had the history of the whole community in his farmhouse. He left a wonderful heritage. I sit in his rocking chair and reminisce about him. When I look at things I never thought they'd come from Irving. He had sleigh bells for horses in winter. There's nothing like getting in a horse-drawn cutter on a cold night, under a blanket, and hear the sleigh bells." Why did Irving do it? "He did it because he loved it. Look what he left us, eh?"

In the collection was something the original Pathfinders might have encountered—a jailhouse door from the North West Mounted Police barracks just outside of town. Not that Haney and Wilby would have been arrested for allowing their pilot to hunt a day before the season began, but they did drive by the NWMP post where, until 1922, the police chased horse thieves and cattle rustlers.

> As we stopped before the little quadrangle forming the barrack square, the place looked to be deserted. Close to the gate, however, we found a couple of men sweeping the path and dressed like rough and tumble vaudeville eccentrics, or some fantastic creatures out of the pages of "Alice in Wonderland." One could have played a game of chess with ease on their garments, which were baggy and patterned with immense black and white checks. The style gave utmost freedom to bodily movement. Comfort before elegance, and yet fanciful, airy, unenslaved!

The men, it turned out, were prisoners, and when he tried to strike up a conversation with them, they were silent. Wilby was interrupted by a soldier who explained that they were forbidden to speak, and marched the men off to the guardhouse. For what it's worth, the Pathfinders must have seen the same door that now hung as a museum piece in the schoolhouse, which they also must have seen.

As they set off for the Alberta boundary at Walsh at 9:30 a.m., their way was hampered by gophers darting in and out of the fields and sitting up in the wheel ruts. They dared the Reo to run over them, said Wilby, "as they dare the badger to interfere with them while their sharp teeth saw through the wheat stems and lay whole tracts to waste...In Montreal they would probably have selected the quiet and safe retreat of the street-car track." Wilby said the gophers were in "Olympic training"—the Summer Games had just been held in Amsterdam. The car would sometimes be chased by horses that "gradually tail off to the pastures again when satisfied as to our harmless eccentricities. Often, however, they would gallop a short distance ahead of the radiator, playfully hurling huge clods of earth into our faces."

The only thing that hurled itself at cars in our day ended up as roadkill—on this stretch a red fox who was probably trying to follow a chicken across the road and got caught in headlights. Our car was driving well, after Lorne had set up the brakes, tightened the wheel bolts and gave it some grease. The two bolts that held the headlights, for some reason, were gone. At the RV site, the folks who ran the place were so enthralled with the Reo they refused to take any money. The woman said it was her way of travelling—she had never been anywhere, but she has seen the world by listening to the people who come through.

The treeless cattle country on which we had embarked was strikingly beautiful in its shades of brown and purple. It was a day to amaze at the ever-changing blanket on Mother Earth. Every so often you could see alkali seeping up onto the ground, and a cow scratching its shoulder up against a hydro pole. The scene, Lorne said, was just like the Old Testament claim of cattle on a thousand hills. If it were not for the highway, a guy on his cellphone, and the big sign welcoming us to Alberta, it could have been 1912.

Perhaps on no other day did we feel as close to the Pathfinders. Whether it was the weather, staying in the same hotel, or even our mood, we couldn't have been more in tune with Haney and Wilby. Even what Wilby wrote could have been written by me, if I had his gift of glibness, his eye and his psychedelic specs

The day was superb. A rim of purple-blue hills rimmed the west and flanked us on both sides. Little white houses with red roofs stood out here and there against the blue sky. A long train snaked a line of black across the pinkish earth, and occasionally a badger peeped out of his yawning and dangerous burrow in the dun roadway...The short-cropped grass had a dull golden sheen, picked out by the delicate pale green of the sage brush. We were in the region of the bunch grass which cures itself, and turns to hay before it is cut, and we were ringed around for many hundreds of miles by the plains which had been the paradise of the buffalo.

A train with two engines in the middle, heading for the Pacific, also snaked past us and tooted its horn; other than the dearth of red-roofed houses, it was scary how much we were in their footsteps. I even felt closer to Wilby, the pompous Brit, and started in my mind to rehabilitate him, claiming that his jingoistic opinions were common in his day. What really won me over was his concern for the buffalo trails, what he called the

ineffaceable, eternal trail of the departed monarch—a dark brown line a foot or so wide and several inches deep, running parallel north to south with countless similar lines at distances of from fifth to a hundred feet. Pencil lines in the vastness of the country, but their very persistence seemed to prove the reality of the Red Man's dream of the buffalo's return. Here the creature had found refuge from the colder latitudes to the north and east. Even to-day, under the protection of the warm Chinock winds from the Rockeries, this portion of Alberta is ideal ranching country.

Having reached Alberta (the only province to bill Lorne for his tourist info — "No wonder they have a $2 billion surplus"), Lorne could smell B.C. The speed limit had increased to 110 km/h, which prompted Lorne to boast, "We can really open it up." Evidence of what happens when people open it up came by on a flatbed truck: an expensive Range Rover was crushed like a packet of cigarettes.

As if it was a tip of the hat to what the original Pathfinders experienced, a truck with train wheels went down the railway tracks.

By 1:30 p.m. Haney, Wilby and Wise found Medicine Hat amid the trees of a pocket canyon, and descended in a breeze that blew poplars "out of their stiff perpendicularity." We went through the same valley, and found the stark green of the park stood out against the gold and brightness of the afternoon. It was now known as The Gas City, for its role in the natural gas industry, but Wilby deemed it among the more sophisticated of Prairie towns. By his description, you'd think he had found a woman to his liking: "Well-dressed women, lacking the hard settled look of the 'fighting women' doing battle with the Prairies beside their struggling mates, were shopping or chatting over an ice at the confectioner's. There was a general air of well-to-do-ism, as agreeable as it was striking."

While they spent until 4 p.m. there, we carried on to Bow Island, home of what looks like the World's biggest golf club, and Pinto McBean, whoever that is, a giant bean for the city that claims to be the bean capital of Canada. On the way we saw a '37 Chev and some alfalfa fields, still green yet bundled up for hay. It was nice to see the green again. Bow Island is south of Old Geyser, where gas was discovered three years before the Pathfinders arrived. As the trio drove through, a line was being laid from there to Lethbridge and Calgary. When reserves ran out in the 1920s, it became a storage centre.

The highways in Alberta were sponsored; we passed the "Christian Community Church—Caring for Highways" sign. It raised the question of whether the congregation regularly picked up litter on the highway or just prayed for those who used it. We'd see a sign later that said: "20,000 Alberta traffic injuries a year: Something has to change. We can make it happen." Peter Findlay, who was now driving, said he felt out of place not having a cracked windshield—it seemed like every other car or truck had a cracked windshield. Out west, he said, they decorate their windshields by hanging garter belts from the mirrors, but cracking them was something different.

When the wind picked up, Peter said he now understood the dust bowl and how during the drought farmers could do nothing more than watch their land blow away. For a while we were in sugar beet country, and then we came to "Taber Corn Capital of Canada." The Pathfinders had a late evening meal of fried eggs and coffee here, "served by the ubiquitous Chinaman of the Canadian west, who never fails to 'produce' no matter what the hour of day or night," said Wilby. They were determined to make it 70 kilometres to Lethbridge that night, so they ventured into the blackness, their headlights catching sight only of telephone polls, railway tracks and a flag cabin for trains. It was a night of glorious stars, but their truest marker by which to find Lethbridge was the wind—as long as it blew in their faces, they were heading due west. They were not hounded by gophers or badgers, but blackbirds, meadow larks and a bat.

While his engines hummed monotonously, Wilby was inspired to write

> The cry of the Indian, the thunder of the buffalo hoof, the crack of the murdering rifle, the tramp, tramp of trapper feet, the creak of the Red River cart, the howl of wolf and coyote, the flight of the hawk, the voices of the homesteaders—how many sounds mingled in fancy with that monotonous hum and whir!

The engine's hum may have been louder because when they travelled through uninhabited territory, they could gain more power by opening up an exhaust cutout—it was louder but no one was around to complain. They were also able to make good time because Alberta had pledged $1.25 million towards road-building in 1912, including the improvement of the Medicine Hat to Lethbridge south trunk road. Thus, when they arrived in Lethbridge at 10:30 p.m. they had covered 313 kilometres, a record for one day's travel.

Haney seemed to be caught up in the success of the day, writing in his diary that he was "feeling fine, just got out of bath." With Wise aboard, it seemed the focus had switched from the irritation of being with each other, to a determination of reaching their goal.

Meanwhile, for us the south trunk road had become No. 3, Crowsnest Highway, heading for Crowsnest Pass. It was good to get away from the Trans-Canada, even though someone had decided to make No. 3 a four-lane monstrosity. We passed a sign for the 1885 Turkey Track, a 36-inch gauge train track that used to carry coal from Lethbridge. The CPR took it over and converted it to the standard 56.5 gauge—the width of two horses' behinds. On our way to Lethbridge we chased down a potash train, filled up with gas for only 53.9 cents a litre (compared to the 70 cents we paid in Quebec), saw oil pumpers, dairy and cattle farms, and other farms raising llamas and buffalo. It was like a microcosm of the province advertising itself to us. Peter said the stock market reports on the camper radio are all about grain through the Prairies, and he marvelled at how little had really changed in cars since the Reo was built. "All the things they tried in cars, the basics are still the same. The push button gear shifts...the best place for gearshift is still on the floor over the transmission."

When we arrived the Reo had a date at Dr. Gerald B. Probe Elementary School, where some students had been following the trip on the Internet.

October 2 — Lethbridge

Haney, Wilby and Wise had arrived so late that plans for a reception had to be put off, but they were not without a welcome. By the five-metre oak-and-mahogany bar of the Lethbridge Hotel, Wilby had been buttonholed by several intriguing characters, including a Lethbridge journalist who wore under his coat the Khedivial star and the medal with bars for serving under General "Chinese" Gordon in the Sudan campaign of 1884–85. Another man had left a country parish in Scotland for his health, and another had earned and lost a fortune in England, and was now trying to earn a second fortune from the soil. Wilby would have heard tales about the Calgary rodeo that year, dubbed "The Greatest Outdoor Show on Earth"—it was the first Calgary Stampede. Yet another man, whom Wilby called a Man of Statistics, gave him a crash course on the Prairies. He trotted out facts on millions of hectares of arable land, and how many thousands of ships would be needed to import immigrants needed to till the soil, the first foot of which, the man said, "was worth more than all the mines in the mountains from Alaska to Mexico, more than all the forest from the boundary to the Arctic Sea, and more than the Bank of England."

A man next to Wilby said the long distance between homesteads on the Prairies necessitates a horse and buggy, which is a great perch to sit and chat with your neighbour from. "Why I've known a couple of men to sit with the reins in their hands for more'n half a day, discussing family affairs, transacting business and eating dinner," said the man, "and pretty comfortable they were, too." Wilby countered that the farmer's isolation prevented him from enjoying community life of gardens, lawns, lectures, churches and saloons without some form of transportation, an argument that was common among people on the Prairies who took to cars more quickly than any other part of Canada.

After a night at the Lethbridge Hotel, Mayor Hatch, Alderman Charles Bowman, who was one-time agent for the Macleod Stage Line, John Taylor of the Board of Trade and Dr. Campbell of the Canadian Highway Association accompanied the Pathfinders to the Mounted Police barracks, where they checked out stables of big-boned horses, more cavalry than Indian-pony type. The mayor gave Wilby a Lethbridge pennant, and several photos were taken. In speeches, Hatch went on about the need to obliterate the terms "east and west" with one highway, saying "the people of Canada are beginning to wake up to the need of a highway which will cement it together in one solid nation." Since the mayor had stolen his stock lines, Wilby expounded upon the great city of Lethbridge, saying he was surprised when he arrived the night before to find "such a clean, well-lighted city, the prettiest he had seen since leaving Toronto." He added that the highway would one day be successfully completed because his trip had shown where the problems are, and had also shown that they could be overcome.

The Pathfinders embarked in high spirits on this crisp morning for the Rockies. While Haney was chipper in his diary, Wilby wrote of a "strange physical and spiritual elation. The long journey to the mountains did not appear so long as before. The prospects of danger and difficulty ahead were exhilarating. Fatigue was trifling, and the Pacific close at hand."

We felt the same way as we headed, in a bit warmer weather, toward Frank, on the border with British Columbia and the mountains. Lethbridge's Oldman River prompted a soundtrack of "Old Man River" and "Moon River" for our morning imitation of Haney and Wise—who played the spoons and also liked music—and when we saw signs for Head-Smashed-In-Buffalo-Jump, Lorne broke into "Buffalo girl won't you come out tonight, come out tonight..." Head-Smashed-In-Buffalo-Jump was near our lunchtime goal of Fort Macleod which, with Lethbridge and Maple Creek, was one of the early posts of the North West Mounted Police. The police, many of whom were ex-British soldiers, were first called out in the 1870s to stop the trading of poisonous whiskey for buffalo robes at Fort Whoop-Up, which was close to Lethbridge. Their directions were off, and when they finally found Fort Whoop-Up, there was no evidence of malodorous moonshine. The police continued on to Fort Macleod, which became the first NWMP fort in the territory that would become Alberta.

It was also a day for the Reo to flaunt its fenders. We were meeting members of the Alberta Reo Owners Club at Auntie Lynda's Restaurant in Fort Macleod, that is, if we could get there. Lorne had to steer the car at an angle to compensate for a bracing headwind, especially the gusts. Because of his *alopecia*, he could have used goggles "You never know how valuable eyelashes are until you lose them."

We passed Debbie's Road Kill and Grill Café, which made Lorne wonder if they served skunk or porcupine, two of the more common roadkills we had seen. A 1931 Reo Royale in the parking lot was obviously on its way to greet us. "The Reo made cars until '36," said Lorne, who was relishing the thought of seeing some of Ransom Eli's offspring. Obviously thrilled to be getting back to his home province, and the completion of his quest, Lorne got a kick out of what one woman told Irene. "When you're in the mountains," she complained, "you can't see the sky unless you look straight up." To someone who revelled in the beauty of the mountains, and the perspective it gave him, he wondered what people saw in the vast flatlands of the Prairies.

If Wilby had his share of characters at the Lethbridge Hotel, we had ours at Auntie Lynda's. We met 75-year-old Harry Urwin, a recycled teenager, who owned a '38 Lincoln Zephyr with a V12 engine that is also known as a Stinking Heifer. His '47 Dodge truck, he said, "was in the film *In Cold Blood*, you know, by Richard [Truman] Capote." He also had a '60 Cadillac hearse that was in the movie *Finder's Keepers* and a '50 Nash air flight that was Pullmanized—the Mounties called it "The Shaggin' Wagon." To complete his collection, he also had a '64 Lincoln Continental and a '57 Crown Victoria. "I lost my wife 11 years ago," he said. "She was always complaining about me buying another old car. I'd say it was better than peeing against the wall. Lots of guys go to the bar. I never did that, or at least not much. Cars are a fun thing."

He did go to the bar every so often during the Second World War, when he wasn't at sea for 32 months. "I was sick only once, and that was from drinking too much." Harry hadn't seen a boat until he joined as a 19-year-old, taking a train for 36 hours to get to the coast. The navy was "a million-dollar experience for $1.50 a day. One time we were stationed at St. John's, Newfoundland. At the time kids didn't have to go to school. We were there for two weeks getting refitted. I used to organize the ball team. One kid hung around the jetty so he became my bat boy. His family were as poor as church mice. He was wearing a pair of dungarees, and he hadn't had a bath in a month. His teeth were so bucked he couldn't close his mouth. We gave him pork chops for dinner—he hadn't seen them before. His eyes would bug out when we gave him pop, tea, jam, sugar and bread to take home. We would have been in shit if anyone found out, but what the hell. He stuck to me like shit to a blanket. When we sailed he stowed away. We had to order a bum boat to get this kid off. I'm sure I was crying when they picked him off the ship. He was, too. I never saw him again. I was always going to go back, fly to St. John's, to see if I could find that kid. I don't know his name but I have a picture of him."

During the war Harry had a camera his sister gave him—he had to turn the film in to make sure he didn't take photos of any war secrets. He had pictures of submarines in Halifax that never saw the light of day, but his most vivid images are the ones his mind paints of the USO in New York City. "We never knew how long we'd be in, but I could phone a lady in the USO at 10 p.m. and tell her there'd be 250 guys looking for companions, and there'd be 250 girls there. We never paid a cent. We use to go to Gus and Andy's. I never knew one from the other. They owned a half interest with Gil Lamb, the movie actor who was in *Anchor Aweigh*. I could remember him wearing a polo jacket, queer as a $3 bill. There were 10 or 12 of us. We ate a lot, drank a lot, and he picked up the bill. I also remember stealing a cab in New York City from Ligget's Drug Store. The cab was sitting in front of the store. I hollered for the cabby, he didn't show, so we took off. I'm going the wrong way on a one-way street, in a stolen cab. Next day I didn't go to shore—I was scared shitless."

The couple across the table went through their youth fearlessly. Tommy Fraser, 83, raced Fords, even though he was a GM dealer for 45 years. He still owns a service station he goes to each day. He's used to tinkering—that's how he outraced his competitors. "Everything with the Model Ts or As had to be original, but you could turn the manifold upside down to get more air input. From '41 to '51 I raced the half-mile, whether it was the Calgary Stampede chuckwagon course, Red Deer, pretty well all over the province. I won two Alberta championships in Calgary. One in Elmont." He took off the watch he won, a Gruen Curvex. "It's been a wonderful watch. I wind it up for special occasions." Its back reads *Presented by Union Tractor Equipment Co. Ltd. Tommy Fraser, Winner, Model T Race 1, Edmonton, May 24, 1947*—50 years ago. The Alberta racing commission honoured him for starting auto racing in the province, but he was also the amateur "rassling" champion in 1935–36 for Alberta. When he wasn't rassling cars he was rassling bodies.

Tommy was driving a '29 Reo Mate, with a compartment at the side for golf clubs, but he also had a '52 Muntz Jet. The builder was known as "Mad Man" Muntz, who put together the better parts of different cars. He had Ford running gear, chassis, Lincoln engine, and it was convertible. Muntz built 175 cars and only 75 still exist. It had a three-ton truck motor, and the body was its own design, like a Curtis.

Tommy's wife Ivy would be 82 in a few days, but she started riding an Indian motorcycle as a 16-year-old. "When other mothers complained about me setting a bad example, my mother chased them off the property with a broom," said Ivy. "She said 'I think she's just as good riding that bike as she'd be out with a bunch of drunken boys. I wish I could have done that when I was her age.'" Ivy said the motorcycle kept her on the straight and narrow. "I never drank or smoked—I couldn't afford it. I had to buy gas for the motorcycle. It was an Indian pony-style. I drove it all over the countryside. I used to ride it to see Tommy. My mother thought it'd get me past the foolish age to get married—I married at 22."

After lunch Joe Asuchak took us out to his farm in his 1932 Model S Reo. "I bought my first Reo in 1959 for $10," said Asuchak, who farms cattle and a little bit of grain. "Each time I was going to restore it with a bit of money, another Reo came along. My brother was a scrap iron dealer. He bought it for $5 and wanted to double his money. It's still in my shop in pieces. Body is done but the engine has to be fixed. In the winter I head north to work in the oil patch, so I don't get much done."

Lorne told Joe about the '24 Reo Roadster that met us in Ottawa and the '53 Reo truck, and about the Ransom Eli Olds museum he went to in Lansing, on the way east. Lorne said Olds was a more interesting character than his contemporary Henry Ford. "I don't think Olds was as much a fanatic as Henry Ford," said Lorne. "He liked to live outside of cars. Ford was pro-German in WWI and anti-Jewish. Ford was ruthless. Olds was a real gentleman. Ford was so cheap he wore socks that needed darning—he just put them on backwards."

At Asuchak's farm, past the round green bales of alfalfa hay, we came upon a shed with a '35 Reo Royale and a '29 Flying Cloud, a '30 Flying Cloud, a Model 25, one equipped with a Trippe Senior light that points in the direction the car is turning. Joe, 59, also had a '30 Packard, Model 726, that he picked up in Saskatoon for his second wife Lynn. "I always wanted a Packard," said Lynn, 44. "When I was a kid I saw a Packard commuter, I thought it was beautiful. I always told Joe I wanted a Packard and he bought me one. It was used as a rum runner; the booze was under the floorboards. It could outrun any cop car. The original owner had a still in his hardware store in North Battleford. Every old car has its story. They're like people; they're fascinating." Lynn opened the back door to reveal a huge back seat. "Show a woman over the age of 60 this and she'll giggle," Lynn declared. "I'm sure a lot of courting went on in these cars."

Wise stands tall in the Reo just before entering British Columbia at Crowsnest Pass. Wilby is crouched behind the Reo writing because of the wind whipping through the pass. The 1997 Pathfinders had been buffeted by 100 km/h winds before finding an old road next to the modern road entering the Crowsnest.

Most of the hotels the original Pathfinders visited had become strip joints or run-down city inns, if they were still standing. The Coldwater Hotel in Merritt, B.C., was an exception. The only major change in 1997 was the "Pub" sign, which Wilby didn't need in 1912–he could smell a drink from the city limits.

Following the Thompson River north to Ashcroft and, after crossing Pavilion Lake Road, sitting above the majesty of the Fraser Canyon. One could only imagine what Simon Fraser and his men felt when they happened upon these rivers in the early 19th century.

Top and above right: Haney (and Findlay) posed for a photo at an Indian cemetery north of Ashcroft, B.C. His father, Albion Joseph Haney, was fascinated by Indian burial sites. Jack took him to the ones around Niagara when his father visited him in St. Catharines, Ontario.

Right and above: We duplicated this 1912 photo from Pavilion Lake road as well as we could, but the mountainside on the right was chopped back to allow a wider road when we arrived in 1997.

The first mixing of Atlantic and Pacific waters in Vancouver.

Wilby was mesmerized, as was the 1997 crew, by the beauty of Cameron Lake on Vancouver Island, and the knowledge that this joy-ride of joy-rides was nearing its end.

Back out in front of the Rattenbury-designed Parliament buildings in Victoria, B.C., for the last shaking of hands. The original duo didn't earn the A.E. Todd medal for being the first to cross the country wholly within Canada [that would not happen until 1946], but Todd did manage to give them a Canadian Highway Association pennant.

The final mixing of the Atlantic and Pacific waters in Victoria, B.C., at Cattle Point in 1997, and Oak Bay in 1912.

One of their cars had been in the Indiana Jones movie *Temple of Doom*, while the Reo '32 Model S, the one Joe picked up in California, was the exact car Edward G. Robinson used in an advertisement for Astro Glide. But Lynn acknowledged that Joe's fascination with cars had its drawbacks. "That shed over there," she said, pointing to a shed with more old cars, "that was my new house."

In another barn they had a Reo Speedwagon, and next to it, Tommy's son-in-law, Sunny McMillan, was expounding on the difficulty of fighting brushfires in a Prairie wind. Sunny was a bronco-rider and chuckwagon racer. "The chuckwagon races started with the original roundup for feeding cowboys. Some of the outfit had races to get back from the camp. That evolved to using thoroughbreds and developed into a sport where you can get sponsorships for more than $100,000. Over four wagons were sponsored for $100,000 for the 10-day Stampede."

Sunny, 57, is an outrider—a guy who helps pitch the tent or set up camp. Each racing outfit has four outriders for the "half mile of hell." "We lose a couple of horses a year, sometimes one of the outriders gets killed. The winner gets $50,000. Ian Tyson sings about the 'Half Mile of Hell.' They play the song at the Stampede. There'll be eight or so in a race—32 heads of horses and 20 men. Gives you an idea of the panic. A racehorse will run into a wall without putting brakes on."

All of a sudden, cars seemed more civil.

On the horizon a serrated line of foothills beckoned. Someone pointed to Chief Mountain, where a love-crazed chief once threw himself to his death. Peter and I would soon be in those foothills. We had no thoughts of throwing ourselves off mountains, yet the wind had other ideas. The only way for us to motor on was to put the roof down and lower the top half of the windshield. The wind gusted up to 100 kilometres an hour into our faces, so much so that my sunglasses wrapped flat around my face, cutting the bridge of my nose. When I turned to the side they flew off, sailing 50 metres through the air. It took five minutes to find them.

The Pathfinders visit to Macleod was along the historic Macleod Trail, which afforded a scenic panorama of the Belly River valley:

> The trail crossed a river by a magnificent bridge and then entered a
> canyon, where the road wound high above a stream before it finally
> debouched to the level plains again, close to the remains of old Fort
> Kipp. Far to the west we could see the dim white-capped wraiths of

the Rockies, over which hung fleecy clouds that curiously imitated the snowfields of the mountains. Close at hand, sheep and horses were abundant, and a man passed us with a dead coyote chained to the back of his little motor-car. Not far to the south lay the Peigan and Blood Indian Reserves.

The Reo stopped at Macleod at 2 p.m. "mud-spattered and weather-stained and loaded with luggage and traps, spare tires, gasoline and equipment of all sorts, but looking very 'fit' and business-like," said the *Macleod Advertiser*. The Hon. Malcolm McKenzie, MLA, Mayor Stedman and other prominent citizens took care of their "creature comforts" at the Queen's Hotel while the car "imbibed a little oil and gasoline at the garage. Then at three o'clock [Haney said it was 4 p.m.—he didn't turn his watch back an hour] the western journey was resumed. Neil McCaig acted as pilot as far as Pincher Creek. The departure of the pilgrims was quite an event and a big crowd was on hand to watch. The Mayor affixed a large red pennant, inscribed with the word 'Macleod' to the transcontinental car which fluttered conspicuously in the wind as it headed a little procession of automobiles through town."

Wilby was described as "grey-haired, sun-tanned, alert, energetic and intensely interested in his adventure. The driver is F.E. Haney, a young man with a deeply tanned face and an eagle eye." The escort accompanied them for nearly 10 kilometres, which would have placed them at Howe School due north of Macleod. It was there, I later found out, they stopped and took photos with schoolchildren. We had asked all across the Prairies if anyone recognized this photo in Wilby's book, but its location was a mystery. It wasn't solved until research at the Alberta archives in Edmonton revealed it was the Howe School, given away by the location of the barn. It was necessary for everyone to ride saddle horses to school (schools are marked now by huge parking lots for students' cars). In the photo, the Reo has its top lowered and its windshield folded down, and the tonneau is full of schoolboys. In the background, the schoolgirls are standing in the entranceway to the school, while four children sit on horseback. For some students who had long hikes to school, the Reo must have been looked on with wide-eyed envy.

The story Haney's wife tells after the trip is that Wilby didn't want to mess around at the school, but to carry on. They would lose their way three times that night. In *Motoring* magazine, Haney wrote that they entered the beginning of Crowsnest Pass near Cowley just as it was getting dark

The road winds in and out, up and down. Our pilot suggested a hinge in the centre of the car to facilitate making some of the turns. Near Frank we narrowly escaped going into a torn out bridge. We had lost the road and were playing blind man's bluff around some large stones. We finally came to the conclusion that we were getting no nearer Vancouver so we stopped to collect our few remaining wits and look around. Our guide climbed out of the car and went prowling off into the dark, but soon returned with the information that a light could be seen around the hill behind us. We soon had our directions again and found that we were only a quarter of a mile from a small town and three miles from Frank. Before reaching Frank we had to go through the Big Slide.

At 10 p.m. they made it to Frank, scene of the 1903 disaster in which part of Turtle Mountain tumbled into the valley, killing more than 80 citizens. The Frank Sanatorium or resort hotel, in a wider part of the valley, was left intact. For the Pathfinders, it was the most expensive hotel of the trip; Haney and Wise shared a room for $7. In a magazine Wilby wrote: "The sight which presented itself as the car picked its way among the giant boulders beggars description. Some of these fallen 'pebbles' by the roadside dwarfed the machine to pigmy proportions." Wilby would be glad to get into British Columbia, lest more of the mountain descend upon them.

We made slow progress against the wind, and understood why we had seen modern windmills in the valley near Cowley as we rose through the foothills. On the way up we had our last look at the golds and browns of the patchwork Prairies set against a big blue sky.

The sanatorium no longer existed. I spent the night at the seen-better-days Bellevue Inn. It had a karaoke night downstairs, so southwestern Alberta serenaded me to sleep. I was tempted to put my name in to sing "King of the Road," or perhaps songs that were big in the Pathfinders day, like "By the Light of the Silvery Moon" or "Memphis Blues," but the temptation lasted for a millisecond. In many ways the original Pathfinders were lucky—at least they didn't have to contend with karaoke.

One of the newspapers we had picked up had a photo by David Bly of a road heading toward a mountain with the caption: "When you reach the far horizon, there'll be another—that's the joy of life's journey." And that was the joy of this journey. We had enjoyed the rolling hills and rivers of the Maritimes, the history of Quebec, the grandeur of the St. Lawrence, the many textures of Ontario, and then the Prairies, which everyone said you had to get through quickly because you'd enjoy B.C. The Prairies were mesmerizing, and yet, the big enchilada awaited us.

Near Macleod Alberta, the Reo stopped at a school where the students climbed all over the Reo, much to Wilby's chagrin.

The trio who would tackle the mountains of British Columbia, finally together: Haney, Wilby and Wise.

The Reo crossing the Continental Divide on its way into British Columbia.

Wise relaxing while the Reo stopped near Princeton, B.C.

AUTO ON FIRE, October, 1912, Greenwood, British Columbia—On Sunday evening while driving his auto from Midway to Greenwood, Dr. Maclean had a thrilling experience. When a short distance from Midway a fire broke out in the engine box. The doctor saw a chance that his $1,300 motor car might be cremated, so he became extremely active, and with the assistance of E.R. Redpath, who was riding with him, they finally smothered the fire with a fur robe, and clay that they scooped from the side of the road with their hands. After the fire was out they walked eight miles (13 kilometres) to Greenwood, procured another car, and towed the disabled machine to its garage in this city.

BOWEN'S BLUES, October, 1997, Bowen Island, British Columbia—During her 77 years, Jean Jamieson has seen this green refuge in Howe Sound transformed from a summer picnic spot to the daily destination of hundreds of car commuters. "Now we've reached a turning point," said Jamieson. "Traffic congestion is becoming a problem. The beaches are becoming crowded and dirty. We find ourselves going to other islands for the beaches and trails we used to enjoy." About 1,750 vehicles are registered on Bowen Island, giving the island a vehicle-ownership rate slightly higher than that of car crowded Vancouver. There are five lanes of pavement on the only commercial street on Bowen—the street that leads to the ferry terminal —but it doesn't seem to be enough space during the rush hours. The morning line-up for B.C. ferries 70-vehicle ship begins at the ferry dock and continues the entire, half-kilometre length of the town of Snug Cove.

Chapter 13

Beautiful British Columbia

October 3—Frank/Blairmore

Our first stop, on what would be an eerie morning of trying to duplicate photos from 1912, was the Frank interpretive centre where we looked across the valley at Turtle Mountain and gained some perspective on the 74 million tons of rock that fell onto the vulnerable town at 4:10 a.m., April 29, 1903. Ron Swan's story came to mind. Some time ago in Frank he'd met a woman who was the slide's only surviving person. She was a baby and for some reason had been thrown clear. She was almost 90 when he met her, so she wasn't around when we arrived. The slide looked like it had taken place in ancient history, as if the rocks had been chiselled from the mountain by a glacier. It became even more eerie when we took the Old Frank Road across the boulders. It wasn't hard to find a rock for Lorne to pose on, as Haney had done standing on a boulder that dwarfed the Reo.

The next shot was easy to locate, because not all mountains move, at least not the Crowsnest. The unmistakable peak was easy to find, as was an old road next to the highway, which might have been the route the trio was on in the original photo. In it, Wise is in the back seat, and Wilby is crouched down behind the car, writing. Without having taken the trip, you'd have thought Wilby was hiding from Wise, but after feeling the wind come whipping through the valley, there's no question why Wilby is crouched. He obviously wanted to write without having the pages of his notebook flap in the wind.

Wilby found Frank to be a melancholy little community that seemed
to have lost all heart or pride since the terrible disaster of a few years
before. Death and disaster might reappear at any moment, and Frank

had been counselled to betake itself to a site more convenient for this earthly pilgrimage. Everybody was fully conscious of the danger, but everybody looked up at the great, bare slopes of the slide and out at the white sepulchre of rock across the valley, and prepared to take his chances, pending—what? Children were still going to school, men to their work on the railroad that had been temporarily obliterated; tradesmen were bartering their wares with the wonted air of men who had never known the terrors of a cataclysm. A road had been cut through the debris, and as I stood looking up at the mass of rock that towered above, a little boy and girl drove a rig unconcernedly by and disappeared behind a fallen rock-monster fully thirty feet (10 metres) high.

The Pathfinders enjoyed the commodious and superior hotel at Frank, and a few kilometres down the road in Blairmore, they were met by local garage man A.W. Robbins, who told them he had heard about their coming by telephone from Pincher Creek. Robbins told them a pilot car had waited all day for them, but the man left, saying he was "mighty sorry" he missed them. Instead, Robbins led them to the next town where a pilot, the mayor, chief of police, parson, townfathers and old-timers of Coleman greeted the trio. It prompted Wilby to exclaim: "Such spontaneity of welcome! Such faith in the coming of a highway across Canada as these men of Coleman showed, while they crowded around a mud-stained car from Halifax to offer their hospitality and to shake hands again and again!"

The new pilot was W.H. Murr, owner of the Coleman Hotel, who good-naturedly had to teach these Easterners how to make it through the deceptive grades of the mountains. At one point Murr told them to "Pile out" as they attacked a wooded, narrow ascent, a three-kilometre climb to the summit and the entrance to British Columbia. "After that there's another climb along a narrow road over a chasm," he said, laughing boisterously at the thought of the passengers having to help push the Reo into the most westerly province. Murr seemed to take joy in the passengers jumping out to lighten the load or to help push the Reo, or to hang on to its sides, hood, wheels, top—anything—to stop it slipping backwards. They found a lake, the source of Oldman River, and entered British Columbia on a downgrade.

"Odd, isn't it?" said Murr, "to enter the mountain province downgrade instead of upgrade? But you always have the doubtful consolation in these parts that you never go down without having to go up again afterwards. I suppose that's a little way the earth has of compensating itself."

Eighty-five years later, we never had anything like the 25-percent grades they tackled, but we saw where the old collieries were, the mountains with a sheer face of poor-grade coal staring at us, and the pungent smell of burning rubber as we made our way into B.C. And just as in 1912, the wind that had been blowing strongly on the other side of the Continental Divide was now calm, allowing us a breezeless ride toward Fernie. The Divide was more dramatic than the earlier north-south split between water going to Hudson Bay or the Great Lakes. Here, clearly seven-eighths of the way across the country, we'd come to a place where water would flow either to the Pacific or back toward Hudson Bay and the Atlantic. We saw a coal train chugging its way west, a sawmill with a beehive burner, a lime factory and a natural gas pumping station. Add in the breathtaking beauty before us, the river alongside the road, the aspen trees turning gold and yellow before a backdrop of evergreens, and one couldn't help but think it was an immensely rich province. While the trio had their warnings from Murr, road signs told us not to mess with the road—"Carry chains or use good winter-tread tires ahead"—and one sign we didn't have to worry about "Photo radar."

Haney's morning was preoccupied with coming over "fierce hills." They had a seven-kilometre climb to the summit of the Crowsnest, which they did in low gear with no signs of the engine getting hot. "Going down the other side with gear in low and the spark off we found the grades so heavy that we had to stop a number of times to allow the brakes to cool off." The trio made it to the coal town of Michel at noon. Michel and Natal, another bleak coal town, had been replaced by Sparwood in 1964, when the Kaiser Corporation started strip-mining coal. It boasted the world's largest truck—10 metres high—and we could see pillars from the old bridges over to the mines.

The air was cool, which had reminded Lorne to tighten the hose on the radiator that morning, because of metal shrinking with the cold. It was Lorne's province, and he was even bouncier than normal at the thought of making it down the home stretch, like he was sitting hand-on-fork for a long-awaited meal. "Think we really are going to make it now!" he exclaimed, although I'm sure his fingers were crossed. He also knew the roads, noting one of the province's most beautiful drives was from

Cranbrook north up the Columbia River Valley to Golden on the west side of Rockies. When the Pathfinders came through, the Kootenay Central Railway had just opened a route from Cranbrook to Fort Steele. The train to the historic town of Fort Steele, scene of a 19th-century gold rush, would enable businessmen and farmers to market their products, miners to get at the nearby quartz and gold, and it had tourism potential. Lorne said the motto of the CPR's Van Horne was: "'We can't bring the scenery to the people so we have to bring the people to the scenery.' That was the gist behind the CP hotel in Banff."

At the Fernie tourism office we were met by reporter Maureen Kafer, who was a bit of an adventurer herself, having lived in Dawson City, the Northwest Territories and around British Columbia. "When you leave home you seem to leave everyone standing still. You're moving forward. You're not an armchair traveller, you're there to experience their world, and then it becomes addictive. Those are the reasons why, when you come back, it's so hard to relate. Your mind has been expanding, and you never see things quite the same way again." Dawson City was her favourite, because time had stood still there. "All those characters you read about in Jack London books are still there on the Bonanza Creek banks where they discovered gold." Instead of prospectors, hippies live in tents by the creek. They fashioned meals from what they could scrounge. Maureen said she had some of the finest potluck dinners, sitting on furniture they picked out of the dump. "We were living more real, like it was the early 1900s. Making a loaf of bread isn't like buying something in grocery store. Your day is full, there's no TV."

Her story resonated as I had lunch in the old railway station, now an art gallery-restaurant-theatre, listening to a jazz CD play selections from "Come Dance with Me" to "Wand'ring Star." Part of my own fascination with Wilby, Haney and now Wise was thinking of what the world was like in 1912, a few months before my father was born. Being the son of older parents, and having a natural affinity for the past, I'm not naive enough to think they were the good old days, but it seems as if we have lost some of the elements that made life more pleasant over the century— the sense of community, the ability to walk places, the connection to the wilderness.

Fernie had an old city hall and courthouse, but when the musketeers came through, it had just been rebuilt after a forest fire. On their way into town they had seen charred and ashen-grey trunks and blackened earth for nearly 30 kilometres. It all fits with the legend of the town founded by William Fernie. When the prospector noticed the daughter of a local Indian chief wearing a necklace of coal, Fernie found the location of the coal deposit and started the Crowsnest Pass Coal Company. The chief declared the valley would suffer from fire, flood, strife and discord. Fernie not only suffered from fires but mine explosions and floods.

Murr, the man of mirth, left at Fernie. About 10 kilometres west the trio had their first flirtation with disaster. During an afternoon of intermittent rain, Haney wrote in *The Echo* that "we came within an inch of going over a 300-foot precipice. At this point planks are laid over the gravel. When the planks are wet the climb is difficult, and skidding is easy, with a more than usual possibility of a spectacular disaster." At dusk at Fort Steele Junction they met the press and a large contingent of Cranbrook automobilists. The contingent would have been larger if not for the rain.

The Reo was flying the pennants of Halifax, Toronto and Lethbridge and bore the name of the Canadian Highway Association, and the trio, said the local newspaper, "did not in any way look much the worse for wear. Mr. Wilby kindly explained the way all the equipment was packed away in the car, as nothing whatever could be seen of the weight he must necessarily carry for such a trip. The total weight of the car reached 3,280 pounds."

The entourage arrived after dark at 8 p.m. and were entertained at the Hotel Cranbrook by the local automobile association. Wilby told them the trip from Wardner to Cranbrook was like passing through a park. When the road from Banff to Golden is completed, Cranbrook "will be the key to the finest piece of scenic touring in all British Columbia." That night there was much debate about how the trio should get to Kootenay Landing, where they would take the ferry to Nelson—which, to this day, is one of the better ways to head west. Some of the men said the road was impassable. "Ship your car at once," suggested a prominent townsman, "and we will take a run in my machine to Golden, along the Kootenay Valley." Others claimed that, save for a bad place or two, the whole route might easily be covered. "Mr. Wilby listened to all parties, but being determined to make every mile possible in his own car, did not commit himself to shipping his car."

We also had rain and we were also met outside Cranbrook by a stunning collection of cars, but none that the Pathfinders would have known. There was a 1940 Ford V8 yellow convertible, a '27 red and blue Chev coupe, a '35 Plymouth PJ, a blue '35

Haney and Wise and a pilot clearing rocks from their path on an excuse for a mountain trail.

Haney and Wise and, in the back seat, W.H. Murr, owner of the Coleman Hotel, who good-naturedly had to teach these Easterners how to make it through the Crowsnest Pass. They are beside a lake in the pass that is the source of Oldman River.

Ford with wire wheels, and a '47 114 Mercury 8. Its owner, Ken McLean, explained that Ford and Mercury split after the war. "Ford had the Ford and the Monarch, while the Mercury just had a big Merc and needed a smaller car. In '46–'48, they had 114 Merc and then they came out with the Meteor in 1949."

Lorne's friend George Ferris Dowling, a retired mechanical engineer who met his first wife in the back seat of Lorne's car, found me a hotel other than the Hotel Cranbrook. The 99-year-old hotel had become run down.

October 4—Cranbrook

Cranbrook was so enchanted with the Reo's arrival that it tried to give the threesome a tour of the area. Instead, on finding out that the trio must carry on, local drivers organized their cars into a huge crescent outside city hall. In one of his stories, Wilby wrote that "a crowd lined up on the sidewalks; and the Mayor, whose wife presented me with a pennant, called upon the ex-Mayor to deliver a little oratory suited to the occasion." The local newspaper said Mayor A.C. Bowness had a sore throat, so he asked P. DeVere Hunt to speak. The ex-mayor said it was a red letter day for Cranbrook to be welcoming the Reo, "forming as it does another strong link in binding the East and the West together." Wilby wrote: "Of course I had to respond. It was a singular and even note-worthy event—this tribute to a motor tour and to the Good Roads Movement by a generous public demonstration."

Wilby said the town was "about the size of a man's pocket-handkerchief, a mere village in dimensions. A hotel, of which the landlord was my genial friend of the flask, a railroad station, a modest town hall, a few more or less sleepy stores, a form-less back street or two, a chaotic pavement, and a YMCA building built and maintained by the CPR—that was all." But he felt the people had a good work ethic, character and entrepreneurship, even if they didn't have all the social graces. "Social advantages are accumulative," he wrote, "not fashioned by the waving of a fairy wand while the shovel and the axe are still in the hands of the moulders of life."

That morning I spent with one person who was trying to write the history of Cranbrook, and one who had lived it. Marvin "Skip" Fennessy, a retired postal worker, had a committee together to write the history of Cranbrook, but it folded when two members succumbed to Alzheimer's disease. Among his interests were old trails that went through British Columbia, including the Dewdney Trail that went from Rock

Creek near the Washington border, through Salmo and Cranbrook to Fort Steele and Fisherville. "The Americans came up that way for the gold rush," said Skip. "In 1846, when they designated the 49th parallel, they had to come up with a Canadian route so miners with gold wouldn't have to travel in the States. The trails were from Walla Walla, Washington, and from Jennings, Montana. The trail was named after Edgar Dewdney, who became Lieutenant Governor of British Columbia. Right now we're trying to reclaim possession of the trail for the Canada Trail." It would have pleased Phil Latulippe, the cross-country runner from Quebec.

The most interesting story Skip told was about the Lower Kootenay native band that has been in the Kootenay valley for 11,000 years. "They didn't have a written language until the last 20 years, but their speech and habits and livelihood were totally different from other natives. They had immigrated from Russia over the Bering Strait, and stayed here because everything they needed was on the valley floor. They lived by the water with a sturgeon-nosed canoe. The only other one like it is in Amar, Russia. The Smithsonian has proven that."

As for the route the Pathfinders took to Yahk and Creston, Skip said it would have been "nothing but a cow trail. The road wasn't put in until the twenties, and they had to blast that through rock. There were areas where a pass did go down by the lake. The actual road was put there by Bedlington-Nelson Railway in 1901, but it didn't last all that long." It turns out that some of the early highways took up the routes of railways gone to seed, sort of like the modern rails-to-trails movement.

Al Hunter was old enough to remember the original trip in 1912, but he wasn't in the area then. Born March 1, 1901, the 96-year-old drove down to the Cranbrook train station, which is now a museum, to talk about cars and how much the world had changed this century. His grandfather, William Hunter, had a livery stable in London, Ontario, and brought the first automobiles to that city. He knew Canada's first prime minister, John A. Macdonald, and made his money renting horses to the Tories. When they lost power in 1896, Hunter had enough money to start buying McLaughlin carriages from the McLaughlin boys. He then bought a Pierce Arrow and a McLaughlin, introducing the cars as taxis.

"Everybody in those days said, 'Go west young man, go west young man.' It was 1904 when we came west from Toronto on the settlers' train. It took six days to get to Calgary. We had got a wagon and horses, just camped downtown until my father found a place for us to homestead. We spent our first four years northeast of Cochrane, in Simon's Valley. My dad then went railroading with the CPR. In 1910 he used to run through here on the Spokane Special from Calgary."

When Al was learning to drive, it was in a Studebaker that had the brake lever outside the car. In those days it took two days to go the 130 kilometres from Calgary to Banff, so they used to stop at the Morley Indian Reserve to spend the night. "Now they do it in an hour. It used to take four days to drive from here to Vancouver even in late 30s. It's amazing what's happened in our century, especially last two or three decades." Al started with Bell Telephone in Chicago in 1919 and became such a communications expert he was summoned to the War Department after the December 1941 bombing of Pearl Harbor to help with communications around the Panama Canal. "I drove a lot in South America and Africa, so I quite appreciate what you're doing and admire you for it." The road to Yahk, he said, "is quite modern now. Even in 1931 it was still more gravel and dust and boulders. It was not much improved until after the war. Nothing was done through the 1920s through this area. They didn't have money. During the Depression they had CCI camps, where they put unemployed people in the bush with tents where they could behave, and they worked on roads. On the other side of Moyie, they paid them 50 cents a day."

When I asked for his phone number in case I had to check something later, he said, "if you need anything, you better get it now." At 96, he didn't plan ahead. "You're really doing something that's remarkable. I wish I was going with you."

He did, in a strange way. The driver of the pilot car this 1912 day for the trio was J.R. McNabb, manager of the Kootenay Telephone Lines Ltd. Al Hunter had come to the Kootenays after the war to modernize their telephone lines.

The Pathfinders didn't get away until 2 p.m., with an English fruit farmer named Mr. R along for the ride in the Reo to Creston. "From Cranbrook," wrote Wilby, "I was escorted out of town by a cavalcade of automobiles that accompanied me several miles into the forest. Then, having been told that there was 'a devil of a road' somewhere ahead, I was bidden a kindly farewell and abandoned to the chaperonage of a plucky, little pilot-car. The swamps and forests which lay ahead of us had never before been attempted by an automobile, and our chances of crossing them were not considered good, but together we faced the first seventy miles of this cheerful hundred with the do-or-die spirit which the occasion demanded."

Wilby said, "the way led along mountain sides, by steep, winding curves, and up precipitous hills," where the Reo sometimes refused to venture without the aid of block and tackle. To get to Ryan, which no longer exists on the map, the Reo slithered down a mountain to a little wooden bridge at the entrance to the swamp at dusk, forcing the travellers to light their acetylene headlights. They rested a bit, facing a narrow track filled with rock, mud and watery potholes. Wilby had telephoned ahead for a team of horses, but it was nowhere in evidence. McNabb allowed the Reo to go first. If trouble loomed, the pilot car could always turn back.

In his book, Wilby blamed the Reo's weight for the car's repeated refusal
to stand on end. The light, fleet-footed pilot-car lent embarrassment
by friskily skipping up the hills on top-speed, while we had to jump
the moment we changed into second, or to push with all our might
when the driver dropped into "low." But it was not bad sport, even
hauling on the tackle, and scenery left little opportunity for dullness.
Eye and mind were stimulated by the magic of the mountain setting,
while muscles were stretched to their utmost.

Wilby paints a picture of being the extra set of muscles, ever at the ready, to help the car across, but that contrasts tartly with the impression that Haney's future wife Annie had. She tells of Wilby never lifting a hand to help Jack, and cited the one-man block-and-tackle Jack made to help him through the Maritimes. Sometime after Regina, when they picked up Wise, the Reo got stuck and all hands were needed. "They had fun with Wilby then," said Mrs. Haney. "Wilby actually picked up a shovel. They were stuck many times before but he had never done a bit of work. Wise, who had a dry sense of humour, looked at Wilby and asked, 'Do you really mean you're going to work?' Wilby dropped the shovel and stormed off." What works against that anecdote taking place in the mountains is that the enormity of the task before them would have taken all their teamwork.

Our journey to Creston would include a 300-metre drop in altitude, which seems like a long downhill trek, but it also included ups before the downs. Besides, said Lorne, the headwind would keep us at our normal cruising speed. While Wilby had the sensation of an explorer reaching forward into virgin land, with "scarcely a hut and seldom a puff of smoke to humanise the lonely valleys," we were travelling on a Saturday, being passed by tourists and finding several homes on the route, including a row of shacks just off the road. They would have elicited a plea from Wilby to spruce themselves up in order to improve the highway.

Meanwhile, the Pathfinders were in the midst of their longest day; indeed, it could have been their D-Day. They continued on in darkness, plunging through a thicket and denting the engine's overflow pan on boulders and roots of fallen trees.

> Often we plunged along at angles which no motor-car was ever intended to take, inwardly praying for the advent of the horses. We were buried to the flanks in the slough and at times both cars sank to the hubs, listing heavily, grinding and ploughing their way, pounding the tyres to rags, while the engines roared and groaned and the wheels angrily shot the water in inky spindrift over men and trees. How we longed for the smooth prairie trail, where our flight had been made musical with the song of the motor as it purred and hummed to the undertone of the wind! When at last a human voice hailed us out of the darkness and we saw the huge shadows of the long-expected horses between the trees, not a voice was raised in protest at the caution which had kept man and beast away from the scene of our trials.

By 8 p.m. the team of horses had led them into Yahk where they faced another dilemma. They could stray into the United States to get to Creston, or they could cross 22 kilometres on railway track to Kitchener. While a panting locomotive and big freight cars loomed out of the shadows, the trio crossed the tracks to enter a gloomy-looking inn. They managed to get a greasy "rough-and-tumble" supper amidst the trainmen and, incongruously, a girl who was toying with a typewriter. Wilby did some reconnaissance to discover that no trains were expected—barring a possible freight or two—for the next few hours. Officially, it was forbidden to take the tracks, so they asked no direct questions, and volunteered no hint of their intentions.

Farther along the trail they found the campfires of a road-gang. The workers told them where they could find a level crossing to get on the tracks. McNabb, who would try to return over that hellish road to Cranbrook, wished them good luck, adding "We'll have that road fixed all right for you by the time you come again!" Wilby said they needed five minutes to bid a fond farewell to McNabb, who had endured with them their most trying route, and ten minutes "to stoke the inner man"—for the courage to direct their Reo into the unknown. They had reasoned that if a train came either way, and there was no way to pull off the tracks, they would leap from the Reo and consign it to the junk heap. It would be the end of the Reo's brave journey, but that was the chance they had to take. Mr. R, the Cranbrook fruit rancher, must have thought he was travelling with daredevils, or had got more than he bargained for from his jaunt to Creston.

Our venture to Yahk was fairly civil. The Yahk Diner was serving burgers, borscht and carrot cake, but we opted for Irene's sandwiches in the Yahk Provincial Park. For the sake of duplicating photos, Lorne steered the Reo onto the tracks for a monotonous jostling that would be intolerable for the modern commuter. For the trio who had spent two days bouncing through the mountains, it would have been extraordinary but not unexpected.

In fact, Wilby talks about how the adventure on the rails, which commenced around 9 p.m., soon seemed like the norm.

> We were astride the glittering rails which were to lead us along the intense darkness of the Yahk Loop. There was a gasp as one felt the first forward plunge of the car and the white path of acetylene light shot before us into the immense shadows of that forest wilderness. Four pairs of eyes strove to pierce the distance ahead and behind; and every nerve was strained in listening for a possible monster of steel and steam which might dash down upon us at any moment from around a curve or catch us in its swift career from behind! Muscles were tense, ready for the leap to a precarious safety at the first sight of an approaching headlight. And yet, strangely enough, there seemed just then nothing novel in the situation. It was as if we had always motored on a railroad—so paradoxical is Man! After all, danger was no greater there than at every turn of the crowded city thoroughfares, where no one knew from what direction it might come. Here, every fibre, every cell, was ready for it.

Haney drove with one wheel inside the tracks. He began crawling slowly from one sleeper to the next, then on a downward, curving track, he had to use all his weight on the brake to stop the car from careening into the darkness. In a magazine piece, Haney said that in "some places these ties stick right out over the embankment, with a steep slope of three or four feet of ballast, and then a sheer drop of 500 feet (160 metres)." Wilby said the foursome endured "incessant and infernal jiggling and jolting that shook the teeth and vibrated through the spine. The jaw rattled slightly as when a man shivers with cold. One felt as though in speaking there was a danger of biting the tongue at every attempt at articulation."

The fourth man in the car, whom Wilby calls a fruit rancher, Haney calls a railroad man who knew the line. "It was very dark, and what we couldn't see about the ticklish points in the landscape he would tell us. I was just as glad in some ways that I couldn't see them. We could distinguish the shadows of the tree tops, right underneath us almost, in some places. The railway grade was so steep at certain turns, the car would run without its power. This is the heaviest haul on the Crow's Nest Pass line of the Canadian Pacific."

Sometimes the wheels got stuck in the frogs of the switches, which led to a madcap rush to jack the car above the level of the rails and fill the holes with stones. The spikes which keep the rails attached to the ties cut the two back tires to shreds. When they finally reached a lonely and darkened Kitchener railroad station in the forest just before midnight, they awakened a youth who showed them the Government Road to Creston. While they loudly proclaimed triumph, it would take another three hours to cover the 19-kilometre run along the Goat River Gorge, where they had to use the block-and-tackle three times on one hill alone. "The wheels would turn, but the car refused to climb," wrote Haney in *The Echo*. "It was like asking her to climb a wall of wet, loose gravel. The road runs along a steep mountainside. When the wheels threw up the stones some of them could be heard rolling down and bouncing on the rocks until they got to the river, four or five hundred feet below. Swinging around some of the corners on the slope we had barely room to pass, even with the car just crawling, owing to the narrowness of the road and to the washouts. We were mighty glad of our traction tires at some of those places."

At Goat River Gorge, the Findlays and I stopped for some photos. It hardly seemed like a rushing torrent, but maybe the water had been diverted in the last 85 years. A railway bridge crossed the gorge, and even though it was a short crossing, I was reluctant to climb on top to take a better photo of the gorge for fear a train might dash down upon me or catch me in "its swift career from behind." Having seen evidence of old roads and the height at which the train tracks swept down from Yahk, my respect for the Pathfinders doubled.

At 2 a.m. they found a road through a valley which led them into Creston by 3 a.m. Without concern for those in the land of nod, they honked their horn at the success of becoming the first car to arrive from Cranbrook. They roused inmates of a dimly lit bar at the Burton Hotel, and the proprietor served them "the loving cup" to celebrate the occasion before they went to bed. While they stood at the bar, Mr. R said, "Lucky thing we came over the tracks in the dark. Those precipices are bad enough to look at from the train, but in daylight in a motor car—Excuse me!" Having been suspended sometimes 160 metres above the valley, it was good that Haney, who was afraid of heights, found out after. All he could say in his diary was: "Had h__l of a time getting to Creston which we reached at 3 o'clock the next morning. Fourteen miles on ties, and up some fierce hills."

After fixing two flats and cajoling the car on its most adventurous day, the Pathfinders slept soundly that night. We arrived about 12 hours earlier than did the intrepid adventurers, and all we had to do was have Creston Big-O Tires fix the flat on the trailer—which they did for free.

October 5—Creston

Wilby makes little mention of this day or the next in his book. "There was no straight road westward; at times there was no road at all," he wrote with exclamation. "I was compelled to make a detour of 300 miles to cover 65! To again entrain my car for 20 miles at Nelson! Occasionally to make my own path! And horses and rafts were still in requisition in the emergency of mud and river-bank!"

It is easy to speculate what might have transpired:
- he may have lost his notepad;
- he had been carrying letters for the Governor General, who was in Nelson at the same time; if he had been snubbed, he might have ignored the Nelson trip;
- his editor might have wanted to cut somewhere, and chose Nelson;
- he might have wanted to downplay the fact that he ended up on a ferry;
- his muscles might have been so sore from all the physical activity of the previous day that he was too tired to take good notes; then again, he looked chipper in photos at Nelson and at the Indian village, so he couldn't have been too exhausted.

He had enough of a recollection to mention this day's Kootenay Landing expedition in two magazine articles. "The next day," Wilby wrote in *The Motor* magazine, "when we made for the Nelson steamer at Kootenay Landing, was a repetition of the last, inasmuch as it offered real 'pioneering.' There was no recognized road to travel, only a trail that meandered past Indian tepees into the broad Kootenay Flats, and then left us. There were two broad rivers to ferry. One way was a real navigation with a real pilot through lofty sedges and amid stranded log booms, for the flats are formed by a low-lying valley which is generally under water, and which engineering companies have repeatedly tried in vain to recover from the deep recurring floods. The waters had just receded when we arrived. The wide river at the second ferry was running low, and some twenty feet below the mud banks was a log raft. To get the car down to the level of this raft was a Herculean task that required all the strength of five men, with the aid of stubbing posts, ropes and planks. Once on the raft, we were paddled and towed across, and a team hauled the machine up to terra firma again. But there were moments when the career of the long suffering vehicle bade fair to end in a watery grave."

Haney, ever since he began sharing a double room with Wise, says very little in his diary, other than the basic departure and arrival times, and "fierce roads" or "bad time," getting somewhere. But local newspapers filled out more of the details, and Haney said much more in the magazine pieces he wrote, which dwelt largely with the challenges they faced in British Columbia.

This morning they were aiming for the Crow boat to Nelson, but first they had to bask in the success of their previous night's ride on the rails without being dismissed by a locomotive. With a few local enthusiasts following them, they took to the rails of the Bedlington-Nelson line of the Great Northern—which had run from Spokane, Washington, to Kuskonook, B.C.—to re-enact their daring stunt for their cameras. Haney says in *The Echo* that their intention when they awoke was to ship the car by train to Kootenay Landing. While waiting for the train, "an old fellow came along and heard our story. He proved to be a trapper who had come over from Kootenay the week before. He said 'thars a way, but yer gotto know it.'" The man, Wymont Williams, jumped in the Reo and directed them to the Kootenay river ferry, near a picturesque Indian Reservation of huts and tepees, and then along an old lake bottom that usually has one to five metres of water in it, but goes dry by fall. Except for a few puddles and stranded driftwood, and Haney stopping to pick up what he called in his photo album of the trip his "lucky horseshoe" (Lorne had that same horseshoe attached to the grill of our Reo), nothing stopped their progress until they came to the Kootenay River again.

"The only way to cross," Haney wrote, "was on a log raft, and the raft was on the other side. We made a lot of noise, and at last stirred up somebody in a little shack across there. A little girl of eleven years old came over in a canoe. Her father owned the raft, which he used for cattle. He was three miles away. The little girl paddled us across, and then jumped on an Indian pony and galloped away to bring her dad. She could ride all right."

The girl summoned her father, rancher I. Lewis, and three men to help get the Reo down and then up the almost straight, four-metre-high banks with the use of a block and tackle. The earth was soft, so they had to lay planks like a chute, and to pull the car up on the other side, horses were needed. Wilby sounded like a watcher rather than a doer when he told the *Nelson Daily News* "It was one of the most trying tasks I have ever seen undertaken." Through mostly high grass, Haney drove the Reo, and I. Lewis, to Kootenay Landing, which they reached by 5 p.m., one minute before the Crow boat was scheduled to leave.

Knowing the trials of the original Reo, Lorne and I felt a bit guilty breezing along a well-paved road. Our departure from Creston involved a nod to the past—a '51 Ford and horses at the side of the road. The theme this day was something the Pathfinders could relate to—the generosity of strangers. The campground people refunded the overnight fee of the Findlays, and the guy who ran Big-O Tire refused to accept any money for taking three nails out of the trailer tire. My encounter with goodwill came from a local historical society member who opened up the Creston Valley Museum the night before. In it we found two unpublished photos of the original trip that were misidentified. They show the trio in good form, posing with a Kutenai Indian chief and others impressed by the Reo's arrival in Creston.

If October fourth was the Pathfinders' most harrowing day, the fifth had to be the most beautiful—it was for us, even under cloudy skies and showers. The valley before us, between the Selkirk and Purcell Mountains, seemed like heaven on earth. Exactly 100 years before the Pathfinders arrived, Welsh fur trader David Thompson explored this land and mapped it; then he put those careers behind him (he moved back to Montreal with his wife and three children and drew maps until he died poor and blind in 1857). Since 1912, engineers have finally figured out how to keep flooding to a minimum, so where the trio had found a muddy ride to the ferry, we saw an array of prosperous farms.

At the southern tip of Kootenay Lake, the view was breathtaking. Long-needled Ponderosa pines shot up into our horizon above the valley, as did the red and green needles of the Western Red Cedar, an evergreen whose needles start to die and turn colour in the fall. Tall grasses filled the meadow, and only now, in what seemed like a late autumn compared to Ontario, the poplar trees were turning a dull yellow, and maples stood out red and orange against the evergreens. The mountains bled water: Scanta Creek, Akokli Creek, Crawford Creek. Fresh snow sat on a peak on the opposite shore, which was an undeveloped bower of bliss that made you crave to lie down on its cushion of trees. A passing car awoke me from the reverie; its licence plate, Beautiful British Columbia, seemed like an understatement. All Highway 3A needed was the removal of its hydro wires and poles.

It was days like this that you could understand how Wilby and Haney could endure all the stress of their personal warfare, the dangers of the road, and still smile for photos—not that Haney was a smiler. Nature's balm was being applied to them each day. Although our biggest problem was dealing with faulty cellphone connections and computer hook-ups, we also benefited from our slow slide through the countryside. It gave me the idea that every car adventure should be done with a governor restricting how many kilometres you could cover each day.

Lorne was quick to point out that you couldn't have done this trip with just any car, either in 1912 or 1997. As we wove along the shores of Kootenay Lake, up small hills and down around curves, the Reo responded to Lorne's touch at the wheel. He said "Not many old cars could steer like this." Some turkeys walking along the highway reminded Lorne of what he saw on television—a new group out to protest our inhumane treatment of turkeys. Lorne, who was shaking his head at the inanity of it all, yelled to the turkeys, "Watch out! Thanksgiving is next week."

At Crawford Bay, where golf courses and artisan shops beckoned, the mountains were drenched in the mystery of the clouds. We could have caught an earlier ferry— we arrived one minute before its departure, just like the Pathfinders —but we were scheduled on a later trip. A sign warned us of the six- to eight-degree grade on the hill going down to the ferry. The Pathfinders only wished they had such a hill when they tried to embark on a raft to cross the "Kootenai" River.

On the ferry we met Ron Welwood, a librarian at Selkirk College in Nelson who had delved into the story of the Reo when he put together a historical brochure on Nelson. Born in Penticton in 1940, he grew up in Port Alberni and was educated at the University of British Columbia. He spent two years at the National Library where he honed his love of history and of Canada. On board ship he said, "I think every Canadian should drive across Canada once."

As we crossed the narrow 120-kilometre-long lake to Balfour, a 35-minute trip, Welwood told us about the Bluebell Mine up the lake that produced silver, lead and zinc, but closed in the 1970s. On the west side of the long north-south arm of the lake is the Ainsworth Hot Springs. Someone had recently caught a 29-pound trout in the lake, but it is noted for its kokanee, or freshwater salmon. On the western arm, toward Nelson, there used to be a CPR Hotel and a golf course on the mountain. It had an elevator down to the stern wheelers, or paddle steamers, that brought rail passengers up from Creston way. CPR owned the smelter and the mines in the area, but they were now all closed as was the hotel, which had been turned into a sanatorium after the Second World War.

We disembarked at Balfour and headed, in the rain, along the north shore to Nelson. Welwood, who had the enthusiasm of someone who had discovered his own Shangri-La, pointed out old mining roads veering off up the mountain, the old fruit ranches on the upper benches, and explained how they'd bring the fruit down to the ferry and ship them with the CPR. One house perched on the hillside turned out to be the top of the *S.S. Nasookin*, the Crow boat that was brand new when it carried the original Reo up Kootenay Lake. We passed Red Fish Creek, one of the spawning channels for the kokanee, and marvelled at the large fir and hemlock that decorated the south shore, which is accessible to humans only by water. Of course the coyote, elk, bear, wild turkey and deer, which commonly invade the backyards on the north shore, would have no problem with mobility or trespassing on the south shore.

Nelson was a gem, arguably the most beautiful town we visited. Nestled around the end of the lake's western arm, and rising partway up a hill they call "evening ridge" are 350 heritage homes, even though a heritage home is only about 100 years old, the age of the town. Founded during the rush for nearby copper and silver, it was named not after Horatio but Hugh Nelson, the lieutenant governor of B.C. Not only does the town have a great feel to it, but it also has a great smell—the scent of

Wilby messes with his box camera as the trio prepare to stage a photo on the railway tracks in Creston to record their derring-do of the night before.

The Reo and the only other cars in Nelson outside the Strathcona Hotel, which no longer exists.

blackberries, broom and mountain ash. Residents are quick to mention that the movie *Roxanne* was filmed in Nelson and that a man named William Pratt— later known as Boris Karloff—got his start as a stagehand in Nelson (his first acting performance was in Kamloops). But they're just as quick to tell you about the famous architect who designed several buildings in town as well as the B.C. legislature and the Empress Hotel in Victoria. The architect, Francis Rattenbury, is just as well known for his demise—his wife made off with a young scoundrel named George Stoner who ended up killing the 67-year-old Rattenbury.

Outside Rattenbury's courthouse, and kitty-corner to what was the post office and is now the city hall, is a statue of John Houston; a forward thinker, Nelson's first mayor died two years before the Pathfinders arrived. He envisaged an electrical tram system for the town, feeding off the hydro-electric plant the city boasted.

It seemed like the entire town was the result of a forward thinker, that it was close-knit, that it rebuffed the car culture to maintain a sense of community. The thinker, it turns out, was Mother Nature, as Jack Haney's grandnephew pointed out. Jack Leyland, a 72-year-old artist living in Nelson, is the son of Annie Haney's sister. At a luncheon at Nelson's Prestige Inn, Jack talked about how the slopes of the surrounding Columbia Range kept Nelson a tight-knit city. "It's not like the sprawl of Kelowna, an abomination to drive through on your way to Vancouver."

We wouldn't be going through Kelowna, but south toward the border at Rossland. When the Pathfinders arrived here at 8:30 p.m. that night, a trip south by car wasn't a foregone conclusion. They were met by all the cars in Nelson—two— and were directed to the Strathcona Hotel. It was here that a debate raged about how they could continue westward. In the audience were the two automobile owners, members of the board of trade, Mayor Annable, W.R. McLean, MPP, a roads superintendent and a bridge superintendent. The summation of advice was to take the train to Castlegar and then drive to Rossland.

October 6—Nelson

With 350 heritage homes, Nelson had a good choice of bed and breakfasts, and an engaging group for the "Inn the Garden" breakfast table. The Spokane couple had just moved from Portland to get away from the city and traffic congestion. I offered that Portland was better than most cities because it had a public transit system, and they were trying to do things about road widths and traffic calming to make it more human. The Spokane man said he wanted his car and enough room for his garage. I suggested garages spread out cities and made them more hostile. The man from Spokane said you need your car to go into the garage because the world outside is too scary. The other Americans nodded their heads.

A mother and daughter at the table were originally from La Jolla, a pretty seaside town just north of San Diego. The mother kept talking about traffic congestion, and how they widened the highway to Southern California but nothing stopped the congestion. Lynda Stevens, the proprietress of Inn the Garden, a home built in 1900, said that widening highways has been deemed a bad solution, because if there are lanes, cars will fill them. The daughter said she wanted to move from La Jolla because she'd get in 20-minute traffic jams coming out of her small street. Then she realized that there were 6,000 people living on her block because of all the four-storey condos. She moved to the village of Sand Point in Washington, where she works for a catalogue company and her husband is a fiction writer.

Lynda said she was glad for the protection of the mountains in Nelson. "It is still a town." A town, apparently, with a sense of humour. While I was debating the future of life as we know it, the Nelson mayor had persuaded Lorne and Peter to bring the Reo down to the mall within town, where they had the big Turkey Bowl-Off. Participants bowled frozen turkeys at two-litre pop bottles.

In 1912, the "protection" of the mountains also made it difficult to connect anywhere by car. What the Pathfinders debated the night before was whether to drive to Bonnington along the Granite Road, cross the river on a ferry and then go via Crescent Valley and Pass Creek to Castlegar. But they wondered about the difficulty in crossing the river on a ferry, the dangers in using the railway track at Slocan Junction if they crossed the bridge at the rapids, and possible trouble in using either the Doukhobor ferries or the Columbia River railway bridge at Castlegar. Because any setback could have meant the loss of another day, they had the Reo shipped on a 9:30 a.m. freight-train flatcar to Castlegar. H.H. Cleugh would act as pilot as far as Rossland. H.W. Robertson, president of the two-member Nelson Automobile Club, pinned a Nelson pennant on the Reo and photos were taken.

It appears the trio climbed aboard that freight train themselves, because Haney mentions departing from Castlegar after the train arrived at 11 a.m.

Outside Castlegar we were met by members of the Columbia chapter of the Vintage Car Club of Canada who escorted us to a motel parking lot where city officials met us. Castlegar boasts about being right between Calgary and Vancouver at the crossroads of the Kootenays, with hot summers, snow in winter, good golf courses and ski hills. You can golf and ski at the same time. We saw a 1960 V8 Silver Rolls-Royce Bentley S2, a '47 Silver Dodge, Special Delray with suicide nob on the steering wheel, a '57 Blue Chevy Bel-Air and a '55 green and white Olds '88. Each had a story behind it, but none more gripping than Ken Schmidt's.

Schmidt's Olds '88 was the same model of car that saved his life in 1963 when he was living in Redcliff, Alberta. One day, while driving his '55, two-door hard-top on Highway No. 3, he faced two cars coming the other way in a drag race—a '55 Pontiac and a '56 Ford. The Pontiac hit him head on at 155 kilometres an hour. The Pontiac driver, a married man with a wife and four children, died of his injuries, but not for a year. Schmidt had a caved-in chest, broken ankle and 38 pieces of glass in his eye. "The doctor was amazed I didn't lose my sight," said Schmidt, a 70-year-old retired millwright. "If it would have been a different car, I wouldn't have been around. They had a frame in them a foot deep—that saved me that day. I had just dropped my kids off at swimming, or it could have been a tragedy."

The tragedy came a year later, in 1964. His son Gary, 12, went with his cousin for a sleigh ride February 9 and both disappeared. A chinook wind had warmed the river. The ice was only a half-inch thick. "As soon as the ice broke for the winter, we found the body of our seven-year-old nephew," said Ken. "I looked for Gary for three months. We even hired an airplane to fly up and down the river with my cousin, a photographer in the Canadian Air Force who was trained to spot things. People have written and said he's living in Calgary. I went up and I couldn't find him. I think it's possible. At the time there was as much evidence to say he could be alive. I found my gloves he was wearing. One on the edge of the ice. There was a branch broken as if he tried to save our nephew. Maybe he felt so guilty about losing his cousin that he didn't want to come home. We just don't know. When we got the letter it was even worse. You don't know whether they're pranks or not."

His wife Adeline was shaking her head in the background, as if her husband had lost perspective. "Life goes on," she said quietly.

"We believe in the supreme being," said Ken. "There's a reason for it all."

Adeline looked up with sorrowful eyes: "I don't believe he's alive. We were too close for him not to want to come home."

Our stop was only 20 minutes, but it was not unlike other stops where we were like strangers, again standing on a bridge, waiting for someone to tell us their stories. The bridge we were on was a road across the country, and once the talk of old cars broke the barriers, the desire to connect with other humans took over.

While Irene prepared lunch, Ray Kosiancic, who owned a silver Rolls, drove me to the old railway station, which is now a museum. His grandfather was one of the first in the valley in 1902, coming from Pittsburgh where he was getting 5 cents an hour in a steel mill. He heard of gold mines in Rossland where they were offering 10 cents an hour, so he worked two years there, saved $600, and then applied for land. "There was no road to the land so the CPR lent him a hand cart. He was pumping away to his land, and when the handle came down on a butter box, it snipped off his middle finger." Losing a finger didn't affect his foresight. His grandfather bought three valley properties, guessing that one day Castlegar and Trail would be one city. Sure enough, Castlegar spreads along the highway, like one long strip mall toward Trail, 26 kilometres away. The sprawl saddened me. A town with so much going for it, where you need a car to get around, has no sense of place.

Lorne had to fix the water line that connects to the radiator—"brass gets brittle when it gets old," he said—so Ken Schmidt offered to take Peter and me to the site of a Doukhobor Heritage Museum, an old Doukhobor suspension bridge, which was being built as the Pathfinders went through, and to the tomb of John Verigin, an early Doukhobor leader who fought for Doukhobors to live by their own laws. Wilby makes mention of them because Leo Tolstoy had dedicated the profits of *Resurrection* to them. Wilby says Tolstoy mistook their fanaticism for "Christian socialism." As the Pathfinders went through, they were in the news for refusing to register any births or deaths, and what Wilby called "their defiance of the commonly accepted laws of sanitation." The Doukhobors gained further notoriety later in the century for going around naked and blowing up telephone lines and bridges.

The Pathfinders' trip south was over "steep, breakneck hills and sand slides high above the Columbia River," wrote Wilby, which would have been a lot more powerful and contained a lot more salmon before the building of the Roosevelt Dam on the American side of the border. Haney said their road was full of "corduroy stumps, sand and stones" down to Trail, where they got a tour of the smelter operation, before making the big climb up the hill to Rossland—Haney wrote that it was an 11-kilometre climb up nearly 1,100 metres in altitude to the highest town in Canada—where they dropped off their pilot H.H. Cleugh.

Ken Schmidt piloted us south to Trail, where we tackled our biggest climb, 11 kilometres up an 8-percent grade. The car overheated on the hill—"When you go too slow you don't get the air going through the radiator to cool it off," explained Peter—so we created our own smoke in the home of the Trail Smoke-Eaters, the famous hockey team. Where we stopped was once known as "watering hole corner," because several cars had to stop for water there. The view was captivating, a chance to examine the layout of the massive smelter operation, and see comparatively smaller trees dotting the mountainsides—evidence of a time when smoke from the smelter and the sulphur it emitted killed all the trees in the valley.

At Rossland the Reo dropped me off downtown and I hitched a ride with Tim Smart, a 40-year-old employee at the smelter. He said it is one of the largest zinc and lead smelters in the world, but they also do gold, silver and germanium, a black dust that is a big seller right now. Germanium was originally a byproduct, but now one barrel (300 to 400 pounds) is worth $250,000 American.

Smart drove me out to the border crossing at Paterson, where the Pathfinders ended up that night. They had no means of getting across to Grand Forks within Canada, so they decided to make a V-cut into the States, following the Columbia River down to Marcus, and then up to Cascade. One of the tires that was badly torn by the Yahk railway adventure burst with a loud bang outside Rossland. "Then the startling discovery was made that we had not a sound inner tube in the car," wrote Wilby in *The Motor Magazine*. "Laboriously the old tube was patched up, and when twilight fell we had progressed no further than the Canadian Customs House at Paterson. Here we were cordially entertained for the night by genial Mr. Wood."

An old boarded-up house stands at the crossing. It might have been the place the Pathfinders stayed. After a quick conversation with the American agent and a lengthy wait, we made a U-turn to get back into Canada.

That night at the Flying Steamshovel pub, I ran into Larry LeSergent, 36, of Grand Forks. "Nothing better than a wake-you-up shaky." He was rhapsodizing about huckleberries, two cups of them, a splash of milk, throw in an egg, two teaspoons of sugar, cut up an apple or even better a peach, and blend it up. "You won't want blueberries after you taste huckleberries." Larry is a student at a cooking school in Nelson, and knows how to savour the pleasures of the forest. "I hunt, grow a garden and collect herbs and mushrooms. I can hear a bird and tell you what it is without seeing it. I've spent all my life in the bush." He has a country twang to prove it, and rattles off the names of trees—white pine, Jack pine, yellow pine, Ingleman and Blue spruce, hemlock, mountain juniper—as if they were members of his family. "There used to be gold mining back in six-shooter days, a lot of gun-play. Around Grand Forks you can still pan gold and show colour every time. Rock Creek has the best jade in North America, and you can even find gold streaks in it."

He was born and raised in bush around Grand Forks, again near the border, but it's a border he has been unable to cross in 14 years. I asked "Waaaah?" and he said, "Yankee border trouble. Let's put it that way." He started fighting forest fires at 13. "My uncle was the fire warden. In those days you'd walk in with a piss tank on your back and a polaski—an implement with a hoe on one side and an axe on the other. With them you'd try to fight fires." He also worked as a lumberjack, but he had to get out. Holding a chainsaw gave him carpal tunnel syndrome. "I miss those days. That used to be my life. I got hit by a tree in '87. It fudged me up for a couple of years. Fishing is the number one killer of workers, logging is number two."

We were now buddies, so I asked him about the border guard confrontation. "I told him, 'Don't show your face in the Forks or I'll whip you like a red-haired stepchild in broad daylight in front of the women and children.' Another time a guard pulled a gun on me. My friend had to hold me back. That's when I was young and foolish," he said, nodding his head. When I told him what we were doing, he responded with a chuckle "To drive 40 miles an hour across Canada—that's fudging scary." Obviously, we were going too fudging slow.

YOUNG DRIVER WINS GRAND PRIX, October, 1912, Wauwatosa, Wisconsin

—Caleb Bragg, a wealthy young Cincinnati driver, won the fourth International Grand Prix automobile road race with a Fiat car after a sensational last lap brush, in which Ralph De Palma's Mercedes car was overturned and De Palma was seriously injured with a punctured stomach. Bragg captured the race from a field of 12 starters, which included the country's most widely known drivers of heavy cars. Only six cars finished. Bragg's speed average for the race was 69.3 miles per hour (111 km/hour), five miles (eight kilometres) an hour below the record set the year before in Savannah, Ga. by the late David Bruce-Brown, who died earlier in the week during practice. Bragg covered the distance of 409 miles (656 kilometres) in five hours, 59 minutes and 25 seconds.

POPULATION GROWTH RAISES FEARS OF GROWING TRAFFIC CHAOS, October, 1997, Vancouver, B.C.

—Vancouver's population will grow by 240,000 people in the next 25 years, but poor transit and transportation links and a desire for affordable single-family homes will make urban sprawl inevitable. If sprawl is to be maintained, travel across the eastern boundary into Greater Vancouver during the peak hour of the morning rush should not exceed 5,500 vehicles south of the Fraser River by 2021. Since 1992, the number of vehicles during this hour has increased 21 per cent to 3,240, from 2,685. Traffic volumes are increasing five times faster at this location than anywhere else in the region. At this rate, the 2021 target will be surpassed by 2007.

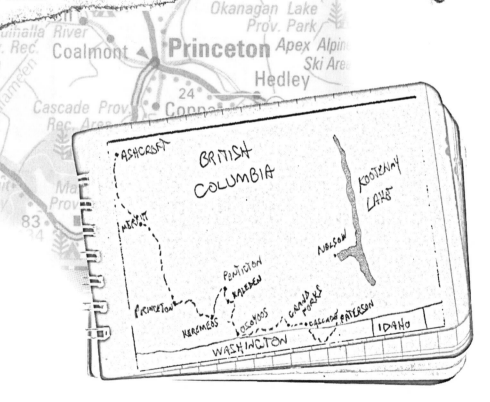

Chapter 14

The Valleys of the Okanagan and the Similkameen

October 7 — Paterson/Rossland

What kind of sleep did the Pathfinders get this night, in what Wilby called the "grass widowerhood" of William M. Wood? They arrived at 5 p.m. so they must have eaten there that night. Did Wood have confiscated food? Confiscated booze? Wilby says, "Customs officer Wood would hear of nothing else but that the motorists should partake of his hospitality until morning, and a right good hospitality it was in spite of the temporary grass widowerhood [he was temporarily away from his wife at work] of the genial official."

Did they have any misgivings about finally veering off into the United States? Were they hung over when Lorne Campbell, the Rossland MPP, drove up in his friend's Cadillac that morning to meet them and give them instructions? Wood had phoned Campbell the night before for advice, so the MPP drove out to the customs house with a reporter from the *Rossland Miner*. Campbell gave Haney directions on how to get to Grand Forks. The *Rossland Miner* said: "Wilby spoke feelingly of the kind manner in which he and his party were entertained by Mr. Wood without cost, as he said he was not keeping a hotel. While in Paterson Wilby took two photographs of Mr. Wood's house and the two autos which he will use afterwards to illustrate his written story of the journey across the continent."

Although there were a few beers consumed at The Flying Steamshovel, what gave me a headache the next morning was the TV news. U.S. President Bill Clinton had already declared his conviction that the science on global warming "is solid," that the climate is warming at a more rapid rate "due in large measure to a dramatic increase in the volume of greenhouse gases going into the atmosphere." He went on to say something must be done to make sure future generations have the chance to enjoy the world as we have, and that could lead to demands for fewer emissions from cars. *The New York Times* was reporting that morning that the heads of General Motors, Ford, Chrysler and the United Auto Workers were all at the White House to vent their dissatisfaction with Clinton's stance on global warming.

Alex Trotman, Ford's chairman and chief executive, was particularly critical of Clinton for considering legally binding limits instead of voluntary targets, *The New York Times* reported. "That would be bad for the auto industry in terms of jobs and the economic vitality of this country," Trotman told reporters outside the White House. Stephen Yokich, president of the 800,000-member United Auto Workers Union, also voiced concern that restrictions on cars could lead to job losses. From what we had seen across the country, the auto industry is already responsible for a huge change in the way we live. Now, when the very existence of life on this planet is at stake, they were telling the U.S. president not to mess around with the car industry —we employ too many people.

That morning I made a quick visit to the Rossland museum. Trail miners were among the first to car pool. As a cooperative they bought seven-seater taxis that would take them home from work. I saw another item in the paper about a speaking engagement by Virgil O. Stricker of the First Church of Christian Science. After writing *A Motor Tour Through Canada*, Wilby's next book was *What Is Christian Science?* It made you wonder whether Wilby heard Stricker lecture on this trip and decided it was topical enough for a book.

While I was drifting back in time, Lorne thought the Reo's time was up. He filled the radiator with warm water and was "horrified" when he cranked up the motor and saw water spurting out of the back of the engine block and splatting against the firewall. "There goes the trip!" was his first thought. It turned out the water he drained the night before had collected in the car's belly pan and submerged the engine flywheel. When the engine started the flywheel picked up the water and threw it up against the firewall. Before collecting me he drove a bit up the old Cascade Highway. It wasn't around in 1912, and had been superseded years ago.

Instead of duplicating the run into the United States, Lorne decided that a 1912 Reo should finally go from sea to sea wholly within Canada. We took Highway 3B, otherwise known as the Nancy Greene Highway, named after one of two Canadian

Olympic champion skiers from Rossland—Greene got a gold in 1968 and Kerrin Lee-Gartner in 1992. We climbed to our highest altitude at Bonanza Pass, 1,575 metres above sea level. It prompted Lorne's rendition of "I'm sitting on top of the world..." Other signs indicated that nature was still king of the hill. There was a "Road closed" barrier for blizzards or accidents, and a "Frost warning bridge deck ahead may be slippery." Fresh air filled the lungs from the coolness in the mountain shadows. The high for the day was 13 degrees Celsius, so the Reo climbed with no worry of overheating. The Reo's only problem was the altitude—it coughed a couple of times as if gasping for oxygen.

Slash-burning, or burning of stumps and branches after a clear-cut operation, marred one side of the mountain, but overall it was a spectacular day to be climbing into the clouds. When we descended into the stunning panorama of Christina Lake, it was as if we had been touched by the gods. The narrow lake that glistened before us made us want to spread a blanket for a weeklong picnic. It was a place I'd never heard of, part of the routine beauty of B.C. Awaiting us, besides the beauty, were Lincoln and Sylvia Sandner and their 1914 Overland Touring Car, the local fire truck, a Model A Ford, an MG and schoolchildren. Peter wowed the children with a talk before we headed in to a scheduled lunch at Mama Mitri's restaurant.

At lunch Cliff Kohn, 74, told me about working every mile of the Greenwood to Osoyoos road, starting in 1946 and ending in 1952. They had to hack through rock and hard pan, or solidified clay, in a monumental battle to put a safe route between the two cities. After lunch the Findlays carried on to Grand Forks, while the Sandners offered to let me see what the Pathfinders experienced south of the border.

All the villages the trio went through that morning were too small to have a newspaper, so no record of their trip through the United States exists. According to Haney's diary they took Wood with them to Bossburg, while the *Rossland Miner* says they took Wood to Northport. Both are villages inside the Washington border. "We crossed river," Haney writes, referring to the Columbia, "on ferry and drove through States to Cascade. We had one of our rear tires go out up about 15 miles out of Cascade, result of railroad," again referring to their Yahk adventure.

Their route south would have been through Northport, where they would have had access to both a railway bridge and a cable ferry to get across the Columbia, to a trail that would have led them as far south as Marcus or perhaps Kettle Falls. They would have crossed the northern tip of Roosevelt Lake or the mouth of the Kettle River and then followed the Kettle River north through Boyds, Barstow, Orient and Laurier to Cascade, back in Canada.

Lincoln Sandner, 88, drove me to his house in his right-hand drive Overland and I pretended to feel safe, which was difficult when he said his rearview mirror was useless with the roof on. I casually felt around the door and the top of the seat to determine what I could use as a base when I launched myself to safety. Lorne had talked of Lincoln using car engines in his family's sawmill, a shingle mill they ran at the far end of Christina Lake for 48 years, but it was common in those days to bastardize cars to have them run farm implements or the family washing machine. On the drive Lincoln told me he bought his first car about 46 years before I got mine—he bought a 1929 Essex; my dad gave me a '66 Pontiac Laurentian.

His wife Sylvia, a youngster at 78, drove us in a modern car south of the border. Lincoln, in the passenger seat, was an encyclopedia of local information, talking about the road being popular during the bootlegging days. Sylvia said that in the 1950s, "We used to come square dancing in this country, at a schoolhouse. They'd come to us and we'd go to them." I gave them a recap of the Reo's trip, and Sylvia said her music teacher Marion McPhail was the one who survived the Frank slide. "She was the baby they found in a baby carriage on top of a pile of rocks." It made me wonder if she was the same woman the Swans ran into in Frank, or maybe there were several who claimed to be the baby who survived the Frank slide.

The Sandners found an old road south of the border. It was one of the eerier parts of the trip. Unlike the Canadian side of the border, where there's a reason the population clings to the southern border, there's no reason for Americans to cling to the border on the north, so the area is largely vacant. On an old dirt logging road, cut through the tall fir and pine trees, it could have been 1912—how fresh it all must have seemed to them, the smell of trees, the chance that a bear might pop out from behind a tree, the possibility that the road might end and they could be lost in the middle of nowhere for the night. As much difficulty as they had so far getting through British Columbia, each day must have been invigorating, and the fact they had to veer into the States shouldn't have bothered them at all. The A.E. Todd medal, which they had hoped to get for being the first to cross Canada wholly within Canada, would have been lost, but they would have known they were still pioneering a route, regardless of the 49th parallel.

When the Pathfinders reached Cascade, road superintendent E. Spraggett was waiting for them—all day. With Spraggett as pilot they made it into Grand Forks by 8 p.m. and checked into the Yale Hotel. At a reception that night, Mayor Gaw of Grand Forks presented them with a pennant and the trio "expressed themselves as greatly pleased with the roads of Grand Forks."

The 1997 Reo was also met by the mayor of Grand Forks, otherwise known as the Pot-Smoking Mayor, Brian Taylor. He showed up on Comet, his seven-year-old Morgan gelding, wearing black leather chaps, a beaverskin tophat, tuxedo tails, cowboy boots and a snakeskin bolo. Like Nelson and Rossland, Grand Forks was celebrating its centennial, so the mayor "put extra effort into it" to show up in style. He led them to the park where speeches were made, and Lorne thanked him for leading the tour into town with less horsepower than the Reo. When I arrived I sank into the *Grand Forks Gazette* archives where I discovered that the manager of the local smelter in 1912 owned a car. He put an ad in the Grand Forks paper to say if anybody has a horse that's skittish around cars, "just wave and I'll pull over."

The Boundary Bandits Car Club, which organized a 1929 fire truck to meet the Reo outside of town, had a reception for us that night at the old Grand Forks railway station, that is no longer a station but a restaurant. Bruce Mark, the club president, said his love for old cars is a way of connecting with his brother, who died 10 years before in an accident with a Firebird. "When I go out to the garage to work on the car, he's there with me. I have his name on one door, mine on the other."

October 8—Grand Forks

This was the day Lorne had been waiting for. The old Penticton boy was coming home. He was going to get a chance to see his mother and family, his old hometown, his old school. Although the Pathfinders only made it as far as Fairview that night, we would carry on to Penticton, where they ended up visiting the next day. Besides, Fairview didn't really exist any more. At the time, said Lorne, the once prosperous mining town, with several hotels and saloons and the local seat of government, had begun to fade. The buildings burnt down or were torn down, leaving the jailhouse and not much else.

With Spraggett aboard at 9 a.m., the Pathfinders left Grand Forks, a town known for its beautiful homes, large lawns and luxurious gardens. Spraggett had received many compliments for the east-west road through town, which W.A. Johnstone, grand master of the Oddfellows of British Columbia, deemed to be "the finest stretch of straight roadway" he had seen during his 30 years in B.C. Spraggett directed the Pathfinders up the big hill at Phoenix, which Haney said was a 923- to 1,077-metre climb. Going down it to Greenwood "we near burned the brakes out," he said. After lunch, John R. Jackson, MPP for Greenwood, followed the entourage in his "big" car as they went west through the Kettle Valley, where they found "fine roads and dull weather," according to Wilby. "The hills are steep by the old mining camps up in the clouds and there is a lot of shoulder to the wheel business which sets drivers and passengers blowing like grampuses in the short spells of rest amid those lofty altitudes. Spraggett is careful to explain that these roads are back numbers and not on the route of the coming Canadian Highway."

Peter started the driving this day, past the slag heap the town of Grand Forks is selling off, and unfortunately past our first deer of the trip, a dead Bambi-like baby all scrunched up with its eyes staring at oncoming traffic. At Greenwood, Peter stopped at the local school and gave the kids a spiel when they crowded around the car. When the Pathfinders came through it had 2,000 residents, 100 businesses and a 1,000-seat opera house, thriving on the existence of nearby copper mines. Peter noted that it was no longer thriving because it had no lights at its ballpark—a humorous reference to the New Brunswick woman who felt her hamlet was a village because it had lights at the park.

On the way there we stopped and took photos of two brick Doukhobor houses. It was on this stretch that Wilby stopped and visited one of the Doukhobors' communal houses. He issued a backhanded compliment, saying the "desirable colonists" are "spreading like locusts in the Canadian west." In his book he writes:

> As we drew up at one of the community houses of this Russian peasantry, close to Grand Forks, some of the strange, immobile, shapeless creatures who form the women folk of the colony came forward and arranged themselves gawkily in front of the entrance, a motley collection of children clinging to their skirts. The house had about a dozen rooms and probably sheltered as many families. House and women were equally uncouth. The latter were apparently ignorant as well...How incongruously their appearance contrasted with those noble tenets which have made successful farmers and colonisers of a

people who work to enrich not themselves but the community; who abhor war; who neither steal nor covet; who scorn to work for wages and who own nothing but that which belongs to all!

In his *Travel* piece Wilby writes that he visited a Doukhobor house with "unlovely females" and children who "lined up spontaneously and mechanically" when they saw Wilby's camera. One woman gave them a couple of watermelons. "They recognize, apparently, only obedience to their spiritual head; but they have votes, and could be a factor in politics. It is said that there is a disposition to leave them alone because of the desire in some quarters to take advantage of their political support, which one day may become a considerable power, providing that the Doukhobors survive the consumption and other ills that are rife among them."

The Pathfinders couldn't ignore Doukhobors because debates about them dominated local newspapers. The same issue of the *Grand Forks Gazette* that talked about the Pathfinders being presented with a pennant also had a story headlined: "Douks At Old Game." The story was about a band of Doukhobors who went to the provincial insane asylum in Manitoba to liberate several members of their sect who had been confined to the institution. "The Doukhobors are adopting the methods that attracted so much attention several years ago. They loiter around the asylum grounds and divest themselves of their clothing. The police had arrested several of them, but the Doukhobors are threatening that 3,000 of them will protest."

As for divesting oneself of clothing, a pickup truck went by with a guy and gal virtually in the driver's seat. With such economy, the front seat could have held six. A German Shepherd in the back turned its head to watch us, as did the girl.

The temperature would only get up to 10 degrees Celsius this day, and the coolness led to the smell of wood smoke wafting over a mountain village. The cool seemed incongruous with the description Lorne gave me of our lunch destination — Osoyoos, near the American border at the southern tip of the Okanagan Valley. It has rattlesnakes, warm temperatures, everything to qualify it as a desert. "It's hot and dry, a wonderful resort with a Spanish flare to it," said Lorne. "My mother's brother was chief customs officer there after he got back from World War I."

At Anarchist Mountain, named after a farmer on the mountain who was a real radical, Wilby wrote that it overlooked "one of the finest waterscape views in British Columbia." For Haney there were 20 switchbacks to negotiate, as well as bad sand at the bottom. He said the road "is good on the surface most of the way, but it makes balloon ascensions—three assents of over 3,000 feet each and were only 30 miles (50 kilometres) nearer our destination at the end of the day." We had only a few, well-graded switchbacks, and we were met by some of Lorne's relatives on top of the mountain in Bridesville, including his sister Shirley and his brother Ray, whom Lorne seemed to look up to. In 1937, while he was still 16, Ray left home for Ontario with a friend in a '32 Chev pickup. The truck broke down in Dubuque, Iowa, and it took all their money to re-babbitt the rod bearings. In Ontario they worked on farms and eventually got into trucking. Ray enlisted in the army in Chatham, Ontario and got de-mobbed in Vancouver. He drove big equipment for 35 years as a trucker.

Ray was also interested in the history of the automobile, and history in general. He tramped some of the old Hudson Bay trails with a man who was mapping the route. Most of them were deer and game trails or native trails. He told me Osoyoos meant "the narrows," and that the word came from the Salish tribe that inhabited the Okanagan. The valley was now known for its orchards of apples, peaches, apricots and cherries, which prompted ongoing banter between a guy from Canada's fruit capital in Niagara and those Niagara-wannabes in B.C.

At lunch I learned about natives who ride bareback down the Washington side of Anarchist Mountain as part of the Omak Stampede. A couple of the horses usually get killed, so animal lovers have been trying to ban it.

We took the old highway to Fairview, as the Pathfinders must have, and then we left the former gold-mining town behind for a quick visit to the Oliver Museum. A huge entourage of antique cars from the Okanagan chapter of the Vintage Car Club then ushered us to a reception at the BCAA building in Penticton. As Peter wrote on the web page, "Penticton is Lorne Findlay's home town and many people were pleased to recognize the efforts of a local citizen."

October 9—Fairview/Penticton

Wilby was anxious this morning to be heading west, but in Fairview he was met by another road superintendent, Turner, who just had to show him Penticton and the roads of the Okanagan. The *Penticton Herald* said Wilby "looked fit and his only anxiety appeared to be to get to Vancouver by Saturday morning." Prominent citizens met the Reo on its arrival. The trio stayed for an hour before heading west.

Just as Turner was proud of the area's roads, Ray Findlay was proud of the area's history and beauty. While Lorne and the Reo visited his old school in Kaleden, Ray wheeled in from Kaleden to give me a tour of Penticton, talking about how the bench-lands have been developed in the valley, and development is still trying to stretch further up the hill. He drove me down main street and lamented that there used to be a wonderful view of Okanagan Lake before a new hotel blocked it. "It's immoral, almost. I don't know how this hotel was allowed to be built." The movie *My American Cousin* was filmed here, partially because the woman who wrote the story, Sandy Wilson, was from nearby Naramata. We drove to Munson's Mount lookout point where Lorne and every other young buck in Penticton came with their sweethearts to watch the submarine races. It had a tremendous view of the lake and slopes if any-one had ever bothered to look above the dashboard.

The boat that plied the Okanagan lake was a sternwheeler named *Sicamous*, now permanently docked in Penticton. When Ray's mother Iva arrived in 1910 as a 14-year-old, she came to the town of Sicamous on the main CPR line, took a smaller train line down to Okanagan Landing near present-day Vernon, and then took the *Sicamous* down to Penticton. She would have been a 16-year-old in Kaleden when Wilby, Haney and Wise went by. Penticton also had a mural of the sternwheeler, an old car and a horse-and-buggy.

Ray had directed us the day before on the old Okanagan Brigade Trail. It was so-called because, in the early 1800s, the Hudson's Bay Company organized a brigade of horses, sometimes 100-, 200- or 300-horses strong, to go north with goods to trade with Indians in New Caledonia, as northern B.C. was called. "They brought furs down the Fraser River to Fort Alexandria on canoes," said Ray. "The brigade met there and went south via Fort Kamloops through Osoyoos and Oroville to the con-fluence of the Okanagan and Columbia near Brewster, Washington. There weren't dams on the Columbia then, so they used huge canoes to take a ton of furs by boat to Astoria, Oregon, and then by ship to Europe."

We went to Trinity Lodge Seniors Home where we saw a confluence of wheel-chairs around the Reo. This is the home of Iva Findlay, mother of Lorne, Ray and five other Findlays. Iva was a frail 101, and not as alert as she once was.

"Hi Sweetie," said Lorne. "Remember when I drove you in the Reo?"

"To the *Sicamous*?" said Iva.

"No," said Lorne, speaking loudly but gently. "That was with the Auburn years ago. To the Kaleden Hotel. I drove you and dad in that car."

Iva, whose father was a road foreman who put in the main road through Kaleden, had been all dolled up by the staff for the occasion. Lorne, who was sitting clasping his mother's hand, told her she looked pretty. "They curled my hair," she said, matter-of-factly.

The Reo was creating quite a stir with the other residents. One man said, "Mighty God isn't that wonderful." Another man, being pushed out in his wheelchair to the car, patted his slippers along the ground as if to try to get outside faster. "I can remember as a boy in England seeing a car like that." When told this car was a 1912, he said, "They sunk the *Titanic* and raised this?" Clem Battye, another resident, once ran the fruit-packing house where Lorne worked. Clem made his way out quickly to the car, prompting another resident to say, "Clem wants to drive that car." He said he was born in 1900 and lived in British Columbia all but 10 years of his life. He looked down as if to cry. "Don't go away....I learned to drive in 1919 on a car that was called a McLaughlin Buick." His story was interrupted by Mary, a short woman made shorter by her hunchback. She did the cranking motion as if to start it, and said, "That car's as old as me. Our first car was this style but much smaller. We travelled to and from Blackpool to Cheshire. We had a bit of an accident coming back. I was young. Good Lord!" She managed a closed-lip smile, as did they all, staring at a car that peeled back layers of memory.

Our escort out of town led us down a magnificent rolling road through woods and hills toward Keremeos. Because of the number of people who wanted to drive in the Reo, I ended up in a 1951 Buick 8 Dynaflow, whose front looks like a missile. I needed a target out front because it had one of those floating steering wheels that Fred Mertz kept turning every which way just to go straight as the Mertzes and the Ricardos went to California on the *I Love Lucy Show*. Just outside Keremeos I was relieved of my driving duties, which was probably more of a relief to the car's owner. Jean McFarland, the wife of the owner and organizer of the Reo's receptions in Penticton, stepped out of the Reo to say, "When they built this, if they only knew all the joy it would bring people."

At Keremeos, the trip was all about joy. We were met by a high-wheeled 1880s bicycle known as a Penny Farthing, and two 1927 Model Ts that looked like jalopies. Their owners were dressed as hillbillies. The Reo has always been a smilemaker, but it was hard not to smile at the sight of it all. Parson's fruit stand, where we stopped in the middle of a town known for its fruit orchards, sent us on our way up the Similkameen River with some of B.C.'s best apples. We stopped briefly at a large rock on the side of the road that has been a native landmark for centuries. The three Wisemen stopped to get their photo taken there, as did we, but the rock was full of graffiti with a sign next to it saying: "Please respect this native historic site."

In his book for the Reo company, Wilby wrote: "Mountains and lakes—and pretty towns like Penticton and Keremeos, nestling snugly in their valleys!—all these and the hills and the twists and turns and snakings and windings up hill and through dale were but the work of a summer's day for the valiant Reo." But in his own book he is more elaborate:

> Threading forest paths like the woodland scenes of a fairy play, past swirling pools and the icy blue waters of silent lakes and of rivers that rushed through canyons and ravines, now dropping to valleys flanked by towering walls of granite and sand, now climbing towards snow-capped peaks, we pursued a road that followed the line of least resistance and took us more often north and south than westward. Pine-clad hills and slopes, lovely in the soft nuances of autumn foliage, gave place to perilous divides and the sites of abandoned mines. Again and again placid vistas, beautiful in their domesticity, were succeeded by all that was wild and rugged and stamped for ever as Nature's undisputed own.

Members of the Marauders Car Club of Princeton picked us up in Keremeos and piloted us into their town. It was originally called Vermilion Forks, for it is located at the confluence of the Similkameen and Tulameen rivers. The town was having problems because its mine closed last year, leaving about 1,000 people on employment insurance and prompting Vancouver to send its welfare cases up there for cheap rent because 200 homes were for sale. In recent years it was known for its mining, logging and cattle ranching, but in the Pathfinders' day it was known for its red ochre, which drew natives from as far away as the Prairies to Vermilion Bluffs to gather the red soil to make paints and dyes.

A reception was held for us at the Princeton Hotel, which was likely the hotel the Pathfinders stayed at, even though other hotels existed at the time. You could no longer stay in the rooms; they were a bit rough, said owner Steve Brodie. The structure was made out of huge logs dragged down to the river by horses and floated into town. The original owner had a 1917 Dodge Depot Hack, like a station wagon, to take guests back and forth to the train station, and he also kept a Chinese labourer in the basement to fire the boilers, a situation which epitomized the mistreatment of Chinese in the early days of Canada. "The Chinaman was mistreated," said Brodie, "continually thrown downstairs." He directed me to the dank, scary-looking basement and showed me a bloodstain and a black hair in the wooden pillar at the base of the stairs. "That's a piece of his hair. He died at bottom of the stairs."

The hotel story that preoccupied locals was about its owner Brodie, who had an extremely young wife for a family of nine. It turns out the wife was his Czechoslovakian nanny for two months. Leaving his wife for the nanny created a bit of a stir in the small town. One woman in town yells out "Naannneee" every time she sees the young woman, which elicits an Eastern European finger.

That was one of the stories picked up that night from the town's Writer's Club, a gathering of four people that included a tall gruff man who sneered at the suggestion they recruit more members, a quiet man who was probably the most prolific writer of the group, a cigarette-smoking single mother with "special person" and first-husband problems, and Margaret Stoneberg of the local historical society, who dug up copies of the Similkameen and Hedley newspapers from the adjoining room. The *Hedley Gazette* said "superintendent Turner and Mr. Wilby sped into town on Turner's Case car. They were pacing the Reo in which Mr. Wilby has made the long trip from Halifax. A little later J.R. Jackson's car from Greenwood, with Chief Constable Dinsmore on board, drove in with the word that the Reo had sustained a puncture and they were changing the tire. Mr. Wilby, who is in position to know something about Canada's roads, said B.C.'s roads are the best in the Dominion. Mr. Wilby's diary of the trip should make a most interesting volume."

Ironically, the Reo followed the same route as the Welby stagecoach, which was a year away from folding, unable to cope with the competition from cars.

Haney, in his diary, said they were "piloted by Turner in a McL car," which probably meant a McLaughlin Buick. Because he knew cars better than the newspaper man in a rush to deadline, it was probably Jackson who had the Case car. He said they arrived at "7 p.m. over good roads and fair grades."

October 10—Princeton

The *Similkameen Star* said the Pathfinders would have a good road from Princeton to Nicola "which is becoming familiar to all local motorists. At Spence's Bridge he will likely load his car and cross the Hope Mountains on the CPR, and the Fraser Valley has a good road for the final stretch." Wilby was preoccupied with his dilemma at Princeton. Before his journey he was told the east-west Hope-Princeton road was under construction, and that he would not be restricted in his journey by the Hope Mountains which now separated him from the lower Fraser Valley.

In his magazine pieces, Wilby writes that "Princeton, with its forbidding and insurmountable barrier of the Hope Mountains directly in the line of my path to Hope, is the next landmark in my memory. There was nothing to be done but to make a wide detour to the north to Spence's Bridge and Ashcroft on the Thompson River, and thence through the Marble Canyon to Fraser River Canyon. By following the Fraser I should reach Lillooet and Lytton, whence I could get to Hope by way of Keefer and Yale—a total distance of 300 miles in order to make 65! When the Princeton to Hope boulevard, now under construction, is completed this long detour will not, of course, be necessary."

In his book Wilby said that Princeton had little as yet to offer the traveller in the way of fare or accommodation, despite being on the direct route from the United States boundary to the Cariboo country. The route west was

> inaccessible by motor-car. Only one or two precarious packhorse trails, much visited of blizzards, led over the mountains, and there were many places along these lofty trails where it was impossible to find footing for any kind of car. The projected government trans-provincial highway will strike south along the Similkameen River and thence west by Silver creek to Hope on the Fraser. Only a short trip of this route had been completed from the western end, and between the two extremes lay a dense thicket of mountain forest.

"The finished Princeton-Hope road will be a revelation in mountain-road construction," Turner explained to Wilby. "You'll find it some day quite a different affair from many of the old roads you have traveled, which are so steep and impracticable that we have had to abandon the majority of them as too expensive to keep up. You see the old roads were constructed by hand labor, and the province, too, was short of money. Today we are eliminating all pitches and aiming to have the best of surfaces with minimum grades and low altitudes—nothing over seven per cent, you know— and a road available nine months of the year."

Wilby says steep mountain grades begin almost immediately outside Princeton and "get mixed up with the clouds and mountain tops until the Tulameen River far below begins to look like a mere trickle. The grades beggar description, and there are sheer drops down to the canyon stream from the narrow ribbon of the road 3,000 feet above sea level, which have a knack of getting on the nerves and sending a shudder down the spinal column of even a Reoist."

Our day started with typical generosity. Ernie Lawrence, who owned the local lumberyard, had put the Reo in his yard for night-time protection, and John O'Rourke, an old sanitary disposal man, wanted to meet me with a book that explained all the parts in a Reo, and how to fix them. The man had clung on to a small piece of history, and now had an opportunity to put it to use. I photocopied the pages in Ernie's office.

The couple who visited the Findlays the night before had sold Lorne a '26 Essex for $20. It was one of Lorne's first ventures with an old car. He kept it for a while, did a paint job with a roller, and then sold it. He also told the story of John Hudson, the Keremeos gypsy, who fixed a Model T engine in his kitchen. He took out a wall to get the whole car inside, which made the Manitoba story of the guy with a Reo in his dining room all the more believable.

We were on our way to Merritt and the Nicola Valley through ranchland. Some of the ranches sold venison or wild sheep meat; we'd see moose antlers on a barn, horses and cattle grazing on hillsides. One lake, Guildford, was a mysterious blackish green, while the only mystery on Allison Lake was what the lone angler would catch with his two lines. With a backdrop of aspen turning gold and yellow, and griebes or loon-like birds leaving the lakes for the coast before their webbed feet get frozen to the soon-to-be icy lake, there was already a sensation of yearning for the trip not to end. This world of sightseeing in the bosom of such beauty was the best of all possible worlds, and it was nearly over.

The roads, of course, enabled us to enjoy such beauty, but it didn't come cheaply. A roadside sign said: "Your tax dollars at work." It was another road rehabilitation, and the taxes will continue to be at work in the never-ending battle to keep roads navigable. We were on another Hudson Bay trail, now Highway 5A, rolling towards a reception in Merritt on a sunny day. Another sign asked us, before an 8 percent grade down a long hill "Brakes adjusted?" Lorne had the pipe at the ready to attach to his brakes. The Reo was missing that morning, owing to the choke staying on and fouling the plugs, but after it got warmed up with all the hills, the problem cleared and, as Lorne said, it ran like new.

We stopped outside Merritt, as the trio did, to take photos of a wonderful valley opening up along the Nicola River. But that was not the end of our photo duplications. In town we were met at the historic home of Matthew Begbie Baillie, a 19th century circuit court judge whom Lorne said was "very just, but very tough and became known as the 'Hanging Judge.'" From there we were led by a parade of pipers, a red-coated Mountie, Second World War veterans, Rocky Mountain Rangers Cadets and members of the Historical Society to the Coldwater Hotel where we duplicated another photo from 1912. The hotel existed, almost unchanged from its backdrop of 85 years before, and we were met by two friends of the Findlays whom we'd meet again and again—Fran and Jan.

While we had taken the more modern road along Allison Creek north, the Pathfinders chose to follow the road along Tulameen and Otter Creeks which rose 960 metres and looked down "from a dizzy height of a narrow corkscrew road to a torrential valley clothed in firs." At Granite Creek, site of the present-day Coalmont, they saw the spot where two million dollars worth of gold had been removed through placer mining. In the Reo book Wilby said a pilot named Thomas led the Reo car 50 kilometres along this breakneck road and then at Canyon House they were met by a car containing Merritt men A. Jackson and H.S. Cleasby. Reaching the same vantage point as we had, Wilby's heart leapt with admiration at the view "of the broad sweep of the Nicola Valleys, exquisite in their soft loveliness and rich in their panoramas of hillside ranchlands." Just like we had experienced, "Merritt hospitality was not to be denied," Wilby said.

At Spence's Bridge, where many had suggested they put the Reo on the train to Lytton (the towns were also connected by an unnavigable Thompson River), they learned they could get to the Fraser River farther north along Cache Creek. The *Merritt Herald* said "the absurd scenic railway route over or, we should say, through the snow on the high Hope Hills, was not considered on this occasion, and in any case it would have been absolutely impassable." Joseph Burr, a government agent, took over as pilot, leading the Reo along the western bank of the Thompson to the beginnings of the old Cariboo Trail at Ashcroft. The river, Wilby wrote, is a torrential stream whose water "seemed too green to be real, the banks too steep and rocky for human passage, and the river roared and rushed and boiled so self-consciously that it was obviously waiting for soaring poets and temperamental dramatists to chronicle its moods."

In the Reo book, Wilby compliments the car during this journey, saying "an incautious turn of the wheel, a too swift negotiating of any one of the countless down grades and curves overhanging river or valley would have meant instant destruction for both car and occupants. But Reo reliability was now a part of our consciousness." Of course, he failed to mention the reliability of Haney. In *A Motor Tour*, he expanded with great detail on the Thompson, saying

> How such a river must have despised automobiles and the other trumpery details of travel! The Thompson, I know, took a dislike to us from the first. It rolled up the earth of the road-bed as one might twist hair into curl papers. It buckled and warped and wrenched the path into semblance of a flapping ribbon. It tossed the path about like a shuttlecock, bending it back and forth until often we seemed to be returning to Spence's Bridge. Then it dropped us to water level and tried to drown us; next it endeavored to pitch us into a cleft in the rocks, or to shoot us up into the sky again. Failing in these tactics, it threw a lofty wall of rock and a careful arrangement of trees and bushes as screens. To all seeming, there was an end to the path and the tour! But the path merely lay hidden. When we found it again, the river, obviously incensed, straightway broke a spring leaf on the car, forced us continually to adjust the carburetor to the changing altitudes, and kept us generally shivering with anticipation for the next catastrophe. Suddenly aware of its impotence to do us further damage, the Thompson melodramatically shot out of sight and left us to struggle on alone through the bunch grass and rabbit brush of lordly cattle ranches and high plateaus.

We wholeheartedly agreed with Wilby's observations 85 years later, although the modern route, almost sadly, was without such travails. It gave us an even greater appreciation for what Simon Fraser must have experienced, and what so few people in the world have shared, coming upon this untainted and uninhabited wonderland. When they returned across the Atlantic, how did they describe it to their mates in the pub? It's easier to imagine the workings of a supreme being after such an experience, or to understand the glazed look of the mountain climber who has communed with the gods.

Ashcroft seemed off the beaten track, down over the Thompson across scrub land one would expect to find near a desert. The sign outside town said "Gold Country," and Lorne pointed out what used to be called Chinatown, where the Chinese lived to work in gold mines. After the railroad came through, Ashcroft was in the right place at the right time, and many prospectors, instead of going to the gold fields, settled there. It would not have been a good place for Haney to broadcast his name. Only three years before, outlaws Dave and Bill Haney robbed a train just east of town and escaped on a boat down the Thompson. Dave, the leader, was killed by a policeman, whom he had shot simultaneously. Bill Haney finished off the cop and escaped over the hills toward Nicola, never to be seen again.

Wilby felt Ashcroft was a back country outpost only then being tapped by railroads. The new and still unfinished Grand Trunk Pacific bisected the trails that led northward, and he felt the town was neither Anglo-Saxon, Tudor nor Norman.

> They were decidedly Oriental. The sandhills above the river, the intense blueness of the sky, the deep green of the firs upon the mountains, the strange unearthliness of the boiling contorted stream—all these combined to suggest a landscape in Algiers or Egypt. No traveler, in face of this general bizarreness, could remain long indoors in Ashcroft. There was little civic conventionality about the main street. There were low huts, with tiny windows and doors, occupied by "Chinatown." There were shops with wooden roofs projecting over the side walks to give shelter from sun and rain. On the side streets, private houses were fenced off, seemingly with the laudable intention of keeping out wandering kine and dogs, and keeping in unornamental wild flowers and weeds. In a corner above the river-banks, however, I came across a garden of old-fashioned flowers, lovingly tended by the rector of the little Anglican church. In the illusion of distance and elevation, it

was not difficult to imagine that the draught horses moving slowly along the highway against the dun yellow background of hills were camels or to endow the human beings by their side with something of the mystery of Bedouins.

The Ashcroft that Wilby described only had four more years to live. In 1916 three-quarters of the town burned down. But his comments about Bedouins were not unrealistic, as the world of the Cariboo Trail was explained at a museum that rivalled that of Maple Creek's.

Haney near Greenwood, B.C., fixing a flat tire that stemmed from their perilous ride on the railway tracks, which tore two of the tires to shreds.

American customs and immigration at Paterson, B.C., where the trio spent the night thanks to the grass widowerhood of United States agent William M. Wood.

The people of Penticton wanted to give the Pathfinders a tour of every new road in the area. Wilby opted for a shortened tour because he vainly believed he could reach Vancouver by the 10th.

MOTORISTS TURN TO CLOSED CARS, October, 1912, Vancouver, British Columbia—

With the coming of the rainy weather interest of automobile owners and prospective purchasers is centred on closed cars. During the last several days dealers in Seattle have received a large number of inquiries concerning coupes and limousines. In the street there is noticeably an increase in closed automobiles than what has been seen in the summer months. While the weather on the coast is not so severe at any time of the year that driving in a touring car or roadster is uncomfortable, nevertheless there is a strong demand for the coupes and limousines. Design and construction of machines have progressed to a point where the cars can be adjusted to suit the whims or needs of the most exacting

OXYGEN BAR'S MARKETING IS BASED ON MORE THAN THIN AIR, October, 1997, Vancouver, B.C.—

Stressed, depressed or just looking for a little pick me up? Consider a radical new alternative oxygen. The premise of the new business Planet Oxygen is simple. Oxygen is essential for survival, "but the fact of the matter is," says owner Bill Greenway, "the air quality in our cities has deteriorated significantly." Oxygen bars give customers a chance to sniff undiluted oxygen sans the pollution of everyday life. Sit down at one of 38 ports and stick a tube up your nostrils, just like in the hospital, and inhale oxygen from a pair of 85,000 litre tanks through a humidifier bottle. The oxygen enters the blood's hemoglobin and saturates the tiny air sacs around the heart. Greenway says "It's like taking your car in to the mechanic and getting new plugs."

Chapter 15

The Fraser Path to the Pacific

October 11 — Ashcroft

Who knows what conversations Wilby had that night he arrived in Ashcroft, but his dreamy visions of camel-riding Arabs on the horizon may have been induced by a disastrous experiment half a century before. Two-humped or Bactrian camels were introduced to B.C. during an earlier gold rush, but they couldn't handle the hard road. Their feet became so sore they had to climb Pavilion Mountain, to the north-west, on their knees. They also had bad breath which the mules couldn't handle. On the camels' first trip up the road they met a pack train of mules. Long before they met, the mules got a sniff of the camels. A cook who was riding the bell mule was bucked off with all his paraphernalia, "the train stampeded to the three winds of heaven and did every fool thing except climb trees."

That was one of the stories the Ashcroft Museum had to offer. Run by Helen Forster, the museum details the growth of Ashcroft as headquarters for Cariboo freight teams and stage coaches, beginning in 1886 when the British Columbia Express Company transferred its base from Yale. The teamsters, mostly single men who often slept in their wagon boxes or in the hay lofts above where their horses stabled for the night, drove teams north from Ashcroft at 4 a.m. on a Monday and reached Barkerville, 500 kilometres away, by 3 p.m. on Thursdays.

The explorer in Wilby must have been tempted to continue up the Cariboo Trail, either by a sense of history or a sense of adventure. Pioneers in these parts, like the first guy to introduce cattle or the first white man in this or that valley, were dying of old age at the time of the arrival of Haney, Wilby and Wise. The trio could not help but hear stories of the characters that peopled the trail, such as Stage Billy, who drove stage out of Ashcroft and would have been 77, still 32 years before his death when the Pathfinders went through, or F.J. Barnard, who took the early mails into mining country from Yale to Soda Creek in 1861 for $2 a letter, and from there to Quesnel by Indian canoe. Fifty years before, he started a pony express—one small cayuse with mail on his back. A year later, in 1863, he put on a two-horse light wagon after the government built a road into that country. In 1864 he put on the first four-horse stage connecting with the North Fraser canoe service at Soda Creek.

Wilby wrote that the "wild frontier life of the Cariboo Trail, along which the heavy eight- or ten-horse freight teams still ply to the far off goal of Soda Creek or Fort George, is like nothing else which either Canada or the United States affords."

Because Haney had to fix, for the second time, the seat in which the spring or shock absorbers sat, the Pathfinders spent the morning in Ashcroft, giving Wilby a chance to explore the town, pontificate about its images, and dream he was back in Cairo, where he worked as a foreign correspondent. He was daydreaming when

> a jingling of bells, and the cracking of whips in the direction of the bridge brought an abrupt end to my dream. A number of wagons, with long spans of horses, were pulling out of town, moving slowly up the winding road. They formed one of the picturesque freight caravans which for years, in conjunction with trains of pack mules, have plied along the Cariboo trail between Ashcroft and the gold district of Soda Creek and Barkerville. Shooting past them hurried the automobile "stage," a huge red-painted affair, great of horsepower, which of late has disputed service on the Cariboo trail.

The car was one of B.C. Express Company's seven-passenger Winton touring cars—bright red with yellow trim, just like its stagecoaches—which ran regularly from Ashcroft to Soda Creek. "When they first started using cars, the freighters used to laugh because inevitably they'd find a car stuck in the mud that they'd have to pull it out," said Lorne. "By the time the trucks came in, the chain drive trucks, well then that crushed everything. You couldn't hardly give a horse away." It was 1913 when the Pierce-Arrow solid-tire trucks ran from Ashcroft to Soda Creek. Each truck carried seven tons and took three weeks to make the round trip. After each trip the wheels had to be sent to Vancouver to be retreaded. As for passenger transportation, Lorne said the Winton 6s made the stagecoaches redundant.

The Pathfinders got away by noon on a 17-kilometre run up the road to have lunch at Twelve Mile House. On the way they stopped for Haney to have his photo taken at the arched wooden entranceway to the Bonaparte Indian Cemetery, which was enclosed by a picket fence. His father loved visiting Indian burial grounds, so Jack probably had the photo taken for his dad's sake. Lorne stopped at the cemetery to get his photo taken, too, but the wooden archway was badly in need of a paint job, and it was now surrounded not by pickets but ugly and ubiquitous chain-link fencing. The nearby forest-covered mountains, where slow-moving clouds seemed to rest a while, acted as protection for the ginseng farms on the valley floor. Lorne says the farms, which have exploded in popularity in the last 15 years to serve Vancouver's Asian population, are easily spotted because the crops have to be sheltered from the sun under black vinyl netting. Also, you can smell them. After spotting the rabbit bush Wilby referred to, and before we turned westward we smelled ginseng again, which prompted Lorne to quip, "We ought to be healthy by the time the day is over." We also passed two tractor-trailers at the side of the road which precipitated a stop for a photo with the Reo out in front.

Wilby, Haney and Wise also passed big haulers—the same wagon train they had seen earlier that morning that carried canned meat and bedsteads.

> A team of eight or ten horses drew a couple of waggons and a trailer. Built high and narrow, the waggons were loaded with every conceivable object of utility for the hardy frontier. What could not be jammed under the huge canvas cover was rammed at all angles into the sides; what could not be rammed was apparently slammed—anywhere; and what could not be slammed was unceremoniously hanged by the neck to the sides, the top, the underside, the back, the front, the axles and the horses' harness. The driver, the least important part of the load, was perched high above all other earthly things except the hills.

Wilby said the rigs were so jammed that other men, dressed in flannel shirts, greenish-yellow or grey trousers and top boots, had to walk alongside. One of them hitched a ride with the Pathfinders, sitting side-saddle on one of the back doors. He had been freighting "ever since he was a kid. It's a good life as far as it goes. I've got my own team and a bit of a ranch, with a shack and some good beef cattle, and you've got to show me somethin' that has this thing beat. Of course, there are times when a fellow wants to pull out and quit doin' the same durned thing that doesn't seem to get you anywheres in particular. I've tried to unhitch sometimes, and every time I've come back to the road. It didn't matter so much before, but now I'm married and got a kid it's kind of hard—the road pullin' me one way an' the missis and the kid the other. It's only becoz of them that I ever go home at all. I guess there's nothin' better for me than this road, and I'll live and die on it."

The love for the road appealed to Wilby, who himself had been travelling for the last 10 years: "The call of the road! How many of us must answer that summons! What matter whether it reveal only a few hundred miles of its length to a sturdy freighter, or a continent to an automobilist."

The wooden-framed inn or wayside house where they stopped for lunch had been reconstructed as the Hat Creek Ranch, but it was closed for the season. The 1912 building had an entrance porch covered in creeper, and dormer windows peeped out of the slanting roof. Inside was a general store and the owner was holding court in a side room at the head of a table of Cariboo teamsters. A rib roast smothered in onions sat before them. Then Wilby seems to fall instantly in love with a "neat-looking girl" who jumped out of a light express wagon that drew up, and

> ran out and dropped a letter in to the mail bag. She was a pretty crea-
> ture, rather self-conscious in her well-coiffured hair and high-heeled
> shoes, and conveying the impression of having "got up to kill." What
> the damsel imagined she might 'kill' in Cariboo country remained a
> puzzle all during the meal, where she acted the role of waitress
> whenever a guest was too occupied to slide the bread, pickles and
> butter along the table. The meat formed another puzzle until mine
> host volunteered the explanation that we were eating venison which
> he himself had "brought down" only a day or two before.

Perhaps after 50 days on the road, Wilby was missing his wife, but it was the first time he spoke so admiringly about a woman. Most often he went out of his way to show his love for the landscape, his reluctant goodbye to the Cariboo Trail, the "great beauty" of Hat Creek's winding "through woods and past small lakes, with occasional settlements and signs of farming. At one point the road and the limpid waters of a lake squeezed themselves through the attenuated valley, but not without some evidence of friction and ill-feeling."

Hat Creek was the most northern point of the trip, and from there our path was west by southwest along Hat Creek or Pavilion Lake Road. At the point where the waters squeezed through the valley, we took photos to duplicate poses struck by the original Pathfinders. Again, the mountain in the background identified the location, but the corner of the hill going down to the roadside was chopped off so we weren't so "squeezed" as we made the turn. The mystical aspect of the view was that Lorne, in the midst of giving a bus tour, stopped to take a photo of the scene, long before he had connected it to the trip of Haney, Wilby and Wise.

After a brief snowball fight at the only place we encountered snow, we had lunch at one of the oldest general stores in British Columbia. Pavilion was built in 1862, 50 years before the Pathfinders arrived, to serve the miners heading for gold in Cariboo country. Despite the references in Wilby's book that the road "neglected to warn us of the magnificent scene Nature was preparing," I was still unprepared for what lay ahead of us. I had a working knowledge of the tales of Simon Fraser, but I had no idea of the visual feast his expedition enjoyed. Wilby writes that a

> tremendous sweep of road dipped down to vast solitudes. Then we saw a deep cleft in the earth, somewhere within which, though hidden from view, coursed the torrential Fraser. Directly before us, enormous benches of colored rock and soil receded upward from ledge to ledge and slope to slope. In the course of a million years, the river had worked its way down over these benches to the lower levels, leaving noble terraces of green carpeted earth, on which grew dark and shapely firs and golden poplars, and whose faces formed towering escarpments of bare rock shaped into castles and impregnable walls of natural fortresses. We moved on and down. Through a huge gash in the dun-colored earth far to the right, there flowed a tiny rill of slatey-steel edged with white. It was the mighty Fraser, a thousand or more feet below. Crawling out of an abysmal and gloomy channel into light.

The view makes you wonder how Wilby composed himself enough to write about it. The modern vista has been smudged by hydro pylons and wires, but its depth and breadth leaves a sensation that must afflict those who visit the Grand Canyon, that we are but a millisecond in the history of the mountain runoffs that created the chasm. It's a view that would inspire Icarus to devise wax wings to soar off the slope to explore its crevices, its muscular sides. While daydreaming about the beauty of it all, we were overtaken by Brian Moore, not the author, but a Salmon Arm man who set out that morning to catch up to us. Moore marvelled at our feat, but I was struck by what mysteries lay at the feet of all this glory, the site where rapids forced Fraser and his party to beach their canoes and proceed on foot.

The modern road is paved and gave us a view above, and then below, what the original trail must have been—a narrow road clinging to the mountainside above certain doom, enough to give James Stewart vertigo. At times, ours seemed just as precarious, especially when Lorne had the Reo on the shoulder to allow a car to go by, and I looked out the passenger side to find a steep cliff beneath the running boards. The farther south we went, the more we saw of the Fraser. Although Lorne and I debated whether Wilby had gone off the deep end in his floridity about the Fraser being milky green, it was correct at that stage of the river.

We arrived in Lillooet three months and 189 years after Simon Fraser did, although he would have had a more arduous journey down the river that would later be named for him. It would be the stomping ground of fur traders for 50 years after Fraser, when the gold seekers arrived. At first, the town was known as Cayoosh Flats, because it provided good grazing for the Indian ponies known as Cayuses.

Near Lillooet, the trio passed crowded Indian huts and "swarthy women," wearing white head-cloths, blue skirts and pink baggy blouses, who worked arable patches of land next to the huts. But after a 4 p.m. departure from Lillooet, night approached, and the road became more tricky as it dodged mountains, creeks and loose stone from what must have been tremendous rock slides. Halfway between Lillooet and Lytton, about 25 kilometres from their destination for the night, the owner of a wayside inn told them to be on the lookout for freight teams coming along the winding precipitous trail from the south. Into the dusk they drove, in what would be a journey more dangerous than that of the railway journey at Yahk.

> With lighted lamps we crept warily along the unprotected precipices above the river. At last we heard through the darkness ahead a high-pitched voice. I sprang cautiously down. Nothing could be seen. After some time a light waggon containing an Indian and his squaw appeared round a curve directly in front of us. Gingerly the car backed out upon a jutting ledge to let them by, and they passed us

indifferently while we anxiously watched our rear wheels, all but poised over space. Again we cautiously advanced. Then came the sounds of bells and our lights flashed upon the huge canvas tops of the expected freighters with their long string of horses. The waggons carried no lights and one marveled at the miracle which kept them on the roadway. Had the horses taken fright a catastrophe would have been inevitable. We backed again. We stopped the engines. We held our breaths. The freighters crawled past, half asleep!

Haney, of course, was the one with all the pressure on him, the one who had to make a split-second decision whenever the weak acetylene lights caught any sight of danger. That is, until the acetylene gas tank was empty. Then they were stuck on a dangerous curve, in total darkness, still 16 kilometres from respite in Lytton. They couldn't camp there, and their kerosene parking lamps, attached at the height of the windshield, could not shed enough light for them to advance, that is until they decided to detach the kerosene parking lamp and have Earl Wise ride with his stomach on the right fender. On the modern road one would be reluctant to tempt riding along its steep cliffs at night without headlights far above the river. As for the remnants of roads we could see on the cliffside, we realized the danger was greater than Haney conveyed in two magazine pieces

A little oil remained in one of our oil lamps, and with its aid Mr. Wise was able to pick up the trail. We came very near going over the precipice, 200 feet into the Fraser River, at one sharp turn. The light ray fell on a spot across a nick in the canyon, and we thought it was the road. We stopped just in time. When Mr. Wise noticed where we were he gave the danger signal—"Whoa!" I understood what he wanted as soon as I heard it. Anybody within a mile of us would. As it happened the pilot was on the fender nearest the edge and when he found himself in the attitude of an aviator he concluded it was time to take a seat on the other fender for a while. As I didn't enjoy this kind of travelling any more than he did, and while Mr. Wilby said nothing, I think we were all glad to reach Lytton.

Haney, in comparison to Wilby, seems sanguine about the whole adventure. He calmly warns motorists heading in that direction to make sure they have enough acetylene, because they ended up without lights all the way into Vancouver. Wilby, of course, captures Wise's courageous stretching with a bit more drama.

> Taking one of the oil lamps, he stretched himself at full length along the mudguard next the outer edge of the road, reached out his arm so as to bring the lamp close to the ground, and boldly gave the signal "Go ahead!" Ten miles on one's stomach, holding a light over a sheer drop of hundreds of feet is a devilishly unpleasant role! Inch by inch we crept on. Moment by moment the poor fellow grew stiffer. A sudden jolt and it seemed as if we must throw him down the bank. A flicker of the light, and it seemed as if we all, car and passengers, were already over the brink. We were incessantly rounding a series of bluffs, twisting and turning in short, sharp curves that shut out the road ahead. Conversation languished. The unfortunate man progressing on his stomach gave vent to his emotions only in occasional grunts.

Lytton, where Fraser and his men obtained new canoes from the natives, gave the Pathfinders of 104 years later a hot supper and shelter, both of which seemed in peril if not for the "gymnastic feat" of Wise. With but a three days' ride to Vancouver, the trio had seen the worst of their trip, and survived.

October 12 — Lytton

Lytton ended up being a lightning rod for Wilby's disgust for anyone who had a chance to drink more than him, especially the Swedish prospectors who came here via the Australian gold rush. They dominated the town's bars and liked Copenhagen snuff, although they didn't sniff snuff like 18th-century gallants, Wilby scoffed. They chewed it like Americans, and expectorated the fluid, by gosh. Some of those, who had drunk so much as to find themselves on the wrong side of the law, found themselves at the courthouse and prison that the Pathfinders visited that morning. There Wilby found "a tall, fine-looking soldierly type of Anglo-Canadian" who loved gardening and loved keeping his prisoners clean by means of a hose.

> In the pound, though, was a real-life reminder of those who weren't so lucky in gold country. In the pound there lay the half-burned hat and trousers and the broken pipe of a poor unfortunate whose dead

body had recently been dragged from the river as the result of an accident to a scow. The man had been hastily buried in a little fenced-off whitewashed cemetery, decorated with wooden crosses, and every one said he was lucky even to have the luxury of a burial. The boiling Fraser "ran on its edge," and rarely, if ever, gave up its dead.

The Pathfinders were prevented from taking the old road south along the Fraser, because the railroad had beaten them to it—one of the few times, and one of the last times this century, that the railroad won out at the expense of automobiles; in 1997 power lines competed for the best route along the Fraser. The Reo thus had to be shipped again on a flatcar from Lytton to Yale.

Yale, 12,500 years ago, was the site of one of the earliest known communities in North America. After 1863, it was the start of a trek for Cariboo freighters who delivered hydraulic equipment, flour, champagne, whatever was ordered, to miners 640 kilometres away in Barkerville. One of the most famous was Cataline, or Jean Caux, a character not unlike the one the Pathfinders met outside Ashcroft. A native of the Basque region of France who always carried a Mexican knife in his boot, he was one of the old-time mule packers, the province's most famous, of whom it was said, if given enough rope he could pack a piano on the back of a mule. He had trains as long as 16 to 48 mules, each carrying 250 to 400 pounds, and his trains made it to Barkerville within a month despite forest fires, blizzards and washouts.

Wilby described the character they met as "Prognathous of jaw, with huge neck and shoulders, and fingers that were eloquent of the massiveness of his frame." Cataline was a shorter version—a heavy-set guy with powerful shoulders and arms, a barrel chest, so strong he could handle a recalcitrant mule with ease. He wore blue jeans tucked into fine calf boots, a stiff-bosomed white shirt covered with a black frock coat to his knees, a scarlet sash around his waist, and the whole topped off with a broad-brimmed toreador hat on his shoulder-length black hair. He never wore socks or mitts or any covering over his ears and all winter long he would emerge from his cabin stark naked, roll in the snow, rubbing it all over his body, and then saying, as he went back in, "She's good, oui!"

He spoke a hard-to-understand jargon composed of English, French, Spanish, Chinese and Shuswap. He employed all nationalities but preferred the husky north Chinese—white men kept quitting to dig gold, the Indians left after being paid, but the Chinese were hard workers and reliable. He would use Catalonia as an expletive (the source of his nickname). His language was lurid, so when he really lost it and began swearing in several languages, he put on quite a show. He lived on bannock, beans, game and raw herbs and weeds steeped in vinegar, and slept under the stars, and was proud of his citizenship and his friendship with Judge Matthew Baillie Begbie, the hanging judge. We had seen Baillie's hanging tree the day before in Lillooet, although only two unfortunate souls were ever hanged from that tree.

At 9:30 a.m. the Reo picked me up at the riverside hotel and we were off towards a succession of greetings, as the Findlay family members began to show themselves in earnest. The previous night's hockey game, in which Wayne Gretzky scored four goals in a clash against his old friend Mark Messier, was a subject of conversation, not so much for the feats of The Great One, but for the succession of car ads. Nissan was advertising its Pathfinder with an ad that showed it in a traffic jam, and then suddenly the mountain opened up and the four-wheel drive vehicle found itself driving across country with all the freedom in the world. In our context, the ad was almost nostalgic, looking for a time when freeways were free, and you didn't have to go off the road or find a backroad to feel free in a car. Because of the preponderance of cars, cars meant restrictions—some wise ones, like seatbelts, but most of them stifling like traffic jams, the annoyance of finding parking spots, red lights, stop signs, crosswalks, speed limits, red lights, stop signs, solid yellow lines...

The trend in 1997, through sales and advertising, was toward off-road, four-wheel-drive vehicles, although most drivers would never take their car or truck off a road. To consumer experts, most owners of these sport-utility vehicles had bought too much car, but the auto companies didn't care. It was just the latest gimmick, as Lorne knew, in the long history of selling cars with images that appeal. In 1997, the ads appealed to drivers to have a car that took them away from the frustrations of the road. In the early part of the century, explained Lorne, they were about being adventurous, and hip, and sexy. The four classic auto ads, he said, included the woman in a car "Somewhere west of Laramie," done by an avant-garde painter, with a woman driving a Jordan Playboy with her scarf flying behind the car.

We stopped for photos on Jackass Mountain, which earned its name when an ass slid down the mountain while carrying supplies. At times we were talkative and then we'd go silent for long stretches, just enjoying our last moments on the road. Lorne said he had some anxiety about finally making it home. He had regrets about the trip ending. "This," he said, "has given me a great amount of pleasure."

Just north of Boston Bar we met Lorne's older sister Babs, his youngest brother Ken, and their spouses Don and Laine. We carried on to the Bar, named after the American city, where we took the aerocar or airtram across the Fraser and what is known as Hell's Gate—so named by the early explorers for the number of men lost while trying to negotiate this stretch of the turbulent river. Lorne knew the staff of the restaurant because he had taken so many tour groups there. Peter had a surprise visit from two schoolchildren—their parents drove up from Vancouver to meet the car, and then they planned to pan for gold in the sandbars along the river.

Ken Findlay, 61, was also a truck driver. He remembered a snowstorm north of Lillooet in which he was ahead of a line of trucks cranking down the road toward their produce deadlines in Vancouver. With the help of his CB and some low gears, they all made it through safely. That was as recent as 1987. He told the story with such passion, I had new respect for the truckers' role in the nation's commerce.

The 1912 trio went south from Yale for 24 kilometres on a route overgrown with fern and bush, but that seemed like a minor obstacle compared to what they had been through. Wilby joked that the road veered away from the Fraser to take a winding route through the forest, lest the railroad decide to expropriate it.

> It lay buried under leaves, twigs and pine needles. For years apparently no vehicle had been driven through these glades. Another decade of abandonment, and it would be absolutely impassable. The soil was soft, and there were a few inclines where the wheels of the car could scarcely get sufficient purchase to take us to the top. A splendid avenue, originally built, I understand, by the British engineers—one of the highways of empire—is fast going to the dogs!

The threesome made it down to the point across the Fraser from Hope, and traversed the river on the Lake Gibson ferry with the help of Mr. Gibson. Gibson, wrote Wilby in the Reo book, "is a name familiar to everybody who has used pack and saddle horse across the Hope Mountains." Mr. Gibson was kindness itself to the Reoists, giving them a public reception and dinner at Hope as well as a tour of the Hope end of the Princeton Mountain road under construction. If this road had been completed, and the Reo not been waylaid at Winnipeg by what Haney called "Jupiter Pluvius," the Reo may have reached the coast in the 40 days Wilby had projected.

Our final Fraser Canyon stretch, through seven tunnels, was interrupted after a climb up the hill near Lake of the Woods. By the roadside a crowd held up a sign saying "We've missed you—Grandma, Grandpa, Peter." It was most of the Findlay family—the children and grandchildren of Lorne and Irene. It was a grand reunion for the folks who hadn't been seen in 10 weeks (7 for Peter).

On reaching Hope we were introduced to the Fraser Valley, which we'd take the next day to Chilliwack. For the moment we hung tight in Hope, escorted into town by a few old cars and an old highways department truck. That cold, wet night the Findlays snuggled into two motor homes, a tent and two station wagons, had a barbecue, marshmallow roast, games for the kids and a dark, scary walk through five abandoned railroad tunnels. My night included walking back and forth in the rain to get sustenance at a nearby garage—the modern general store. In my loneliness, missing my own family, the rain meant the coast was near.

October 13—Hope

On this day Haney's fellow workers in St. Catharines were celebrating the centenary of the death of Sir Isaac Brock at the Battle of Queenston Heights—an event that was regarded by some as the birth of Canada.

Haney, who had all but given up any extensive diary entries with the arrival of Wise, did note that on their arrival in Hope, there was a ballgame in progress. Wilby says the inhabitants were at a "football match at the back of the town, and, from the appearance of the streets, most of the houses had gone with them as a precaution against burglars." Maybe Haney had told Wilby it was a ballgame, meaning baseball, and because Wilby was only familiar with English football, he thought it must have been a soccer game.

Hope, in 1912, was little more than the Hudson's Bay outpost it had once been. In fact, the wooden, box-like Hudson's Bay building was still standing when the Pathfinders arrived. Wilby heard stories of how the traders ripped off the natives by standing a long musket on end and expecting a similar height in pelts for the gun— the longer the barrel, the more the pelts.

Mr. Gibson, owner of the ferry, gave them a tour of what had been built from this end of the Princeton-Hope road. Haney wrote that he "unloaded the car," which must have meant taking off all the extra baggage and tools, for what would be a joy ride "up Yale Road to get some pictures. Got stuck on hill for an hour on account of loose gravel." Five kilometres up the road they abandoned the Reo and mounted "tough, wiry Indian mounts of uncertain age," wrote Wilby. Haney didn't like horses—he felt they should be out in a field—but he joined in. A photo of Wilby on a horse led to the myth they disassembled the car in Princeton and carried it over the Hope Mountains on horseback (that was one of the suggestions heard in Halifax, and a tactic used by the Flanders '20, which won $1,000 and a gold medal for being the first car to drive from Seattle, Washington, to Hazelton in northern B.C.).

Nevertheless, their horse jaunt over undulating ground had Wilby thrusting forward into the pommel of his saddle and back against the cruppers. He was especially unnerved by one of the packhorses which insisted on imitating a bucking bronco. The Hope-Princeton road, which they expected to finish the next year, would not be completed until 1950. Completion delays became such a joke that people in the area created a jingle:

> *When dad was a lad, he worked on the Hope-Princeton Highway.*
> *When I was a lad, I worked on the Hope-Princeton Highway.*
> *Now I'm a dad who has a lad, who works on the Hope-Princeton Highway.*

Gibson's description of the recent rise and fall of Hope was not an unfamiliar story of the time. Two Americans came up to Hope and ventured in the direction they were headed—to Steamboat Mountain, about 58 kilometres outside of town. Just before the snow fell, they said they had struck a huge vein of gold. One of the two men opened up an office in Hope while the other went to Vancouver to sell shares in what they deemed to be a new Klondike. Gibson recalled that

> the ferry from the railway station to the town began working over-time, bringing in the young and old, the women and kids, and all the people who wanted to live and die in Hope as millionaires. Junk and furniture they brought along with them kept us busy for months. Hotels filled up, houses went up. Even then people slept all over the place, out of doors—any old corner was good enough. Hope had a population it had been waiting for for years....When spring came

along, some of the boys went ahead to take the first look and bring back news to the eager, waiting crowds. But Mr. Yankee didn't wait for their return. Both he and his pard in Vancouver cleared out. Lucky they did. Everybody wanted their blood. The bubble had burst; the bottom fallen out of the boom. For there wasn't any gold in that Steamboat except the bit of ore the sharks had brought with them from Nevada to salt the mine.

The misery created by the false mine—by chance, in 1997 thousands of people got taken in by talk of a Bre-X gold mine in Indonesia—nearly wiped Hope out.

Before a 1938 Buick escorted us to the Trans-Canada Highway on our way to Chilliwack, we witnessed an accident—a woman pulling out of a parking spot downtown. We continued on, heading south between the Cascade Mountains, which come up from California, and the Coastal Range. The mountains were more warmly clothed in trees, but they were being pushed aside as we headed into the Fraser Valley. The river itself drops 25 metres, and it has created its share of fertile islands. With some flood control after the bad flood of 1948, the islands are now productive. Lorne said they'd be a good place to look for gold.

We saw a rare road sign, this one for Likman Tires: "Going Bald?" Lorne explained that road signs aren't allowed in B.C. "When you do see them, it's Indian land. They realize they could make a whack of money putting up billboards." Lorne was still telling stories about cars. With a '38 Buick in front of us, he talked about the '37 Buick Coupe he once had. It was called an "opera coupe" because it had back seats that folded out of the sides. Overall, though, Lorne was becoming more British Columbian again, getting in more shots about disparity between east and west, taking on a more Western attitude toward Quebec separatists.

We got off the Trans-Canada at Popkum, taking the Old Yale Road through Rosedale to Chilliwack, which was named by the Indians for "where the rivers meet"—the Fraser being joined by the Harrison River due north. On the way in we passed another Agassiz Experimental Farm, which reminded us of our blissful day in Indian Head. The parking lot at the Travelodge at midday was full of cars from the Antique Chapter of the Vintage Car Club of Canada—a 1911 and a 1913 Cadillac, a 1912 Model T Ford, a 1912 Oakland and a 1931 Model A Ford. If that wasn't enough pleasure for car lovers, there was a gas war in Chilliwack: a litre cost only 48.6 cents.

Although Wilby and crew didn't get off until 2 p.m., there was no rush; they were told to take it slowly into Vancouver so they could be feted at luncheons and dinners. In what the *British Columbian* called "an easy day," the Chilliwack mayor and auto club members met them in Rosedale. Wilby said "friends were waiting to escort us into town, where pilots and photographers from New Westminster were in evidence. Before us, the mountains stood aside at last, and showed a broad, open, level valley leading to the goal." The *Vancouver Sun* said Thomas W. Wilby of New York, an officer of the Touring Club of America, arrived at 5:45 p.m. His trip, the paper said, "has been fraught with intense interest and more or less danger."

For us it was Thanksgiving, a holiday that wasn't statutory then, nor even broadly observed. We had our dinner at the motel, where Lorne's oldest brother, Alf, joined us. We had a lot to be thankful for the bounty and freedoms of the country itself, our success in reaching Chilliwack and reaching it safely. Later that night we'd learn that a bus on an outing to see the fall colours plunged into a ravine in St-Joseph-de-la-Rive, Quebec, killing 42 seniors and their driver. It was the worst traffic accident in Canadian history.

October 14—Chilliwack

On a day the Pathfinders had long been waiting for, they left Chilliwack at 8 a.m. amidst an entourage. They went due south to the Vedder Crossing, where they stood for what turns out to be one of their better photos with T. Eastman, secretary of the New Westminster Auto Club and a relation of the photography clan who must have had some good film. Haney's face is enlarged slightly because of a boil in his mouth, but the momentousness of the day makes the photo so compelling. Haney wrote in his diary "saw some great fish in Vedder River," an observation that must have resulted from that stop. The *Chilliwack Progress* said that several motor car owners who escorted the Pathfinders to Vedder Crossing left him at the bridge so he could continue on with his pilot, G.A. Gilley. The newspaper said:

> It was an undertaking that but few who were able to afford the expenses of the trip cared to attempt. It meant a journey of over 5,000 miles, a large portion of which seemed impossible for a horse, let alone a motor car, and that the adventurer should have succeeded in accomplishing it in less than seven weeks is marvellous. The car

looked businesslike with its cargo of block and tackle and other wrecking supplies, but it was fit for a return journey. Those who had expected to find a derelict were astonished at the serviceable condition in which they found the machine. Dr. Wilby in successfully accomplishing the trip has become famous. His name has been in all the papers of Canada and his photos are sold in all the towns along the route of his travels. The Chilliwack photographers were not behind their brother professionals and they too sighted their cameras on the machine. Even the smaller fiends were around and took their little snapshots, and the results are being displayed in many windows. The person who did not see the pathfinder and his car, or who has not a photo of them, is looked upon as strictly out of it.

Wilby, in his book, wrote that "prosperous farms and tidy villages now filled the landscape; there were huge fields of hops, where Indians were still at work among the tall vines, symmetrically fenced fields of clover, herds of sleek Holstein and Jersey cows—all the adjuncts of a conventionally smiling countryside."

The World says Wilby gripped the hand of Alderman Baxter of Vancouver who had ridden over to New Westminster to greet him, and Wilby expressed his huge delight at hearing the name Vancouver and learning that he was so near to the end of his long, arduous journey. At the automobile association's lunch for them at Westminster's club rooms, Haney was introduced as Wilby's able assistant, and Wise as an auto expert of Regina. Wilby, believe it or not, said B.C. roads were the finest he had traversed since the start of his trip. He emphasized the importance of constructing east/west highways to stop traffic heading north and south. *The World* says that except for a stretch between Lytton and Yale, the journey from Halifax was made in a Reo. The primary object of the journey was to establish the possibility of such a trip. Wilby sees no reason why any man of ordinary motoring ability could not make the same journey with the proper equipment.

An entourage that included auto club members, aldermen and newspaper reporters left New West city hall at 2:45 p.m. with great difficulty because of dense crowds that thronged about the car labelled "Halifax to Vancouver." Dr. Elliott S. Rowe of Vancouver's Progress Club piloted them "through a devious way from the Royal City to Vancouver," via the Westminster Road, Broadway and Granville street to the Vancouver hotel where Mayor Findlay awaited. Mr. Wilby stepped from the running board as it drew up at the steps of the hotel. His first move was to note the figures shown by the mileage meter 3,870. An admiring crowd jostled for a better view of the machine and the active man with the iron grey hair and moustache who had directed it across the continent on its record-breaking trip. Photographers were perched at every convenient vantage point and reporters contested for the opportunity of an interview.

It appeared that the reporter from *The Sun* got the best interview, for Wilby was described as "a journalist and novelist as well as an automobile and good roads expert. One of his recent books, *On the Trail to Sunset* is now on sale in Vancouver bookstores. *A Yankee Pilgrimage* is about to be given to the American public, while a further work, entitled *Seeing Uncle Sam's Country from the Tonneau* will be published shortly." As far as my research could find, there was no record of the latter two books ever making it to the book stands.

But *The Sun*'s most stunning disclosure is that "the laurels and honor which accrue to the conqueror will be divided between Mr. Wilby, Mr. Wilby's car and Mr. Wilby's mechanician. During his trip Mr. Wilby drove the car practically all the way, but to Mr. F.V. Haney, the mechanical expert who accompanied him, he gives most of the credit for his success." Wilby may have still been drunk from his luncheon if he was claiming to have driven all the way. What he might have said was that he drove in the Reo all the way, except when he jumped into pilot cars for short jaunts into town, just like I jumped out three or four times to take short rides in other cars. But the biggest revelation, is that Wilby might have admitted to someone that he gives Haney "most of the credit for his success." Was it a misprint? Or did someone slip Wilby some truth serum? Or did he receive so much adulation his conscience told him he had to deflect some of the praise? For someone who had no record of sharing the spotlight with Haney, it was quite a revelation.

> *The Sun*'s description of the arrival was also the best. It said the Reo was stained with the evidence of strenuous travel, covered with mud and oil and grease, but with every component part performing its allotted function regularly and efficiently as the day it left the Nova Scotia coast, the Halifax to Vancouver Reo automobile, bearing the banner of the Canadian Highway Association with Mr. Thomas Wilby at the

wheel, drove up in front of the Vancouver hotel at six minutes to four o'clock yesterday afternoon. The total distance traveled was 3,900 (miles). No tour by motor car has caused more widespread interest. The difficulties attendant upon the expedition were almost incalculable. Mountainous, unmarked country had to be traversed, watercourses crossed where there were no bridges, country traveled where there were no trails or paths, and in many cases railroad rights of way and grades taken in lieu of roads. It meant the survival of the fittest. A slight defect in mechanical construction, a moment's relax of vigilance in driving over dangerous trails, and the object of the tour would have been at naught. Wilby and his mechanician Mr. F.E. Hanley, were both deeply tanned by exposure to all sorts of weather, but beyond that there was little to indicate either in the crew or the car the magnitude of the undertaking or the unusual nature of the trip.

The mayor's wife tied a banner with the word "Vancouver" emblazoned upon it to the Reo's windshield support. Wilby, whom another paper described as looking "the picture of health," presented the letters he picked up along the way. From Halifax, Mayor Bligh wrote that he hoped the highway would "not only bring the different provinces into closer relations, but help to weld all parts of the Empire indissolubly together." Mayor G.A. McGaughey, North Bay, penned: "The importance of securing a national highway from coast to coast is a matter of great national importance. I might say a matter of great national necessity. It will encourage our public and influential citizens to visit one another and thus become better acquainted with the necessities and possibilities of this great and flourishing country of ours." Mayor W. Geary of Toronto wrote: "We in Toronto are much interested in anything that would tend to bring more closely together the East and the West, and more solidly to unite the different parts of the Dominion. To my mind, the establishment of a transDominion highway must work towards this end." T.P. Regan, president of the New Brunswick Auto Association, wrote: "The man who builds a good road will be remembered long after the other men of his generation are forgotten." And John Ferguson, a vice president of the Canadian Highway Association, noted: "With the deepest regret I had to assist the bearer of this letter to ship his car from North Bay, capital of the district of Nipissing, to Sudbury, capital of Sudbury district, a distance of 79 miles, there being in many places absolutely no trails or roads, and the best being impassable, which is nothing short of disgraceful in districts so rich in natural resources as we are blest with."

At the reception at the Hotel Vancouver, where they stayed, Wilby was met by Warren Gould of the Seattle Automobile Club, who wanted to make a similar trip himself next year, and according to newspapers, "he had a most interesting conversation with the pathfinder on the road question." Wilby said they averaged 120 miles a day over the first half of the trip, considerably less for the rest, averaging about 90 miles a day overall. He said railways were operated by companies for the benefit of the companies and not for the public as in the case of government-constructed roads. He expected to see the time when roads would practically replace rail in the matter of passenger traffic. In his *Travel* article, Wilby wrote about this Vancouver day, saying he received "salvoes from the cameras, a public meeting, pyrotechnic displays of newspaper headlines—what a difference from that far off day when I had taken my seat for the first time in the car and given the order to head for the Pacific! I felt like Alice in Wonderland when she drank from the mysterious bottle and swelled to unexpected proportions of importance."

The Findlays and I were in our own Wonderland, with not as much attention, but just as much satisfaction. The mountains, which had been with us for two weeks, seemed to rise out from the clouds reclining on their benches to say farewell. We didn't meet any member of the Eastman clan, but we saw some anglers and their dogs standing in the Vedder River fishing. In the distance was Cultus Lake on the ledge of the mountain. The land we were crossing, said Lorne, was "now called Sumas Prairie. Until 1923, it used to be called Sumas Lake. A series of dykes and canals turned it into farmland." Pointing at an elevated level of land, Lorne added, "This used to be an interurban tram line—the longest in North America, from Vancouver to Chilliwack. They built the track high because of the lake. They'd bring Fraser Valley milk and fruit in on it." Along for the ride was Lorne's grandchild Stephen, age five, who interrupted "Grandpa, you know everything."

Stephen's task was finding roadside animals, and although he missed a coyote in the field, he spotted sheep, llamas, goats, horses, and some black and white cows which may have been the descendants of the Holsteins that Wilby said made the countryside smile. Scenes of goats crossing the road in front of us, immigrants picking corn and a farm called "Mootel," made it seem like we were in rural Canada, not next to the largest conurbation west of Toronto. Cascades were behind us, the valley was spread out and the Coastal mountain range rose on the far side of the valley. Lorne, like Dr. Rowe, had found a "devious" route along Powerhouse Road, where the old powerhouse was for the tram system, to the Old Yale Road. As a bus driver, Lorne came this way to the Abbotsford airport when planes couldn't land at Vancouver because of the fog. The old highway went through Aldergrove, which had become a ghost town after they moved the No. 1 highway further north. But from my vantage point it was the start of suburbia, a continuous strip mall into Greater Vancouver. We saw a '31 Model A sports coupe with rumble seat; it looked like a rag top but it was really a hardtop. Here we were met by Jack Haney's grandsons, Paul and Brian Haney Masterson, and great-grandchildren Tammy, 27, and Bart, 28. Tammy, Bart and Brian piled into the car for the run to New Westminster city hall.

At New West we stopped at the Quay, a marketplace where we met Mayor Helen Sparkes and had lunch. The Royal City was once a great river port, but the ships got too big. Across the road was a parking garage from the sixties spread out along the side of the road near the waterfront, as if the purpose was to give cars a view of the water. We stopped briefly at the Burnaby Speedy Muffler. There was a quick exchange of speeches, which allowed Stephen, who is not shy in front of a crowd, to step up to the microphone: "I'm really glad my grandpa's home. He's that guy that drove across Canada. He was on TV and the radio. I just want to say that I'm proud he did that." It was one of the better, and shorter, speeches we had heard.

The way to Vancouver city hall passed one of the more spectacular sights on the trip. The kids at General Wolfe Elementary, Peter's school, evacuated and led a charge around the block chasing the Reo in full flight. The students' enthusiasm and joy were staggering. It was a taste of the mayhem that Wilby and Haney created 85 years before, for at the city hall, only a few people straggled by the car. Acting mayor Alan Herbert welcomed us to the city, but all those faces seem to be the same, as were their comments. What I liked best were the narrow lots of the old houses near city hall, and the back lanes that put cars in their place. For a city that has been overrun by bad planning, here was an example of good planning on the doorstep.

In Lorne's diary, he wrote: "Successfully home at last thanks to a truly great automobile—the Reo. How good it felt to make and eat a meal and go to bed in our own home!!" Haney made his last entry in his diary this night, saying "New Westminster had a lunch for us and then we left for Vancouver which we reached 4 p.m." It was a simple sign off, never doing justice to the moment. In the end, Haney was doing what he did the entire trip—he left the rhetoric for Wilby.

Wilby checking out the completed portion of the Hope-Princeton road on a horse that insisted on imitating a bucking bronco.

Haney, Wilby and Wise. The quality of the photo is so good because the man on the right is an Eastman of Kodak-Eastman fame. He died in the First World War.

USED MOTOR CAR PROBLEM OVERCOME, October, 1912, Seattle, Washington—

What to do with the accumulation of used cars, cars traded in towards later models has been the unanswerable problem for automobile dealers all over the country since the birth of the industry and particularly since the motor car has come into such universal usage. The Seattle Automobile Clearance Association will put all used cars under one roof and hold a sale for 30 days each fall. Strange as it may seem, dealers are left with the higher class and more mechanically perfect car at the end of the season—the ones that have had the hardest usage and longest service are readily disposed of to the smaller merchants and made into delivery cars.

LUXURY IS A CAR YOU CAN WORK IN, October, 1997, Detroit, Michigan—

Back in 1923, Rolls-Royce accessorized a stately Silver Ghost with a gun rack, a large spotlight and a Gatling gun so its owner, an Indian prince, could hunt tigers. In 1995, a Silver Spur was created for a businessman who wanted all the comforts of the office when he was on the road. The car had a fold-out fax machine and printer, a walnut case for a laptop and slots in the ceiling for filing paperwork. Since what passes for luxury in the 1990s is the ability to work all the time, many Rolls-Royces are being designed as portable offices, not just portable bars. Younger magnates are ordering theirs with five phone lines as well as a fax and an outlet to plug in a computer for the Internet, CD-ROM equipment and computerized navigation systems.

Chapter 16

Vancouver to Victoria

October 15 — Vancouver

As Wilby suggested, newspaper headlines were full of pyrotechnics. Blasted across the top of the *Vancouver Sun* were the words: "Across Canada by automobile, Thomas W. Wilby finds route for transcontinental road." *The Daily News Advertiser* said< "4000 Miles in an Automobile," with a photo at the top of the page of Wilby being greeted in Vancouver, with Haney sitting behind the wheel of the Reo. *The World* had a front-page photo of Wilby, his topcoat pulled back, his hat at a jaunty angle, with the caption, "Canadian Pathfinder," right next to a story about the World Series between the New York Giants and the Boston Red Sox going to an eighth game. There were separate stories on the durability of his Dunlop Tires, but little or no mention of the Reo, which upset Haney. He felt the Reo deserved all the credit, and for all the pontificating Wilby did, he studiously avoided being quoted about the Reo. Perhaps the company had disappointed him, or didn't come through with the money he wanted, but the Reo company didn't get nearly the attention given the Canadian Highway Association. Either Wilby had his blinders on, or he expected the car to make it because he had few problems going across the United States in his Mudhen.

Amidst the fooforaw, Wilby was in his element. Throughout the trip, he told a reporter, "I don't believe I saw more than one per cent of macadamized roads. We found the worst roads around North Bay, Ont. where on two occasions the car was damaged and had to lay up for repairs. We had to pull the car out with block and tackle on 12 occasions, and twice had to be pulled out of the mud by horses. As for tires there is still one of them in use now that we started with, one being badly cut in Ontario, and two of them being torn to ribbons on the ties between Yahk and

313

Kitchener, B.C. We also used up about six inner tubes." His recap of the trip said that seven weeks of Maritimes rain had turned the red clay and gravel roads into a batter. "When we got to Quebec we were more or less out of the rain belt, and we found dusty roads, and a very good wagon trail along the St. Lawrence." One difficulty that must be remedied are the road rules which force the driver to switch from the left side in the Maritime provinces, to the right in Quebec and Ontario and to the left again in B.C.

Whether intended or not, Wilby left the impression with at least one reporter that the car only had to be entrained once, and that was in B.C. Otherwise, it made it across on its own. He is even quoted directly as saying they had to make "repairs to the car in general after having encountered seas of mud between Winnipeg and Fort William. Every mile of the way was covered by the car under its own power, with the exception of a stretch of 20 miles near Lytton, which necessitated having the car placed on a flat car and shipped by rail. At no time did we have the slightest problem with our engine." Railways, as he was fond of stating, "bind the provinces together, but it remained for a roadway to still further cement them."

In the afternoon, the Reo made a run through the city and out to Kitsilano beach to dip the wheels of the auto in the Pacific, the same ceremony having been performed on the Atlantic coast. We too dipped our wheels this day, just down from Kitsilano beach. Lorne lives in Kitsilano, so we also stopped at a ceremony unveiling a new wooden sculpture as its gateway. Jim Kostyniuk, who spent more than two years constructing images on large logs, intended to symbolize driftwood and the town's history of logging and century-old fir and cedar trees. The first tier represents the Salish community of natives, with their log houses and long canoes. The second level includes the older buildings, houses and storefronts of Kitsilano that can still be seen, and a rendition of the first train that came through, known as Engine 374. It was at the beach for many years, said Kostyniuk, and it is now at the roundhouse on the water's edge. The third tier is the horizon view from Kitsilano, Stanley Park, freighters, the mountains. Kostyniuk said Kitsilano, named after the Squamish Indian Chief Khahtsahlanough, has an older cityscape with a strong community spirit: "One way of hanging on to it is the idea behind this sign," he said, meaning to cherish the past without obliterating it, yet welcome progress.

Our first collection of Pacific water was done at Vanier Park, where Lorne drove the front wheels into False Creek, on the edge of English Bay, so that I could pour half the bottle of Atlantic Ocean into the Pacific, and then refilling it for the symbolic gesture of uniting both coasts with our trip. A reception followed at the nearby Vancouver Archives and Museum, and then I had little time to savour the moment. I ended up on a float plane to Victoria to reach the archives on time.

Peter dropped me off and took pictures of the Reo in the Gastown area from which Vancouver sprouted. The city was incorporated in 1886 and burned down shortly after. When the railway came to Vancouver in 1887, the city quickly became an important seaport, and 110 years later, it had become a magnet for people wanting to take advantage of its natural beauty. At the time the Pathfinders went through, lots were being given away to prospective residents of nearby White Rock.

Then Peter went by his school for a rousing reception. The Wolfe Advanced Band, which Peter usually conducts, played a rousing rendition of "O Canada" while the entire school waved flags. The school is between Manitoba and Ontario Avenues; Peter joked if it was one block further east it would have been Montcalm School.

Wilby's reception, referred to as "a smoker," would be at the new digs of the Progress Club at the corner of Richards and Hastings streets, an event being hosted by the Progress and Vancouver automobile clubs. Mayor Findlay hailed Wilby as a trailblazer whose name would live in Canadian history, and added that nothing brought better returns than scenic highways. Dr. Rowe said the time is near when a cross-continent trip would be like "taking a drive over to see the folks." Wilby rose to hearty applause. One of the joys of the trip, he said, was to discover that there was a justification for what the Holy Writ and classic legend said about apples—B.C. apples were worth crossing the continent for. He was pleased to accomplish the trip with the sacrifice of only one life that was a chicken's. The further west he got on his tour the greater cordiality he experienced. He was a lover of the road and it ever lured him. His speech was largely reprinted in one of the newspapers:

> The continent has been crossed—not by portages and canoes and weary toil of endless months, as in Mackenzie's days, when in 1793 the first transcontinentalist caught a glimpse of the golden strand of the Pacific and inscribed his name upon the rocky boulder overlooking the ocean goal, but in the comparative luxury of the tonneau. But the work is not over. It is hardly begun. The true crossing of Canada is yet to come. At present one can do little more than show the way

and the Canadian Highway looks very much like a dream. But men will come after me and complete my work, for dreams and ideals are, after all, the real things in life. Inch by inch the great white way of Anglo Saxon civilization will be wrested from mountain pass and beetling crag, from sandy waste and alkali slough, from winding pass and dizzy height, stretching its way from the Silver east to the Golden west, along trails left by our pioneer fathers to their ceaseless march toward the setting sun, until the last link is forged in the 4,000-mile chain. Then and not till then will Canada be a true nation. The road will consolidate, will unite East and West, will wipe out all difference, racial and distinctions. The confederation of Canada will not become historically complete until we have a Canadian Transcontinental Highway to take up the work of nation building at the point where the railroads left off. This transcontinental highway unlike the railroads, will be a people's highway, built for the people. Thus in a true sense it will be a national highway. A transcontinental highway will be essentially an All-Red Route. It will have great significance as a military road. The idea of a trade union of the British Empire has presented itself largely because of the potentialities of the Canadian west. It will take practical form when a transcontinental highway shall span from East to West, and shall open up new belts of land and be a great and constant natural asset, the extent of which can not be gauged.

When his speech ended, Wilby passed on letters from the Halifax and Quebec boards of trade. Already, plans were being made for the final leg across Vancouver Island. The Vancouver Auto Club sent Mr. Harold Johnston, an esteemed citizen of Nanaimo, a telegram stating: "Thos Wilby, will leave here Wednesday morning on way to Alberni. Can you arrange reception by Nanaimo Auto Club and supply pilot for trip? Am wiring A.E. Todd, Victoria. He may arrange to go over road."

The Pathfinders had little to do other than be feted and celebrate. Earl Wise, who had helped them hurdle the mountains, left on the train for Regina, where he was reunited with the love of his life, a divorcée from Lansing who would marry again before Earl, at 36, had the chance to walk down the aisle with her in 1925.

October 16—Vancouver

The town of Nanaimo, on the island, took great pleasure in being part of the Pathfinders' trip. The *Nanaimo Free Press* gave a play-by-play of the Pathfinders' movements, from his Vancouver arrival to taking the island ferry. The next day the paper took great pride in saying Wilby was well-feted at the Windsor hotel.

> Doubtless when this skilled journalist writes the story of his journey, he will not overlook the honor shown him in Nanaimo. Whilst his feat of traversing the Canadian continent is a wonderful one, it is not so hazardous as that of the hobo who, from his uncomfortable position on the brake beam of a freight, peeps through the trestle bridge at the miles of torrent and gullies below into the perils of which he fears every moment to fall. Road making is a great step towards civilization. The Romans who built the great North Road from London to Edinburgh were the first pioneers to open out Great Britain and their highways remain today testifying to the excellent work of nearly 2000 years ago. Labor was cheap in these days and very abundant, all the unfortunate Britons received in remuneration being in the shape of lashes from the invaders' whips. Times have changed vastly since then. The Roman of former history who rode ruthlessly over the plebeian Briton or matched his might courage and log spear in the arena against the feeble short handled sword of his Anglican prisoner, is now a Dago trundling along his narrow load of cement at two and a half dollars per day.

Luckily, newspapers have changed for the better. But when "the skilled" one wrote his book, he had more subtle racist slurs, though the later chapters were not as rife with condescending comments.

That morning Haney, Wilby and the Reo took the $9 *Princess Patricia* ferry to Nanaimo during a rainstorm. In the Reo booklet, Wilby said they were met by a pilot car from the Victoria Automobile Association and Mr. Inglis from the *Victoria Daily Times.* "Alongside were Mr. Sherwood, M.P. and Mayor Shaw to conduct the party to the hotel, where the festive board was spread."

It's not clear whether Dunlop paid for the stories, but *The Daily Province* wrote about Dunlop traction tread tires as though it were an advertisement. "The first tire that Wilby changed was in Ontario, after having run over a broken bottle, which went through the tire and tube. Over corduroy roads, rocks and through veritable seas of mud, Wilby pushed his car and never once did his tires give him the least trouble. After coming off the ties in Kitchener, it was found that the two rear tires, the driving tires, had to be replaced. *The Province* examined the lone remaining tire from Halifax and found that the tread was scarcely worn at all and in no place was the fabric showing through. The Dunlop Company guarantees every tire leaving the factory for 3,500 miles. They were just ordinary stock, Quick detachable tires, size 35 by 4, and were not made to order for Wilby."

The Findlays managed to get the Reo over to the Island without my help, not that I was ever any help. It went over the Lions' Gate Bridge, which crosses the Burrard Inlet, and on through West Vancouver to Horseshoe Bay, where the B.C. Ferries terminal is located. To make the crossing cheaper, the Reo was placed on its trailer for the first time since Toronto. The *M.V. Queen of Cowichan* took an hour and forty minutes to travel 25 kilometres across the Georgia Strait to Departure Bay, just outside of Nanaimo. The escort was not a pilot car from Victoria but pre-1916 cars from the Malahat Challenge Planning Committee, including a 1911 Russell that was built in Toronto by the CCM company, now better known for its bicycles and sporting goods. The Malahat Challenge is an annual car tour of the island by pre-1916 cars. Lorne noted the next day that there are only five or six Russells in existence, and only two or three in private hands. Other cars on hand were a 1912 Cadillac speedster, a 1913 White and a 1915 McLaughlin Buick.

After a crazy day at the archives, I left on a bus not knowing where to find the Findlays. The Windsor Hotel, where Haney and Wilby stayed, still existed near the wharf, but unbeknownst to us it is now the Dorchester Hotel and is one of the swishest places in the city. Two $20 taxi rides later, I found the Findlays at a Best Western motel on the north side of Nanaimo, yet another victim of bad modern planning. [The fast four-lane arterial roads make the city inhuman. Sure enough, the local paper explained that schoolchildren are having such a hard time crossing one of the roads speeding through town that they all have to be bused a short distance. Councillors against the move said this will lead to everyone being bused. It doesn't take a genius to realize rising taxes are the natural fallout of a badly designed city.]

In one paper, Wilby regurgitated that, other than between Lytton and Yale, he had motored all the way from Halifax. He took another shot at trains, saying "travel by auto is more leisurely, and leads to a more intimate acquaintance than rushing through the country by train. I look for the time when such a trip as we have just made will be a common affair."

That day in 1997 there was nothing leisurely about auto travel in Gerlach, Nevada. A jet-powered car driven by British air force pilot Andy Green broke the sound barrier in the Black Rock Desert 200 kilometres north of Reno. The 35-year-old pilot made back-to-back runs at a speed of 1,228 kilometres per hour, edging that day's calculation of the speed of sound—which varies according to weather and altitude—by 24 km/h. It was almost 50 years to the day Chuck Yeager ripped through the sound barrier in a rocket-powered plane.

October 17—Nanaimo

A misreading of earlier material on this day, which is probably my fault, led to what would be one of our longest drives of the trip. Mind you, it allowed us to escape having to spend another night in Nanaimo, because the original Pathfinders went from Nanaimo to Port Alberni and back to Nanaimo on this day. Smart-alecks that we are, we did that and continued on to Victoria. It meant an early start.

The way out of town was marred by billboards, which meant native land. Then we passed through Coombs, which was tacky and just too Clifton Hill-ish, as in the tacky part of Niagara Falls. Goats stood on the roof of one tourist joint known as the General Store. Lorne was shocked there were so many new buildings he didn't recognize. Can't say I would call it progress. When Wilby went through, he was impressed that a Salvation Army colony had turned 800 acres into a model settlement of 20-acre farms.

As for beauty, you'd think after 8,000 kilometres you would have seen it all, but after Coombs the island invoked new levels of elation. The huge Douglas firs of Cathedral Grove, which the Pathfinders had stood in front of for 1912 photos, were just as majestic, although Wilby and Haney seemed to find a much larger trunk to stand before. The firs stood with their treetops in a fog, or low-lying cloud, as if they were rockets waiting for the countdown. These trees, in what is now called H.R. MacMillan Park, were the backdrop for one of Wilby's post-trip indignities. In his book, *A Motor Tour Through Canada*, there is a photo of Wilby standing in front of two cars with three men in the background, two of them up against a Douglas fir. Haney is nowhere to be

When Wilby saw this photo of himself in Cathedral Grove, he commented: "The big timbers have grudges against men and turn them into gnomes."

found. There exists, though, the same photo by the same photographer—Vancouver-based Broadbridge—with everyone in the same poses, except Haney is seen leaning up against the Douglas fir. It doesn't take a detective to surmise that Wilby had Haney air-brushed out of the photo in his book. Not only doesn't he mention him by name, but he makes sure his picture is nowhere in the book. Of all the photos that exist about the trip, there are some great ones with both Haney and Wilby in the same picture, but none is used in the book. You could argue that Wilby might not have had access to them, but Broadbridge had some of the photos of the two of them together. In fact, of the 34 illustrations throughout the book, Haney's silhouette appears in three of them, but he is either so distant from the camera or his face is obscured. There are at least two other photos where you expect to see Haney's head, but the background is blurred or indistinguishable. Bad photography or good airbrushing?

We reproduced another photo at Cameron Lake. Again, we found the location because of the mountain silhouette, but unlike the photo from Hat Creek, road engineers had chosen to reclaim land rather than cut into the hillside. Duplicating this photo was so important to me. It would be one of my last chances to jump into the developing fluid of those old photographs. In the original, Wilby is looking off into Cameron Lake in a contemplative pose, as if he too was going to miss the wonders the country had presented him. When I think of Cameron Lake, even now, I am filled with a burning sense of yearning.

Wilby found what he called

> Lordly scenery and land and sea-scapes of unsurpassed beauty, ideal gravel roads through forest of giant pine and if—that was Vancouver Island, a paradise of the motorists. Our way led along a fringe of kingly preserve, and for miles we traveled through a veritable forest tunnel of timber, the car dwarfed to insignificance by trees which shot up to the sky and barred the sunlight from spreading banks of fern and flower. The way followed closely the first trail blazed years ago through this solitude and now marked by immense stumps, sooner or later to be torn by dynamite from their anchorages. We emerged from the forest into the open at the head of Cameron Lake, where an automobile skirted the south shore and was often almost crowded into the water by towering crags.

The 1912 run to the western coast of the island was fraught with the decision of whether to go to Alberni, population 300, or Port Alberni, population 600. In late summer, the issue of who would have Mile 0 on the Trans-Canada Highway became the subject of heated debate in the towns. A milepost was erected in one place and stolen by the other, to the point where they tied a bull mastiff dog to the post to make sure no one would take it. Just before they arrived, the rivalry between Alberni and Port Alberni had even gained national attention in *Collier's Weekly*. Wilby noted, with irony, that the "outward symbol of a road that is yet to weave province with province, to interlace people with people," needed a bull terrier to protect its first sign from those who might want to steal it.

The Alberni board of trade heartily welcomed Wilby and entertained him and his party at luncheon. Wilby had warm praise for Vancouver Island roads. The *Alberni Advocate* said Wilby's speech concluded with thanks to the board of trade for their welcome and luncheon, and though he had far larger gatherings along the way, there had been none that impressed him more with their hearty goodwill and the sincerity of their congratulations. MPP J.C. Wood followed, having just returned himself from the interior of Vancouver Island looking for places to build roads. He spoke of the journey's great importance to the country. After lunch the party headed along an old logging road and veered off toward Great Central Lake, the farthest one could drive west in Canada at the time. The 50- to 60-kilometre jaunt took them to the Ark Hotel. Wilby acknowledged that the hotel was the most unique he had encountered on the entire trip, a reference which has baffled modern historians.

The story of Wilby reaching Alberni went over the AP wire. Vancouver and Victoria journalists were there along with Houston of the *Nanaimo Herald* and C.H. Gibbons, the well-known special correspondent. Wilby put the Alberni/Port Alberni squabble, and the significance of the day, in perspective in his book:

> A few years more and the transcontinental motorist will find a post
> yet further west than Alberni, on the actual western shore, looking
> out across the blue Pacific to an unobstructed view of the horizon
> beyond which lies the Orient. Some day, too, he may journey north-
> ward through the interior of the island, following the Great and
> Buttle's Lakes to the newly-laid-out National Reserve, Strathcona
> Park—a great provincial domain of 240 square miles, abounding in

glacial lakes, forests, lofty peaks, and a flora and fauna quite equal in natural beauty to anything on the American Continent. Some day, yet far in the future, he may supplement his motor trip across Canada by a tour on a Pacific highway stretching along "the slope of the two Americas, from Arctic to Antarctic; a great broad, smooth well-engineered road, extending continuously from community to community and absolutely free to use of all."

Before we could reach Alberni, we had to climb a mountain, the Alberni Summit, and we had to deal with steam coming from the radiator. Sure enough, it was another broken water line from the radiator. It took Lorne only 10 minutes to fix it. When we were greeted just above the town by Mayor Gillian Trumper and the Golden Oldies Auto Club, a smell was in the air, but it wasn't our brakes. Turns out it was the pulp mill. Port Alberni had the province's first pulp mill, and one can only imagine what it smelled like 85 years before. The club escorted us to the edge of Alberni canal where Wilby said salmon "leaped in great parabolas on their way to the spawning grounds"; at the time British Columbia was processing six million cases of salmon a year; Canada's fisheries were the most prolific in the world.

Lorne had constructed a Mile 0 pole so we could re-enact the photo of Wilby and Haney standing beside the infamous sign. The town was now known as Port Alberni, so there was no more squabbling about being at the end of a highway. It's claim to fame now was being known as "The Gateway to the Pacific Rim"—Mile 0 in a westerly direction. An enthusiastic crowd had gathered, including some folks who were older than the Reo. One of them was Meg Trebett who used to do a lot of writing for the paper *Twin Cities Times*. She was born seven miles up Beaver Creek Road in Beaver Creek on April 5, 1908. She said she "came down for a ride." Other characters were about, including an old guy in railroad cap and overalls who reminded us to "Watch out for photo radar."

On the way back we could smell the brakes coming down Alberni summit. The sun was now out, and it played off the river rushing down alongside the road and it had burned the fog off Cathedral Grove, so now strands of light made it through the forest, creating church-like sanctums at ground level. Peter said a New Year's Day storm, with winds as high as 120 kilometres an hour, had cleared out a lot of trees in Cathedral Grove. The Visitors Centre had suffered a lot of damage. It was October, nine months after the storm, and we could still hear the chainsaws of clean-up crews. Every so often among the firs and cedars were golden maples, sitting like a well-organized bouquet against the green backdrop. Colour also sprung from the greenish-blue waters of Cameron Lake. In reproducing the photos the wooden barriers that Wilby had leaned on had been replaced by New Jersey turnpike concrete—practical, but hardly aesthetic.

In Nanaimo, we saw other concrete roadside barriers—to stop the sound of highway traffic infringing on the city's sprawling neighbourhoods. At least they were made to look like wooden fences, unlike Ontario's mess of walls along its busy highways near Toronto. Next to the city's bike route, and the dessert delicacies named after the city, it was the best thing Nanaimo had going for it.

The trip south was jubilant. Every so often we could smell freshly cut lumber in trucks that could carry only two or three of the massive logs at a time. We stopped right on the 49th parallel in the town of Ladysmith, whose lumber company provided the posts when the Victoria Automobile Club first erected 300 road signs on the highways to Nanaimo and Alberni in June of 1912. The Ladysmith cenotaph reminded me of the one in Parrsboro, N.S.—too many names of fallen soldiers for the size of the place. We carried along to Duncan, where Wilby and Haney had stopped at a hotel for photos. Now Duncan is noted for its totem poles and having the world's largest hockey stick—it's leaning against a Canadian flag pole. An old man in Duncan told us: "Congratulations, you've done a marvellous thing."

Led by a Model T speedster, an escort from the Victoria chapter of the Vintage Car Club of Canada, we drove down Malahat Drive at 75 kilometres an hour, with a stunning view from on top of Malahat mountain overlooking Saanich peninsula and Mill Bay. Lorne and I couldn't contain our smiles. Maybe it was lightheadedness bred by mountain air. The sun was shining, Lorne's dream was about to be fulfilled. The engine sang as if it wanted to return to explore the shadows in those Alberta hills, find the source of those Ontario rivers, or just to retrace those 8,000 kilometres to Halifax Harbour. A photographer from the *Victoria Times Colonist* drove alongside and took some photos of the Reo in motion. The Reo had made it, never giving us any problems that Lorne couldn't fix within an hour. We didn't even need haywire, a staple of those early motoring days, although we did have bungee cords. We had more problems with computers and phones along the way than we had with the Reo.

Above is a photo by Broadbridge of the Pathfinders and their entourage in Cathedral Grove on Vancouver Island. Inset is the identical photo which appeared in Wilby's book, with no trace of Haney leaning against the huge Douglas fir. Good airbrushing? Or did all those men hold that pose?

Granted, the Reo is much simpler to understand, but had I been responsible for getting the Reo across the country, it wouldn't have made it.

Victoria in the sunshine is one of those cities that sparkles. At the stoplight near the B.C. legislature, our destination, Lorne asked the taxi driver in the next lane, "Where's the Reo dealership?" The taxi driver, who must have gone to the Lorne Findlay School of Quick Retorts, said, "It's about 100 years that way."

At the legislature we were greeted by a government minister and we reproduced some photos. It would have become tiresome if the car hadn't elicited such joy everywhere we went. Just looking at it made me wistful that we'd soon be parted. I stayed at The Empress, feeling tired and anxious. Eight thousand, two hundred and twenty-eight kilometres, and I loved every one of them.

October 18—Nanaimo/Victoria

The *Nanaimo Free Press* said a large assembly stood outside the Windsor Hotel to witness the departure of Wilby on his motor trip to Victoria. "The car, which was loaded with pennants bore none more beautiful than that presented to the intrepid autoist by Mrs. John Shaw, the souvenir being accompanied by a few gracious words from that lady." The photo of the departure will "be long treasured as a memento of the historic journey from the Atlantic to the Pacific. An outburst of cheering marked the departure of the pathfinder who smilingly acknowledged the honor paid him by the pivot of progress."

Nanaimo, sometime during the century, must have turned heel on the "pivot of progress." Haney and Wilby, the latter wrote, drove through a "region of copper and coal mines, and lands which harvest the big timbers, through the trout paradise of Duncan." There Mayor Beckwith of Victoria and A.E. Todd, he of the A.E. Todd medal, awaited to pilot them "over the famous Malahat Drive winding along an arm of the sea to the capital!" They arrived at 3:30 p.m. and Wilby delivered two final pieces of mail: Manitoba Premier Roblin's missive for Sir Richard McBride, premier of British Columbia (it was given to the attorney general, acting premier in McBride's absence), and Winnipeg Mayor Waugh's note for Mayor Beckwith, which included greetings "from the Hub City of Canada to you at the Gateway of the Golden Pacific." Of course, Port Alberni is the Gateway to the Pacific, but let the Albernians argue about that.

On arrival at the buildings Mr. Wilby showed off a flask containing Atlantic sea water. After the party had been photographed he and his friends went down to the shore and emptied the flask into the Pacific ocean, the first time the two oceans have been mingled in this latitude by the aid of man.

The speedometer, as Wilby called it, now read 4,200 miles, or 6,720 kilometres. The discrepancy of our odometers of 1,500 kilometres meant that we had driven across northern Ontario instead of taking boats and trains.

We still had 16 kilometres to travel that morning to Cattle Point in Uplands for another mixing of oceans. We began at a Speedy Muffler shop, and then went on to Victoria's Mile 0 marker, where several vintage cars had gathered through the organizational skills of John Ratel of the British Columbia Automobile Association and the local Vintage Car Club chapter. As Wilby said at his last stint at Parliament: "More speeches, more cameras..." The last ride was a heady blur, past wind-shaped shoreline trees, up Beacon Hill, past a yellow Model T with a quail-like sounding horn, up Cook Street to Rockwood, where we were invited to sign the guest book at Government House, home of the B.C. lieutenant governor. The neighbourhood's Garry oaks, which grow there and in California, gave it a great allure.

By now we were leading a parade of cars on a flowing ride along shorelines, looking across at islands of the Juan de Fuca Strait or back behind us at a midnight blue '38 Olds, a green '31 Chevy Deluxe coupe or a silver '35 Packard owned by Lorne's oldest son Ken. When asked the inevitable question about his sentiments, Lorne said he felt "a sense of accomplishment, sense of relief, and sense of 'Am I ever glad I'm going home.' I've been feeling overwhelmed at everything from Fraser Canyon on. And I still don't know why." Lorne had the pressure of making sure the Reo made it; all I had to do was sit in the passenger seat, keep my eyes and ears open, and take notes.

The excited gathering at Cattle Point gave me the feeling that we had, indeed, accomplished something, or at least Lorne had. He had completed what Haney had tried so hard to do—to get that Reo 8,244 kilometres across the country, without the aid of trains or horses or diversions into the United States. Haney, who drove his only 6,720 kilometres, would have been proud. Peter's wife Teresa took the final frame of our attempts to duplicate 1912 photos—with nine people hanging off the Reo, I poured Atlantic water from my perch on front of the car.

While we retreated to Schwartz Bay for the ferry back to Vancouver, Wilby and Haney were to be guests at a dinner in their honour or, at least, "In honour of Thomas Wilby, Esq. On the completion of the First Cross-Canada Automobile Run, at The Pacific Club, Victoria, B.C. 18th October, 1912, at 8:15 p.m." The evening began with Grape Fruit Oysters on Half-shell. White Cream of Asparagus Soup was being served, so was the Sherry. It was followed by a Fish dish of Boiled Salmon with Sliced Cucumber, and then the Entree of Filet of Beef, Aux Champignons, with some Claret to wash that down. Champagne accompanied the Joint of Roast Island Turkey with Cranberry Sauce, Vegetables of Cauliflower, Petit Pois and Mashed Potatoes. When that was consumed, it was followed by Sweets of English Plum Pudding with Brandy Sauce and Maraschino Jelly, Coffee, and of course, Liqueurs.

Taking a page out of Wilby's book, Haney told a reporter for the *Daily Times* "that Malahat Drive was the finest road he had driven along, the best built and with the finest regard to the showing off of the exquisite scenery of the vistas which stretch out before the eyes at every turn." One could only assume Haney was acknowledged at the dinner. After the toast to the King, A.E. Todd, president of the Victoria Automobile Association and vice-president of the Canadian Highway Association, B.C.'s deputy minister of Public Works, spoke, and then the floor was cleared for Thomas Wilby, speaking on "The Canadian Highway as it Exists Today." He was described by the *Daily Times* as being "an excellent after dinner speaker, and has a gift of happy expression which renders his post-prandial efforts well worth listening to. He shared with all Englishmen the love of the open road, and it had long been a dream of his, this winding ribbon of road leading through the heart of the most scenic country in the world." With "trenchant phrases" he described the challenges of the bogs, the corduroy roads and almost unmarked trails.

As if to clear up any misconception left by newspapers on the mainland, Wilby made it clear that he did "not actually motor across the continent, but he did the next best thing," reported the *Daily Colonist*. "He did it all save the section of New Ontario from Sault Ste. Marie to Fort William, which he traveled on a steamer. The reason for this is that there are no roads in that territory and it would have been impossible for any motor car to have got through the bush. But with this exception Mr. Wilby did the rest of the tour and his car, while a little weather-beaten, was in excellent condition as it finished its trip of 4,200 miles." OK, so he didn't totally clear it up, because he didn't mention the Reo's four train rides (North Bay to Sudbury, Fort William to Selkirk, Nelson to Castlegar, Lytton to Yale) and eight ferries (Lévis to Quebec City, Carillon to Point Fortune, Cutler to Blind River, Soo to Port Arthur, two on the Kootenay River, Kootenay Landing to Nelson, Vancouver to Nanaimo). The papers noted that Wilby was accompanied by an official photographer, Richard Broadbridge of Vancouver, "who has secured a series of remarkable photos of scenes on Vancouver Island, which will be added to the others taken eastward and published in a book which will tell the story of this record-breaking tour."

With the trip over, Lorne's friend Geoff Crowe and I jumped in Ken Findlay's Packard for the trip to the ferry. Crowe was expounding on how cars were identified with happiness. "Cars in those days were brought out to go to grandpa's, for special occasions, to go to the swimming hole. The car wasn't used for daily driving; it wasn't used for daddy to drive to work." His love for cars was no sooner expressed than we detected a flat tire. The Packard had dual side-mounted spares, but it took Geoff and Lorne's son Ken less than 15 minutes to change the flat. We couldn't get the car raised high enough with the jack, so they used some ingenuity and dug a hole to get the tire in. Unfazed by it all—changing a tire on the side of the road would have been an ordeal for me—Geoff maintained that all you need with an older car is a tool box. No problem.

While the original Pathfinders had champagne and champignons, we took the ferry's fare in a rather unostentatious diner-style way, and then retired to cabin seats. The ferry went between Galiano and Main Island through Active Pass. When its horn blasted, the sound echoed off the islands' trees. We saw a seal, which almost made up for never seeing a live moose, but I was drawn out onto the deck by the seagulls. Some squawked as they followed in our wake, but others soared beneath an old plane flying overhead, riding the drafts of the wind in seemingly outstretched joy. I wanted to be up there myself, celebrating the moment, but instead I leaned on the handrail with a smile as wide as the ship. This was my second ferry ride, but I would have liked two more—we missed the ferry ride in Quebec City across the St. Lawrence, and one across the Ottawa River from Carillon. Wilby rued the necessity of the Kootenay Lake ferry, but 85 years later it was still a worthy route. In my mind ferries were great, transporting hundreds of people and their cars across wide distances, so those people could return home or begin their own cross-country treks. Others, like myself, would be heading for the train; still others would be heading for the airport. And that, I thought, is what transportation should be all about. The landscape should be shared by different modes, the most suitable for the topography.

On this, Wilby and I would probably agree. He didn't believe in obliterating buffalo trails. He felt different transportation modes should work together. In his book's final chapter, though, he pushed the idea of the car taking its rightful place.

It was after the car had been stripped of the appurtenances of travel—after the speeches of the banquet at the Pacific Club—that I strolled out under the stars to the Douglas obelisk in the Parliament grounds. The tall simple shaft stood out grey against a background of fir and jewelled sky. With difficulty I made out the inscription: "Erected by the People of British Columbia to the Memory of Sir James Douglas, K.C.B., Governor and Commander-in-Chief from 1851 to 1864." Sir James Douglas, Factor, Governor, Dreamer! Douglas who had pre-visioned the day when vehicles would make the crossing of the Canadas to the Pacific! Linking east with west—a trail from Hope to the Kootenay across the Rockies, meeting at Edmonton a similar road built westward from the Atlantic—a great highway should cross the continent by which emigrants from the Maritime Provinces might have easy access to British Columbia. As in the days of Sir James Douglas, so now Canada needs the Transcontinental Highway for the unification of her peoples. Had I not seen them—Scotchmen, Irishmen, Welshmen, Old and New Englanders, United Empire Loyalist descendants, picturesque Habitants, the mixed races of the prairies and the mountains, thousands of incoming farmers from the great Republic to the south? Were they not as isolated from each other as if Eastern and Western Canada were worlds remote and unrelated? What might not a connecting road accomplish for such diverse elements as these in common purpose, in common ideals? Does not Canada, as much as India, or Algiers and Tunis, or indeed Europe itself, need that continuous thoroughfare from border to border which has ever stood for unity and strength?

Wilby foresaw the day when Canada could broadcast itself to the world as a tourist Mecca, when with the advent of a perfect road from sea to sea, good hotels and wholesome little wayside inns would be as plentiful as the scenery. If the word got out, through the work of aggressive tourist promoters, the world hurriedly "packs its suitcases and trunks, it ships its motor-cars, guns and fishing tackle and trots off to Canada." He ends *A Motor Tour Through Canada* by suggesting what a tourism promoter might say:

> "Just take a journey along our new road. Longest bit of macadam in the world. Better stop at some of the new health resorts along Lake Superior or by the Lake of the Woods. You can also take a little run round Timagami or Algonquin Reserves. By the way, you'll find the prairies sign-posted now, you know—no getting lost or mud-bound. Gumbo's a thing of the past. Don't miss, of course, a tour of Strathcona Park on Vancouver Island. What? Oh, never mind now about the way to get back! I know what's going to happen to you. You'll so fall in love with British Columbia that you'll settle down there."

Displaying their pennants outside the customs house in Nanaimo, B.C.

ENGLAND WILL EXCHANGE TRAM CARS FOR GASOLINE MOTOR VEHICLES—MORE ROADS NEEDED, October, 1912, London, England—A revolution in public transit involving the doom of London's electric tramways, the rapid extinction of the horse for purposes of haulage, and an entire revision of the primary duties of railways is predicted for the near future by one of England's leading traffic experts. Sweeping changes may include the establishment of new main roads across England, the institution of a chain of motor services between towns, and a considerable reduction in the passenger rates for short journeys on the railways of the kingdom. English people, too, may adopt a new variety of holiday, and instead of gestating for a fortnight at the seaside, take holiday motor trips at popular prices, traversing the entire country by a chain of public vehicles running between the towns. Many inland towns pleasantly situated, hitherto neglected, would then rise into fame as holiday resorts.

TIME TO STOP RESISTING RAPID-TRANSIT SYSTEM (letter), October, 1997, Seattle, Washington—On my recent business trip to Los Angeles and San Diego, three people asked me about our developing highway crush and why we resist the use of rapid transit. While in Long Beach, I happened to watch the Blue Line pull out on its way to L.A. From what I was told, ridership is way over projection. While riding on the greatly enlarged Long Beach Freeway, I saw something that appeared to be the bus version of what Chicago has on the Kennedy Express-way—express buses that just go up and down the freeway, stopping at stations in the middle of the freeway, where riders go down stairs to take local area buses. This was L.A., home of the one-person, one-car syndrome, but they've had enough of all this traffic.

Epilogue

Victoria to Kyoto on the Tokaido Road

October 19 — Vancouver

Thomas Wilby, having exhausted acres of newsprint with his words, took the rails this day to Montreal, where he would switch trains and head south to New York. You could do that in those days—take a trip across the country by train any day of the week, and have good connections south or east or west. In 1997, I was prevented from leaving until the 20th, because trains head east only three days a week. When Wilby left, he took with him the two suitcases Haney had let him borrow, and never said as much as thanks to the man who made his book possible and his trip successful. All he did was wave goodbye.

This recollection of their parting long lived on in the Haney family, such that when Jack Haney's wife died in 1989, 77 years later, she still felt bitterness toward Wilby. This was confirmed that day by Haney's daughter Ferne, who lived just a Skytrain-ride away in nearby Surrey. Her husband Bob Hicks picked me up at the station. We had dinner at a restaurant and then retired to their trailer. Ferne was fighting cancer, and had had surgery on August 27, the day Lorne and I began following her father's tire marks from Halifax.

"My dad never spoke much about the trip," said Ferne, who saw the three pennants her father kept and his photo album of the trip, which his wife had turned over to the B.C. Archives. "When he did he called Wilby 'Sir Thomas,' but he never said a bad word about him. I grew up thinking Wilby was royalty." It was Ferne and her husband who began to piece Jack's trip together in the 1960s. When Jack returned to St. Catharines—he took the TransCanada train on the morning of the 20th—he was finally given some credit. The Reo Company held a dinner in Haney's honour at the home of Reo manager U.E. Lazelle. The invitees included a foreman of each department, members of the Reo Sales company, two newspapermen and a local church minister who liked Reos. At the front of the dining room were the British Union Jack, Canada's flag at the time, and the American stars and stripes. It was supposed to signify the international nature of the company, but the reporter thought it signified the American Haney driving the Canadian car. It could just have easily represented Haney and Wilby. Jack was given a gold watch and fob and Lazelle told him a cheque for $50 was awaiting him on his desk. The St. Catharine's *Daily Standard* said Jack told the gathering of his trip in a modest, lucid and interesting manner

> Mr. Haney took his hearers across the continent with him. He encountered almost unbelievable difficulties on the way and many times was tempted to turn back, but he hung on, and finally got there. Naturally, the worst part of the road was through the Rocky Mountains, and he and his car and the newspaper man, Mr. Willoughby, who was travelling with him, had many narrow escapes. Frequently they just missed going over precipices in darkness. Countless times they lost their way or got mired, or came plumb up against an obstruction, which litterly [sic] was a stopper to them. The staunch Reo car did about everything but fly. It jumped ditches, climbed stairs—there was one place where a corduroy road was laid stair fashion—it turned around corners in the Rockies where a slip would have meant death and destruction hundreds of feet below; in fact, it did everything it was asked to do and more.

After these accolades, Haney was sent to some auto shows with the Reo still clinging to its dirt and tools. Ads depicted the route and suggested readers meet Haney and "shake hands with him. He deserves it." Among the Reo world records the company boasted about in its magazine, the *Reo Echo*, it said the Reo "holds the honor of being the first automobile that entered a score or more of Canadian towns and cities in this world's record sensational run." Old-timers in St. Catharines say the car that had toughed it out over endless obstacles ended up as a truck. Reo turned over its factory in St. Catharines to produce shrapnel shells for the war effort, and Jack left with a wonderful letter of reference.

In May 1914 he married his sweetheart, Annie Swan, who had kept his spirits up with letters during his two-month absence, responding to Jack's regular updates of his progress. She was the type who did woman's work, and let Jack mess with the men's work. When Jack had an appendicitis attack during a hunting trip, he had to teach Annie to drive the car home. "He started it up and got her going," said Ferne, who was born at the end of 1915, "but she couldn't stop it. A neighbour said, 'I think Annie's having trouble.' I never saw her drive a car again after that."

It's difficult to say what Jack learned from the trip—you could argue that Wilby taught him how not to live the rest of his life. Whereas Wilby had shown his impatience with children, and never had any himself, Jack loved to have kids jump all over the car during the trip, and had two of his own—Ferne and his son Lowell, who was born in 1918. Whereas Wilby had shown intolerance and snobbishness during their eight weeks together, Haney was progressive in fighting racism.

"My dad gave me a lickin' when I stuck my tongue out at Clarence Harper," said Ferne, referring to a black man who worked for her dad. "The kids dared me to do it. Every Christmas dad made us go up the street to Mr. Harper's house. Mother knit him socks because he had such big feet. Dad trusted Harper. He was so much of a friend. He and another black guy showed up at the door to take Lowell to the fair. Mother didn't know what to do but dad said let him go—'Lowell will have a good time.' Dad would say 'Mother was airing me out; she didn't like my friends.'" He liked listening to his Philco radio while sitting in his favourite chair, but he wouldn't listen to Amos and Andy, a popular radio show at the time, because he didn't like its depiction of blacks. "He thought they were putting the black people down," Lowell said later. "He wouldn't let anybody make racist slurs. That wasn't tolerated."

Wilby didn't turn him off cars, though. Jack started a taxi garage with two other men, dabbled one winter with returning to North Baltimore, Ohio, to take over the Campbell garage he once worked at, but decided to return to St. Catharines and start his own garage. He had the first car in St. Catharines with side windows, because he built it. While working for the garage he would take a car home at noon and let it idle while he was having his lunch. When he heard a noise he didn't like, he rushed outside to make adjustments. He would do this two or three times during a meal, and return to work without having wasted any time. His son Lowell remembers the ritual Sunday drive, including the one time the car went dead and the lights went out. Jack always had chewing gum with him, so he took a fuse out from under the instrument panel, removed the foil wrapper from a stick of gum, wrapped the fuse in the foil and replaced it. The car ran again perfectly, said Lowell. "If we came on rain we'd stop and lock the curtain buttons on the grommets. We'd be sitting there with the rain spraying in as if we were at Niagara Falls. Father would motor along, happy as the day is long."

Another ritual was the summer drive up to Huntsville near Scotia Junction, as soon as school was out. Singing as he drove north, he was one of the first to make the pilgrimage by car to what is now cottage country; it meant plenty of detours to avoid road construction. "Dad felt the best place for kids in the summer was on the farm in Huntsville," said Ferne. "We had a wonderful time." There, Jack taught his children to be self-sufficient, how to handle a rifle and how to make the most of a fishing rod on Lake Nosbonsing. He had a reputation as a marksman and regularly bagged deer and quail. The Hicks have a photo of Jack holding a wolf he had shot. "Dad was a good shot," said Ferne. "When they got a bear in a trap, they usually asked dad to come out and shoot it because if you had a bear in a trap, you had to shoot it before it got you." He also played horseshoes and crocono with his children, and was known by everyone, especially his employees, as a good-natured sort.

He continued to be a pioneer, not only with new cars, but also by helping to promote a Niagara airport. In 1928, the government gave Jack and his partner two gypsy moth planes to start what is now the Niagara District Airport on the edge of St. Catharines in Niagara-on-the-Lake.

Jack's father had a stroke in 1917 and was partially paralysed for seven years before he died. Jack suffered the same fate. For seven years he put up with coronary thrombosis, which limited his ability to work and climb stairs. His uncle Alfonso Valdo Heneig, whom he was named after (the Swiss name "Heneig" became Haney in America), died and left him $7,000. Annie Haney wanted Jack to go to the States for an operation, but he refused. He preferred to put the money in the bank. "If dad passed out," said Ferne, "I was supposed to give him a bit of whiskey the doctor had given him. If he woke up before I gave it to him, he'd have none of it. Dad didn't drink. He suffered so much pain." On one of his last trips to his garage, the new owner was drunk and yelled at one of the girls. "Dad got mad," said Ferne, "and he passed out. The agitation had brought on another heart attack. He was incoherent for a night and then returned to normal, but he never left his bed again." He spent his final days listening to his political hero, Franklin Delano Roosevelt, on his Philco.

Ferne said he looked like an old man before he died on March 26, 1935, two weeks after his 46th birthday.

Ferne said that Jack told Annie he would have handled Wilby better had he been older. He had obviously seen Wilby's book, but he never saw his name or his picture inside. Another mechanic at the Haney Garage gave Annie a copy of *A Motor Tour Through Canada* that was hanging around the garage. Annie was furious for 77 years, until her death in 1989, that Jack Haney never got any credit for his pioneering efforts for Canadian roads. A few weeks after her death, my small book, *Jack Haney*, was published, and the Canadian Automobile Association launched a good driving award in Jack Haney's name.

October 20

The Findlays returned to their lives, and to their Baptist Church this morning, where, amidst all the angelic singing, they were honoured for successfully completing their trip. Peter's family was also there, as were some women who met us on the trip. One of them, Jan Essig, even read a poem she had written, called "A Song of Two Reos": "Oh, sing a song of Reos, Nineteen and twelve of year, Oh, come and crank the handle, And set it off in gear! Two times with great adventure, she crossed the nation wide, First time with brave Jack Haney, Last time, the Findlays guide. With hist'ry resurrected, Towns jumped to life again, To welcome Lorne's fine Reo, And to remember when..." It went on. 'Tis the thought that counts.

I was off to research at the Vancouver public library, and a chance to examine what I had photocopied in the papers. A story from the *Alberni Advocate* said the Victoria Auto Club made a strong protest to the Canadian Highway Association because the car's sign said "Halifax to Vancouver," when it should have said "to Victoria" after all the money that club spent on Wilby. "We are however," said the letter to the CHA,

> particularly surprised on receiving what we suppose is an official
> final photo of completion of tour (showing car with many pennants
> spread over it, and Mr. Wilby and driver) to note that the wording
> "Halifax to Vancouver" is given prominence and that the driver of
> the car is so posed as to hide both the Alberni and Victoria pen-
> nants—the only pennants in the whole photo that are hidden. The

matter was explained to Broadbridge and Wilby when they were here, with instructions that no further photos being taken with Vancouver as a terminus. We hesitate forwarding you this letter of protest as it may cause some idea of inter-city jealousy. Our pilot car for Mr. Wilby took care of him for between 250 and 300 miles, and our total bill of expense in connection with Mr. Wilby while on Vancouver Island is nearly $300. Under all these circumstances we feel that we have a right to make a strong protest.

They wanted the Highway Association to refuse to publish any photos that indicated Vancouver at the terminus. Kerr of the Highway Association replied that the "Halifax to Vancouver" sign was painted on at the Reo factory in St. Catharines, and that the association couldn't suppress the photos of a commercial photographer like Broadbridge, who took the photos at considerable personal expense. Still, few of Broadbridge's photos existed in archives, and the Vancouver library didn't have any.

After my stint at the library, Irene prepared a lovely farewell dinner, with a bit more ammunition than she had in the camper. Then Geoff Crowe dropped me off on the eastbound train. Except for the Findlays, we were all on the train now—myself and the ghosts of Haney and Wilby.

Wilby's book, *A Motor Tour Through Canada*, was published in New York, London and Toronto in 1913. It was dedicated "To the companion of unforgettable motor journeyings through American desert and wilderness, My Wife." Neither Haney nor the Reo Motor Car Company, are ever mentioned by name in his 290-page book. Wilby did write a small pamphlet for the Reo company, but other than his one compliment to Haney in the Vancouver paper, he goes out of his way to avoid mention of the Reo or Haney. Who knows what irked him—Haney's view of democracy, that Haney expected to be treated like an equal instead of tugging his forelock? Or did he expect a bonus from the car company that he never received? Or was he still upset he got stuck with a "damned American driver"?

In its review of the book, the *Times Literary Supplement* compared Wilby's attempt with motoring accounts by Count Maurice Maeterlinck, who won the Nobel prize for literature in 1911, and Emilio Marinetti, a futurist and future fascist.

There is nothing in Mr. Wilby's account of his tremendous tour which recalls either Maeterlinck's eloquent sympathy with the soul of his 30 horse power car or Marinetti's ecstatic realism for ever expanding itself in terms of a meridional Whitmanese. On the other hand there is rather an excess of commonplace philosophy and a vast amount of useful information for those who think of following in his wheel tracks—a wild adventure which shall be postponed, so far as we are concerned, until Mr. Borden's road-making policy is being carried out.

The review says Wilby is shrewd and to the point, especially on his belief that Canada should advertise for poets as well as farmers, but it doesn't like his sense of humour, the thrice telling of his Manitoba mudman story, and says he should stick to descriptions of the landscape, which are "much more decorative than the reproductions of hack photographs" in the book. *The New York Times* said, "Mr. Wilby is always entertaining, because he was always interested; and he has, moreover, a whimsical slant in his mind's eye, and he likes to turn a neat phrase." Another review, in the *Boston Transcript*, says Wilby's "descriptions of scenery and people in the country towns and rural districts throughout the Dominion are full of interest, and his photographs especially of the western provinces are very beautiful."

The attention paid Wilby in Boston leads me to believe he must have had friends who worked for the *Transcript*, which also reviewed his next book, *What Is Christian Science?* Wilby never professed to be religious, but reviews of his 1915 book say "his claim is that he writes from outside the church, but he does not claim he is a disbeliever" in the teachings of Mary Baker Eddy, the American who founded Christian Science in 1879. The church itself appreciated "its friendly tone and obvious attempt to be as fair and accurate as possible in its portrayal of Christian Science." Wilby never became a member, but he did work for the *Christian Science Monitor* in Boston beginning in 1917, a year after returning to America after an absence of three years.

In May 1914 Wilby wrote a fictional story for *Century* magazine called "The Rise of Menai Tarbell," an artist who conjures up a ludicrous style of art called "lunism"— he must have drawn on the experiences of his short-lived engagement to New Zealand artist Frances Hodgkins. In early 1914 he toured Belgium for *Travel* magazine, just before the Great War. It results in a humorous mix of travelogue and jingoistic war banter. It begins: "As good luck would have it, we happened to be touring in the kingdom of Belgium some months before there broke out the war which was to inundate the drugged and wooded Ardennes with the troops of the German Kaiser and accomplish the humiliation of Brussels. I suppose that very map of Brabant smells of gunpowder." He describes one city hall as "a beautiful example of the late Gothic renaissance, and one dreads to think of what the policy of the 'jack-boot' might find it well to do upon the city's glorious hall or upon the stately tower of St. Rombaud."

Wilby must have returned to the auto tour business, for he writes, in a 1914 edition of *The Car*, about touring English homesteads of American presidents in a car with enthusiastic American tourists. From December 1917 until July 1921 he was a copy editor and editorial writer at the *Christian Science Monitor* in Boston, but in the Roaring '20s he resumed his travelling ways. He spent 12 months with Agnes on the French Riviera and in England, and in September 1923 he fell ill and went to Bath, which still had a thriving spa. There, on November 17, 1923, he died at 10 Johnstone Street. His death certificate said he was 53 years old, in keeping with his bogus line that he was born in 1870, which is contrary to his birth certificate. His obituary in the *Bath Chronicle* called him a widely travelled journalist,

> the first man to cross Canada by motor car from coast to coast, the whole distance being covered in the car except for one impassable district. This was regarded at the time—in 1912—as "some feat." The trip was not undertaken on behalf of the Government of Canada, but during its progress it was accorded official recognition, and Mr. Wilby was honoured with the freedom of some of the cities he passed through, and was often received by Mayors and feted en route. The trip was made in the interests of good motoring roads, they being then not good, and in some cases non-existent. The funeral took place on Tuesday at Bathwick Cemetery when the Rector (the Rev. H.F. Napier) was assisted by Dr. William Walker Rockwell, of New York, a long-time friend of the deceased.

Wilby's death only made one known obituary in the United States; that was, again, in the *Boston Transcript*. It said he was survived by his wife and two sisters—Mrs. Fred Stanforth and Mrs. Wisker. It also said his goal in writing the book, *A Motor Tour Through Canada*, was to "unite the country politically, socially and commercially." That might have been some reconstructive history—the schtick he stuck to after the trip—or perhaps he wanted a united Canada to fight off a takeover by the burgeon-ing United States. Maybe he really did care, after all. In *The Car*, he admitted

> the Cause got into my blood. The people were demanding a road to
> unite their shores, to connect their markets, to open up their scenery
> to the cosmopolitan tourist, to make them independent of the slow,
> vexatious railroads, to release cities and towns from splendid isola-
> tion, to bring them untold days nearer to the Orient and the Occident.
> One felt the bigness of the idea—that there was something in it that
> lifted it above the narrowing, vitiating influence of politics and
> brought it out on the broad stage of "Welt-politik."

October 21

What plagued me on the way home was that, since I had read his book 10 years before, I hadn't given Wilby much respect. I embarked from Halifax thinking he was a pompous, racist git who trotted across Canada as if he were Henry Stanley belittling the natives on his way to find David Livingstone. Without having seen what obsta-cles he had to overcome, I regarded his speeches as exercises in arrogance. But his effort was much like a Western explorer with a Sherpa guide trying to conquer Mount Everest—sure it couldn't be done without Haney as his guide, but all the endurance and decision-making had to be there to accomplish the task. I never forgot that we had smooth roads; their experience was a daily bone-jarring, teeth-rattling exercise. To add to their tedium, they were haunted by the fear of failure. We were never far from help or all the advances of the 20th century. In what was now a harmless drive along Highway 11 from Scotia Junction to Trout Creek, the Pathfinders could have been stranded there for days, or had their car smashed to pieces had they not used their ingenuity and their wit.

My sympathies grew for Wilby, for I had walked, finally, in his shoes. I heard some of the same sounds, smelled the same vegetation, saw many of the same sights, and made the same steps of anticipation into the Reo each day—sliding the lever of the door over, stepping up and in and then clicking it shut behind me. At some point, we both had to put our affairs with Canada, these long wonderful slides across the country, in perspective. He probably experienced the same glowing sensation at the back of his mind, the same smile of repose as I did thinking of the magnificence we had seen. I could forgive him his florid descriptions of lapus lazuli waters, indigo hills and purple sands. I couldn't blame him so much for his jingoism; it's what he was brought up with. For that matter I too defended Ontario just as the Findlays defended British Columbia. There's a tendency to protect your own, what you know, defend where you came from. Wilby, to his credit, was not so jingoistic that he couldn't criticize his homeland.

Perhaps, too, I hadn't given motor cars their due. It was the flexibility of the car that enabled us to hopscotch along Nova Scotia lakes, through the marshes and covered bridges of New Brunswick to witness the majesty of the Saint John River. The car drove between the St. Lawrence and the narrow lots of the seigneuries. It undulated with the ungulates grazing on our way to Ontario. The Reo pulled up on Parliament Hill, lunched at Fort Henry, boomed up Bay Street, caterwauled through cottage country, interrupted the tantalizing textures of the Canadian Shield and ploughed along Prairie fields. Reverentially, the car climbed the foothills, where we heeled at the haste of a chinook, and then boldly, but cautiously, crossed the B.C. mountains, diving down into valleys and onto ferries, both to Nelson, the jewel of the trip, and to Vancouver Island, the trip's terminus. This hulking Reo had created such bliss, not only for the Findlays and me, who experienced the nation, but for all those people who ran their hands over the Reo's fenders and upholstery.

The car is instant gratification, not only to ride in, but to look at. We saw more than 1,000 vintage cars during our trip, and just as many car fanatics. At the gatherings I was always a bit perplexed by the devotion to a machine, but by trip's end I had a pretty good idea why the old automobiles were so important. It started in Halifax with Eric Davidson, for whom cars meant memories of his early days of blindness, when his father described them to him, and he ran his fingers over them in junkyards; then, for his lifetime, he was known as the blind man who could fix cars. Near Economy Mountain in Nova Scotia, we met Burt Fulmore and his mesmerizing yellow '34 Chevy cabriolet with a rumble seat. He thought it was special because his uncle had a '34 Chev, but on this day the hubbub over his vintage cars made his family forget his wife's bout with cancer [as of late 1999, she was winning].

Cars also provide jobs—we saw several car factories, hundreds of taxis and car dealerships—such that one in seven jobs in Canada is connected to the car. Vintage cars are also a burgeoning business, whether it was a museum in Kingston, Ontario, or Francis Xavier, Manitoba. Cars launch a trillion conversations, whether it was the Reo as icebreaker in St-Andre-de-Kamouraska, or in Quebec City, where it introduced us anglos to francophone car lovers, with whom we had more in common than the media or the Parti Quebecois would lead us to believe. Cars provide frivolity— the Sunbeam fanatic at the Winnipeg car club forever having to explain his favourite car was not a vacuum cleaner, or the woman on the Alberta farm postulating on how many women had done their courting in the Packard's palatial back seat. "Every old car has its story," she said. "They're like people; they're fascinating."

All across the country people wanted their parents' cars—a sentimental attachment to their first ride in a car, or a connection to long-gone loved ones. No place was that more evident than at Castlegar, B.C., where Ken Schmidt told a story of just trying to connect to the past, to a loved one, to a significant moment in his life—his Olds '88 saved his life in a head-on collision with dragsters, and it was the last car his 12-year-old son was in before disappearing on a sled near an Albertan river. It was one of dozens of tragic stories told to us by car lovers on a trip that coincided with the death of Diana, Princess of Wales, in a car accident. For the most part, cars, especially vintage ones, are associated with joy. It made us want to cheer, posthumously, for Ike Clarkson on the Manitoba-Saskatchewan border and for Jean-Marie Paradis just west of Quebec City. Their foresight saved cars of yesteryear, seeing value in what other people considered junk. We're all much richer for it.

But because of the ongoing comparison with 1912, the largest story of that year, the *R.M.S. Titanic*, grew to be an entirely apt parallel. In many ways, the goals for the car, and its subsequent domination, were much like the *Titanic*'s pompous boasts— people thought they could dominate nature with human ingenuity. For the 8,000 kilometres we drove we saw the havoc cars wreak with nature and the way we live, yet we glide along oblivious to the iceberg—perhaps the ice ages—ahead. We should find a way to live better with cars, or prepare for our comeuppance. It was like the item from the North Bay paper in 1912 about "Abuse of the Auto"—the car is intoxicating, yet like other intoxicants, too much of them leads to a hangover; retribution for excess. The car's promise has been obliterated by its problems.

The most obvious was the way our cities have been devoted to cars. As American social critic Lewis Mumford said in 1957, we sacrifice the city for motor transportation, just as 19th-century cities subjected themselves to the railroad and factories. In defiance of lessons the past should have taught us, we "are butchering good urban land as recklessly as the railroad builders did in laying out their terminals and marshalling yards. But the notion that you can free the motorcar from all restriction in the city without devastating the city's living spaces is a delusion that will probably cause a lot more damage before it dies." Most cities we visited, with the notable exception of Nelson, B.C., were unattractive, in many cases moats of asphalt and tarmac. The average city devotes 30 to 50 percent of its land to the car; in Los Angeles, where General Motors made sure it ripped up streetcar lines to promote car usage, two-thirds of sought-after land is given to motor vehicles. Wilby let us know how grand the entrance to Montreal once was; now it's a nightmare of drive-thrus, strip malls and big-box stores.

The overall effect is ugliness, which German philosopher Friedrich Nietzsche says, reminds man of "deterioration, of danger, of impotence. His sense of power, his will to power, his courage, his pride—they decrease with the ugly, they increase with the beautiful." Tolerating such ugliness can only lead to less vigorous and more downtrodden communities.

But it's not just the aesthetics. The car influences almost every aspect of our lives, and it is insatiable. With each impact, it demands duplicates of itself. The car allows cities and towns to spread, sprawl makes public transportation inefficient, thus creating the need for more cars. More cars elicit wider roads. Wider roads separate neighbourhoods, and make being a pedestrian or cyclist more precarious and less desirable. Fewer people walk. More people lead sedentary lives—then we need health clubs and personal trainers, because we never get any regular exercise, unless one has a standard gear-shift. One-third of us—the poor who can't afford cars, and children and seniors who can't operate cars—lose mobility. A study comparing kids in a walkable Vermont town and kids in a Los Angeles suburb show the L.A. kids watch four times as much television—they aren't easily mobile, so they rely on the safety of their couches. Most of all, it works against the idea of community. As the custodian said at Eastern Passage, once isolated across the harbour from Halifax: "This place really growed up. I don't think there's any land to build up any more. Twenty-five years ago I knew everybody. Now I don't know anybody."

Cars affect traditional ways we interact, whether it is by meeting someone on the way to school or the cornerstore. They abandon places not designed for them—the most poignant had to be the Sudbury car dealership, one of Canada's oldest, that had to move from downtown because of a lack of parking. Usually downtowns lose; instead we create a mall world that is selective in who it invites inside its doors. And the very act of creating parking to feed these monsters, as we saw in Sault Ste. Marie, creates scary places. In Canada, enough land has been covered in asphalt and cement to cover Nova Scotia and Prince Edward Island. The preponderance of pavement makes us reluctant to venture out without a car, again promoting yet more car-use. And not in cars like the Reo, all open and slow and an easy platform from which to have a conversation with a pedestrian; they're fortresses on wheels not meant to slow down and idle for street chats, like a horse and buggy. We spend so much time in cars, an average of 11 workweeks each year, the phenomenon has spawned the popularity of audio books and adult bibs for drivers—more than half of McDonald's revenues are collected through drive-through windows. Some cars are better equipped than cottages—they are veritable second homes. Most have air conditioning, and some have coffee makers, televisions, computers, fax machines, electric razors and the ubiquitous telephone. I, myself, have been guilty of flossing, phoning, changing clothes, shaving, reading and eating while I was supposed to be driving.

So many people have bought into the idea of not leaving home without taking home with them, our dependence on cars is staggering. In Canada we have one of the world's highest ratios of autos to inhabitants (neck-and-neck with Australia, Italy and Luxembourg behind the United States). Half of all Canadian households own more than one car. Four out of five people go to work by car. Canadians travel some 15 billion kilometres per year on one million kilometres of streets and highways. We don't even walk to the cornerstore anymore—one-third of our trips go to errands and chores. The inevitable outcome is gridlock, and anger, and road rage. When someone is busy flossing or chatting, and they end up denying us a lane, or a parking spot, or the chance to save 3.5 seconds, road rage simmers. We cut them off, or pull out a gun and blow them away, like the Haitian in New Jersey whose flat tire delayed traffic. And these are only the early days of the road-rage rebellion. It is no wonder squeegee kids, and other peddlers tapping the windows of gridlocked motorists, are loathed on first sight.

We'd be able to put up with loss of community, loss of our finer architecture and pretty public spaces if the car delivered what it promised. At one time cars spoke of freedom, freedom to escape from the farm, freedom to go for a Sunday drive without being restricted by whether your horse was fed or healthy, and freedom to roam where no railway tracks had been laid. Cars were a means of escape, escape from our homes, where we are, what we've become, where we grew up. But the freedoms began to erode when the second car was built. There were traffic rules to follow, stop signs and stoplights. As cars became affordable, more people bought them, and the trend accelerated. Congestion is supposed to quadruple in the next 20 years. The answer is not more lanes, as the Californian woman I met in Nelson attested to. Cars only fill them, slowing the overall ability to make your way from A to B. The greater mobility of the car has a "paradoxical effect of lengthening how far people go rather than saving them time," wrote Jane Holtz Kay in *Asphalt Nation*. "In the late 80s, time use surveys found little difference in average commuting times in the car-heavy US and the nearly car-less Soviet Union. Soviet citizens walked or took the bus a half-hour each way; Americans, living in distant suburbs, drove the same amount of time."

We fight the onslaught on our neighbourhoods and freedoms by convincing ourselves, hopelessly, that if we get a faster, bigger, safer car, we can manage. And now the idea, pushed by the Honda ads, that you need a car that can create its own road, and that you can drive out of traffic jams with your own route. The popularity of 4-by-4s does not have everything to do with people looking for a sexier version of the van; it has more to do with the illusion that if you want to get away from the rest, you need the road less travelled, whether it's down the sidewalk or across a field, you need a vehicle that won't bottom out on curbs or get stuck in mud sloughs—something that would have made Haney's chore a little easier.

But if going off-road is the way of the future, that will perpetuate another problem with the car—stratification of people as car-owners and car-wanters, further stigmatizing those without cars, relegating them to the bus. The Amish believe, says a brochure from Amish country in Pennsylvania, "that cars pull people apart, and that a car distorts its owners' sense of self-importance in a world where humility is a necessary virtue." Cars become a means of social climbing. In poor neighbourhoods it is not uncommon to see expensive cars outside shacks. With a car, you don't have to take the bus or ever trip across poor people. Especially when I had a column, I was always amazed talking to wealthy or upper-middle-class people who had no idea of homelessness—they travel in air-conditioned cars, phones to their ears, to automatically opened garages in tony neighbourhoods. They never walk where they might trip over someone sleeping in a cardboard box. "Sequestered by income, deprived of parks, bankrupting Main Street for malls, we no longer rub shoulders with our neighbours, rich or poor, deprived or thriving, that tousled mix of age, race and experience," writes Holtz Kay. "All of the same breeds fear of the other, and the everyday intercourse of public life, the plural, multicultural world of a civil society, vanishes." A car-dependent society underscores and enhances the divide with a lack of mobility. Woodrow Wilson, as president of Princeton University in the early 1900s, suggested a ban on cars to prevent a further split between rich and poor. As much as cars promised to bring families and friends together, slowly but surely they are dividing us up, and killing us.

During the 53 days of our trip, more than 600 people died on Canadian roads, including pedestrians—Don't step off the curb, especially in the suburbs—and a further 33,000 were injured in accidents. You can't make too much of that, though, because transportation has always been a dangerous exercise—in 1912, there was the *Titanic*, and trains had an abysmal record of running over people or injuring them in accidents. The way cars really kill us, though, is by pollution. Cars tap our biggest resource, our air, for their internal combustion engines. High levels of carbon monoxide have been linked to congestive heart failure in older people. Air pollution and global warming kill about 16,000 Canadians a year, say scientists who maintain that environmental problems cause 1 in 13 deaths. A David Suzuki Foundation commissioned report says the death tolls could rise if the problems are ignored. By 2020, it predicts, 700,000 people worldwide will die prematurely each year from air pollution. "These people are dying, and it's directly attributable to the burning of fossil fuels," said Jim Fulton, the Foundation's executive director.

My oldest brother Robert, who plied the highway to and from Los Angeles for five hours each day, did so while suffering from bronchial asthma. He died at age 56. But you don't have to be in a city to experience the pollution. North America has a 15th of the world's population, but produces a quarter of its vehicles and a quarter of its carbon dioxide emissions. Parking lot runoff and road salt get into our water table. Road salt deforests roadsides and sterilizes the soil, making it hospitable to weeds. Ragweed prospers under the reign of salt, which explains the increase in allergies.

You can live in a distant outpost and still be affected by acid rain. In our lifetime we've had to stop swimming in some lakes, and not leave home without slopping our exposed skin with sun goop. The situation is like the cotton magnates of Uzbekhistan who drained the feeders of the Aral Sea to irrigate their cotton fields, shrinking the sea and creating a wasteland where once there was the fourth largest freshwater lake in the world. We are coming to grips now with the smokestacks of the 19th century industrial revolution. Will it take as long for us to recognize what the car is doing to us? Will change only come about because of a catastrophe? If you care about cars, you'd want to do something. If you care about your community you'd want to do something about it. If you care about the world as we know it, you'd do something about it.

One of my few regrets on the trip was not meeting Tooker Gomberg of Edmonton, who travels throughout Canada doing street theatre in traffic jams, wearing a gas mask and a white decontamination suit. His main function is to issue pollution tickets to drivers. We need something to jar us from our traffic-induced stupor. The status quo will literally kill us.

What I didn't realize when I began this trip is that I wasn't in Halifax, but Tokyo, making my first steps along the Tokaido Road heading for Kyoto, as Paul Millington explained to me in Halifax's Pier 21 [the pier has since been turned into a national shrine for immigrants]. The car has given us enormous freedoms, it has given us jobs, it has enabled us to see the world in all its magnificence, but it is like the devil—as people called it at the beginning of this century. When you sell your soul to the devil, there's a cost, and the cost was clearly spelled out at the Kyoto conference shortly after my trip. The Kyoto Protocol called for reductions in the output of carbon dioxide and other heat-trapping gases thought to warm the Earth's atmosphere. American oil companies and members of the U.S. Senate have been fighting against it, arguing that the science is uncertain and it would lead to grave economic consequences. But some low-lying nations in the South Pacific feel their entire countries will be swept away if global warming continues to raise sea levels. Already, scientists claim global warming is damaging the fragile ocean food chain, leading to skinny polar bears on Hudson Bay and weakened and smaller West Coast salmon. As we were coming down the Fraser River in 1997, three out of four sockeye-salmon running upriver died, as opposed to the normal mortality rate of one in 20. Global warming is a problem we must face, whether the heads of the big three automakers like it or not.

But scaring people about environmental disaster won't work on its own. To get people to change their car-led ways, we should show them how it affects their wallet. We spend as much on our car each year as we do raising a child, anywhere from $5,000 to $9,000 up front and half as much in social costs. If drivers were taxed to accurately reflect how much we spend on roads—seven dollars for every dollar we spend on public transit—it would encourage more compact land use and thus promote more public transport. By paying a more accurate cost for petrol, Europeans are aware of the costs and don't drive as much.

But even if cars are making us poor and killing us, we've known about the threat for 40 to 50 years, and we've done little to stop the onslaught. And each year, cars become more difficult to give up. As Moshe Safdie said in *The City After the Automobile*, "As cars shaped the city, so the city itself is now shaped to require cars." We're like heroin addicts unable to put down the needle. James Howard Kuntsler went one step further in *The Geography of Nowhere*, saying: "Everywhere in America, cars had destroyed the physical relationships between things and thereby destroyed the places themselves, places people love, yet Americans could not conceive of life without cars."

However, there is evidence of a willingness to change. United States Vice President Al Gore has preached against sprawl, and several Republican governors, who typically don't like to hinder market forces, are picking up on Gore's "smart growth" mantra, talking about tight, multi-use neighbourhoods and improved rapid transit. So far, around the world, more than 70,000 urban dwellers are sharing cars, and, most significantly, the new urbanism trend is growing. Maybe it's because developers discovered they could make just as much creating tight-knit communities as they could on sprawling green-field developments. But the demand is there, whether it's in Toronto, Niagara-on-the-Lake or Calgary. Even Disney got into the act by creating Celebration, Florida. People want walkable communities where every trip doesn't start and end with a car, or places where they can park once and park often— in vibrant downtowns they only have to park once and can tackle several different tasks without hopping from big box to big box parking lots. The key is to integrate stores, housing and workplaces to reduce the need for cars even more. An area where you can get by walking and cycling is a healthy place to live—the only fuel you burn is your most recent meal. Such collective living around nodes would be a natural for a rail link, just as railway stations once were hubs for compact living.

W.J. Fulton, deputy minister for Ontario roads in 1961, had the answer, if anyone was listening to his speech at the Canadian Good Roads Association meeting that year in Banff: "Air travel has affected both the road and the railway and the railway is again influencing road transport with its piggy back operation and in Canada, the Seaway will affect other forms of transportation. At present, these different modes of transportation are developing independently and to avoid future conflict, there should be a growing interest in integrating these various forms of transportation into systems that are both functionally and economically more efficient than anything our present disjointed approach has been able to produce."

Sixteen years before Fulton, noted city planner Henry Churchill wrote in *The City Is the People:* "The lack of integration is responsible for a good part of the traffic difficulties which beset cities. The planner who takes traffic counts and recommends a series of street widenings and lights and intersection remodelings is like a doctor who takes bloodcounts and then recommends an old-fashioned bleeding. Solution must be by way of complete diagnosis: railroads, markets, docks, airports, congested areas, and recreational areas must be brought into some kind of proper relation with each other, the lines of future growth plotted, and controls put into effect."

It we could devise optimum links between airports, railway stations, cars buses and ferries, we wouldn't have to build and maintain 12-lane highways. If one thing became evident during Ontario Premier Mike Harris's downloading of responsibilities from the province to municipalities, it is that Ontarians can't afford their road network—and with no attempt to rein in green-field development, that burden will only grow. Days when newspapers for Regina and Winnipeg boasted of riches waiting for entrepreneurs who wanted to turn farmland into a suburb are long gone, or should be. We must re-look at land, and its real value. Land should not be looked on as a possession, but a responsibility, to be used wisely for the good of the community, and the perpetuation of life on earth.

On that morning of the 21st, I awoke as the train made its way northeast toward Yellowhead Pass. The cross-country passenger train takes the lower grade route toward Jasper instead of through southern B.C. and the Crowsnest Pass, nor does it cross the Continental Divide at Kicking Horse and Rogers Passes, as most motorists now do on the Trans-Canada Highway. The bulky snow-capped mountains made you want to scratch at the window, to break out and explore. You are like Tantalus, being shown so many fruits of the country, only unable to reach out for them. If only I had a car to take me and my hiking boots to where I wanted to go. Therein lay the dilemma —the car so valuable in connecting us, one of the greatest inventions of the last century, yet I couldn't just enjoy the trip, what should have been a celebration of the car, without thinking of its consequences. I was disappointed the car didn't just become a useful alternative to the horse, but sought to destroy the competition, the streetcars, the intercity trams, the trains, and is even taking a run at buses, directly if not insidiously, creating such spread-out towns that it makes it financially awkward to run a bus route. Fewer routes, fewer passengers, the spiral downwards, the increased need for the car, where poor families and slow-witted students feel they have to work just to support their car.

I began work on this book in an old house in Niagara-on-the-Lake, across from the mouth of the Niagara River, where at night I could hear the lonely clip-clop of horses hooves taking tourists around town in a calèche. Most of the writing was done in a tight neighbourhood of Toronto, where cars were crammed on the street outside, even though the lovable College streetcar was a few metres away. At other times I worked while on commuter and passenger trains, a hydrofoil and a catamaran. Some of the services were unsustainable, and thus inefficient, because too many people enslave themselves to their cars, and there was no organization to combine the transit efforts to keep me commuting to Toronto. I was forced to move.

What I learned then and during the trip was how important our connections were, our links, our roads. Road-building had been abandoned with the advent of the train, and the trip of Haney and Wilby, said the *Western Canadian Motorist* in 1913, precipitated Canada and the United States to compete "in the most friendly way for the honor of completing the first great highway across the continent, from ocean to ocean. There is something elevating in the thought that these highways are being constructed in the cause of peace and the furtherance of goodwill and progress, and in this way are in striking divergence from the system of the old world, where the road-builders were the conquerors or leaders of dominant peoples, whose foremost thought in the construction of a road" was for military reasons.

But, as Wilby said, our new roads to the West should not have eradicated the old buffalo trails. Our new modes of transportation shouldn't obliterate our old, just like e-mail shouldn't eradicate the letter. Our links define us as a society, just as our cars define us as individuals. The train connected visitors right away to our town centres. With the emphasis now on cars and planes, whose first interaction with the town is on its fringe, the soul of our cities has been abandoned. The car demanded it, but we didn't have to say "Ready, Aye, Ready." George Martin and Peter Freund, in *The Ecology of the Automobile*, point out that "the auto is a source of pleasure and unprecedented mobility for many people, but its overuse and misuse create problems. Once utilized, technologies do have ecological and social consequences."

If we could turn back the odometer on the car's progress, we wouldn't have allowed General Motors to buy up streetcars and tear up their tracks. To give us more freedoms, town planning would have been more strict. All future planning would have been around tight neighbourhoods, where kids can walk to schools and their parents could walk for groceries. Neighbourhoods would have been built around transportation nodes, so getting from place to place, city to airport, airport to train, could all be done without the help of a car. With the car in its proper place, able to tackle unique routes and Sunday drives, one could dream of crossing the country in many ways, to run like Latulippe, take the canoes of the Malecites and Choctaws, portage like the fur traders from Lake of the Woods, see it from the bar car, the dome car, or the comfort of a train's rolling bedroom. And if we don't like to sleep on the train, we should be able to get off in Kenora, like Jack Haney did. Each time we want to connect from canoe to train, there should be a car to take us to places like Ignace's Lone Pine Motel, to watch sun set on summer over a small lake.

Can you blame it on the Reo? The Reo's success prompted others to publicize the need for a national highway—in 1913, Donald Gooch drove his Austin from Montreal to Vancouver, not hesitating to drive into the States when needed or to jump on a train or boat across much of the Great Lakes. (The first successful crossing, wholly within Canada, did not happen until 1946, when Brigadier R.A. MacFarlane and Kenneth MacGillivray drove an Oshawa-built Chevrolet sedan from Louisbourg on Cape Breton Island to Victoria in nine days.) And Wilby's speeches might have hastened the growth of provincial highways a few months, emboldened some minister to demand more money sooner, and made the public readier to hand over their world to the car. In 1919, Ottawa added roads to the department of railways and canals, and it revived Borden's 1911 bill. The 1919 Canadian Highways Act initiated the spending of $20 million on highway construction and improvements over the next five years. Each province was to receive a minimum grant of $80,000 annually, with further funds allotted by population. The Trans-Canada Highway Act of 1949 ensured the completion of a national highway, even though it didn't take seven years and $150 million to complete—more like 13 years, $1.4 billion and counting.

However, neither Wilby nor Haney nor anyone else could have predicted the car's dominance of our world. Wilby and Haney were searching for an all-red route, a highway wholly within Canada, but they have left us with an all-red route of a different sort—red lights, red stop signs, red taillights, the red of anger and blood, a red-brick tangent of a deadly mentality from which there are no evident exit ramps.

Jack was 23 on his historic journey, unwittingly halfway through his short life. His daughter Ferne Hicks died a year after the re-creation of the trip. Nothing ever turned up on the fate of Thomas Wilby's papers, if he had any. His wife Agnes did not remarry. For at least eight years after he died, Agnes spent every second summer in Bath, staying at a friend's house and visiting her husband's gravesite.

Earl Wise, the gangly guy who nearly died guiding the Reo above the Fraser Canyon at night, outlived them all. He eventually returned to Lansing, and between Michigan State College and University of California at Berkeley, he got an engineering degree at age 39. He became a highway engineer and helped design stretches of one of North America's most beautiful roads, old Highway 1 along California's coast. He died in April 1954, one month after retiring at age 65, leaving a wife and daughter behind. Just before the book was published, a subdivision was going up on Earl's old family farm in Lansing. It is called Wise Estates, but some wiseacre who had seen a country full of urban sprawl would prefer it be called "Unwise Estates."

As for the Reo? Like other old car companies not attached to the Big Three, it floundered. They stopped making cars in 1936; its truck business was later absorbed by the Diamond company, which stopped making the trucks in 1974. The Reos, like many old cars, are painted on the sides of buildings in empty downtowns, or end up in museums where they look as shiny as they once did in a showroom—so full of promise.

Endnotes

Each chapter includes the use of several newspapers, both in 1912 and 1997, and general use of Wilby's books—*A Motor Tour Through Canada, On the Trail to Sunset. 'Cross Canada with the "All-Red" Route Reo*—and his articles in *The Car* (December 18, 25, 1912), *The Motor Magazine* (January and February 1913), *Travel* (February and March 1913), and *Colliers*. Also, Haney's articles are from the *Reo Echo* (December 1912) and *Motoring* (January 1913).

Chapter 1 Page 10: *Saint John Daily Telegraph*, Aug. 30, 1912, *Toronto Star*, Aug. 24, 1997
Halifax Herald, Halifax Morning Chronicle, Century Magazine.

Chapter 2 Page 28: *New York World*, Aug. 27, 1912, *Halifax Chronicle-Herald*, Aug. 26, 1997
Halifax Herald, Halifax Morning Chronicle, The Nova Scotian (weekly *Chronicle*), *The Truro Daily News, Moncton Transcript, Moncton Daily Times.*

Chapter 3 Page 46: *Truro Daily News*, Aug. 29, 1912, *Toronto Globe and Mail*, Aug. 16, 1997
Saint John Evening Times/Star, Saint John Globe, Saint John Daily Telegraph, Fredericton Daily Gleaner, Woodstock Dispatch, Woodstock Press.

Chapter 4 Page 66: *Quebec Chronicle*, Sept. 1, 1912, *Ottawa Citizen*, Aug. 24, 1997
Quebec Chronicle, Quebec Daily Telegraph, Montreal La Patrie, Montreal Gazette, Montreal Le Devoir, Progres-Dimanche, Le Soleil, New York Times, International Herald Tribune.

Chapter 5 Page 86: *Montreal Gazette*, Sept. 3, 1912, *Montreal Gazette*, Sept. 3, 1997
Ottawa Citizen, Ottawa Evening Journal, Cobourg World, Toronto News, The Toronto Globe, Toronto Telegram, Toronto Star, Toronto World, Toronto Sun.

Chapter 6 Page 104: *North Bay Daily Nugget*, Sept. 16, 1912, *Globe and Mail*, Sept. 11, 1997
North Bay Nugget, Sault Star, Sudbury Journal.

Chapter 7 Page 124: *North Bay Daily Nugget*, Sept. 12, 1912, *Sudbury Star*, Sept. 11, 1997
Sault Star.

Chapter 8 Page 144: *Vancouver Sun*, Sept. 16, 1912, *New York Times*, Sept. 16, 1997
Page 160: William Michelson. *Man and His Urban Environment: A Sociological Approach.*
Fort William Daily-Times Journal, Port Arthur Daily News.

Chapter 9 Page 162: *Vancouver World*, Sept. 21, 1912, *Winnipeg Sun*, Sept. 21, 1997
Page 178: *Macleans* (September 1912).
Manitoba Free Press, Winnipeg Tribune, Winnipeg Telegram, Portage La Prairie Weekly Review, Weekly Manitoba Liberal.

Chapter 10 Page 180: *Manitoba Free Press*, Sept. 23, 1912, *Globe and Mail*, Sept. 27, 1997
Page 185: Anne Collier, *History of Portage.*
Manitoba Free Press, Winnipeg Tribune, Winnipeg Telegram, Portage La Prairie Weekly Review, Weekly Manitoba Liberal, Brandon Sun, Moosomin World Spectator.

Chapter 11 Page 200: *Regina Leader*, Sept. 26, 1912, *Regina Sun*, Sept. 28, 1997
Regina Leader, Moose Jaw Herald, Swift Current Sun, Maple Creek News.

Chapter 12 Page 220: *Vancouver Sun*, Sept. 11, 1912, *Lethbridge Herald*, Oct. 2, 1997
Medicine Hat News, Lethbridge Daily Herald, Macleod Advertiser, Blairmore Enterprise.

Chapter 13 Page 244: *The Ledge, Greenwood*, Oct. 3, 1912, *Vancouver Sun*, Oct. 4, 1997
Blairmore Enterprise, Fernie, Cranbrook Herald, Cranbrook Prospector, Cranbrook Herald, Creston Review, Nelson Daily News.

Chapter 14 Page 270: *Vancouver Daily News-Advertiser*, Oct. 6, 1912, *Vancouver Sun*, Oct. 6, 1997
Nelson Daily News, Trail News, Rossland Miner, Grand Forks Sun and Kettle Valley Orchardist, Grand Forks Gazette, The Ledge, Greenwood, Penticton Herald, Similkameen Star, Hedley Gazette, Merritt Herald, Nicola Valley Advertiser, Ashcroft Journal.

Chapter 15 Page 290: *Daily News-Advertiser*, Oct. 12, 1912, *Vancouver Sun*, Oct. 4, 1997
Chilliwack Progress, New Westminister Times, Vancouver Sun, Vancouver Daily Province, British Columbian, B.C. Saturday Sunset, Vancouver Daily News-Advertiser.

Chapter 16 Page 312: *Victoria Times*, Sept. 28, 1912, *Victoria Times-Colonist*, Oct. 17, 1997
Vancouver Sun, Vancouver Daily Province, British Columbian, B.C. Saturday Sunset, Vancouver Daily News-Advertiser, Nanaimo Free Press, Alberni Advocate, Victoria Daily Colonist, Victoria Daily Times.

Epilogue Page 332: *Daily News-Advertiser*, Oct. 19, 1912, *Seattle Times*, Oct. 19, 1997
St. Catharines Daily Standard, Bath Chronicle, Globe and Mail, Vernon Daily News, Crossland Daily Townsman, Boston Transcipt, The Nation, New York Times, Times, Literary Supplement.

General use was also made of *Motor Age, Motor Magazine, Motor Life, The Travel Magazine, The Automobile, Vintage Vehicles, B.C. Historical News.*

Photographic Credits

Page 10: Courtesy of St. Catharines Historical Museum
Page 55: From the *Nova Scotian*; Courtesy of St. Catharines Historical Museum
Page 94: From Ferne (Haney) and Bob Hicks
Page 95: Hicks; Hicks
Page 153: From Wilby's box camera
Page 171: From Nicol's box camera
Page 189: Hicks
Page 209: Courtesy of St. Catharines Historical Museum
Page 229: Wilby
Page 242: Wilby; bottom—Hicks, BrianByrnes, Courtesy of the Creston Historical Museum
Page 253: Nicol
Page 260: Hicks; Eisemann
Page 273: Courtesy of the Creston Historical Museum; Courtesy of the Nelson Historical Museum
Page 288: Eisemann
Page 299: Eisemann; Penticton Historical Museum
Page 321: Courtesy of St. Catharines Historical Museum; Byrnes
Page 330: Courtesy of Broadbridge Collection
Page 335: Courtesy of Broadbridge Collection; insert—Nicol
Page 341: Courtesy of St. Catharines Historical Museum

Colour Plates:

Section One
Page 1: From the *Nova Scotian*; Nicol
Page 2: Nicol; Nicol
Page 3: Nicol; Lorne Findlay collection
Page 4: Wilby; Nicol
Page 5: Wilby; Nicol
Page 6: Nicol; Nicol; Nicol
Page 7: Findlay; Nicol
Page 8: Hicks; Nicol

Section Two
Page 1: Wilby; Nicol
Page 2: Courtesy of the Merritt Historical Museum; Nicol
Page 3: Nicol; Nicol
Page 4: Hicks; Nicol
Page 5: Courtesy of the National Archives, Ottawa; Nicol
Page 6: Broadbridge; Nicol
Page 7: Courtesy of the National Archives, Ottawa; Nicol
Page 8: Courtesy of the National Archives, Ottawa; Nicol

Bibliography

Adams, Joseph. Ten Thousand Miles Through Canada. Toronto: McClelland & Goodchild, 1912

Beauvau-Craon, Charles. La Survivance Francaise au Canada: Notes de voyage. Paris: Emile-Paul Freires, 1914

Bosanquet, Mary. Saddlebags for Suitcases: Across Canada on Horseback. Toronto: McClelland & Stewart, 1942

Carrel, Frank. West and Farther West. Quebec City: Telegraph Printing Co., 1911

Carver, Humphrey. Compasionate Landscape. Toronto: University of Toronto Press, 1975

Chrysler, Walter P., and Boyden Sparkes. Life of an American Workman. New York: Dodd, Mead & Co., 1937

Churchill, Henry S. The City Is the People. New York: W.W. Norton & Co., 1962

Collins, Robert. A Great Way to Go: The Automobile in Canada. Toronto: The Ryerson Press, 1969

Copping, A.E. Canada Today and To-morrow. Toronto: Cassel and Company, 1911

Dobbs, Kildare. Ribbon of Highway. Toronto: Little Brown & Company, 1992

Durnford, Hugh, and Glenn Baechler. Cars of Canada. Toronto: McClelland & Stewart, 1983

Fitzroy, Yyonne. A Canadian Panorama. London: Metheun, 1929

Freund, Peter and George Martin. The Ecology of the Automobile. Montreal: Black Rose Books, 1993

Galt, George. Whistlestop: A Journey across Canada. Toronto: Metheun, 1987

Gomery, Percy. A Motor Scamper 'Cross Canada. Toronto: The Ryerson Press, 1922

Gordon, Charles. The Canada Trip. Toronto: McClelland & Stewart, 1997

Guillet, Edwin C. The Story of Canadian Roads. Toronto: University of Toronto Press, 1966

Jacobs, Jane. The Death and Life of Great American Cities. New York: Vintage Books, 1961

Kay, Jane Holtz. Asphalt Nation: How the Automobile Took Over the Nation and How We Can Take It Back. Berkeley: University of California Press, 1997

Kuntsler, James Howard. <u>The Geography of Nowhere</u>. New York: Touchstone, 1993

Lindamood, Jean, ed. <u>Road Trips, Head Trips and Other Car-Crazed Writings</u>. New York: Atlantic Monthly Press, 1996

MacLennan, Hugh. <u>Barometer Rising</u>. Toronto: McClelland & Stewart 1989

Michelson, William. <u>Man and His Urban Environment: A Sociological Approach</u>. Don Mills, ON: Addison-Wesley, 1970

Mumford, Lewis. <u>The Highway and the City</u>. Toronto: Mentor Books, 1964

Mumford, Lewis. <u>The City in History</u>. New York: Harcourt, Brace & World, 1961

<u>Official Automobile Road Guide of Canada</u>. Toronto: Ontario Motor League, 1912

Pound, Arthur. <u>The Turning Wheel: Story of GM through 25 years, 1908-33</u>. Detroit: General Motors, 1934

Pullen-Burry, Bessie. <u>From Halifax to Vancouver</u>. Toronto: Bell and Cockburn, 1912

Roseland, Mark. <u>Toward Sustainable Communities</u>. Ottawa: National Round Table on the Environment and the Economy, 1992

Safdie, Moshe, and Wendy Kohn. <u>The City after the Automobile</u>. Toronto: Stoddart, 1997

Sansom, Mary J. <u>A Holiday Trip to Canada</u>. London: St. Catherine Press, 1913

Strang, Herbert, ed. [pseud,]. <u>Adventures in the Far West: Canada's story</u>. London: H. Frowde and Hodder & Stoughton, 1912

Vernede, R.E. <u>The Fair Dominion</u>. London: Trubner and Co, 1911

Walker, Eldred G.F. <u>Canadian Trails</u>. Toronto: Musson, 1912

Washburn, Stanley. <u>Trails, Trappers, and Tender-Feet in the New Empire of Western Canada</u>. London: A. Melrose, 1912

Wilby, Thomas William. <u>On the Trail to Sunset</u>. New York: Moffat, Yard and Company, 1912

Wilby, Thomas William. <u>'Cross Canada with the "All-Red" Route Reo</u>. St. Catharines, Ontario: Reo Motor Car Co., 1912

Wilby, Thomas William. <u>A Motor Tour Through Canada</u>. London: John Lane, 1914

Acknowledgments

For the genesis of this book, credit must go to the diligent work of Arden Phair, curator of collections at the St. Catharines Historical Museum, whose enthusiasm for the 1912 trip was intoxicating. He epitomizes the best of a trait found in many archivists, historians and librarians across the continent. I turned my newspaper feature for the Burgoyne family at *The St. Catharines Standard* into a small book because of Lou Cahill, the godfather of Canadian public relations whose love of country made sure Jack Haney became a reality.

I vowed then, in 1989, to duplicate the trip. In December 1996, Lorne Findlay wrote me to say he was preparing to back his car into the Atlantic on August 27, 1997, so Lorne is ultimately responsible for the trip taking place, and for that I can't thank him enough. With sponsorship from Speedy Auto Services, financial support from Trimark Mutual Funds, and publicity from the Ontario Editorial Bureau, Edwardian clothing from the Stratford Festival and support from I-star Internet, VIA Rail and Bell Mobility, we embarked on our odyssey to be greeted with more generosity from friends and strangers across the country. There are too many people to mention, but those who come to mind include Geoff and Gord Crowe, Norman Brunt, Rod Burgland, Frank Hoyt, Ann Pullen, Burt Fulmore, Wellsley Crossman, Bob Esterbrook, Dave Kennedy, Doug Steeves, Larry Albert, Vincent MacDonald, Elmer Mulherin, Daniel René, Jacques Boutin, Jean-Marie Paradis, Dave Gurney, Jil McIntosh, John Sherwin of the Niagara CAA, Robert Spence, Patsy McVickers, Isabel Hobbs, Guy Emond of Apple Auto Glass, Herv Rector of Rector Machine Works, Fred Petit, Sophie Munro and her class at Bonnycastle, Chuck Ingram, Marg Kentner, Jim Higham, Jolene Fleming, Les Green, Gerry Dyck, Doug Keith, Bob Meyers, Dot and Russ Kelly, Earl Boan, Dick Meaker, Chad Jedlic, Ray Wiskar, Joyce German, Maple Creek, Karie Cupolo and the Wilsons, Joe and Lynn Asuchak, Tommy and Ivy Fraser, George Ferris Dowling, Jim and John Usher, Creston Big-O Tires, Rob and Krista Reyes, Scotty's RV Park, Ron Welwood, Lincoln and Sylvia Sandner, Bill and Ruth Cooper at White House B&B, Alice Glanville, Ray Findlay, Charles and Jean McFarlane, Steve Brodie, Ernie Lawrence, Kim Leclair, Pat Lean, Fran Giberson, Jan Essig, Debbie and Brian McKinney, Rick Funk, Archie Miller, Ken Haugen, Brian Byrnes, Bruce Schappert, Marilyn Amos, Sonja Drinkwater, Derek McGregor, Bruce Hopkins, and John Ratel of the B.C. CAA.

At archives and museums, I'd like to thank: Wanda Lyons, New Brunswick Archives, Nan Harvey, Colchester Historical Museum, Heather Allen, Cumberland County Museum, Kim Forbes, Sault Ste. Marie Museum, Ted Stremel, Manitoba Automobile Museum Elkhorn, Man., Rosemary Anderson, Maple Creek, Donny White, Medicine Hat Museum and Art Gallery, Linda Cerney, City of Lethbridge Archives, Dave Whitaker, Cranbrook's Canadian Museum of Rail Travel, Lois Price and Dollie Kaetler, Creston and District Historical Museum, Joyce Austin, Kootenay Museum, Rossland Historical Museum, Christian Cook, Penticton Museum, Margaret Stoneberg, Princeton Museum, Nicola Valley, Helen Forster, Ashcroft Museum, Dorothy Dodge, Lytton Museum, Christine Meutzner, Nanaimo Community Archives, David Goode, Alberni, Jacqueline Gyssen, Alberni Valley Museum, Gary Mitchell, deputy provincial archivist, British Columbia, , Barbara Dawson, Ohio Museum, Caroline Johnson and Marie, National Motor Museum, Beaulieu, England, R.E. Olds Museum, Lansing.

Among the dedicated librarians I encountered were: Gail Benjafield, St. Catharines, Ont.; Ron Welwood, Nelson, B.C.; André Cochrane, Quebec National Library; Nada Nehes, Sudbury; Gwen Kraft, San Luis Obispo; Helen F. Bender, Boston; Terry McCormick, Pontiac, Michigan; Sarah R. Brooks, Flint, Michigan; Tony and Marie Keck, Erie, Pa.; Dan Kirchner, Mark Patrick, Detroit; Stuart McDougall, Philadelphia, Pa.; and Blair Poelman and Stephen Young, Mormon Family History Library, Salt Lake City. A general thanks goes to unnamed toilers at Buffalo Public Library, New York Public Library, Michigan State University Library, Bath (England) Public Library, and Bodleian Library, University of Oxford.

Thanks to two of the most determined researchers: Dennis Gannon in Washington D.C., who helped me track Wilby's American wanderings; and Betty Childs Klaviter in Lansing, Michigan, who helped me find Earl Wise's daughter. Also, Rheanne Smith in Alberta for tracking down that Macleod schoolhouse.

Auto clubs that helped us along the way include: Golden Age Automobile Club (Truro), Antique Auto Club of New Brunswick, Les Belles Autos d'Hier Inc., Reo Owners Club of Ontario, Lakehead Antique Auto Club, Manitoba Classic and Antique Auto Club, Vintage Cruisers Auto Club, Western Manitoba Pioneer Auto Club, Inc, Regina Antique Auto Association, Frontier City Antique Auto Club (Swift Current), Alberta Reo Owners Club, Marauders Car Club, various chapters of the Vintage Car Club of Canada. Antique car connoisseurs who helped: Peter Weatherhead, Toronto, Lloyd Brown, Toronto, Clarence Coons, Ottawa, Glenn Baechler, Wellesley, Ontario, Mr. and Mrs. Clarence Rutledge, Oregon, Jim Neal, Lansing, Jack Perkis, Syracuse, Trent Wilson, North Carolina, Ralph Dunwoodie, Sun Valley, Nevada.

The families of the participants were of inestimable help. They include Bob and Ferne (daughter of Jack Haney) Hicks, Isobel and Lowell (son of Jack) Haney, Stanley Read (great nephew of Thomas Wilby), Henry and Mary Ellen (daughter of Earl Wise) Eisemann, Lorne, Peter, Irene and the rest of the Findlay family who worked in the background, and all the Nicols, from Annie to Annika.

Others who inspired me or helped me with information or advice include: Sarah MacLachlan, David and Stevie Cameron, Robert John Collins, Margaret McBurney, Nina Callaghan, my friends and former colleagues at *The Standard*, including Murray Thomson, Doug Draper and Janet Davison, Wade Hemsworth, Hamilton, Jane Holtz Kay, Charles Lascaibar and David Andrews, Boston, Roy McGregor, Ottawa, Paul Feris in Port Colborne and Curt McConnell, Lincoln, Nebraska.

This book became a reality because Kim McArthur of McArthur & Company cherished Canadian history and believed in publishing Canadian authors. I'd like to thank Kim, Sherie Hodds and Molly Helferty and the rest of the McArthur staff, as well as my editor Pam Erlichman and the book's designer, Michael Callaghan.

There are countless others from Peggy's Cove, Nova Scotia to Cattle Point on Vancouver Island, and from Brookline, Massachusetts to Salinas, California, who helped in the enormous task of trying to recreate this trip, but they will remain nameless.

HALIFAX T...

1912 1997

THE ALL-RED